Recorded Music

Recorded Music
Philosophical and
Critical Reflections

Edited by Mine Doğantan-Dack

**Middlesex
University
PRESS**

First published in 2008 by Middlesex University Press

Copyright © Middlesex University Department of Music

Authors retain copyright of individual chapters

ISBN 978 1 904750 277

A CIP catalogue record for this book is available from The British Library

Cover design by Helen Taylor
Typesetting by Carnegie Publishing Ltd
Printed in the UK by Cromwell Press

Middlesex University Press
Fenella Building
The Burroughs
Hendon
London NW4 4BT
Tel: +44 (0)20 8411 4162: +44 (0)20 8411 4161
Fax: +44 (0)20 8411 4167
www.mupress.co.uk

To John and Yasemin
with love and devotion

Acknowledgements

I WOULD like to thank John Sivak, Managing Director, and Celia Cozens, Managing Editor of Middlesex University Press, for their enthusiastic support for this project from the moment of its inception. Matthew Skipper has been particularly helpful in preparing the layout of the book. My colleagues at Middlesex University – Dr Peter Fribbins, Dr François Evans, Professor Susan Melrose and Professor Francis Mulhern – deserve special thanks for continuously encouraging my research projects. Peter Williams from the Lansdown Centre for Electronic Arts at Middlesex University has been most generous with his time in providing expert assistance during the preparation of the accompanying CD. Dr Craig Ayrey provided discerning advice during the proposal stage of the book. I am also grateful to all anonymous reviewers for their critical evaluations. Throughout the preparation of the book, my parents Esin and Fahrettin Doğantan, my brother Dr Murad Doğantan, and my cousin Mehmer Bayraktar have continued to nurture my passion for making and thinking about music. My very deepest thanks go to my husband, John Dack, who magically creates time for me to be a full-time mother, professional pianist, and a music theorist. This book would not have seen the light of day without his ardent support. I dedicate it to him and to our baby daughter, Yasemin, who arrived in the middle of it all, with devotion and love.

Professor Dr Mine Doğantan-Dack

Contents

MİNE DOĞANTAN-DACK

Introduction

In an article he wrote in 1878 for the *North American Review* and titled 'The
Phonograph and its Future', Thomas Edison 'for the first time appear[ed]
in propria persona to discuss and comment upon the merits of one of his
own inventions', (Edison, 1878: 528) the phonograph.[1] Admitting the difficulty of
predicting with certainty how the recording process might be applied in future, since
its 'possibilities are so illimitable and the probabilities so numerous', he wrote that
he was himself 'in a somewhat chaotic condition of mind as to where to draw the
dividing line' (Edison, 1878: 527). In the article, Edison nevertheless enumerated the
potential uses of the phonograph that he deemed most significant. His list, which
strikes the twenty-first century reader as rather eccentric, included: dictation of
letters for business purposes, eliminating the need for a stenographer; obtaining 'an
unimpeachable record' of the testimony of witnesses in court; recording of books
read by an elocutionist, to be used in 'asylums of the blind, hospitals, the sick-
chamber, or even with great profit and amusement by the lady or gentleman whose
eyes and hands may be otherwise employed'; the teaching of elocution; preservation
of the sayings, voices, and last words of the dying; the preservation of languages;
manufacturing of dolls which may speak, sing, cry or laugh, and of animal toys
supplied with their natural and characteristic sounds; production of a phonographic
clock that would 'tell you the hour of the day, call you to lunch and send your lover
home at ten'. Practically all of these potentials have, of course, been realized. What
is most remarkable, however, is that the documentation and representation of
music and musical performances, which became during the course of the twentieth
century the most basic and culturally dominant application of the recording process,
appeared in a rather inauspicious position in Edison's list and was presented within
an unlikely scenario: 'A song sung on the phonograph is reproduced with marvelous
accuracy and power. Thus a friend may in a morning-call sing us a song which shall
delight an evening company' (Edison, 1878: 533).

For me, as for practically anyone alive today, an everyday phenomenology of
the pre-recording era is simply not available. As far as the student of performance
research is concerned, recorded presentations and representations of music and
musical performances have always been part of individually and collectively
remembered daily life. Though we can speculate how musical life in the West must
have been in the absence of recording, we cannot claim to proceed from the same
kinds of experiential bases as our great grandparents when it comes to exploring
and theorizing about current musical practices. We can nevertheless feel confident

in assuming that the wide-spread availability of recordings has transformed the relationships of composers, performers, and listeners with music in ways that undermine an unquestioned acceptance of the historical continuity of musical (and musicological) thought between the age of recording and earlier eras.

While sound recordings are ubiquitous in our contemporary culture, their acceptance as valid documents for musicological research did not happen early on and naturally during the twentieth century. One of the pioneering researchers to study early recordings in the context of musical styles, Robert Philip, noted in his recent book *Performing Music in the Age of Recording* that when he decided to write a PhD dissertation in 1968 on changing orchestral styles from 1920 to 1950, based on a detailed study of recordings from that period, he was told by a professor of Music at Oxford that such a topic could not be recommended to the Faculty as appropriate for research (Philip, 2004: 1). Given that recordings and performances often implicate each other ontologically, a dismissive attitude towards recordings is partly a result of the secondary role musical performances have traditionally been assigned within musicology, which places its foundations on the tangible score. In the absence of empirical methods for analysing recorded sounds, which became available only very recently, recordings could not give musicologists the epistemological assurance they would gain from scrutinizing notated music. Over the last decade, this situation has started to change and academic programmes at universities are more willing to accommodate research projects that involve using recordings as data. Studies of changing performance styles (e.g. Day, 2000; Philip, 1992, 2004) and of the history of recording technology and its effects on music (e.g. Chanan, 1995; Katz, 2004; Welch and Burt, 1994) now constitute established research areas within a larger project identified as 'musicology of recording' (Cook, 2007). In spite of these developments, no single book to date has explored the philosophical and critical issues surrounding the nature and uses of recordings from the multiple perspectives of listeners, composers, performers and ethno/musicologists in the form of an anthology. *Recorded Music: Philosophical and Critical Reflections* aims to fill this gap, and provoke ways of theorizing about recordings.

The seventeen chapters of the book are organized in five main sections. The first section, comprising Chapters 1 through 6, are about ontological and aesthetic issues related to sound recordings. In Chapter 1, Andrew Kania presents an ontological study of three musical traditions – classical, rock and jazz – in connection with recordings. As Western music theory and philosophy of music have been largely concerned with classical music, assumptions and arguments made in the context of this tradition are often carried over to rock and jazz. But do classical, rock and jazz music really have identical ontologies? Do 'works', 'performances' and 'recordings', which at a first glance appear to exist in all three traditions, refer to the same kinds of ontological phenomena in each genre? Kania argues that the term 'recording' in fact names different kinds of ontological entities in classical, rock and jazz. 'A recording produced in one artistic tradition', he writes, 'is a different kind of thing from a recording produced in another tradition'. Basing his arguments on the conventions and implicit rules behind the production of recordings in classical, rock and jazz practices, he explains why what we hear on classical recordings are best regarded as performances, and why rock recordings do not represent performances but rather the works of art in that tradition. In this picture, jazz recordings are closer to classical ones in representing performances; the two traditions differ in that jazz has no works that can be instantiated in multiple performances. Kania closes the chapter by briefly outlining the aesthetic implications of his ontological project.

William Echard's main concern in Chapter 2 is the ontological nature of the relationship between musical works and recordings. He proposes to reconsider this relationship through the concept of virtuality developed by Gilles Deleuze, and challenges the widely held assumption that a musical work pre-exists a recording. Each encounter with music involves categories of thought that evoke movement, gesture, narrative structures, or personas – identified by Echard as 'energetic-spatial icons and indices' – and is an actualization of a virtual musical object, which is not to be equated with the musical work. Scores, performances, recordings, and even analyses, do not actualize a musical work that is ontologically prior; they are rather instances of a set of potentials for becoming. The unconventional ontological picture that emerges from Echard's argument thus reduces the differences between recordings and other forms of musical actualization, including scores and performances, to a minimum. Since each instance of musical actualization presents the listening subject with a unique, unrepeatable phenomenon, the often-expressed idea that recordings generate sameness in repeated hearings is unwarranted. Echard thus puts forward a significant counterclaim to standard discussions of recordings by denying, in line with Deleuze, the possibility of repetition without difference.

In Chapter 3, Colin Symes approaches the question of what a recording represents from the perspective of their aesthetic status: do recordings constitute original artworks, or are they copies and imitations in some sense? What are the implications of mechanical reproduction for the aesthetics of music? Basing his discussion on Nelson Goodman's theory of authenticity in the arts, and on Glenn Gould's speculations regarding the possibilities opened up by studio techniques that allow 'creative cheating', Symes explores the connections between classical recordings, forgeries and copies. He asks whether recordings can turn music into an autographic art, where the original is always aesthetically distinct from forgeries. His position is that since recordings can imitate or fake certain properties of a performance, they possess certain autographic properties. 'Differentiating what is fact from fiction in reference to recording', he concludes, 'rests on knowing their history of production and knowing their perpetrator's motives.' He proposes to categorize recordings as 'auto-allographic'.

Is there a deterministic relationship between technologies and the perceptual–

behavioural habits of those who engage with them? Associated with Walter Benjamin's famous essay titled 'The Work of Art in the Age of Mechanical Reproduction', the thesis that technologies have inherent tendencies such that a particular technology leads to a particular aesthetic mode of consumption forms the core of Theodore Gracyk's critical investigation in Chapter 4. Contrary to Benjamin, who claimed that technologically reproduced art is marked by a loss of 'aura' – the tradition or social context surrounding the original – Gracyk argues that sound recordings do not always erase the aura. Since recordings document not only a source 'reality', but also a human perspective on what is recorded, it is impossible to eliminate the aura completely. In fact, according to Gracyk each era of recording has its own distinctive aura, inviting reflection on its social origins. Through the human element in them, recordings can 'magnify the power of the documented performances'. Because recordings both document and transform reality, they do not imply a unified aesthetic response. The claim that different people would eventually experience all recordings in the same way is simply not tenable. The multiple aesthetic stances taken by listeners reduce 'the likelihood that the technology will have a unitary social effect'.

If the relationship between recordings and listeners is thus much more complex than is generally assumed, the relationship between recordings and those who record, i.e. performers, is anything but simple. In Chapter 5, Anthony Gritten considers digital sound recordings from the performer's perspective, and explores how the phenomenon of singularity that is often evoked in reference to live performance is affected by the repeatability of recorded performances. Are the reflective judgements which a performer has to make during a live performance, and which determine the event's singularity, replications of pre-conceived judgements, perhaps learnt from recordings of other performers? The core point in Gritten's argument is that for the performer musical knowledge is essentially rooted in performing live. One might be tempted to believe that one can save time by learning about musical works via recordings, and take a shortcut between practising and performing. However, there are no shortcuts for the performer, who must make reflective judgements anew every time she goes on stage. Whatever role recordings may play while a performer prepares for a live performance, Gritten argues that 'the virtual time of the performance imagined and prepared by the performer prior to going on stage (and indeed while performing) counts for nothing until actualized there and then on the spot'.

The last chapter of the first section, Chapter 6, is a historical study by Marc Battier, who presents a fresh perspective on the motivations that generated an aural culture permeated with sound recordings, by presenting evidence that the aesthetic potentials of the first recording device, i.e. the phonograph, were conceived from the moment of its inception not only by musicians but more significantly by poets, writers, film makers, art critics, music critics and visual artists. The emergence of a new aesthetic that put sound, noise, and aural perception at the centre of artistic creation, and the development of an aesthetics of recorded sound and music is historically bound up with non-musicians. In discussing the role played by the phonograph in the creation of music during the twentieth century, Battier presents a taxonomy: these include the capacity of the phonograph for conservation and for the representation of artificial life, the creative possibilities of the capture, authenticity of the medium in eliminating intermediary forms of representation for music, presentation of new materials for composition, disc itself as the artistic medium, possibilities for exploration in collaboration with scientists, creating music without instruments, and the disc as work of art. 'If the notion of sound has become a fulcrum in the twentieth century', he writes, 'it is largely due to the possibilities offered by the phonograph'.

The second section focuses on genre-specific studies, while at the same time continuing to explore some of the ontological and aesthetic issues already introduced in the first. In Chapter 7, Michael Frith contributes to a relatively unexplored research area by evaluating the ontological status of recorded organ improvisations. His main concern is whether organ improvisations that are fixed by recording can be regarded as works. He presents his main argument – that '[r]ecordings of improvisations… allow the listener to experience a living tradition of a musical practice rather than of objects, i.e. works' – against the historical background of improvisatory practice before the age of recordings, and a critical evaluation of some 'classic' recorded organ improvisations, particularly those by Charles Tournemire.

The implications of recording improvisations are especially pertinent to jazz practice, which forms the subject matter of Chapters 8 and 9. Bruce Ellis Benson's focus in Chapter 8 is on so-called jazz licks – short recognizable melodic motifs, or phrases – and their relationship to recordings. Borrowing of licks is a fundamental aspect of jazz improvisation, and Benson's argument brings out a paradoxical situation created by the recording of a lick: once recorded, it becomes fixed and associated with a particular performer, while its availability via recording opens up new possibilities for its transformation in the hands of other performers. 'Dissemination via recordings makes licks common property of the jazz community'. Using Edmund Husserl's conception of the origins and continued existence of geometry, Benson points out the impossibility of pinpointing the exact origins of a lick, or the exact point in time when it appears as that particular lick. To illustrate his argument regarding the identity of licks, he examines the first two jazz recordings, both of which were the subject of lawsuits.

Tony Whyton's focus in Chapter 9 is on the historical reissues of jazz recordings and their relationship to the aesthetic status of jazz. He argues that current jazz practice is dominated by historical recordings, and identifies the consumer desire for myth-making and icon worship among the ideological motivations for promoting historical jazz. His case study of John Coltrane's studio recordings for the Impulse!

label released in 1998 shows how these motivations frame the design and marketing of the product. An important implication of the heightened aesthetic status attributed to the genre by the veneration of historical recordings is that jazz artists today are evaluated against historical benchmarks while they are also expected to be original. As the ontological status of jazz is changing due to the significant role recordings now play in the practice of jazz musicians, Whyton calls for a reconceptualization that would give recordings rather than ephemeral performances the central role.

In Chapter 10, Tony Gibbs and John Dack present a study exploring the aesthetic assumptions that underlie the ways recording practices in popular, classical and electroacoustic genres create virtual acoustic locations and environments. While the established recording practice in the classical genre imposes a uniform temporal and locational identity on the recorded piece of music, thereby inviting the listener to believe that what she hears is a performance that took place in a particular location at a particular time, recording practice in pop and rock deliberately undermines temporal and locational singularity by creating multiple acoustic environments. In these genres, it is completely acceptable for a single recording to appear to have been created in several locations and thus in an asynchronous fashion. In the electroacoustic genre, compositional motivations override any concern for the creation of a sense of singular performance, or event; here, sounds are used on the basis of their compositional potential, and the aesthetic impact of the music often arises from the way the electroacoustic composer chooses to interact with real and virtual spaces.

The third section of the book, 'An Ethnomusicological Interlude', consists of a single chapter, Chapter 11, written by ethnomusicologist Robert Reigle, who sets out to explore the ideas and motivations behind ethnomusicological recordings. He discusses how these recordings have transformed some of the assumptions early ethnomusicologists worked with, and argues that recordists have humanistic aspirations, such that their practice is driven not only by concerns for the preservation of musical traditions, but also for generating intercultural understanding and aesthetic appreciation. One of the most significant consequences of ethnomusicological recordings has been the spread of philosophical ideas associated with the culture of the recorded music. Reigle's chapter also includes a chronology of milestones in the history of ethnomusicological recordings.

The fourth section of the book is titled 'Sound Recordings and Naturalized Epistemology' since the authors in this section approach epistemological issues surrounding sound recordings through the evidence of empirical methods, and draw on empirical performance studies and empirical work in sound perception to explore what (and how) we perceive and know through sound recordings. In Chapter 12, Francis Rumsey scrutinizes the concept of 'fidelity', which has been a central concept in defining the function of sound recording and reproduction, and challenges standard notions about high fidelity. He asks whether there is a fixed reference for fidelity, whether absolute fidelity can ever be achieved or even recognized, and more significantly whether this is something listeners desire. Research summarized by Rumsey indicates that experience of sound quality is linked to one's previous experiences and familiarity, and that listeners are not particularly interested in high fidelity: 'The reference point for deciding what is good or appropriate depends greatly on the listening context, mode of listening and application area'.

What does a historical musicologist come to know by studying classical recordings? Indeed, what exactly does she study through recordings? Dorottya Fabian's research presented in Chapter 13 focuses on what classical sound recordings represent, and whether they are valid documents for studying performance styles. Her thesis, supported by empirical evidence, is that sound recordings represent performances. Listening to a recording is listening to a performance, which represents the performer's interpretation of the recorded music. Stating that many listeners actually choose to listen to recordings rather than to live performances, she also objects to the view that the aesthetic reference for all listeners is the live performance. In response to the argument that a recorded performance of a piece of music remains the same while its live performances are always different, she claims that every hearing is different and therefore re-hearing a recording does not imply hearing it in the same way every time. More significantly, she points out that listeners actually choose to revisit idiosyncratic performances.

In Chapter 14 Simon Trezise's concerns are similar to those of Fabian: he is interested in exploring whether recordings represent the interpretations of performers such that the historical musicologist can claim to be familiar with their performances by studying their recordings. His conclusion differs in pointing out that musicologists need to exercise caution when working with recordings: 'There is no reason why we should mistrust every sign of performance we believe we hear', he writes, 'but record's codes cannot be devolved back through a transformational language to live performance without detailed consideration of the medium. Recordings are technical surrogates, artistic identikits of a live performance'. In discussing recorded performances, Trezise refers to the temporality of live performances, which he identifies as the 'performing breath': an unbroken time-line marking the spatio-temporal unity of the performance event. Recordings transform and subvert this performing breath, and consequently technological mediation becomes 'an obstacle to knowing how performers played'.

The final section of the book is titled 'Practising Music, Recording Music'. Here, practising musicians write about the role of recording in their area of expertise, and in their own practice. In Chapter 15, I argue for the urgency of establishing a performer's discourse within the discipline of performance studies, which would give recordings an integral role in representing the performer's voice. While recordings are studied as documents of performances within the discipline, musicologists – rather curiously – do not regard them as documents of the performer's expert musical knowledge. After discussing how the dominant disciplinary discourse misrepresents the performer's identity as a musician, I argue for the necessity of developing a discourse that originates in the act of music making, and provides a textually and musically accurate representation of the performer within performance studies. Towards this aim, I discuss the second movement of Beethoven's Piano Sonata Op. 13 from a pianistic perspective and present my recorded interpretation of it.

By way of setting up the background for a discussion of his 'documentary, radiophonic, electroacoustic work' titled *Ricordiamo Forlì* and composed in 2005, John Young begins Chapter 16 by considering the aesthetic implications of recording for electroacoustic music. The compositional possibilities opened up by recording technology are such that it allows sounds to be treated both as abstract objects and as representations of associative meanings. Both of these compositional possibilities are important for the composer in creating musical signification. Young argues that when used as a creative tool by the composer, sound recording can invite imaginative engagement with the recorded musical materials and function as artefacts of lived experience and memory. He writes that 'acousmatic music can deal with themes of an experiential and phenomenological nature via evocation of images and by allowing us to recognize reflections of lived experience in audio documents'. Aiming 'to make sound recording function as an active extension of our sensibilities', he turns to a discussion of his work *Ricordiamo Forlì*, explaining the compositional techniques and conception behind the work.

In the final chapter of the book, Chapter 17, Sabine Schäfer and Joachim Krebs discuss the compositional process 'EndoSonoScopy', which they developed during the late 1990s using digital sampling technology. After presenting a brief survey of the history of electroacoustic music in terms of the effects of technology on the creative process, they present the philosophical background for their practice originating in the work of the French philosophers Deleuze and Guattari. Schäfer and Krebs are concerned with finding ways of representing the dynamic ways of becoming rather than the static condition of being, particularly in the context of micro-dimensions of animate matter. They identify EndoSonoScopy as a 'specially designed micro-acoustic procedure for the recording and analysis of the largely unexplored and unknown (internal) micro-dimensions of naturally created sounds and noises which employs the sampler as an audio-microscope'. The basic audio material for their TopoSonicCompositions comes from nature, particularly from the animal world.

Several stylistic conventions adopted in the book need to be mentioned: all translated texts that are referenced in a particular chapter are given with both the date of the original and the date of the referenced translated edition at their first appearance in the chapter (e.g. Deleuze, 1966/1988: 100–1). Subsequent references to the same text give only the date of the translated edition. Proper names are given in full when they are first mentioned in a chapter, and subsequently only the last name is provided, except in a few instances where the full name has been reintroduced for rhetorical purposes. Presentation of the discographies in different chapters does not follow a fixed format, but rather the criterion of ease of identification in the context of each chapter; accordingly, some chapters list recordings by performer, and some others by composer.

The broad range of issues addressed, and the multiple perspectives covered in *Recorded Music: Philosophical and Critical Reflections* will no doubt be of interest to readers from diverse backgrounds, and appeal directly to musicologists, ethnomusicologists, and practising musicians, as well as philosophers, sound artists, and recording engineers. It is hoped that they will be encouraged to continue the explorations started by the contributors to this book on the nature and uses of sound recordings.

Notes

1   The *North American Review* has been digitized and placed online at the Cornell University Library as part of their 'Cornell Making of America' project. See: http://cdl.library. cornell.edu/cgi-bin/moa/moa-cgi. For a brief discussion of Edison's article see Chanan (1995: 2–5).

References

Chanan, M. (1995) *Repeated Takes: A Short History of Recording and its Effects on Music.* London: Verso.

Cook, N. (2007) 'Performance Analysis and Chopin's Mazurkas', *Musicae Scientiae* XI (2): 183–207.

Day, T. (2000) *A Century of Recorded Music: Listening to Musical History.* New Haven: Yale University Press.

Edison, T.A. (1878) 'The Phonograph and its Future', *North American Review* 126: 527–36.

Katz, M. (2004) *Capturing Sound: How Technology Has Changed Music.* Berkeley: University of California Press.

Philip, R. (1992) *Early Recordings and Musical Style: Changing Tastes in Instrumental Performance, 1900–1950.* Cambridge: Cambridge University Press.

_____ (2004) *Performing Music in the Age of Recording.* New Haven: Yale University Press.

Welch, L.W. and Burt, L.B.S. (1994) *From Tinfoil to Stereo: The Acoustic Years of the Recording Industry, 1877–1929.* Gainesville: University Press of Florida.

I
Questions of Ontology and Aesthetics

ANDREW KANIA

Works, Recordings, Performances: Classical, Rock, Jazz

I N this essay, I undertake a comparative study of the ontologies of three quite distinct Western musical traditions – classical, rock, and jazz – approached from the unusual angle of their recordings.[1] By the 'ontology' of a tradition I mean simply the kinds of things there are in that tradition and the relations that hold between them. A study of this scope is bound to leave many questions unanswered when restricted to this length. The ontology of classical music has been debated in the analytic tradition for close to half a century, and there has been a growing interest in the ontologies of rock and jazz in the last ten years.[2] The advantage gained by the wide scope, however, is a bird's eye view of the terrain. As I see it, that terrain is quite varied, and looking at it through the lens of recordings throws the differences into relief. I end with some reflections on the consequences of the ontological project for musicology.

One thing I take for granted is that there *are* three such traditions. Their precise individuation would doubtless be a complicated musico-socio-anthropological task, but that it would not be a wild goose chase is suggested by our shared abilities to sort music into these three categories, whether this be in a record store, when identifying the kinds of music we are familiar with, or, significantly, discussing a case that is hard to pigeonhole. Despite what is sometimes suggested, the existence of borderline cases pretty quickly implies the existence of a borderline, however wide or fuzzy.

Another claim I rely on is that a great majority of art produced in a given tradition fits into a single ontological structure. This is not to say that it is of a single ontological kind, but that relations between works, performances and recordings, for instance, are invariant across most of the art produced in the tradition. Though I do little explicit arguing for this claim, the idea is that once I have set out my theory of the ontology of a given tradition, reflection on that tradition by someone familiar with it will convince her that the theory fits the data, i.e. the tradition itself.

Looking at my title, one might think that the ontologies of the three traditions I discuss cannot be all that different. After all, it is not the case that in classical music we have only works, while in rock we have only recordings, and in jazz only performances. All three kinds of entities exist in each of the three traditions, it would seem. These appearances, however, are misleading, if not outright deceiving. There

are different kinds of things that go under the name 'recording'. Although all audio
CDs seem *prima facie* to employ the same medium, the many different ways available
to produce a sound recording belie this first impression. A recorded musical artwork
that sounds like a landing jet will be more impressive if it is constructed entirely out
of a recording of a bleating lamb than if it is simply a recording of a landing jet. But
more than the direct causal provenance of a recording is relevant to its appreciation,
for even two art objects made in exactly the same way will be appreciated differently
if produced in different contexts. For example, it would be unremarkable to find an
unedited studio recording of a harpsichord performance of one of Johann Sebastian
Bach's two-part inventions on a CD of his keyboard works by a leading performer,
while such a recording issued by an avant-garde electronic music studio would be
considered a strangely archaic, rule-flouting work. Just as we might sensibly say that
a CD containing an unedited, relatively transparent record of a sound event is a
different kind of thing from one containing a highly edited and processed recording,
we might also sensibly say that a recording produced in one artistic tradition is a
different kind of thing from a recording produced in another tradition.[3] How we
decide to label these different kinds of things is, naturally, a semantic issue (though
it can also be an ideological one). I will suggest some neologisms below simply in
order to talk more easily about the different kinds of musical things I believe there
are. Though I do not choose my terms capriciously, my focus is on metaphysics rather
than semantics – on the kinds of things there are, rather than what we call them.

The conclusions I argue for are as follows: jazz recordings are like classical
recordings in that we hear performances by means of them; they are, in this sense,
transparent. The kind of performance to which they are transparent, however, differs.
Typically, a classical performance is of a work, while there are no works in jazz, only
performances that share various features with each other. There are works of art in
the rock tradition, but these are the recordings themselves. They manifest songs that
may be performed live, but since these are not at the center of the tradition, they are
not the works of art in the rock tradition.

Musical works

Philosophy of music, like musicology, has historically been concerned primarily with
Western classical music. Most theorists agree that the ontological paradigm of this
musical tradition is that there are musical works, such as Igor Stravinsky's Violin
Concerto, which receive multiple performances.[4] What kind of thing a musical
work *is*, exactly, has been a matter of some controversy, at least among musical
ontologists. Most, however, propose theories that can be seen as instances of more
general approaches to the problem of universals, i.e. the problem of the nature of
things that seem *prima facie* to be individuals in some sense, yet also seem to exist
in multiple instances.[5]

I will not engage here in the debate over which fundamental ontological category classical musical works fall into. Before we look at recordings, however, it is necessary to see that the question of what a musical work *is* is not exhausted by the resolution of this debate. For whatever fundamental ontological category Stravinsky's Violin Concerto belongs to, it is easy to see that the solo violin part of the concerto falls into that same category. It, too, is unitary, in whatever metaphysical sense the concerto as a whole is unitary, and it, too, is multiple in the sense that it has many different instances – some with orchestral accompaniment, some with piano accompaniment, some with no accompaniment at all, and so on. Still, the solo violin part of Stravinsky's concerto is just that – a *part* of the work, not a work itself.

Using the term 'piece' to refer to any unit of music, we can put the current question as follows: what is it that makes some but not all pieces of music *musical works*? Reference to the literature on the definition of art will not help since, again, parts of works are art, yet those parts are not in themselves works of art. I suggest that a work of art must be of a kind that is a primary focus of critical attention in a given artistic tradition. This suggestion is not without its problems. First among them may be the identification of the relevant artistic tradition. Nonetheless, the basic idea, which I believe is sound, is that the *Mona Lisa* is a work of art, in part because it is a painting produced in the artistic tradition known as 'painting', while none of the sketches for the *Mona Lisa* is a work, since sketches are not a primary focus of critical attention in the painting tradition.[6]

The case of classical music, however, shows that there must be more to the piece–work distinction than we have uncovered so far. For it seems plausible that performances, such as those of Stravinsky's Violin Concerto, are a primary focus of critical attention in the classical tradition. Yet, we make a clear distinction between the work and performances of it. The relevant difference here, one that is appealed to in other multiply-instantiable temporal art forms, is between something that is an enduring entity and something else that is a fleeting event. Like works in theatre, dance, and cinema, musical works persist beyond the temporal boundaries of their instances, while musical performances, like dance and dramatic performances and showings of films, are passing. So a work of art must be, at least, (i) of a kind that is a primary focus of critical attention in a given artistic tradition, and (ii) an enduring entity.

It might be objected at this point that I have smuggled some ontological assumptions into the discussion. A certain kind of strict nominalist, for instance, will certainly not accept, at face value at least, the claim that Stravinsky's Violin Concerto persists beyond the boundaries of its performances. To assume so is to assume the existence of some sort of abstract entity. I do not, however, mean to make such substantive fundamental ontological assumptions. Thus far, I have been 'speaking with the vulgar', and while the nominalist may be unable to resist 'thinking with the learned', he must, nevertheless, acknowledge the vulgar distinction between works and performances in some way. I intend to continue to speak in this vulgar fashion. The ontological views I defend below are not fundamental, meaning that they do not stand or fall along with any theory of the fundamental nature of reality. Even if we argue that tropes are all that ultimately exists, we still have to say something about why people go around talking as if there are concrete individuals. Similarly, classical musicians and audience members make a clear distinction between works and performances, and no fundamental ontological theory ought to rule out this distinction. In sum, the views expressed below, while ontological, are not fundamental. They are neutral with respect to various competing fundamental ontological theories.[7]

Classical recordings: recorded work-performances

If the paradigmatic ontological picture of classical music includes works and their performances, it is an open question where we should locate recordings in that picture. It seems to me that the intuitive answer is to locate classical recordings close to performances and I will defend that intuition against two considerations that have led people to argue that, on reflection, classical recordings are more like works than performances.[8]

Before discussing those considerations, let me say something about what I refer to with the term 'recording'. First, a recording is a type: there are particular tokens of a recording, usually referred to as 'copies'. We might each have a copy of Anne-Sophie Mutter's recording of the Stravinsky Violin Concerto. Furthermore, there may be many playings of a single copy; I might listen to my copy every night for a week. What I will refer to as a recording is the type behind each of these tokens, i.e. the sound-event type that is encoded on each copy and instantiated with each playback.

The first consideration that moves people to regard classical recordings as more like works than performances can easily be seen given our discussion of works and recordings above. Recordings are enduring, reinstantiable things. If it is natural to think of a classical recording as a performance, it is equally natural to think of it as a *repeatable* performance. That itself should be enough to give us serious pause, for 'ordinary' performances are fleeting events while works are the types they instantiate. If recordings are reinstantiable sound structures, then it is not obvious that they should not be called works.

The second consideration that leads people to think of classical recordings as more like works than performances is the fact that they are worked on over time. Even if a classical recording were a perfect live recording, in the sense that it gave an aural experience just like that afforded by the live event it records, it would still be a reinstantiable sound structure. But no actual classical recordings are like this. Apart from imperfections in the sound reproduction technology, the sound is mixed from a number of different microphones, parts of different takes are spliced together, notes are electronically corrected or overdubbed, and so on. The extent of these manipulations has led some to think of recordings as more like sculptures in sound than performances – as works of art in their own right.

I will deal with these two considerations in turn, offering arguments intended to lessen their force, leading classical recordings back to their rightful place, away from works and close to performances.

My main argument against the first consideration is that while classical recordings endure and are reinstantiable, they are also *transparent* in the sense made popular by Kendall Walton's discussions of photography:[9] 'to look at a photograph is actually to see, indirectly but genuinely, whatever it is a photograph of' (Walton, 1997: 60). The basic argument for this thesis is that photographs are 'counterfactually dependent on the scenes they portray...[and that the] counterfactual dependence...is independent of the photographer's beliefs' (Walton, 1997: 68). Walton's original statement of this view (1984) has generated much discussion.[10] However, even Walton's best critics grant some version of the transparency claim – that we see the objects captured by a photograph unmediated by intentions in some important respect (Warburton, 2003). I will take for granted that photographs are transparent in Walton's sense. What I suggest further is that there are no relevant differences between mechanical image-reproduction and mechanical sound-reproduction when it comes to considering their transparency. That is, recordings are as transparent as photographs; just as we see things in or through photographs, we hear things on or through recordings. The relevance of this point should be clear. Just as in looking at a photograph we see, say, a single person, even though the photograph itself is a type with many tokens, so in listening to a recording we hear a single performance, even though we may listen to it several times. Though the recording is a multiply instantiable enduring entity, what we hear through it is, therefore, a fleeting event – a performance. For that reason, classical recordings are better viewed as more like performances than like works.

An objection to this argument brings us to the second consideration in favor of viewing classical recordings as musical works. The objection is that even if a classical recording is transparent, what you see through its window is not a single event – a performance – but a mishmash of different bits of different performances tacked together with corrections pasted over certain spots, and so on. Thus, even if classical recordings are transparent, we do not, and ought not, approach them in this way. What we rightly appreciate in a classical recording is the finely honed sonic sculpture we hear on the surface, not the frantic chiseling that we know lies behind it.

This way of putting the objection draws out an important distinction between what I call 'active' and 'phenomenal' performance. These are not two different kinds of performance, but rather two distinct aspects of any performance. As Jerrold Levinson notes, there is 'a well-entrenched *process/product* ambiguity in regard to the concept of a performance. On the one hand, there is the *activity* of producing sounds for an audience; on the other hand, there are the *sounds* that are produced' (Levinson, 1987: 378). I call the activity or process the *active performance*, and the resulting product, the sounds we hear, the *phenomenal performance*. Levinson goes on to claim that:

the thing primarily judged seems to be product rather than process, achieved result rather than activity of achieving it. This is not, however, to imply that one can judge the product in this case – a performance – in *ignorance* of or in *isolation* from the process that issues in it.

(Levinson, 1987: 378–9)

The relevance of these points to classical recordings should be clear. In what follows, I argue that the phenomenal performance we hear on a recording is connected to the active performance of the musicians in the studio in such a way that we are justified in claiming that we hear a performance *simpliciter* when we listen to a classical recording.

For clarification, it is helpful to contrast my view of the relationship between classical works and recordings with that of Stephen Davies, who argues that classical works are of the ontological kind *work-for-live-performance* (S. Davies, 2001: 20–36).[11] I argue instead that classical works are for performance *simpliciter*, and that there are two kinds of performance – live and recorded. This makes my view more attractive than Davies', I believe. For if classical works are ontologically for-live-performance, then a recorded performance of a classical work cannot authentically instantiate it. Most classical audiences and musicians, however, seem to think that a studio recording of a classical work does give them access to a genuine instance of the work.[12] Davies seems to recognize this, and hedges a little, saying that 'such talk relies on our willingness to treat the representations of performances found on recordings as acceptable substitutes for live performances' (S. Davies, 2001: 319). Of course, our pre-reflective intuitions that classical recordings give us access to work instances may be wrong. But, other things being equal, this conformity with our intuitions is an advantage of my account.

The disadvantage, some might say, is that it makes no sense to talk of a 'recorded performance' in reference to classical recordings. One of the oft-cited features of classical recordings marshalled against the idea that they are performances is the looser spatio-temporal constraints on the playings that go on in the production of a recording, as opposed to a live performance.[13] Those who produce a live performance must all play together, in the same place and at the same time, without taking (non-musical) breaks. The argument is completed as follows: these constraints are not respected in the recording studio, and what happens in the recording studio is, therefore, not a performance.

There are two ways of arranging this information into an argument, however. The above argument is *modus tollens*; what follows is a more positive spin. I take quite seriously the practice of treating classical recordings like performances. Most musicians, critics, and audience members think of them in this way. Of course, they also recognize the important differences between live and recorded performances; recorded performances are somewhat idealized performances, but given the initial intuition that recordings are like performances, this can be captured better by the theory that live performances and recordings are two types of performance, rather than two more radically different kinds of thing.[14] The distinction between active and phenomenal performance can help here. The looseness of the spatio-temporal constraints on episodes of musical playing in the recording studio is mirrored by a similar looseness in rehearsals for live performances. In both cases, the point of the disjointed active playings is the production of the best possible phenomenal performance. How the playings contribute to that performance is different in each case, but not in such a way as to justify withholding the name 'performance' from the recording.

Perhaps the most serious charge made against classical recordings, which might lead one to deny they are performances in any sense, is that the way the phenomenal performance on a recording is produced amounts to cheating. In availing themselves of whatever technological means necessary to produce a phenomenal performance that they did not, and perhaps could not, produce live, classical musicians are betraying the centuries-old skill-based tradition they purport to be a part of.

I reject both parts of this charge: classical musicians do not avail themselves of any means necessary, nor do they produce a phenomenal performance they could not produce live. To put it a little more subtly and accurately, it is not acceptable in the classical world to produce recordings in this way. To do so *would* count as cheating, but is not common practice. As I have argued elsewhere, just as the spatio-temporal constraints appealed to by the opponent of classical recordings developed implicitly within the performance tradition, new conventions, also implicit, developed over the twentieth century, putting limits on what is acceptable in the production of a classical recording (Kania, 1998: 37–51). The occasional classical recording scandal is evidence of the existence of, and general adherence to, these conventions. What these conventions try to do is precisely to find a practice that honors both the tradition's ancient valorization of live performance skill and the desire of performers and audiences (not of recent vintage itself!) to hear the best performance possible. Essentially, one should not release a recording under one's own performing name if one would not be capable of producing such a phenomenal performance live under ideal circumstances (S. Davies, 2001: 192–4; Godlovitch, 1998: 26–7; Kania, 1998: 37–51).

A common response to this argument, in my experience, is an appeal to the practices of Glenn Gould. His hands-on approach in the studio is legendary, and even if it is admitted both that some of the stories told are apocryphal and that he is at one extreme of the spectrum of use made of recording technology in the classical world, nevertheless he is not considered a cheat by mainstream audiences. So, it might be argued, the conventions I have outlined above are not in fact in place.

My reply to this is twofold. Firstly, it is not at all obvious that Gould flouts the conventions I have outlined. He established a fine reputation as a live performer before retreating to the studio, and no-one could seriously charge that he was incapable of producing the kinds of performances live that are heard on his recordings. Secondly,

Gould's actions belie a commitment to the classical performance tradition, whatever he might say to the contrary. He clearly believed that Bach should be played on a keyboard, whether on stage or in the studio. He was also clearly well aware of the resources available in the studio for producing recordings that cannot happily be called performances, as his important output of electronic works shows. When producing recordings of classical works, Gould did not come close to doing what he did when producing non-performance recordings, or to what rock musicians contemporary with him were doing in the studio. In sum, Gould is no counterexample to the view of classical recordings as recorded performances that I am defending here.

I have argued that classical recordings, as they are typically made, are rightly thought of as giving access to performances of the works they purport to be of.[15] Although the unified phenomenal performance they give access to is usually not connected to a unified active performance, as in the case of live performance, the conventions for producing such recordings that have arisen in the classical-music world – rooted in the long-standing tradition of live performance – are such that it is appropriate to think of what we hear on a recording as a performance; a different kind of performance from a live performance, but a performance nonetheless.[16]

Rock recordings: tracks

Turning to rock music after a lengthy discussion of classical, it is tempting to see the same ontology.[17] For in the rock world, as in the classical, there are songs that receive multiple live performances, and recordings of those songs. The easiest way to see that this temptation should be resisted is to cast one's mind back to our consideration of what makes a piece of music a *work*.[18] Theodore Gracyk has convincingly argued that the primary focus of critical attention in rock music is the replete soundscape of a recording, rather than the thin sound structure – the song – that is instanced in different performances and recordings (Gracyk, 1996: 1–98).[19]

Stephen Davies has argued that rock is more like classical music than Gracyk allows (S. Davies, 2001: 29–36). His view of what happens in the rock studio is somewhat like the picture I have just painted of the classical studio. Davies thinks that rock songs are written for precisely this kind of studio production, and thus calls them *works-for-studio-performance*. There is no space to go into Davies' arguments here.[20] Suffice it to say that I am sympathetic to his reclamation of the importance of performance skill for rock, but I believe we can find a place for such values in rock without recourse to the notion of a work-for-studio-performance. Thus, what follows can be seen as an extension of Gracyk's account of rock recordings – as the works of art in that tradition – that responds to Davies' concerns about the importance of performance skills in rock practice.

The basic view is that rock musicians primarily make *tracks* – ontologically thick works that are instanced in playings of a copy of the recording.[21] These recordings are at the heart of the tradition. However, a rock track also typically manifests a song

– a thin structure of lyrics, melody, and harmonic structure – that may be further manifested in tracks by other musicians or in live performances (Gracyk, 1996: 1–98; Kania, 2006).

There are two places in this account that leave room for valuing performance skills. The first is in the construction of tracks. It might initially seem that if the performance skills that we value in the production of rock tracks – typically skill in singing, and playing the guitar, drums, and bass – are to be given their due, we must conceive of rock recordings as performances of some sort, and thus should be moved towards Davies' view of rock recordings as 'studio performances'. In fact, there is no need to do this. We often value skills that go into the production of a non-performance artwork; just think of a master's skill with the brush.[22] Moreover, Davies is well aware of this possibility in the realm of recorded music, for he acknowledges that classical electronic works are for playback, rather than for studio performance, while they are often constructed from recordings of performance events of some sort (S. Davies, 2001: 26).

The second place where there is room for esteeming performance skills in rock is, of course, in live performances. Though I see this as an advantage of my account, it might equally be used to raise an objection against it. For are rock concerts not a hugely important part of the tradition? Why, then, elevate recordings to pride of place, and grant live rock performances only a subsidiary role?

This is a difficult question, to be answered on the basis of an unwieldy body of musico-sociological data. I will offer three supports for my view. The first is simply Gracyk's work on this topic. He convincingly argues, as I mention above, that however important live rock is, recorded rock is much more important to the tradition, as evidenced by musical, critical, and appreciative practice.

The second support is a consideration of live rock performances. It is clear that most rock performers, most of the time, perform their songs live in such a way that the sound produced is relatively similar to the sound of their recording of the song (more similar to it than to a recorded cover of the song by different artists, for instance).[23] What this amounts to is, firstly, the same song being performed as manifested by the track and, secondly, the same kinds of sounds used to fill out the skeleton of the song – something like what a classical musician would call 'instrumentation'. On the other hand, it is also clear that most artists do not attempt to create on stage a sonic *doppelgänger* of a particular track.[24] For one thing, this can be done quite well by other musicians, as the performances of cover bands amply show; yet, regular (non-cover) bands do not produce this kind of performance of songs they have recorded. For another, audiences expect live rock performances to differ from tracks in certain ways. Some of the more common changes are an extended introduction, often concealing which song is being performed, added verses, instrumental solos, invited audience participation, and so on. Thus, we can see that live rock performances do not attempt to produce the closest sound possible to a studio recording of a song, but do, nonetheless, take the track as primary in some sense. This is unsurprising, given that the track represents the artists' considered opinion about what sounds good enough to constitute an enduring addition to their oeuvre.

The third support for my view that recorded rock is primary, and live rock secondary, is a thought experiment. It invites you to imagine four different scenarios. Two concern the classical music world, and two the rock music world. For each tradition suppose, firstly, that all recording technology has been destroyed without hope of recovery. Then, suppose an alternate scenario in which recording technology survives, but for some reason all live performances are eliminated from the world. In the case of classical music, the elimination of recordings would not greatly affect the music-making practices of the tradition; this would merely be a return to the old days. The elimination of live performances, on the other hand, might conceivably have an effect, over time, on the kinds of works and recordings produced. (I put this point somewhat hesitantly since, as I argue above, the long history of the live performance tradition in classical music has made its recording practices quite robust.) In the rock scenarios, I would argue, the situation is roughly reversed. With the end of live performances, musicians could continue to make albums as they have for the past several decades. Were the recording studios to be shut down, however, live rock performances could no longer draw on recordings as they do now. A different, more performance-based art would need to emerge were rock to survive. In short, classical recording practice is asymmetrically dependent upon classical live performance practice, while live performance practice in rock is asymmetrically dependent upon rock recording practice. While these thought experiments drastically oversimplify matters, I think they do thereby bring out clearly the basic differences between recordings in these two traditions.

To sum up: rock recordings are sonic sculptures – the works of art in their tradition – and not a type of performance, as classical recordings are. This, however, is consistent with the high value placed on performative skill in the rock world.

Jazz recordings: recorded performances

One of the many things that distinguish jazz from rock and classical music is that it is historically coeval with recording technology.[25] Classical music was a firmly entrenched tradition with centuries of history when this technology made its appearance, while the emergence of rock music, if I am right about its ontology, depended on the existence of a somewhat developed recording technology. The claim that jazz came into existence at the same time as recording technology is somewhat contentious, since there is a tendency to focus exclusively on recorded history. Nonetheless, the impact of such technology on jazz, even in the technology's infancy, was such that it is hard to deny the major role it played in establishing jazz as a widespread and central tradition in twentieth-century American, and arguably global, music.

This close connection between jazz history and recording technology might lead one to regard jazz as ontologically similar to rock music. After all, like rock musicians, jazz musicians exchange and discuss recordings, and learn to play by imitating their favorite recordings. The recording studio has had other wide-reaching effects on the history of jazz. For instance, one of the great early jazz groups – Louis Armstrong and his Hot Five – existed only in the recording studio, since contemporary live audiences preferred syncopated dance music to their hot New Orleans style.

Yet, for all the similarities, there are important differences between rock and jazz approaches to recording; here, jazz seems to be a lot closer to classical music than it is to rock. Just as notation enabled classical composers to create more and more complex enduring musical works, recordings enable the preservation of works with all the replete detail of a sound event. Rock, like classical electronic composition, embraced this aspect of recording technology to the extent that informed rock audiences do not expect rock recordings to be transparent to live performance events. Both classical and jazz audiences, on the other hand, expect the phenomenal performance heard on a recording to be connected to the active performance of the musicians in the right way. Different takes may be spliced together, and extraneous noise removed, but nothing should be done to cause the recording to represent a sound event that the musicians would be incapable of producing live. As live performance traditions, both classical and jazz music have embraced recording technology's ability to represent artists' capabilities in the best light,[26] but both traditions maintain a distinction between authentic recording practice and studio trickery. In both traditions, one is supposed to listen *through* the recording to the represented performance, rather than *to* the recording as a studio construction.[27]

A different reason that might be given to align jazz ontologically with rock rather than classical music is that jazz standards, like rock songs, are ontologically thin; that is, relatively few aspects of an instance of a standard are determined by the standard itself, as opposed to late Romantic classical works, for instance, wherein quite specific instrumentation, tempi, dynamics and even expression are determined by the work (S. Davies, 2001: 20). In fact, Stephen Davies has argued, convincingly in my view, that jazz performances are not rightly called performances *of* the standards they instantiate, since (i) the standards are so thin ontologically, and (ii) the performance is largely improvisatory (S. Davies, 2001: 16–19). If this is so, then one might wonder what the work of art in the jazz tradition is. The standard is not a promising candidate for the reasons just given. But neither is the performance, if my arguments above are sound, since it is a fleeting event. A recording is the obvious next candidate, since recordings provide a way to turn a fleeting event into an enduring object. However, if my arguments about classical recordings are convincing, not all recordings are rightly viewed as enduring objects in the sense relevant to making them works of art. Thus, in order to locate works in the jazz tradition, we might be tempted to see them as similar to rock recordings, i.e. tracks to be appreciated as replete soundscapes, rather than windows on to performances.

This theory does not jibe at all well with jazz practice. If anything, the recording conventions in the jazz world are even stricter than in classical music. This is due in large part to the centrality of improvisation in jazz. Quite apart from these considerations specific to jazz, though, the very project described in the preceding paragraph ought to strike one as odd. Given the aesthetic interest of improvisatory jazz performances, the subsidiary interest of the standards themselves, and the usefulness of recordings in delivering performances to large audiences, why exactly should we be concerned with discovering something that will count as 'the work of art in jazz'? That jazz is an art form without works seems quite in keeping with its valorization of creativity in the moment – an attitude it shares with other traditions without works, notably performance art. If there can be art forms, like sculpture, wherein there are works but no performances, and traditions, like classical music, where there are both, why not accept jazz as a tradition, like performance art, in which there are performances but no works?

Though intended as merely rhetorical, a critic might respond to this question with the fact that 'work of art' is not merely a descriptive term, but a value-laden one. Works of art are the *telos* of each art form; an art tradition without works is an impoverished one. Thus, my view of jazz as a tradition without works lends credence to the elitist view that jazz is 'just' popular art, not worth serious attention.

I think this line of thought is behind many attempts to uncover 'the work of art in jazz', but I also think it is misguided. Firstly, I do not think that 'work of art' need be an evaluative term. Its descriptive and evaluative senses have been clearly distinguished since at least Morris Weitz's seminal work on the definition of art (1956). Secondly, my account has something to say about why these senses get conflated. On my account, a work of art is of a kind that is a primary focus of critical attention in a given art form. If some kind of thing is the primary focus of attention in a human practice, then presumably it rewards that attention in some way. Thus, one might hastily conclude that if an artistic tradition has no works, it has nothing worthy of attention. But this is a bad inference. For according to my view, being of a kind that is a primary focus of critical attention is but one necessary condition of being a work of art. In addition, the candidate must also be an enduring object. Improvisatory performances are the primary focus of critical attention in jazz. That kind of thing is obviously worthy of attention, but it is not an enduring object, and thus cannot be a work of art.

To a critic of my view, this argument may look like a *reductio ad absurdum*. Why insist on this second condition if it costs jazz performances their rightful status as works of art? The reason is one of parity across the arts. If jazz performances are works of art because they are the primary focus of critical attention in jazz, then classical performances must be so too, since they are a primary focus of critical attention in the classical tradition. To agree with this, however, would be to radically revise the way we think about classical music (not to mention other arts involving the performance of works). The other alternative is to deny that the term 'work of art' is univocal across the arts. This would also be a radical revision of our art ontology.

Since, if we are careful, we ought not to infer anything evaluative about jazz from the fact that it has no works, my account is preferable to either of the radically revisionary alternatives.

Consequences for musicology

Musical ontology, as I have practiced it here, is descriptive, both in the sense that it aims to describe how we (really) think about things, rather than suggest new ways of doing so (Strawson, 1974: xiii–xv), and in the sense that it describes extant musical practices, rather than prescribing how things ought to be done. Though I think musical ontology in this sense has intrinsic interest for those to whom both music and abstract thought appeal, it also has consequences for musicology.[28] For though musical ontology aims for the best fit with musical practice, the practice of musicians comes first, audiences second, and theorists, to the extent that they can be separated from the first two groups, a distant third. This is because musicology, like ontology, usually comes last, describing an existing practice (Kania, 2008a). Thus, music theorists (like musical ontologists!) can get it wrong in ways that practicing musicians cannot. Because music theory, like philosophy of music, has focused primarily on Western classical music, when it does turn to other music, such as rock or jazz, it often assumes that all music is ontologically like classical music – a tradition of works for performance. When it does so with an ontologically different tradition in its sight, it can lead itself to error. Thus, an understanding of the ontology of a tradition can help the musicologist to focus on the relevant properties of the object of his attention.

The web of similarities and differences between classical, rock, and jazz is quite complicated. Classical and jazz are alike in being live performance traditions. This results in the similar attitude each takes towards recording technology, using it to produce, in a sense, durable performances. Yet, the classical tradition is centered around enduring works, which are the creations of composers, while in jazz the primary focus of critical attention is ephemeral performances, so that the tradition cannot be said to contain works in the same sense as in the classical tradition. Rock music, on the other hand, while including an important practice of live performances, is centrally a recorded art, whose works are replete recordings that manifest songs which can be performed live, without the works themselves being performances of those songs, and without the songs being works in their own right.

In spite of the ontological dissimilarity between rock and jazz music, it seems that the criticism of those traditions might depart from conventional classical music criticism in similar directions. For it is a consequence of both the improvisational environment in which jazz performances are produced and the studio environment in which rock tracks are constructed that small details of timing and timbre, for instance, can be of great import, and used to great effect. The reasons for this commonality are different, however. In rock, details can be very important because the rock musician has every imaginable timbre at her fingertips. In jazz, details can be very important because the improviser has very little to work with, compared to most of the works performed by classical musicians, and thus every nuance counts.

Two qualifications need to be added to these claims immediately. The first is that such criticism already exists, and is part of the data upon which I build my ontology.[29] One of the things I hope to have done here is make explicit the (correct!) ontological assumptions implied by such criticism, thereby encouraging more criticism in this vein. The second qualification is that the methods of analysis these critics apply to rock and jazz, such as those focused on timing and timbre, can be (and occasionally have been) usefully applied to classical music.[30] Similarly, standard classical musicological tools can be of some use with respect to rock and jazz.[31] The development of these aesthetic implications is an important task, but one for another place.[32]

Notes

1   I conduct a more extensive study of the same topic in Kania (2005), from which many of the ideas in this essay are drawn.

2   A bibliography of the literature on the ontology of classical music would be out of place here. However, in addition to the work on rock and jazz cited elsewhere in the text, see Alperson (1984), Baugh (1993, 1995), Brown (1996, 2000a, 2000b, 2000c, 2002), Carroll (1998), Fisher (1998), Hagberg (2002), Young (1995), and Young and Matheson (2000).

3   For amplifications of these arguments see Walton (1970), and the recent debate over 'aesthetic empiricism' (for example, D. Davies (2006) and Graham (2006)).

4   I ignore classical electronic music for the sake of brevity. My view of that sub-tradition is in accord with Stephen Davies' (2001: 25–9). I disagree with Davies in that I see rock music as ontologically akin to classical electronic music, as I argue below.

5   For an overview of the different kinds of answers given to this question, see Kania (2007: §2.1). An important exception to this approach is Goehr's work (1992). I hope that my approach, though analytic, is sensitive to her concerns about the need for an historical awareness of the musical practice one is discussing.

6   If Leonardo da Vinci produced something qualitatively identical to one of these sketches as a finished drawing, upon which he then based the painting, we would instead have two related works.

7   This distinction between ontological levels raises issues in meta-ontology that are beyond the scope of this chapter. See Kania (2008a, 2008b, 2008c) and Thomasson (2005, 2006).

8   I make no distinction between 'live' and 'studio' recordings in discussing classical recordings. This is partly because many of the things (such as editing) that move people to reject the view I defend below are common to both types of recording, and partly because if I can make my case for studio recordings, then the case for live recordings will presumably follow automatically.

9 Rather than in the sense used by Brown (2005), according to which a recording is transparent if and only if it is sonically indistinguishable from the event it records.

10 See Warburton (2003) for an overview.

11 The hyphens are mine, to indicate the specific nature of Davies' view. It is not that there are classical works and rock works (discussed below), of some common ontological kind, and that the classical ones are intended for a certain sort of performance, while the rock ones are intended for a different kind of performance. The claim is that classical works are of the ontological kind work-for-live-performance, while rock works are of a different ontological kind: work-for-studio-performance.

12 There is a parallel problem for Davies' view of the ontology of rock. On Davies' account, live performances of rock songs cannot be authentic instances of the songs they purport to be of, because in his view those songs are works-for-studio-performance. I discuss these issues in the next section.

13 I make a distinction throughout between playing and performing. I take the concept of playing for granted. That performing involves something more can be seen by considering other kinds of playing, such as practicing. See also Godlovitch (1998: 12–13). For ease of exposition, I include singing and conducting as species of playing. For more on the precise nature of the spatio-temporal constraints on live performance, see Godlovitch (1998: 34–41) and S. Davies (2001: 186–90).

14 There is an analogy between my argument here and Arthur Danto's argument about artistic predicates in 'The Artworld' (1964). While we always thought of live performances as the only kind of performance, with the introduction of recorded performances we see in hindsight that live performances are just one of (at least two) kinds.

15 I am sometimes tempted by a stronger version of this thesis, namely that recordings are themselves performances, not merely modes of access to them. The temptation is the result of reflection on the fact that the performance the recording encodes can only be heard by playing the recording. Thus, the recording is not a mere window on to something independently available, as a photograph of a painting or person is. However, I content myself with arguing for the weaker thesis here.

16 One interesting topic I have not addressed here is the comparative advantages and disadvantages of gaining access to works through live or recorded performance. I address that question in Kania (1998: 78–100; forthcoming).

17 With 'rock', I refer to a broad category on a par with 'classical' and 'jazz', as opposed to a narrow stylistic category on a par with 'heavy metal'.

18 The following material is expanded upon in Kania (2006).

19 I talk of rock 'songs' throughout, although there is some purely instrumental rock; what I say is intended to apply to both kinds. The distinction between 'thick' and 'thin' sound structures was first made by Stephen Davies (1991). The more properties of an instance of a sound structure are determined by that structure, the thicker it is.

20 See Kania (2006).

21 The sense in which one 'plays' a recording is, of course, different from that in which one 'plays' a violin. I trust which sense is operative will be clear from the context.

22 *Pace* the revisionary ontologies of Currie (1989) and David Davies (2004), which see all works as performances in some sense.

23 I ignore unrecorded bands for simplicity. Note that as the technology becomes more accessible, this kind of band is becoming less common.

24 This seems to be Stephen Davies' view of live rock, as evidenced in his comments on my 'Ontology of Rock Music', presented at the *Annual Meeting of the American Society for Aesthetics*, San Francisco, October 2003. On Davies' view, as noted above, rock songs cannot strictly be performed live, since they are of the ontological kind work-for-studio-performance.

25 My focus in this section is on instrumental jazz. I ignore the jazz song tradition, which may be more like classical music ontologically. I note below the possible exception of jazz fusion to my general conclusions.

26 Musicians from many different live performance traditions seem to embrace this idealizing aspect of recording technology. See Frith (1996: 232–3).

27 A case could be made that fusion is a significant counterexample to my thesis that jazz is a live performance tradition. For fusion artists arguably take an approach to recording technology similar to that taken by rock artists, embracing all its possibilities as part of the artistic medium. If this is in fact the case, I would attempt to give an account of jazz fusion similar to an account of classical electronic music. Though the latter is part of the classical tradition rather than the rock tradition for historical reasons, the radical ontological difference between electronic classical music and classical music for performance has made electronic music a quite distinct and autonomous sub-tradition within classical music as a whole. Thus, perhaps the 'war between fusion and other jazz practices' (Brown, 1998: 6) could reach an armistice if both sides acknowledge that each employs a distinct artistic medium.

28 In what follows, I use the terms 'musicology', 'music theory', and 'music criticism' loosely and interchangeably. I intend to refer to any theorizing about music that is not abstract enough to qualify as philosophy of music.

29 For two academic examples, besides the journalistic literature, see Daley (1998) and Walser (1995).

30 See, for example, Cogan and Escot (1976). For a review of the current state of 'performance studies' – the discipline emerging within musicology that is most concerned with addressing these questions – see Rink (2004).

31 For examples, see Covach and Boone (1997) and Schuller (1968) respectively.

32 I am grateful to the editor and two anonymous referees for numerous helpful suggestions, and to Trinity University for financial support during the writing of this chapter.

References

Alperson, P. (1984) 'On Musical Improvisation', *The Journal of Aesthetics and Art Criticism* 43: 17–29.

Baugh, B. (1993) 'Prolegomena to Any Aesthetics of Rock Music', *The Journal of Aesthetics and Art Criticism* 51: 23–9.

_____ (1995) 'Music for the Young at Heart', *The Journal of Aesthetics and Art Criticism* 53: 81–3.

Brown, L.B. (1996) 'Musical Works, Improvisation, and the Principle of Continuity', *The Journal of Aesthetics and Art Criticism* 54: 353–69.

_____ (1998) 'Jazz', in M. Kelly (ed.) *Encyclopedia of Aesthetics*, vol.2, pp.1–9. New York: Oxford University Press.

_____ (2000a) '"Feeling My Way": Jazz Improvisation and its Vicissitudes – a Plea for Imperfection', *The Journal of Aesthetics and Art Criticism* 58: 112–23.

_____ (2000b) 'Phonography, Repetition, and Spontaneity', *Philosophy and Literature* 24: 111–25.

_____ (2000c) 'Phonography, Rock Records, and the Ontology of Recorded Music', *The Journal of Aesthetics and Art Criticism* 58: 361–72.

_____ (2002) 'Jazz: America's Classical Music?', *Philosophy and Literature* 26: 157–72.

_____ (2005) 'Phonography', in L.B. Brown and D. Goldblatt (eds) *Aesthetics: A Reader in Philosophy of the Arts*, second edition, pp.212–18. Upper Saddle River, NJ: Pearson Prentice Hall.

Carroll, N. (1998) *A Philosophy of Mass Art*. New York: Clarendon Press.

Cogan, R. and Escot, P. (1976) *Sonic Design: The Nature of Sound and Music*. Englewood Cliffs, NJ: Prentice-Hall.

Covach, J. and Boone, G. (eds) (1997) *Understanding Rock: Essays in Musical Analysis*. Oxford: Oxford University Press.

Currie, G. (1989) *An Ontology of Art*. New York: St. Martin's Press.

Daley, M. (1998) 'Patti Smith's "Gloria": Intertextual Play in a Rock Vocal Performance', *Popular Music* 16: 235–53.

Danto, A. (1964) 'The Artworld', *The Journal of Philosophy* 61: 571–84.

Davies, D. (2004) *Art as Performance*. Oxford: Blackwell.

_____ (2006) 'Against Enlightened Empiricism', in M. Kieran (ed.) *Contemporary Debates in Aesthetics and the Philosophy of Art*, pp.22–34. Oxford: Blackwell.

Davies, S. (1991) 'The Ontology of Musical Works and the Authenticity of their Performances', *Noûs* 25: 21–41.

_____ (2001) *Musical Works and Performances: A Philosophical Exploration*. Oxford: Clarendon Press.

Fisher, J.A. (1998) 'Rock 'n Recording: The Ontological Complexity of Rock Music' in P. Alperson (ed.) *Musical Worlds: New Directions in the Philosophy of Music*, pp.109–23. University Park, PA: Penn State University Press.

Frith, S. (1996) *Performing Rites: On the Value of Popular Music*. Cambridge, MA: Harvard University Press.

Godlovitch, S. (1998) *Musical Performance: A Philosophical Study*. London: Routledge.

Goehr, L. (1992) *The Imaginary Museum of Musical Works: An Essay in the Philosophy of Music*. Oxford: Clarendon Press.

Gracyk, T. (1996) *Rhythm and Noise: An Aesthetics of Rock*. Durham: Duke University Press.

Graham, G. (2006) 'Aesthetic Empiricism and the Challenges of Fakes and Readymades', in M. Kieran (ed.) *Contemporary Debates in Aesthetics and the Philosophy of Art*, pp.11–21. Oxford: Blackwell.

Hagberg, G. (2002) 'On Representing Jazz: An Art Form in Need of Understanding', *Philosophy and Literature* 26: 188–98.

Kania, A. (1998) 'Not Just For the Record: A Philosophical Analysis of Classical Music Recordings'. MA thesis: University of Auckland.

_____ (2003) 'Ontology of Rock Music'. Paper presented at the *Annual Meeting of the American Society for Aesthetics*, San Francisco.

_____ (2005). 'Pieces of Music: The Ontology of Classical, Rock, and Jazz Music'. Unpublished Ph.D. dissertation: University of Maryland, College Park.

_____ (2006) 'Making Tracks: The Ontology of Rock Music', *The Journal of Aesthetics and Art Criticism* 64: 401–14.

_____ (2007) 'Philosophy of Music', in E.N. Zalta (ed.) *The Stanford Encyclopedia of Philosophy* (Fall 2008 Edition), URL: http://plato.stanford.edu/archives/fall2008/entries/music.

_____ (2008a) 'Piece for the End of Time: In Defense of Musical Ontology', *British Journal of Aesthetics* 48: 65–79.

_____ (2008b) 'The Methodology of Musical Ontology: Descriptivism and its Implications', *British Journal of Aesthetics* 48: 426–44.

_____ (2008c) 'New Waves in Musical Ontology', in K. Stock and K. Thomson-Jones (eds) *New Waves in Aesthetics*, pp.20–40. New York, NY: Palgrave Macmillan.

_____ (forthcoming) 'Musical Recordings', *Philosophical Compass*.

Levinson, J. (1987) 'Evaluating Musical Performance', reprinted in J. Levinson (1990) *Music, Art and Metaphysics: Essays in Philosophical Aesthetics*, pp.376–92. Ithaca: Cornell University Press.

Rink, J. (2004) 'The State of Play in Performance Studies', in J. Davidson (ed.) *The Music Practitioner: Research for the Music Performer, Teacher, and Listener*, pp.37–51. Aldershot: Ashgate.

Schuller, G. (1968) *Early Jazz: Its Roots and Musical Development*. New York: Oxford University Press.

Strawson, P.F. (1974) *Individuals: An Essay in Descriptive Metaphysics*. Garden City, NY: Anchor Books.

Thomasson, A. (2005) 'The Ontology of Art and Knowledge in Aesthetics', *The Journal of Aesthetics and Art Criticism* 62: 221–9.

_____ (2006) 'Debates about the Ontology of Art: What are We Doing Here?', *Philosophy Compass* 1: 245–55.

Walser, R. (1995) '"Out of Notes": Signification, Interpretation, and the Problem of Miles Davis', in K. Gabbard (ed.) *Jazz Among the Discourses*, pp.165–88. Durham, NC: Duke University Press.

Walton, K. (1970) 'Categories of Art', *The Philosophical Review* 79: 334–67.

_____ (1984) 'Transparent Pictures: On the Nature of Photographic Realism', *Critical Inquiry* 11: 246–77.

_____ (1997) 'On Pictures and Photographs: Objections Answered', in R. Allen and M. Smith (eds) *Film Theory and Philosophy*, pp.60–75. Oxford: Oxford University Press.

Warburton, N. (2003) 'Photography', in J. Levinson (ed.) *The Oxford Handbook of Aesthetics*, pp.614–26. Oxford: Oxford University Press.

Weitz, M. (1956) 'The Role of Theory in Aesthetics', *The Journal of Aesthetics and Art Criticism* 15: 27–35.

Young, J.O. (1995) 'Between Rock and a Harp Place', *The Journal of Aesthetics and Art Criticism* 53: 78–81.

Young, J.O. and Matheson, C. (2000) 'The Metaphysics of Jazz', *The Journal of Aesthetics and Art Criticism* 58: 125–34.

WILLIAM ECHARD

Subject to a Trace: The Virtuality of Recorded Music

Orienting remarks

M Y aim in this chapter is to rethink recordings and their relationship to musical works through a theory of virtuality. We often hear and conceptualize music as embodying many entities that could be called virtual: personas, narratives, spaces, gestures, textures, and so forth.[1] The perspective I will describe is not an obvious fit with recordings because it questions the very possibility of properties often taken to be definitive of them, most importantly their repeatability. A complicated argument will be required to bring the divergent strands together, but in summary, the guideposts will be as follows: I will describe ways in which musical activity involves engagement with virtuality, both in the experience of listening, and the ontology of musical works. I will suggest that a commitment to virtuality is consistent with the claim that each musical actualization is entirely particular and unrepeatable, and in addition, that any general features of a musical work are immanent to these particular events and do not need to be seen as prior to them. If we accept this, novel perspectives become available on the relationship between recordings and other forms of musical actualization. In order to develop these themes, I will challenge the idea of sameness in repeated hearings of recordings by arguing that every hearing is a singular event. This position will be supported not only with reference to limitations in perception or memory, but more fundamentally through the ontological claim that repetition always entails difference. This will require rethinking the question of fixity in recordings. It will also be necessary to examine the nature of virtual musical entities with respect to their supervenience upon a wide range of factors, including recordings and other media. The title of the chapter will be explained at the end, since it relies on a co-ordination of all these strands.

Some readers will have already noted a Deleuzian flavour here. In terms of existing literature, my agenda is to combine elements of Gilles Deleuze with elements of contemporary musical semiotics and research on auditory culture. My understanding of Deleuze is focused less on his work with Félix Guattari (although that is where he most directly discusses music), and more on his earlier ontological concepts.[2] Coming from a background in semiotics and cultural studies, I am especially interested in areas of overlap between Deleuze and the sometimes-naturalistic pragmatism of philosophers such as Charles Peirce and Donald Davidson.[3] These links will not be explored in depth in this chapter, but I mention them so that readers will be aware of the ways in which my use of Deleuze differs from some others. A Deleuzian perspective can clarify and even simplify traditional ontological questions, even though this is not a mainstream way of understanding his work.

The word *record* can be used as a noun or as a verb. I am interested mostly in the former – in the relationship between listeners and finished recordings (of whatever format) – although the implications of the two cannot be separated completely. Also, without apologizing, I should note that I am by training a musicologist and cultural theorist, not a philosopher. However, my work has always been guided by an interest in basic ontological questions; what I hope to contribute to this volume is thus a philosophical perspective in the affective rather than the professional sense, and also some insight into how philosophical concepts can be rearticulated and applied in cultural musicology. Because of this, and also because I want to present the outlines of a complicated argument as efficiently as possible, I will not directly engage with much of the existing literature on philosophy of music. This chapter pursues its own agenda rather selfishly, and says little directly about familiar debates that impinge on the philosophy of recorded sound, such as the distinction between allographic and autographic works, or the aura, or the basic question of how music might differ from other cultural practices. I hope, however, that readers interested in this literature will notice how I have often shaped my presentation to suggest perspectives on such issues, without broaching them directly.

I avoid such well-worn topics also because in my repertoire of primary interest – Anglo-American popular music since 1945 – these issues are simply not as pressing as in the Western art music tradition, which has informed most existing philosophies of music. My work is rock-centric, which means that recordings are not secondary or puzzling, but are a naturalized and primary means of musical expression. As Theodore Gracyk puts it, '[r]ock is a tradition of popular music whose creation and dissemination centers on recording technology...In rock the musical work is less typically a song than an arrangement of recorded sounds' (Gracyk, 1996: 1). Furthermore, it is not only in the narrow confines of rock music that such alternative attitudes towards recordings can be found. For example, Alexander Weheliye argues that 'music and orality carried a different weight in nineteenth-century African-American culture. Because alphabetic script did not represent the primary mode of cultural transmission, the phonograph did not cause the same sorts of anxieties about the legibility of music as it did in mainstream American culture' (Weheliye, 2005: 7). For thinkers such as myself, raised on rock and other traditions in which recordings are neither troubling nor secondary, the emphasis in much existing literature on the philosophy of music seems to be put in odd places. I can understand the motivations of such work, in part because my background also includes years of formal training in Western classical music, but I feel drawn to tell a different kind of story.

Because my arguments rest on an unconventional view of musical ontology, I will take the first half of this chapter to explain that view. In this section, recordings will be discussed only in very broad terms, and by necessity there will be some long passages that do not mention recordings at all. However, the kinds of questions to be addressed here – where is music located? can it be repeated? – are motivated by the need for a sweeping theory of recordings. In the second half of the chapter, these motivations will become more obvious as I directly address some issues that commonly arise in the literature on recordings and auditory culture.

What are musical works? ESIIs, virtuality, and refrain

My focus is on musical *works* rather than music more broadly for two reasons. First, the ontological issues I wish to examine will come into sharp relief if we center our discussion on cases in which listeners believe that there is a coherent structure, the work, which pre-exists the recording and to a large degree determines it. Such an attitude is especially common in the Western art music tradition. Second, recording is one of those practices that tend to convert any musical performance, however fluid or improvisatory, into a fixed entity, which then acts as a template to guide further interpretations and performances. This can be seen, for example, in the jazz and rock traditions. In all of these contexts, ideas about recordings imply ideas about musical works. The idea of the musical work will, therefore, be central to my discussion, although I will not in the end adopt the belief that recordings, when used musically, are primarily repositories for clearly delineated structures. The purpose of the following ontological discussion is to establish a more processual and context-dependent concept of musical works, in order to prepare for a fresh perspective on the relationship between recordings and works.

In contemporary Peircian semiotics of music, there is considerable emphasis on how music is *heard as* something else.[4] The most frequent cases to come under discussion are those in which music is heard as gesture and/or space, which by extension leads to discussions of affect (music heard as possessing emotional properties), musical personas (music heard as being itself an agent), and narratology (music heard as expressing deep narrative structures).[5] Although details vary with different authors, the outline of the theory is this: music, like any other percept, is experienced and conceptualized through energetic and spatial categories; and because many different percepts are conceptualized through the same underlying spatial and energetic categories, music can resemble other kinds of spaces and gestures (an iconic relationship), and can also bear discernible traces of its prior contact with agents and contexts (an indexical relationship).[6] I will treat all of these kinds of musical effect together, because they are all instances of energetic-spatial icons and indices (henceforth ESIIs). Since my approach is modeled in part on the work of George Lakoff and Mark Johnson (1999), I will adopt the view that metaphor is one of the crucial mechanisms through which ESIIs are deployed. A metaphor in this view is a cognitive event, specifically a cross-domain mapping. For example, the domain of monetary value (stock prices) can be mapped onto a spatial domain (rising and falling). A similar mapping can occur between the pitch of a sound (the domain of frequency) and a spatial domain (rising and falling again). A mapping of this sort is not only a linguistic phenomenon. It is an event in which one domain is understood or experienced in terms of another. Because they operate as scaffolding for conceptualization, these sorts of mappings are often pre-conscious. Although the effect is dependent on culturally based learning, and can be enhanced through active participation, on some level we do not choose to hear ESIIs in music. They just seem to be there, and they give the music a dynamic, compelling presence, as if it embodied spaces and could even be a kind of agent.

This semio-cognitive model has two implications for our discussion of recordings. First, since there is a profound entanglement of musical experience with other kinds of experience, easy lines cannot be drawn between musical sound and other forms of agency. When we are alone with musical sound, we can still have what feel like inter-personal experiences, and this will complicate our discussion of the sociality of recordings. Second, the ubiquity of ESIIs emphasizes the need for a theory of virtuality. Although sound waves can be straightforwardly understood as occupying the listening space, rising and falling pitches are not occupying that space in the same sense. What then is the ontological modality of ESIIs, which seem connected and similar to actualities and yet somehow different? A theory of virtuality based on the work of Deleuze will be my central anchor in addressing such questions.

Virtuality is an ontological category. Those things are virtual which are real but not actual. Actuality includes everything that might be called concrete, and it also includes concepts and percepts when they are clearly articulated before consciousness. For Deleuze, the formula *real but not actual* does not suggest a lack, but rather grants a positivity: it expands the concept of reality beyond that of actuality. In general, virtuality contains those structures and processes that guide and give consistency to actualities in their becoming, and so I will say that virtualities are made up of *genetive elements*.[7] There are several ways to think about the relationship of the virtual and the actual. For example, a space of possible states is virtual. Think of a musician's hands, and all the possible positions they can assume. These configurations are never all present together, yet the space they describe is arguably a real property of the hands. A topological form is also a virtual entity. Consider the topological form described as approaching a point of minimal free energy. This form corresponds to a variety of physical entities: salt crystals and soap bubbles, for example, both actualize it (Delanda, 2002: 15–16).

Virtuality is immanent to actuality. There is no parallel realm of the virtual, but rather virtuality is a facet of actuality, just as the past is only accessible to us as a modality of the present. While the virtual is immanent to the actual, it does not resemble actuality, nor is it ever directly manifested there. No particular actualization can claim to be identical with its own genetive elements, and the many lines of actualization from a single virtuality tend to diverge and differ from one another. As Deleuze puts it, 'there are merely lines of actualization...each representing an actualization of the whole in one direction and not combining with other lines or other directions' (Deleuze, 1966/1988: 100–1). For example, recall that both salt crystals and soap bubbles actualize the same virtual topological form. Yet, their actual forms do not resemble one another. Similarly, both a score and a performance can actualize the same virtual musical object, but they do not resemble one another although there are rules for transforming one into the other. And to forestall a possible confusion as soon as possible: a musical work is not in this view prior to its actualizations (scores, performances, analyses, recordings, etc.). A work is a projection or understanding based in, and arising along with, specific actualizations. Rather than 'the work' as such, there is a series of work instances that arise as components of particular actualizations. Of course, factors such as memory, notation, and recording technology can allow consistency to develop between such instances, so that the work series made up by linking previous events (positing that they projected the 'same' work) precedes the latest work instance. But even here, what we have is a consistency made between particular instances such that the work series moves in parallel with various actualization series (the recording series, the performance series, the analysis series, etc.) but does not precede them.

Leaving aside the problem of precedence, we should also reflect briefly on what a theory of virtuality might imply about the individuation of artworks. To borrow the question from Joseph Margolis, how can we 'identify different tokens as tokens of the same artwork-type, in virtue of which we may fix the common reference of critical comments' (Margolis, 1980: 51)? I select Margolis' formulation of the issue not only for its clarity, but because the solution he offers is one, which – I will argue – is consistent with a theory of virtuality.[8] His crucial move is the characterization of artwork instances as tokens, and works themselves as types, along with the related argument that types can only exist as embodied in tokens, and that they are in fact emergent from collections of tokens (Margolis, 1980: 54). For example: '[We may credit] someone with having invented "the Brigitte Bardot look" (the type), but that does not mean that there actually evolves a Brigitte Bardot look that has properties in common with its tokens. It means only that the type's tokens have certain related properties' (Margolis, 1980: 73). Margolis sums up the advantages of this view by suggesting that it 'combines the advantages of the embodiment thesis – hence, of an emergent materialism – with the advantages of avoiding the extreme implausibility of platonism with respect to art' (Margolis, 1980: 76).

A type, as described by Margolis, fits the description of a virtual entity. The full set of features defining any particular type seems impossible to specify clearly (types are somewhat obscure), and yet we routinely use types in our conceptualizations without experiencing confusion (they are generally distinct). Types also display a conceptual fertility reminiscent of the virtual, since most types seem able to encompass an infinite number of tokens. In ontological terms, the relationship between types and tokens is the same as that postulated for virtualities and actualizations in two respects: (i) types are non-actual and yet integral to actual tokens; (ii) types are emergent from tokens, yet at the same time serve to provide a ground for tokenhood. I have drawn this parallel between Deleuze and Margolis at such length in part to illustrate that a theory of virtuality need not commit us to an idealist stance. The theory of artworks as types allows for a naturalistic and historicist perspective, from which the individuation of artworks need be no more problematic than the formation of any other conceptual types, and the description of types can be read as an account of the cognitive and cultural processes through which individuation occurs. By suggesting a parallel between this approach and the virtual, I am aiming to highlight the naturalistic tendencies in Deleuze rather than to problematize or complicate the pragmatic approach.

Although I will use a Deleuzian concept of virtuality to think about recordings and musical works, Deleuze himself (working with Guattari) focused his musical comments on what he called the *refrain*. As Ronald Bogue glosses it, the refrain involves three elements: 'A point of stability, a circle of property, and an opening to the outside' (Bogue, 2003: 17).[9] Deleuze and Guattari portray the refrain as a conjunction of various processes: 'A child in the dark, gripped with fear, comforts himself by singing under his breath. He walks and halts to his song. Lost, he takes shelter, or orients himself with his little song as best he can' (Deleuze and Guattari, 1980/1987: 311). This is the first component of the refrain, a point of stability. The second component they compare to a home, the creation of a space. And for the third component:

> Finally, one opens the circle a crack, opens it all the way, lets someone in, calls someone, or else goes out oneself, launches forth...These are not three successive moments in an evolution. They are three aspects of a single thing, the Refrain.
>
> (Deleuze and Guattari, 1987: 311–12)

As with most Deleuzian concepts, the refrain allows for a variety of further moves by interpreters. There are only two that we will need to consider in this chapter. First, parallels can be drawn between the refrain and the model of ESIIs. Consider, for example, the comments by Bogue, who remarks that 'Deleuze and Guattari extend the notion of the refrain to refer to any kind of rhythmic pattern that stakes out a territory' (Bogue, 2003: 17). A refrain, seen in this way, closely resembles a conceptual schema as described by Johnson (1987: 28–30), since it is a gestalt which is distinct, yet abstract enough to underlie a wide range of actual experiences. The refrain also resembles ESIIs in being a fundamentally temporal and spatial phenomenon. This comparison between the theory of cognitive metaphor and the theory of the refrain works both ways; it shows us that the refrain may be understood in terms of cognitive theory, but also that the concept of virtuality can be an appropriate one through which to understand the entities posited by cognitivists. One implication of both the theory of ESIIs and of the refrain is that 'music [becomes] an open structure that permeates and is permeated by the world' (Bogue, 2003: 14). By itself, this simply re-enforces comments already made. It is another aspect of the refrain that will help us to move forwards. In a comment not extensively considered by Bogue or other authors, Deleuze and Guattari suggest that

> the refrain is a prism, a crystal of space-time. It acts upon that which surrounds it, sound or light, extracting from it various vibrations, or decompositions, projections, or transformations. The refrain also has a catalytic function: not only to increase the speed of the exchanges and reactions in that which surrounds it, but also to assure indirect interactions between elements devoid of so-called natural affinity, and thereby to form organized masses. The refrain is therefore of the crystal or protein type.
>
> (Deleuze and Guattari, 1987: 348)

What this suggests is that musical works are best understood as a set of tendencies or potentials for becoming – a set of genetive elements – rather than strict instructions or finished structures for reproduction. Just as genetic information specifies tendencies of development but does not fix all the specifics of any particular organism, the musical work as refrain specifies the manner in which many kinds of actualization should proceed, but does not fully determine any actualization.[10]

I have so far put forward two main proposals about the nature of musical works. First, they are often heard as a play of ESIIs in such a manner that differentiation between musical and extra-musical concepts becomes problematic.[11] Also, the theory of ESIIs suggests that each act of listening is best viewed as a dynamic and always somewhat distinctive encounter. In this view, rehearing a familiar piece of music is like discussing the same topic with the same people on multiple occasions. The participants are familiar and similar themes arise, yet the experience is never identical, partly because you are interacting with dynamic and somewhat unpredictable agents (actual ones in the case of conversation, and virtual ones in the case of musical sound). Second, the work proper consists of virtual genetive elements that are never manifested as such. Although these are very general claims, we can already see how they might complicate certain concepts related to recordings such as repeatability and resemblance, and their ability to provide an adequate site of immanence for musical works.

Where are musical works? Supervenience, singularity, immanence, and consistency

What are the genetive elements that make up the musical work? The more we look, the more different kinds we can find. The full set, from which any particular work would represent a selection, would comprise spatial-energetic cognitive schemas, the physical potentials of instruments and performers, concepts of music theory, and many other factors as well, including all of the social and historical contingencies relevant to composers, performers, and listeners. There is a close relationship between the concept of a genetive element set and that of a supervenience base.[12] Both refer to a heterogeneous collection of elements out of which a complex entity like a musical work might emerge. In both cases, there is a difference of kind posited between the emergent entity and the genetive elements. Notice how, under this view, scores are not necessarily privileged sites of immanence for a work. Scores can specify a certain range of genetive elements, primarily tonal and rhythmic relationships, and also performance movements and timbre to a limited extent. But they do not specify all of the genetive elements necessary for the work to be actualized. They usually leave out, for example, performance conventions passed along through pedagogical practices. They also leave out culture-specific interpretative habits that a composer would expect from an audience. Recordings can store a different range of genetive elements, and so represent a different mode of actualization. Whether we are interacting with scores or with recordings, we are given a base of elements from which to project an understanding of a work, and this base can involve anything that could serve as a mechanism of consistency (bodies, social institutions, memory, etc.). Because no mode of actualization inherently resembles such a large and heterogeneous set of genetive elements, no particular medium in which a work might appear can be seen as identical with the work itself.

In order to move a little closer to recording-specific issues, we need to consider questions of immanence, consistency, and repetition in more depth. As a first step, it is crucial to understand that scores, recordings, and other media do not store musical sounds and musical structures in a straightforward sense. This is because the concept of storage implies that the same entity can re-appear after a period of absence, whereas I want to hold with the view that repetition as such (unaccompanied by difference) is not possible. Any performance of music, including playing a recording, is an event. If we have heard this music before, then the event might feel like a re-occurrence, as if the same music that happened before is happening again. However, each event is particular and unrepeatable. Since the virtual structures that we hear as the work are immanent to these particular events, we might be tempted into thinking that there is a paradox here, under which the terms of consistency, resemblance, and repetition seem to be generated within a singularity. The apparent paradox can be mitigated, however, by remembering that being itself is a dynamic process of continual movement. Consistencies of all kinds are real, but are continually remade in each successive moment, rather than being a reflection or image of a transcendent constancy. Although it might seem odd to evoke Davidson in support of a Deleuzian doctrine, consider what the former has said of events in general:

> When are two events identical? Or, when is one event identical with another? It
> seems only one answer is possible: no *two* events are identical, no event is ever

identical with *another*...The difficulty obviously has nothing special to do with events, it arises in relation to all identity questions.

(Davidson, 2001: 163)

Because each event is ontologically singular, it cannot be that in a literal sense the music 'happens again' when a recording is replayed. But this does not preclude the constructions of consistencies. Davidson goes on:

> Even if one allows only particular, unrepeatable events, then, it is possible to give a literal meaning to the claim that the same event occurs on two or more occasions...Talk of the same event recurring no more requires an event that happens twice than talk of two tables having the same width requires there to be such a thing as the width both tables have.

(Davidson, 2001: 184)

Two tables can be measured as being of the same width. This is a result of applying certain practices of measurement to particular tables and comparing the results of those measurements. However, what persists are the instruments and habits of measurement, which themselves depend upon constant translation and re-inscription.[13] Similarly, if we hear the same recording on different occasions, we experience two singular events and compare them using many cultural and personal habits. These habits allow for a judgment of similarity, which forms a crucial part of the supervenience base for the musical work heard to be in the recording.

It need not be the case that the music itself is preserved anywhere between such events. Even recordings are not best understood as storing music. Rather, they represent one vector of consistency, which allows, given the right context, for certain sounds to be actualized; those sounds are an important part of the set of genetive elements upon which music supervenes. None of this is to deny that we have an experience of persistent musical entities, which appear to inhabit a parallel virtual realm and periodically appear and disappear in actuality. But in order to understand what is happening, and to look at the specific mechanisms of consistency allowed for by sound recordings, we need to move beyond this surface impression, with its attendant ideas of storage, and beyond a belief in the work itself as something transcendent with respect to its moments of actualization.

What are we doing? Metaxis

I have already characterized two kinds of musical entity as virtual: ESIIs and musical works themselves. Strictly speaking, neither of these as we encounter them is virtual, because they are experienced phenomena and are, therefore, actual. However, there is an experiential sense in which such phenomena are close to virtuality, because they seem particularly effective at making us aware of virtuality. ESIIs do this for at least two reasons. First, because they resemble concrete events and configurations, yet are not actual, they raise questions about the difference and line between reality and actuality. ESIIs resemble virtual genetive elements in their tantalizing balance of determination and changeability also because they can participate in a variety of different forms without strictly resembling any of them. Similarly, musical works display a balance of ephemerality and determination. While they are bound up in their sites of immanence, they never seem fully equivalent or limited to these.

I am suggesting that while no phenomenon is in fact more virtual than any other, in practice some of them are especially powerful as tools of metaxis. Metaxis is a term used in performance studies to denote the creation of a state of mind in which people feel as if they simultaneously inhabit two different worlds – in this case, being aware of both the virtual and actual sides of an event. Rob Shields describes metaxis as 'the operation of the imagination which connects the perceptual environment with the virtual and abstract world of meanings which over-code our perceptions' (Shields, 2003: 39). Certain kinds of musical practice and listening clearly emphasize metaxis, but at first glance, making and listening to recordings might not seem to be among them. We will have occasion to question that assumption, after we entertain it first. For all I have said about virtuality and the impossibility of literal repetition, recordings are usually thought of as storage media. We believe that they can accurately preserve essential qualities of a musical event, and that they allow for repeatable experience. When these beliefs are kept in the foreground, recordings almost seem like tools for discouraging metaxis: a situation in which the mechanisms of consistency become naturalized to the point that we lose our awareness of the virtual. Even where this is true, however, it is not entirely antithetical to metaxis, because metaxis represents a dual consciousness, of which such severe actualities form only one half. Recordings can also foster metaxis when we listen to them with the awareness that what they store, and what we encounter in them, are genetive elements rather than finished musical events. The challenge as we move forward and consider issues more specific to recordings will be to keep both halves in view, and to show how in particular instances the use of recordings itself relies on both virtual and actual sides, and can in effect be a practice of metaxis.

Recordings: fixing and difference

I already used the term *fixing* on several occasions. What I mean is any process that tends to limit the range of possible actualizations by arranging genetive elements so as to strongly favor a given outcome; in other words, any case in which factors that construct or emphasize consistency tend to overwhelm factors that might induce variation. The contrary of fixing would be variation or multiplication of possibilities. When these factors dominate, the singularity of each event is more evident. Although it is tempting to emphasize only the manner in which recordings limit and fix musical experiences, they also afford unique sources of variation. As a very rough approximation, consider two families of variation-inducing factors: (i) those contingencies related to the activity of performers (including record producers); (ii) those contingencies related to the interpretative practice of listeners. Almost by definition, the creation of a recording requires fixing the first set. This fixing is not only sonic but also ontological, because it can determine our understanding of what properties a given work should possess. As Gracyk puts it

> the recording process fixes 'everything' for inspection...every sound is now treated as deliberate and therefore relevant. If a performer coughs during a live performance, we dismiss it as an irrelevancy, but if someone coughs on a record, our knowledge that the cough could have been deleted (or another 'take' released) invites us to regard it as part of what is communicated.

(Gracyk, 1996: 79)

It is interesting to note, however, that even here the point of fixing and the degree of fixity are variable. Consider, for example, the historical progression of recording technologies: from live performances recorded by lathe, to live performances recorded on tape, to tape overdubs and editing, to digital editing, to the remixing of given recordings as a mainstream musical technique. This progression seems to push the moment of fixity further and further back. Even though some fixing of the first set of contingencies seems necessary for a recording to exist, notice that the use of recordings can greatly amplify the effects of the second set (contingencies related to listening), since recordings have greatly expanded the number and nature of possible listening practices.

Because fixing places a termination point on the time of performance, it also implies a gap between the time of listening and the time of creation. By treating the record as a trace of some completed process, we are constantly re-inscribing the alterity of that process. However, it is equally true that we often think of recordings as windows onto those times past. Recordings are used both to mark a separation and to circumvent it. The crucial thing is that recordings play an active role in these sorts of negotiations. Rather than viewing them as passive repositories, we need to see them as machines for the creation of a liminal space, between past and present, between the spaces of listening and production. Such a redefinition is not only phenomenological but also technological. Jonathan Sterne, when trying to create a general definition of recording technologies, focuses primarily on the fact that all 'modern technologies of sound reproduction use devices called *transducers*, which turn sound into something else and that something else back into sound' (Sterne, 2003: 22). Although Sterne wants to avoid ontological claims, what I find striking is the way transduction emphasizes linkage, transformation, and liminal space, all of which in turn emphasize the connection between recording technologies, genetive elements, and the singularity of each event.

Of course, the kind of transduction we expect from our recording technologies is *accurate* transduction. There is still a notion of structure and a rule of law, and this is a crucial part of what makes a recording as such. I would suggest, however, that what most listeners are concerned with when they use a recording, setting aside the special case of audiophile listening, is not accuracy of reproduction so much as the possibility of return. This should be understood not in the sense of a reinstatement of something identical so much as a return to some familiar dynamic. I have already argued that the crucial role of ESIIs causes listening experiences to resemble a conversation. When returning to a familiar piece of music, you recognize the space and yet nothing is identical to previous instances. This brings us close to the core argument Deleuze puts forward in *Difference and Repetition*: there is no repetition without difference. On at least one occasion Deleuze described this thesis in a discussion of music:

> Even in repetition, the fixed element is not defined by the identity of an element that is repeated, but by a *quality common* to the elements which could not be repeated without it...The fixed element is not the same, and does not discover an identity beneath the variation, quite the opposite. It will allow one to *identify* the variation, which is to say the individuation without identity...Far from leading the different back to the same, it allows one to identify the different as such.

> (Deleuze, 1986/1998: 72)

Beyond ontology, there are also cognitive reasons that the experience of listening to a recording will never be identical on any two occasions. Gracyk points out that humans do not have a precise memory for subtle nuances of timbre and spatial distribution. In a literal sense, every rehearing of the same recording will be different because it returns us to the presence of elements that cannot have been precisely remembered (Gracyk, 1996: 58–9). While it is true that certain people, for example highly trained performers, can do much to improve their memory of timbral nuance, even for such individuals the experience of actually hearing a sound is far richer and potentially more surprising than the experience of remembering the same sound. I would add that the fluidity of attention is another important differentiating factor. No two listenings will be the same, because it is extremely unlikely that we would direct our attention in the same way on any two occasions.

Recordings: some particular kinds of listening

In summary, my argument has been that recordings do fix a set of genetive elements, but this set is only a part of the supervenience base for music proper, and in that sense recordings do not fix or store musical works. While the repeatability and accuracy of recordings are important, they are not important as ends in themselves, but rather are occasions for the contingent process of return. As with any other form of musical actualization, the use of recordings affords certain kinds of metaxis, and not all recordings will do this in the same way. There are many different ways in which recordings are used: for entertainment, for musical study, for ethnographic and other kinds of research, for dancing, as objects of Hi-Fi enthusiasm, as instruments of torture or rebellion, and so on. My comments on specific uses of recordings will, therefore, be exploratory and preliminary, since a full description of their many different uses would require an extended study.

One way in which recordings can afford metaxis is by serving as immersive environments. Shields suggests that there is a longstanding relationship between experiences of virtuality and immersive environments, and he cites as specific examples *trompe-l'oeil* painting and Baroque church ceilings (Shields, 2003: 9). Metaxis in these contexts involves voluntary projection and exploration of an alternative world, such as the one described in the theory of ESIIs. The paradigm case for this kind of listening is solitary concentrated home listening: the use of records to mirror as closely as possible the behaviour of concert goers in the Western art music tradition. But other kinds of recording-based immersion are also possible. The next best example might be the communion sometimes experienced by dancers in discos, night clubs, and raves. In this case, the experience is not solitary, and attention is not necessarily focused on structural details of the music (although it might be). But there is still a kind of immersion in the music, leading to a liminal state of awareness.

Aside from immersion and metaxis, recordings can be linked to virtuality also in the way they function as active players in processes of becoming. Recall that the refrain was called catalytic and was compared to genetic information. The genetive elements in this case are defined by the way they act within an environment, connecting with the surroundings and refracting them into new configurations, while themselves being reconfigured in the process. The kind of recording use that most obviously corresponds to this possibility is mobile listening through devices such as the Walkman and the iPod. Although these can sometimes be used simply to block out one's immediate environment, it is more interesting to reflect on how they might mediate a particular kind of connection with the surroundings. Such devices are important in defining our subjective boundaries, but these boundaries often amount to modes of interactivity with our environment. When we listen to music while riding a bus or walking through the city, both the music and the environment are transformed. Sometimes both seem to have greatly enhanced potential, and this is also a hallmark of metaxis. Virtualities are never exhausted, and a sensitivity to virtuality is often accompanied by the feeling that there is a wealth of potential below the surface of experience. This is the feeling of quickening sometimes associated with mobile listening.

To finish our discussion of kinds of listening, I want to consider the concept of *schizophonia*.[14] Although this term was created in the context of early soundscape theory and electroacoustic composition, it has subsequently informed discussions of the general relationship between hearing, vision, and the cultural meaning of sound. The argument as generally given begins with the claim that in Western cultures since the Enlightenment, vision has been the privileged epistemic modality. However, as Weheliye puts it, '[w]hen phonographs began to augment and replace live performances and/or musical scores at the end of the nineteenth century, they created a glaring rupture between sound and vision' (Weheliye, 2005: 29). Such a rupture is thought to have produced considerable anxiety, since in an occulocentric culture the loss of visibility is a loss of the most powerful rubric of conceivability. This claim is not particular to Weheliye, but is one of the overarching themes in studies of phonography. Sterne also mentions the 'pervasive narrative' that associates modernism with an occulocentric epistemology (Sterne, 2003: 2–3). He credits Pierre Schaeffer with coining the term '"acousmatic sounds" – sounds that one hears without seeing their source,'[15] and goes on to note how this phenomenon has been granted prime importance by some later thinkers, who are especially concerned with ideas of original sources and original contexts (Sterne, 2003: 20). Sterne is not ultimately convinced, however, and argues that '[a]cousmatic or schizophonic definitions of sound reproduction carry with them a questionable set of prior assumptions about the fundamental nature of sound, communication, and experience' (Sterne, 2003: 20). Some of these questionable assumptions include: an uncritical acceptance of the primacy of face-to-face communication; the idea that other modes of sonic production will be disorienting; and the conception of an idealized, integrated state prior to the development of sound-reproduction technologies.

Although it may be the case that schizophonia was of crucial importance in certain historical and cultural contexts, I suspect it is one of those topics that would not resonate with most contemporary users of recorded popular music. One proposal as to why this might be comes from Weheliye: 'As a direct reaction to this gash between sound and human visual source, a profusion of cultural maneuvers have sought to yoke the two back together; the iconography of record covers and music videos are some obvious examples' (Weheliye, 2005: 29). While there is certainly some merit to this view, I would suggest more simply that the supposed gap is not a pressing issue in popular culture because it does not exist there. Record covers and music videos are only a small part of the overall context in which music is disseminated and understood. Such factors are not just contextual; due to the large supervenience base of musical works, they are actually a part of those works. This would be the ontological argument: by contrast with sound, music cannot be split from its sources because it is made up of those sources. A truly schizophonic experience would involve no acknowledgement that the perceived sounds were musical (although they would remain sonic), and therefore one cannot in principle experience music as schizophonic. Besides the ontological argument, there is the cognitive one already deployed. The central role of ESIIs in listening guarantees that we encounter music as bearing traces of a source. An experience in which music seemed to carry no such trace would not be a musical experience.

Recordings and community: subject to a trace

The only thing remaining is to explain my choice of title. I mean *trace* in two senses. First, in the sense of something relatively fixed that can stand as a signpost and to which we may return. Second, in the sense of something which points beyond itself and bears witness to contact with an external agent or event. We have explored both of these senses of recordings-as-trace. I mean *subject to* in the sense of being determined by or loyal to an outside force. The title is thus meant to evoke in the fixity of recordings something social and even ethical. By *ethics* I do not mean anything deontological, or exactly contractual although that is closer. I mean something more like attentiveness, fellowship, a willingness to be influenced and to nurture influence. Although the ethical dimensions of other kinds of musical practice are fairly obvious, we are not always as aware that there might be an ethical dimension to the use of recordings (apart from issues of cultural appropriation and intellectual property). The dynamic view of recordings I have proposed, in which they harbour genetive elements requiring a participatory and creative attitude for their actualization, brings this ethical dimension into sharper focus.

A trace is only relatively stable. It is subject to changes of its material, to changes of memory and cultural habit, and to vagaries in the constant stream of translations that keep it in existence. And yet, recordings are accepted and used as stable traces. One interpretation of this would be negative, arguing that by treating recordings as fixed traces we negate much of their creative potential and subject them to a rule of law. This is a dimension to be taken seriously, but I would like to emphasize something else. Treating a recording as a fixed trace also involves a certain kind of good faith, because by nurturing claims of fixity we allow for an experience of return and familiarity. It can also involve taking an interest in the processes that created such fixity, using recordings as windows onto other subjects, events, and locations. In many cases, listeners do not dwell on the fixity claim as such, but instead do things that use the fixed elements as originary points for the creation of new events, such as becoming immersed in the music so as to experience it as motion and narrative, or putting the recording into active interaction with the environment.

So who is subject to what? There are many interlocking subjectivities here, and many ways to construe their relationship with the fixity of traces. Again, we can start with the pessimistic answer. Human subjects can be viewed as the product of self-reproducing cultural discourses, subject to the monolithic traces out of which we are constructed. This answer deserves serious attention, but it has already been well explored by cultural theorists, and so without discounting it I want to move on to some less obvious points. Another answer has to do with sites of immanence. A recording always has a location and a material matrix, such that the recording is subject to its own materiality. In practice a recording will always be a trace, whatever other properties it might display. Yet another answer has to do with the fixed elements contained in the recording, although these are genetive elements rather than phenomenal ones. Musical events are subject to the elements fixed in a trace. This is so not only in the sense that musical properties supervene in part upon recorded sounds, but also in the sense that the very idea of a coherent musical work requires that listeners attend to the recorded sounds in a manner that reinscribes consistency. Recordings can be experienced as always the same, but that in itself is an active construction over something which could have been otherwise (the consistency of the work series can be broken in many ways). This is fixity of the trace as subject to active reconstruction in each event. In all these respects, there is a sense of playing with or around a series of fixed points, like being subject to the rules of a game. The theory of ESIIs suggests that we will experience this play as something done not only by ourselves and by other human agents, but also by virtual musical agents. If the overall effect of my argument has been to diminish the differences between recordings and other forms of musical actualization, this was done in part to draw attention to such social and ethical dimensions.

Notes

1   This chapter is a companion to two other texts in which I explore such a view. The first is a book about Neil Young (Echard, 2005). The second is an article outlining how a theory of virtuality can inflect our understanding of musical instruments and the relationships between performers and instruments (Echard, 2006).

2   Although they are not all cited directly, I am drawing mostly upon *Bergsonism* (1966/1988), *The Logic of Sense* (1969/1990), and *Difference and Repetition* (1968/1994), since these are the works in which Deleuze most clearly develops the implications of his theory of virtuality.

3   I mean Peirce's general association with scientific and logical investigation, and not his semiotic theory in particular, which is discussed later in the paper. Readers interested in an overview of Peirce's pragmatism as it relates to science may wish to consult Volume 1 of *The Essential Peirce* (Peirce, 1992), and especially the middle section titled 'Illustrations of the Logic of Science' (pp.109–284).

4   This emphasis comes about because in the Peircian system the action of a sign (A) is to generate further signs, so that the overall process of semiosis creates a new understanding or relationship with that sign (A). A hallmark of this activity is that a familiar mental object (A), when used as a sign, comes to be understood as something other than what it was first thought to be (A').

5   In this brief discussion, I summarize a model developed at much more length elsewhere (Echard, 2005). The most immediate sources of this model are Cumming (2001) and Lidov (1999; 2005). The cognitive element is drawn from Lakoff and Johnson (Johnson, 1987; Lakoff and Johnson, 1999), and Fauconnier and Turner (Fauconnier and Turner, 2002; Turner, 1996). The manner in which these semiotic and cognitive arguments are combined is influenced by Cone (1974), Cox (1999; 2001), Hatten (1994; 2004), Kivy (1980), Larson (2002), Shepherd and Wicke (1997), and Zbikowski (1997; 2002).

6 Throughout this chapter, I am using the term *trace* to mean a material configuration viewed with respect to its formation by a particular dynamic process. My usage in this sense is quite close to what Peirce calls an *indexical relationship*, and is not at all meant to evoke the equally well-known sense of 'trace' developed by Derrida.

7 I use the term *genetive element* to gather together the various sorts of virtual entity that act as causal or constraining factors in actualization. This neologism is not intended to sharpen the definition of such a set, but only to draw attention to the active role played by virtualities in processes of actualization.

8 I have chosen Margolis also because I see him as an exponent of contemporary pragmatism, which accords well with the Peircian dimension of my approach. An implied argument is that there are important parallels between Deleuzian philosophy and pragmatism, although establishing them properly would require another paper.

9 Another excellent overview of the relationship between Deleuze and music can be found in the collection edited by Buchanan and Swiboda (2004).

10 For a vivid but brief description of the interplay between genetic material and environmental factors see Dennett (2003: 170–1).

11 This is a different point from my earlier remarks about the non-priority of works relative to their actualizations. Those earlier remarks referred to the claim that a work, as a virtual entity, is immanent to its actualizations. These current remarks, by contrast, have to do with the way that musical works are experienced and conceptualized, regardless of their ontological status. There is, of course, an ontological implication to these remarks, i.e. that 'the musical' cannot be a fundamental ontological category since musicality is one distinctive way of experiencing and manipulating more basic cognitive resources.

12 Supervenience is an idea that has taken root most effectively in the philosophy of mind, but has also been applied in aesthetics. See Currie (1990), Kim (1993) and Levinson (1990). One way to describe the relation of supervenience is this: 'properties of type A [for example, aesthetic experiences] are supervenient on properties of type B [for example, specific historical conditions] if and only if two objects cannot differ with respect to their A-properties without also differing with respect to their B-properties' (Horgan, 1995: 778). The difference between supervenience and simple reduction is that supervenient A properties and the B properties on which they supervene are always of different kinds. For example, a brain in the state of seeing red will always be physically different from one in the state of seeing green, but it does not follow that the experience of seeing red is really identical with a brain state nor even that a colour experience and a brain state are the same kind of thing. Supervenience is a relationship of dependence but not a reductive one. I will use the phrase *supervenience base* to mean a set of subvenient elements. I prefer this phrase to simply *the subvenient* because it draws attention to the multiplicity of elements upon which any particular entity supervenes.

13 Such a claim need not involve a refutation of the material world, nor will it necessarily begin a slide towards relativism, because nothing in the view denies that there can and will be certain forms of consistency from one measuring act to another.

14 The term was coined by R. Murray Schafer (1969: 43–7) to designate a sound that is heard in isolation from its original source.

15 I treat 'acousmatic sound' and 'schizophonia' as broadly equivalent for the purposes of this argument.

References

Bogue, R. (2003) *Deleuze on Music, Painting, and the Arts*. New York: Routledge.

Buchanan, I. and Swiboda, M. (eds) (2004) *Deleuze and Music*. Edinburgh: Edinburgh University Press.

Cone, E.T. (1974) *The Composer's Voice*. Berkeley: University of California Press.

Cox, A. (1999) *The Metaphoric Logic of Musical Motion and Space*. Unpublished Ph.D. dissertation. University of Oregon.

———— (2001) 'The Mimetic Hypothesis and Embodied Musical Meaning', *Musicae Scientae* 5/2: 195–209.

Cumming, N. (2001) *The Sonic Self: Musical Subjectivity and Signification*. Bloomington: Indiana University Press.

Currie, G. (1990) 'Supervenience, Essentialism and Aesthetic Properties', *Philosophical Studies* 58: 243–57.

Davidson, D. (2001) *Essays on Action and Events*. New York: Oxford University Press.

Delanda, M. (2002) *Intensive Science and Virtual Philosophy*. New York: Continuum.

Deleuze, G. (1988) *Bergsonism*. Trans. H. Tomlinson and B. Habberjam. New York: Zone Books. Original (1966) as *Le Bergsonisme*. Paris: Presses Universitaires de France.

———— (1990) *The Logic of Sense*. Trans. M. Lester and C. Stivale. New York: Columbia University Press. Original (1969) as *Logique du sens*. Paris: Éditions de Minuit.

———— (1994) *Difference and Repetition*. Trans. P. Patton. New York: Columbia University Press. Original (1968) as *Différence et répétition*. Paris: Presses Universitaires de France.

———— (1998) 'Boulez, Proust and Time: "Occupying without counting"', (trans. T.S. Murphy) *Angelaki: Journal of the Theoretical Humanities* 3(2): 69–74. Original (1986) as 'Boulez, Proust et les temps: "Occuper sans compter"' in C. Samuel (ed.) *Eclats/Boulez*, pp.98–100. Paris: Centre Georges Pompidou.

Deleuze, G. and Guattari, F. (1987) *A Thousand Plateaus. Capitalism and Schizophrenia*. Trans. B. Massumi. Minneapolis: University of Minnesota Press. Original (1980) as *Capitalisme et schizophrenie tome 2: Mille plateaux*. Paris: Éditions de Minuit.

Dennett, D.C. (2003) *Freedom Evolves*. New York: Penguin.

Echard, W. (2005) *Neil Young and the Poetics of Energy*. Bloomington: Indiana University Press.

———— (2006) 'Sensible Virtual Selves: Bodies, Instruments, and the Becoming-Concrete of Music', *The Contemporary Music Review* 25(1/2): 7–16.

Fauconnier, G. and Turner, M. (2002) *The Way We Think: Conceptual Blending and the Mind's Hidden Complexities*. New York: Basic Books.

Gracyk, T. (1996) *Rhythm and Noise: An Aesthetics of Rock.* Durham, NC: Duke University Press.

Hatten, R. (1994) *Musical Meaning in Beethoven: Markedness, Correlation, and Interpretation.* Bloomington: Indiana University Press.

_____ (2004) *Interpreting Musical Gestures, Topics, and Tropes: Mozart-Beethoven-Schubert.* Bloomington: Indiana University Press.

Horgan, T.E. (1995) 'Supervenience', in R. Audi (ed.) *The Cambridge Dictionary of Philosophy,* pp.778–9. New York: Cambridge University Press.

Johnson, M. (1987) *The Body in the Mind.* Chicago: University of Chicago Press.

Kim, J. (1993) *Supervenience and Mind: Selected Philosophical Essays.* New York: Cambridge University Press.

Kivy, P. (1980) *The Corded Shell: Reflections on Musical Expression.* Princeton, N.J.: Princeton University Press.

Lakoff, G. and Johnson, M. (1999) *Philosophy In The Flesh: The Embodied Mind and its Challenge to Western Thought.* New York: Basic Books.

Larson, S. (2002) 'Musical Forces, Melodic Expectation, and Jazz Melody', *Music Perception* 19(3): 351–85.

Levinson, J. (1990) *Music, Art and Metaphysics: Essays in Philosophical Aesthetics.* Ithaca: Cornell University Press.

Lidov, D. (1999) *Elements of Semiotics.* New York: St. Martin's Press.

_____ (2005) *Is Language a Music? Writings on Musical Form and Signification.* Bloomington: Indiana University Press.

Margolis, J. (1980) *Art and Philosophy.* Brighton: The Harvester Press.

Peirce, C.S. (1992) *The Essential Peirce: Volume 1 (1867–1893).* Bloomington: Indiana University Press.

Schafer, R.M. (1969) *The New Soundscape.* Toronto: Arcana Editions.

Shepherd, J. and Wicke, P. (1997) *Music and Cultural Theory.* Cambridge: Polity Press.

Shields, R. (2003) *The Virtual.* New York: Routledge.

Sterne, J. (2003) *The Audible Past: Cultural Origins of Sound Reproduction.* Durham: Duke University Press.

Turner, M. (1996) *The Literary Mind.* New York: Oxford University Press.

Weheliye, A.G. (2005) *Phonographies: Grooves in Sonic Afro-Modernity.* Durham: Duke University Press.

Zbikowski, L. (1997) 'Conceptual Models and Cross-Domain Mapping: New Perspectives on Theories of Music and Hierarchy', *Journal of Music Theory* 41(2): 193–225.

_____ (2002) *Conceptualizing Music: Cognitive Structure, Theory, and Analysis.* Oxford: Oxford University Press.

COLIN SYMES

Variations on a Theme of Nelson Goodman as Arranged by Glenn Gould for the Piano Phonograph[1]

The vocabulary of aesthetic criteria that has been developed since the Renaissance is mostly concerned with terms that are proving to have little validity for the examination of electronic culture. I refer to such terms as 'imitation', 'invention' and, above all, 'originality'.

Glenn Gould (1964: 53)

Introduction

THE period from the 1820s to the 1930s was a remarkable one for Western art. One the one hand, it saw the dissolution, in the hands of painters, composers and writers, of those traditions of art that were developed and consolidated since the Renaissance, and on the other hand, it witnessed the emergence of various mechanical devices that would preserve and/or transmit otherwise transient visual and audible signals. Beginning with the camera (1839) and followed by the telephone (1876), phonograph (1877), motion pictures (1895), radio (1901) and television (1924), these devices played havoc with the metaphysics of everyday life and shattered many of the assumptions governing common sense. That their advents produced alarm, generated neurasthenia and incredulity did not retard their acceptance and they soon became part of the *ballet mécanique* of modernity. Their impacts included the normalisation of the mediated experience across myriad cultural domains and the acceptance of the experience of aesthetic phenomena at a distance, at one remove from their original states (Kenner, 1987; Kern, 1983). Aural technologies, which helped to make music a more ubiquitous presence in quotidian life, had a share in bolstering this mediated experience. Indeed, sound, after centuries of being 'occluded' by vision, came of age during this period, and the sciences of acoustic phenomena became firmly established (Sterne, 2003). The phonograph was part of the advance of sound consciousness and played a major role in transforming the entire political economy of music through its capacity to set musical performances in stone and to diffuse them on a hitherto unprecedented scale (Attali, 1977/1985).

In this chapter, I go beyond examining the 'after effects' of the phonograph, about which many musicians uttered jeremiads. For while from the first the phonograph had many apologists, who saw it as a machine without peer in terms of its capacity to arrest the inherently perishable nature of music, musicians, by and large, were pessimistic about this prospect (Sousa, 1906). They regarded the phonograph with dread; if not exactly the devil incarnate, it was preciously close to being so. Underlying this aversion was the fear that the reception of music would henceforth be balanced in favour of recording, a fear, which to some extent, has been realised.

This negative view of the phonograph continues in the parsimonious treatment it receives, certainly from philosophers, who have not given its musical impact the sustained attention received by music on the page, which remains for them the ultimate benchmark of musical articulation (Levinson, 1990).[2] This reflects the continuing ambivalence towards the family of aesthetic phenomena associated with imitative and reproduced works of art, which includes not only recordings but also copies, forgeries, fakes, pastiches and spoofs. What relationship do these aesthetic progeny have to original works of art, and what type of family resemblance and, more to the point, dissemblance, prevails among them? My argument in this chapter hypothesises that the advent of sound recording generated new, more malleable ways of performing, representing and misrepresenting music. Though it does not refer in any direct sense to the phenomenon of sound recording, Nelson Goodman's philosophy of art wrestles with the problems posed by forgeries and copies. It therefore provides a useful starting point to consider the challenges exacted on classical music by the advent of recorded sound, especially when read, as I do in this chapter, contrapuntally against the Canadian pianist Glenn Gould's philosophy of recording. Though I shall specifically deal with those pertaining to sound recording, they are also matters that pertain to other modes of 'recorded' music such as we find on radio, film, television and DVD (Gracyk, 1997). Nor do these issues pertain just to music, for they are also immanent to recordings of poems, short stories and novels: does their representation on record significantly alter their aesthetic status?

Glenn Gould's philosophy of recording

One musician who rose to the challenges of the phonograph and produced in response a 'new philosophy of recording' was Gould, who halfway through his career abandoned the concert hall for the recording studio. It is important here to distinguish Gould's performance philosophy, which Kevin Bazzana suggests is aligned to Goodman's view of music (Bazzana, 1997: 36–7), from his philosophy of recording, which was to provide *post-facto* justification for his phonographic fanaticism. Some have questioned Gould's use of the word 'philosophy' and suggested that what he produced was too homespun to be considered *proper* philosophy. An exception is Geoffrey Payzant whose intellectual biography of Gould (1992) argues that not only is the use of the word 'philosophy' apposite but so too is that of 'new'. What makes Gould's philosophy distinctive is that it represents an attempt to analyze the impact of the long-playing record and tape recording on music. Indeed, behind his decision to become a concert 'drop-out' and to restrict his subsequent musical 'appearances' to on-the-record ones was his irrevocable conviction that recordings would eventually render concerts obsolete.

It has been suggested that Gould's fascination with recording, which eventually encompassed radio, film and television, began in childhood, and was bolstered by his contact, as an adult, with media guru Marshall McLuhan (Bazzana, 2004: 257). He also fell under the influence of another Canadian, the theologian Jean Le Moyne, who averred, unusually for an intellectual, that technology was a force for good; it could place individuals in touch with one another and in touch with phenomena that otherwise would remain 'untouchable' (Payzant, 1992: 70). However, it was the LP release of Walter (Wendy) Carlos' Moog 'synthesised' J.S. Bach[3] that finally convinced Gould of the inherent superiority of recording and caused him to renounce the concert hall. Although he thought that other musicians would follow his example, Gould's prediction of the imminent demise of the concert proved premature. Aside from the obvious – that audiences actually like attending concerts, notwithstanding their sonic and musical failings, and seeing musicians perform – the majority of musicians have maintained an unyielding attachment to the idea that concerts are the apex of musical experience.

One who did was the Romanian conductor Sergiu Celibidache, who more or less at the same time as Gould was championing recording was doing the opposite, and deriding the process and end-result of sound recording. He justified this on two grounds. First, he held that music takes place in time and perishes the moment it is played, and any endeavour, such as recording, that prevents it from perishing, abrogates music's metaphysical essence and is, therefore, indefensible. He saw recordings as an unnatural form of representing music that renders everything 'flat and mediocre' (Celibidache, 2001: 71). Music only ever exists in a live state, or not at all. Second, was an allied idea: that an orchestra and an audience form an organic, holistic unit, which generates a whole series of interacting forces that bear on a musical performance and interpretation.[4] Remove the audience from the picture, as happens in a recording studio, and these forces are absent, and a performance flags.

These ideas were by no means exclusive to Celibidache but have been (and continue to be) espoused by many musicians, who find the pressure of performing in front of a microphone in a studio as not conducive for fine playing.[5] Such reactions lay behind the recent upsurge in releases of classical concerts recorded live, which claim to capture 'the excitement and emotion that you can only experience in a live concert'.[6] Their existence also highlights an important distinction (one to which I will return) between records as documents, which observe, to use an Aristotelian notion, the regular unities of concerts, and recordings – in defiance of their literal meaning – that are made in studios and are composite compositions removing music from its original temporal and spatial settings (Davies, 2001: 316–7; Edidin, 1999: 31).

In many respects, Celibidache's decision not to make recordings was as notorious as Gould's to only *make* recordings. Both decisions stemmed from parenthesising the live concert, and inquiring as to whether there was something about it that was impossible to replicate in the recording studio or, alternatively, that could only be achieved in the recording studio but not the concert hall.

Nelson Goodman's philosophy of art

Although sociologists of art with a special interest in the development of music in contemporary culture have addressed the effects of mechanical reproduction on music (Théberge, 1997; Zak, 2001), this has not been the case with philosophers of art. By and large, they have restricted the compass of their concerns to traditional expression in the mainstream arts: painting, literature and music, with occasional nods in the direction of architecture and dance. The particular issues arising from their mechanical reproduction have been eschewed. This is the case with the nominalist aesthetics of Goodman, which – though a dominant force in late-twentieth-century aesthetics – is not overflowing with references to technology and the arts. One of the few such references – and it is within a footnote – is to 'the electronic media', though it is not original (Goodman, 1976: 190). It refers to American composer Roger Sessions' view that the phonograph allows for the 'exact control of all musical elements'. While Goodman remains silent as to precisely why Sessions had reservations about the technological potentials of the phonograph,[7] he does interestingly assert in the same note, again via a reference, the contrasting view that it may not be possible to subject music to the 'minutest calculation' because of the variables induced by electronic equipment used in recording. I will later return to this throwaway remark when I explore its significance in relation to Gould's phonographic philosophy.

The remark arises by way of a footnote to Goodman's more generalised formulation of a systematic account of the arts, which, because it builds upon the function of notation, assigns classical music an 'exemplary' part.[8] His first account of the arts appears in *Languages of Art* (1976), and the second, more refined one, which rebuts the legion criticisms of the first, in *Of Mind and Other Matters* (1984).

Goodman's point of departure is the identification of the grounds for authenticity in the arts. He argues that 'forgeries of works of arts' of the type perpetrated by the infamous Dutch forger Hans van Meegeren pose a range of problems not just for gallery curators hoodwinked by them, but also for philosophers of art. The lack of any perceivable differences, other than those revealed by X-rays, chemical analysis or a connoisseur's eye, suggests that artistic originality might be an overrated quality. Indeed, as Goodman points out, a copy, in some instances, might actually exhibit superior qualities to an original. Part of the lukewarm response to copies, which are held in much less esteem than originals, could be cultural (Sagoff, 1978: 456).

Artistic dissemblance such as forgery threatens the prevailing codes of aesthetics in at least some of the arts (Goodman, 1976: 100). Goodman points out that the prevalence of forgery is more evident in painting, whereas it is absent in 'allographic' arts like music and literature, which utilise systems of notation for their complete articulation and embodiment. In order to explain this anomaly, Goodman identifies a category of the arts he calls 'autographic' that are 'one-stage' and 'single'. Painting is the paradigm case. It is in essence one-stage because there is always a distinction between an original and forgery, such that 'even the most exact duplication does not...count as genuine' (Goodman, 1976: 113). This is because their histories of production are dissimilar.

Indeed, consummate forgers will often go out of their way to imitate these histories. Van Meegeren, for example, spent many years researching and assimilating Johannes Vermeer's techniques; he also developed methods for aging his 'Vermeers', to hide the fact that they were painted in the mid-twentieth century. His forgeries were an admixture of fact and fiction, of the true and the false, what in literary circles is called 'faction'. To further allay any doubts about their possible provenances, he also enlisted the services of qualified art critics – one of them an expert on Vermeer – to confirm their status and affirm their authenticity (Werness, 1983). In other words, he did not work entirely alone on mastering his scam. Indeed, the existence of *his* paintings helped change, albeit ever so slightly, the profile of the precedent class of existing 'Vermeers', thereby reinforcing their authenticity. But even though he went to extreme lengths to ensure that his 'Vermeers' were accepted as authentic – and for a short time they were – their counterfeit nature was eventually exposed, something that now remains obvious to anyone comparing them with *actual* Vermeers (Gardner, 1982).

The reputation of paintings rests or falls on establishing an irrefutable genealogy, a clear line of descent between a painter and his paintings. In the absence of this genealogy, accreditation from critics, from respectable art institutions is required. In fact, Goodman was often accused of downplaying the institutional factors underpinning artistic authenticity. Certainly, his second account of the language of arts gives them more scope for play, particularly in relation to another binary he holds salient, namely, that between 'execution' and 'implementation'. He defines 'execution' as the 'creation of a work, from the first flicker of an idea to the final touch', whereas 'implementation' is about obtaining public recognition (and it is not always forthcoming) for that creation, about exhibiting paintings, publishing novels and securing performances of musical compositions (Goodman, 1984: 143).

This distinction is particularly marked in the case of notational arts such as literature and music. Admittedly, one of the pitfalls of Goodman's account is its historical blindness to the fact that the notational basis of Western music is a recent development and that the advent of the printing press changed the material conditions of both music and literature in profound ways. A poem, for example, is only complete when it is published, when in effect it is implemented and undergoes multiplication – a fact that becomes more realisable in the context of printing. Of more import, though, is that it matters not in what font or coloured ink the poem is printed; provided that the alphabetical configuration of the *original* poem is uncorrupted, it remains the *same* poem. In short, different 'representations' of the poem do not confer, as they would for a painting, any relevant aesthetic difference. By contrast, the very absence of notation makes paintings resistant to duplication, and rather paradoxically, because their quotient of individuality is higher, paintings are more vulnerable to forgery. Music, on the other hand, is like literature in being multiple, since a score, like a novel, can be printed *ad nauseam*, without attracting opprobrium; but music also has a second stage, i.e. its performance, which, unless it is subject to a recording, is single but not recoverable – a point lost on Goodman. Indeed, music involves a considerable amount of 'secondary artistry' necessary for its full implementation and without which a score remains, necessarily, stillborn. The fact that more players are involved in this implementation means that within music there are more possibilities for its misrepresentation.

With music, contrasting conditions prevail to those of paintings: *only* exact duplications of an original score constitute genuine instances of the score (Goodman and Elgin, 1988: 66). The matter of who actually wrote the score, though not without some bearing, is less significant in upholding this condition. Indeed, the exact provenance of many musical works, particularly during the Baroque era, when composers – George Frideric Handel is a case in point – would routinely pilfer the works of others as well as their own, is often hard to pinpoint, but this does not lessen their standing. Also, it was common for works of this period to be misattributed. Still, discovering that J.S. Bach did not, after all, compose a certain work, that it was composed by his older cousin J.C. Bach instead, does not make it a different work; it only changes 'our epistemic relation to the music' (Levinson, 1990: 227).

With music, Goodman's criterion of an exact duplication also carries over into a performance: for a performance to count as a genuine instance of a score it must exhibit note-for-note compliance with the score. It would not matter how waywardly a score is *interpreted;* as long as it meets this condition, it would be enough to constitute a *genuine* instance of the score. However, as Goodman observes, there are aspects of a score that leave scope for interpretation and are not notational in any conventional sense. Many of Goodman's most trenchant critics have focused on this aspect of his argument stating that its failure to recognise the discretionary aspect of performing weakens its cogency (Davies, 2001: 139; Goehr, 1992: 39). This is another manifestation of Goodman's historically limited vision of music, which fails to account for the fact that in the past, certainly during the Baroque era, such improvisatory elements as cadenzas and trills were parts of musical compositions. Moreover, there are many forms of music, e.g. jazz, where improvisation remains a cornerstone of performance practice. It is only in the last hundred years or so that it has become commonplace for compositions to be written out in full score, and full-compliance with them has become the expectation. But even with the ascendancy of this practice in classical music, such 'auxiliary directions' as tempo markings still leave performers with discretion to interpret a work in ways considered to be either in keeping with, or wildly at loggerheads with the stated tempo. Of themselves these markings do not have an impact on the notational identity of the work, which remains what it is, whether it is played too slow or too fast (Goodman, 1976: 185).

Indeed, Goodman proffers the view that many performances that are note perfect may nevertheless be uninspiring and unmoving, whereas those containing many wrong notes – and which therefore, by his logic, are not genuine instances of a work – might be quite brilliant (Goodman, 1976: 186). Moreover, it is not unknown for conductors and performers to gainsay what a composer actually wrote. At times, they have even had the temerity to revise their works. Anton Bruckner's symphonies are a case in point. Karl Haas, Grzegorz Nowak, Daniel Orel all had a go at improving them. Once this kind of practice becomes the norm, all attempts at 'score preservation [are] lost' and 'we can go all the way from Beethoven's *Fifth Symphony* to *Three Blind Mice*' (Goodman, 1976: 187). The point is that in the metamorphosis of a score into a performance, mistakes and changes are made – some willful, some unintentional – that transgress the 'terms' of the original score. This does not detract from the legitimacy of the performance, which becomes clearer if one makes a distinction between *logical* usage and *ordinary* usage: logical usage demands that a genuine instance of a work occurs only if its performance exhibits unerring consistency with the original score. Ordinary usage, appertaining to the hurly-burly of a live performance, is more forgiving and allows for indiscretions to occur, even willful ones, although they might not, in the end, be genuine.[9]

Some have argued that Goodman's use of the word 'forgery' is wantonly imprecise (Steele, 1977). In truth, a forgery (not as Goodman uses the word) is an exact copy that is fraudulently passed off as if it were an original, as in the case of bank notes and passports. But van Meegeren did not do this. He painted a number of paintings and passed them off as previously *unknown* Vermeers, paintings that appeared to belong to the class of existing Vermeers. In this sense, they were fake Vermeers, *not* forged ones. As Margolis (1983) has suggested, while the category of fakes includes all forgeries, that of forgeries does not include all fakes. Indeed, fakes arguably belong to a more universal class of art objects, that of imitations, which includes various forms of copies. But the latter rarely attract opprobrium and are considered aesthetically licit. Indeed, there is a fine line between a copy and a fake, and depending on the motives of their perpetrator (which are not always known, of course) the one can easily become the other.

For example, van Meegeren set out to deceive the art world and expose the ineptitude of critics (Dutton, 1983). This is not the case with a photographic reproduction of a Vermeer, which, even though having some considerable semblance to its original, is not reproduced with any pretence of being an original. It is hung for its capacity 'to serve instead of the original', not to *serve* as the original (Goodman, 1986: 291). Moreover, there is the question of its scale: it may be smaller or larger than its original.

The same could be said of a phonographic recording of Jean Sibelius' Third Symphony: it stands in lieu of the original performance, and depending on how loud it is played, it might actually reproduce the scale of its sound. However, although people listening to it, over equipment capable of reproducing the amplitude of the original performance, might feel as though they are at the Barbican and the London Symphony Orchestra is in their living room, they will only do so while they have their eyes shut! And herein lies a significant difference between a reproduced painting, which at least looks like the original, and the recording of the symphony, which might *sound* as though it is being played in the Barbican but certainly does not *look* like it. In this respect, sound reproductions of music are attenuated ones, though this deficiency need not of itself abrogate their capacity to stand in lieu of the music, at least, in Goodman's terms. Since scores do not prescribe that a particular concert hall is necessary for their full implementation, it matters not whether the Barbican is seen.

A record that is not a record

Gould argued that 'electronic culture' had blurred the divisions that had once existed between the composer and performer (Gould, 1964: 53).[10] Even the listener, at the very end of the recording chain, now has more say in what music they listen to, how, when, and where they do so – freedoms they hitherto never enjoyed. These freedoms mean that the work on a recording does not necessarily have to end when it 'is dispatched from the pressing factory' (Gould, 1983, 57). 'Creative listeners' can do their own work on it (Gould and Davis, 1983: 57). In fact, Gould's 'new philosophy' addresses the potential of these new freedoms, of the 'dial twiddling' possibilities open to creative listeners, who would have the scope to produce their own recordings, spliced together from different interpretations of the same work; indeed, Gould hoped that record companies would eventually produce kit recordings for this purpose (Gould, 1966: 59).[11]

Given that these transformations are far from trivial, the question arises as to whether any of them has the capacity to change music into an autographic art. Nowhere does Goodman assert that his two categories of art are immutable, or that in the future, as a result, say, of technology, an autographic art could not become an allographic one, and vice versa. Even Goodman could not hope to play god in the ever so strange world of the arts. In this connection, he invokes the *enfant terrible* John Cage as one composer who was possibly turning music into an autographic art. In his pursuit of more libertarian modes of composing, Cage abandoned conventional notation in favour of a graphical system. But because it lacked any 'syntactical differentiation' there was no assurance that any one performance of a work could ever be like any other, which was why Goodman held that Cage's graphical notation was not a notational one (Goodman, 1976: 188). Around the same time as he was developing his graphical system, Cage began experimenting with gramophone records not so much to record music as to generate it. He took a series of frequency records of constant and sliding tones produced by RCA-Victor for test purposes, and through altering their playing speeds was able to produce the novel 'glissandi' that are a feature of his *Imaginary Landscape IV*. Though by no means the first to deploy a phonograph in creative ways, Cage's example highlights the complexity and heterogeneity of phonographic culture: as well as being used to reproduce music, to which Cage objected on industrial grounds (Kostelanetz and Cage, 1989: 281), the gramophone can be used to produce music, Rap being a case in point.

When he consummated his 'love affair with the microphone' in 1964 (Payzant, 1992: 36), Gould also wanted to explore the creative potential of the phonograph. Part of his reason for deserting the concert hall was that he had grown tired of the concert's theatricality and the attendant 'unnecessary affectations' (Mach, 1980: 85). In succumbing to the 'ticket purchasing whims of the public' (Said, 1983: 53), to the 'group consciousness of the audience' (Angliette, 1992: 18), he felt he was turning into a vaudeville artist. Audiences might make a contribution to the music along the lines that Celibidache imagined, but they did so, Gould held, at the expense of the music. Without their distorting presences, he hoped he might achieve more musical integrity; certainly of the music he generally performed.[12]

The recording studio offered more than just a refuge from malign audiences (Bazzana, 1997: 238); for most performers, it offered a place where faultless, impeccably accurate performances could be achieved. This had nothing to do with the absence of an audience and everything to do with the electronic technology that had become commonplace in the recording studios of the 1960s, which had revolutionized the way records were made, and had the potential to change the way music was 'represented' on disc. Instead of being made all of a piece, in one take, as had happened hitherto, which meant musical errors were preserved for posterity, records were now made, much to the chagrin of some musicians, who abhorred the process, section by section, often out of sequence, in short takes, the final recording constituting a concatenation of the most acceptable of the takes. With the manifold editing processes afforded by tape recording, it had become possible to rectify the mishaps made during the white heat of a recording session – sometimes long after they were committed – with the acumen of hindsight, via what Gould called a 'post-performance editorial' (Gould, 1966: 51). Not that Gould needed to avail himself of these electronic opportunities to rectify his playing errors. To the contrary: from accounts of record producers with whom he worked, the many takes he made were invariably note-perfect; they just involved different interpretations (Scott et al., 1983).

Thus, the recording studio provides a radically different frame for performing music from the concert hall, where it is not just the presence of an audience that can make or break a performance but also the physical fatigue of the players at the end of a long and demanding work, e.g. Franz Schubert's Piano Trio Op.99 D898 in B-flat major, which carefully planned recording sessions can overcome (Tomes, 2004: 158). According to Gould, recording enabled the 'inexorable linearity of time', that most limiting of factors, to be overcome (Gould and Davis, 1983: 57).

That phonographs enabled performances to be fixed meant that they could also be *fixed*. Thus, in the quest of phonographic perfection, Gould regularly pirated his own recordings, lifting notes and inserting them elsewhere, even though some sonic deterioration was inevitable and the tape splices involved were potentially audible, even if only by a minority of listeners (Gould, 1987a; Kazdin, 1989). But he was not the only musician to do so. The history of recording post-1950 is littered with examples of wrong notes being changed, notes being added where there were none, of singers supplying notes that neither they nor anyone else could achieve, and so on (Chanan, 1995). The application of these techniques, which Gould saw as akin to 'creative cheating' – hence his admiration for van Meegeren (Gould, 1966: 54) – meant that it was possible to produce performances on records that in Goodman's terms correlated absolutely with the score in being note-perfect performances, which were, in effect, a result of the 'exact control of all musical elements', the most accurate of allographs. As such, they are, quite literally, a world apart from the 'documentary records' referred to earlier and which are free, more or less, of the interventions Gould was endorsing.[13]

Not that all the sounds on a record are necessarily genuine instances of music; Gould's are no exception. His are particularly infamous for such clearly audible intrusions as his squeaky chair, his 'hiccupping' Steinway, and most intrusive of all, his humming in the background.[14] In fact, Gould would have eliminated the latter had an equalization system capable of doing so been available (Cott, 1984: 42). Their presence is a 'signature property' of Gould's early recordings.

Underscoring recording

One of Goodman's observations about music – and it differs in this respect from literature – is that it is a two-stage art: there is the score, which has as its end product a performance, generally at a concert or recital but also, these days, as a recording. He even posits that there might be a third stage, i.e. that of listening (Goodman, 1976: 114). Some philosophers of music have averred that music could, in these terms, be a one-stage art, and have cavilled at the notion that performance is necessary at all (Kivy, 1997); accordingly, it is possible to read a score silently (much in the way books are read) and to *hear* the music, as it were, in one's head, as pure, 'un-instrumented' sound.[15] Another way to listen to music is through a phonographic recording. The fact that many compositions have infrequent live performances because of the conservative philosophies of concert programmers means that those pieces of music that might not otherwise be performed in a concert are accessible to listeners through recordings, though this way of listening to music might not prove to be the best way. This was another reason why Gould felt that the gramophone was a medicine for the musical ills of our time. Moreover, many works, e.g. Frank Martin's *Sinfonia Concertante*, sound better, in terms of their sonic resolution, on record than they do in the unflattering acoustics of many concert halls. And they are, in this sense, 'naturals for the microphone' (Gould, 1966: 57).

Then, there is disc-specific music that can only be performed on record, of the sort pioneered by jazz pianist Bill Evans, who released a disc (1963), utilizing overdubbing techniques, in the 'conversation with myself' genre, of musicians playing along with themselves. Eventually, classical musicians, including Gould, who first used the technique in his recording of Franz Liszt's arrangement of Ludwig van Beethoven's Fifth Symphony, adopted the practice. In order to sonically 'elucidate' parts of the last movement, he transcribed them for four hands, which he played himself. This led to further, more complex phonographic experiments that he called 'acoustic orchestration', which vindicated his view that the 'concert was dead', and that composers would eventually begin to write music with recordings in mind.[16] To this end, he began to make recordings of the piano repertoire that transgressed 'concert hall discourse', and no longer took as their benchmarks the 'best seat in the house' (Symes, 2004). Adopting techniques analogous to those used in film, Gould began to experiment with recording music – if the music demanded it – from a variety of perspectives, and to use the sonic equivalents of close-up and pan shots. For example, he suggested that the opening of Beethoven's Piano Sonata Op.106, No.29, the *Hammerklavier*, seemed to call out for a close-up microphone 'shot' (Gould and Davis, 1983: 292).[17]

In giving 'actuality' to his phonographic convictions, Gould negated the idea that music's second stage was necessarily a performance of the live concert kind. His acoustic experiments added another line of possible musical representation: that provided by the facilities of the recording studio. In his hands the piano *became* the phonograph. Thus, he was demonstrating that it was possible to execute performances of music on record that were impossible in any other way.

Counterfeit discs

It is not clear from Goodman's writings (or those of his many commentators who have attempted to either refine or refute his arguments) how he regards 'recording', i.e. whether it is, in his view, correlative – at least in the terms that count – of the concert experience and therefore a legitimate form of musical performance. If it is not, then Gould's renunciation of the concert was aesthetically indefensible. Clues to the elucidation of this oversight lie in Goodman's analysis of printmaking, which he sees as two-stage and multiple. Indeed, there are some similarities between the way records and prints are made; both are 'stamped' from masters, which, according to Goodman's line of reasoning, is why printmaking and by extension record-making are autographic arts (Goodman, 1976: 118). For, like a print, each record has a clear line of descent from its master and is different from its predecessors and successors.

However, unlike the makers of prints, record companies do not limit the number of copies that can be pressed from masters. They are more like book publishers in this respect – though one might imagine an opportunist record company setting out to raise the value of its discs by individualizing each pressing, limiting their number, numbering each of them and then issuing each with a certificate of authenticity. However, given the complex division of labour associated with recording, it is not clear who would actually sign such a certificate of authenticity: its producer, performer or composer?[18]

The small physical differences that exist between each and every copy of an LP (the option is less clear cut in the case of CDs), and produce, according to the pianist Alfred Brendel (Mach, 1980: 28–9), audible differences, albeit of a very small magnitude, which frequent playing often makes more pronounced, do not in the least effect the capacity to determine whether the music on the record complies with its score. Indeed, given its greater robustness and acoustic perspicacity, there is more of an opportunity to do so. Thus, recording falls squarely within Goodman's notion of an allographic art.

In order to develop the remainder of my argument, I will undertake a thought experiment: much of Goodman's argument about the distinctiveness of painting rests, I have argued, on the 'family resemblance' between forgeries and copies. Although sound recordings also share a family resemblance with copies, excluding instances where recordings of live concerts are made and then released on disc without any further intervention, it is not clear of what they are *actually* copies: scores, live performances, other performances of the same work? And we have already seen that by resorting to modern-day editing techniques, record producers and engineers can make a mockery of provenance information: recordings are made over a period of time and in a variety of places; sometimes even different performers are used. This is particularly true of those more 'inventive' forms of recording, such as Gould's 'acoustic orchestrations', which treat the technical possibilities afforded by the phonograph as a mode of musical re-presentation rather than representation.

Imagine, then, that there has been an unexpected discovery in a Toronto basement: it consists of four previously unknown recordings (R_1, R_2, R_3, and R_4), allegedly made by Gould in the latter stages of his career. Given the cult status the pianist continues to enjoy, their discovery has provoked considerable interest around the world, and stands to gain the record label releasing them considerable profit.

On first hearing, all four recordings display the sonic signatures of Gould's playing and recordings: extreme clarity of parts and attention to detail, the audible incidentals, the 'hiccupping' Steinway, Gould humming along, and so on; even the dry acoustic of Eaton Auditorium, his preferred recording venue. Furthermore, the recordings are on tape stock that Gould could have used (3M's 206) and exhibit the audio 'fingerprints' of his equipment (AMPEX 440 series; Studer-8 track). The four recordings appear to be authentic, but are, in various ways, misrepresentations.

R_1 is a bootleg recording, apparently of a Gould concert, given in April 1963 – one of his last – made, so it is claimed, furtively by a member of the audience, on his Nagra. This is a documentary recording, and though illegally obtained, is neither a forgery nor a fake. It proves to be a spoof, of the type that Gould himself had once proposed to CBS, and which would have involved him imitating a live performance of Vladimir Horowitz, complete with splutters and coughs from the audience, but which would have been entirely produced in his Toronto studio and not in the romantic setting claimed (Friedrich, 1989: 241–2). The alleged bootleg recording, thus violating the terms of trade of bootleg recording, proves to be Gould spoofing Gould. I hasten to add that spoofs like parodies and pastiches (also having some family semblance to copies) rarely provoke any moral outrage. To the contrary, they are often admired for their ingenuity; P.D.Q. Bach's – by the composer Peter Schickele – are a case in point.

R_2 is of J.S. Bach's *Goldberg Variations* made from the many 'out-takes' remaining from Gould's two previous recordings of the work made in 1955 and 1981, and which were spliced together in a remix, as a 'new' recording by a former record producer of Gould's – a sort of 'producer's cut'. As it was Gould's habit to record 10 or 15 different interpretations before 'deciding on a final performance' (Payzant, 1992: 70), his record label CBS (now Sony) would possess a large number of such 'out-takes' in its vaults. It would entirely be in line with Gould's 'new philosophy' that they be released, perhaps in kit form! However, the producer had not undertaken his 're-mastering' of Gould's recordings of the *Goldberg Variations* with any malicious intent, but merely as a phonographic exercise; further, he had not intended to release the result commercially.

With its pan-spotting techniques clearly audible, R_3 is an 'acoustic orchestration' of Beethoven's *Hammerklavier* Sonata. That Gould had contemplated such an orchestration lends credibility to its authenticity. But there is no record of the recording listed in any Gould discography; and an extensive search of the Glenn Gould Archives at the National Library of Canada reveals no such recording. If there had been one, Sony would have been keen to track it down, to include it as part of its Glenn Gould Edition. A leading Gould scholar hazards that the pianist might have made R_3 in secret, at his Toronto hideaway, but suggests this most unlikely, given his derisory view of the *Hammerklavier*.[19]

By way of explanation a record producer comes forward and confesses to making the counterfeit recording, which he was proposing to release on his own label, Partita, with a projected number, CD 318. It transpires that R_3 was a 'recreation' of an existing recording of the *Hammerklavier* Sonata that Gould had made for a CBC radio broadcast in December 1967, and at which the producer had been present. The producer, unbeknownst to Gould, retained a set of tapes of the broadcast and using the latest digital technology 'reprocessed' them as a seemingly authentic acoustic orchestration – including the close-up of the sonata's opening bars. The recording, by dint of its perpetrator's confession, is declared to be a fake – though it is 'genuine' Gould in all but its mode of 'orchestration'.

R_4 is also an unauthenticated recording. It is of Igor Stravinsky's Three Movements from *Petrushka* – a notoriously difficult work to execute, demanding almost superhuman virtuosity of the type Gould was eminently capable of. Its existence is intriguing and also slightly troubling because there is not a single work of Stravinsky listed in Gould's *opera omnia*. Moreover, Gould's detestation of this composer's works in general and those for the piano in particular, is on the public record (Mach, 1980: 98). Thus, there are some questions hanging over R_4's provenance. The information appended to R_4 suggests that it was made in 1979, at the Eaton Auditorium. This was before Gould had begun using a Yamaha rather than his 'trusted' but mechanically defective Steinway CD 318.

However, even though the recording has all the hallmarks of Gould's other recordings, its history of production, which seems genuine, has been faked. It is a van Meegeren recording[20] perpetrated by a young pianist, who wanted to expose Sony's executives as charlatans for not appreciating his talents. A bit of a dab hand at being a musical ventriloquist, he was able to 'imitate' enough of Gould's virtuosic abilities to produce, with some assistance from friends who were part of the scam, a thoroughly convincing set of tapes of the work in all but one measure, the hiccupping piano.[21] By 1979, when R_4 was allegedly made, Gould had eliminated this sonic flaw,[22] and anyone with knowledge of the precedent class of Gould recordings would have identified the un-timeliness of this hiccup. Its history of production was not spotless. Anachronisms are the Achilles' heel of fakes.

Coda

Jerrold Levinson has argued that musical compositions are not, *pace* Kivy (1984), pure structures, but have 'histories of production', that they are 'person and time tethered objects' (Levinson, 1990: 216). The matter of determining their 'factional' status, and differentiating what is fact from fiction, rests, in the end, on knowing their history of production, and on knowing their perpetrator's motives and intentions. This also extends to sound recordings, which offer new scope for musical representation and misrepresentation, along the lines exemplified in R_1, R_2, R_3, and R_4. In these four thoroughly efficacious recordings, their perpetrators had varying intentions, some innocent and self-indulgent as in R_1 and R_2, some more heinous as in R_3 and R_4, but all involving the convincing deployment of fact and fiction. When the motives are unknown, it would be difficult to determine the status of each recording. Indeed, this status can be double-valued. For example, R_1 could have been R_4; spoofs can be fakes, and vice versa. R_3 exhibits another quality of contemporary counterfeit culture, that is, its hybrid character; that through using technology, the seemingly genuine can be falsified.

R_4 also demonstrates that performances (much like paintings) possess autographic properties that transcend notation and that can be faked (or imitated) on a recording at least, where the performer can *only* be heard. It would be far more difficult to fake performances on a DVD and still harder in a live performance – particularly when it involves a dead performer like Gould, even with his penchant for dressing up. Thus, recordings, though on the surface seemingly allographic, also possess autographic properties. Indeed, a sound recording is a combination of both: it is, to coin a word, 'auto-allographic'. This becomes more evident once a performer or ensemble has undertaken enough recordings to establish a precedent class, and enables, say, the qualities of Gould's playing to be distinguished from Van Cliburn's and Sviatoslav Richter's. What is valuable about recording, then, is that it is not a recording of music as such – a score is that – but that of a performance, which though having a notational basis to it, contains many elements, as many of Goodman's critics recognized, that cannot be notated, though they can be imitated and faked. This means that each performance of a musical work, be it on record or live, is different and is therefore, in Goodman's terms, autographic, the most important implication being that it has the potential to be faked: though to what end, other than a malicious one, is a moot point.

Prior to the advent of recording, performances were, in Gould's phrase, strictly take-one affairs; recordings enabled them to be preserved, to be recovered, and, in Goodman's terms, to be multiplied. To bring the chapter full circle, to its epigraph: it could be that in the age of 'electronic culture' such terms as 'originality' and 'imitation' now have 'little validity'. However, it might also be true that in an age where the *performance* of music has the potential to be preserved in entirely new ways, they have taken on new meanings and that the advent of electronic culture has led to new forms of musical representation as well as misrepresentation.

Notes

1   I wish to thank Mine Doğantan-Dack and the two anonymous readers of an earlier draft of this chapter for their helpful comments.

2   This is less true of those Continental schools of philosophy that have explored the 'culture industry', and of which Theodor Adorno is the most celebrated exemplar (Adorno, 1938/2002). Most mainstream Anglo-American philosophers, however, would see his analysis of the phonograph's commodity regimes as ideology rather than philosophy. Another Continental philosopher often mentioned in conjunction with the phonograph, though he wrote almost nothing about it, is Walter Benjamin (Patke, 2005).

3   The CBS LP (S63501), originally titled 'Electronic realizations and performances' but now known as 'Switched-on Bach', was issued in 1968 and became an immediate best-seller. Incidentally, Gould proclaimed it as his 'record of the decade' (Gould, 1987b: 430).

4   This was a view shared by R. G. Collingwood, who thought that recordings placed audiences and performers at an arm's length from one another. Listeners to gramophone records 'overhear' a performance. They do not participate in it as they would at a concert; hence, the musical experience of recordings is an inadequate one (Collingwood, 1958: 323).

5   Pianist Charles Rosen argues that he likes to be 'inside the music' before recording it. Once pressured to record as fillers for an LP some piano pieces by Bohuslav Martinů, which he had not previously played live, he was not thrilled with the result (Rosen, 2005: 38).

6   See the liner notes of Sir Colin Davis conducting Sibelius' Symphonies Nos. 3 and 7 with the London Symphony Orchestra (LSO Live LS00051). The latest manifestation of live recording is the so-called 'take-away concert'. Pioneered by Cologne's Gürzenich Orchestra, it enables audiences to purchase a CD or MP3 download of the concert they have just attended (see Smith, 2006: 10).

7   Sessions' objection to recordings was that they exhaust their interest after several hearings (Sessions, 1950: 70).

8   Goodman's account has a number of shortcomings, not the least of which is its dogged adherence to classical music for exemplars. At no stage does he refer to forms of music that are not written down. For this reason, its application has been limited to classical music.

9   As LPs of the 'world's worst orchestra' – the Portsmouth Sinfonia – demonstrate, performances of well-known classics can depart very markedly from a score and yet still remain recognizable ('Hallelujah', Transatlantic Records, TRA-285). This could be because the mind's ear renders them recognizable.

10 These divisions were less pronounced before musical Romanticism.

11 More interactive CDs are now being released. For example, Nicholas McGegan's recording for Harmonia Mundi of Handel's *Messiah* (HMU 907050.52) allows listeners to reconfigure its performance in terms of variant scores of the work (Bazzana, 1997: 82). However, this is not what Gould had in mind, which was that listeners would have the option of 'mixing' their own version of the *Messiah* from different recordings of the work made available to them, e.g. John Eliot Gardiner's, Nicholas McGegan's, Thomas Beecham's and Trevor Pinnock's.

12 Gould's repertoire inclined toward 'structuralist' composers: Arnold Schönberg, J.S. Bach, and Orlando Gibbons (Payzant, 1992: 82).

13 I would not want to suggest that the sonic equivalent of point-and-shoot applies here because interventions are undertaken to improve live recordings, including those of the aforementioned LSO Live, such as 'patching' sections that are not up to scratch or speed, removing applause and so on.

14 These intrusions are particularly evident on his recording of J. S. Bach's Two and Three Part Inventions, the liner notes of which include a *mea culpa* from Gould (1965), acknowledging, and at the same time justifying the hiccupping piano (CBS SBRG 72277).

15 In reinforcing his argument that music can be read straight off the page and performed in the head without the need for instrumentation, Kivy cites Donald Francis Tovey who claimed that he was once so engrossed in reading the score of a string quarter that he applauded at its conclusion (Kivy, 1997: 215).

16 The classical repertoire is not surfeited with such works. One of the few is Robert Simpson's Symphony No. 7. This was specifically written 'for one man sitting in his chair, listening by himself'. Ironically, he would have to wait almost a decade before one would be able to do that; the symphony was only released on CD in 1988 (Hyperion CDA66280). This presents a marked difference from popular and rock music, which – beginning with the Beatles' *Sergeant Pepper's Lonely Hearts Club Band* – has been composed with recordings in mind.

17   Gould only produced one such 'acoustically orchestrated' LP, Sibelius' *Kyllikki* and Three
     Sonatines (CBS SBR 235908). For their recording, he developed a system of 'notation'
     (Bazzana, 1997: 249).

18   Record companies, especially those in the field of popular music, do actively 'rarify' their
     product by issuing discs in limited editions, although their rarity derives more from their
     'surrounds', from their packaging rather than their sound qualities (Stanley, 2002: 111,
     116).

19   Gould held it to be the 'least rewarding piece that Beethoven wrote for piano' (cited in
     Friedrich, 1989: 139)

20   As performances involve 'putting on an act', the idea of faking one has a slightly odd ring.

21   At a 'recital' organized to celebrate the pianist's seventy-fourth birthday, a Yamaha digital
     piano 'performed' Gould's performance (recording) of the *Goldberg Variations*. Most
     members of the audience were unable to tell the difference ('Software, robotic piano
     replicate Gould's Goldberg Variations', http://www.cbc.ca/arts/story/2006/09/25/gould-
     piano-technology.html?ref=rss). The existence of this simulation suggests an R_5.

22   As he was no longer interested in mimicking the sound of a harpsichord, Gould was at
     pains to eliminate it in his 1981 recording of the *Goldberg Variations* (Forfia, 1995: 37).

References

Adorno, T.W. (2002) 'On the Fetish-Character in Music and the Regression of Listening', in
     R. Leppert (ed.) *Essays on Music*, pp.288–317. Berkeley: University of California Press.
     Original (1938/1970–1986) as 'Über den Fetischcharakter in der Musik un dies Regression
     des Hörens', R. Tiedemann (ed.) *Gesammelte Schriften* Band 14, pp.14–50. Frankfurt am
     Main: Suhrkamp.

Angliette, E. (1992) *Philosopher at the Keyboard: Glenn Gould*. Metuchen, NJ: Scarecrow
     Press.

Attali, J. (1985) *Noise: The Political Economy of Music*. Trans. B. Massumi. Minneapolis:
     University of Minnesota Press. Original (1977) as *Bruits: essai sur l'économie politique de
     la musique*. Paris: Presses Universitaires de France.

Bazzana, K. (1997) *Glenn Gould: The Performer in the Work. A Study in Performance Practice*.
     Oxford: Clarendon Press.

————— (2004) *Wondrous Strange: The Life and Art of Glenn Gould*. Oxford: Oxford
     University Press.

Celibidache, S. (2001) 'Chosen Pieces', in K. Gerke (ed.) *Celibidache!* pp.51–83. Chicago: Facets
     Multimedia.

Chanan, M. (1995) *Repeated Takes. A Short History of Recording and Its Effects on Music*.
     London: Verso.

Collingwood, R.G. (1958) *The Principles of Art*. New York: Galaxy.

Cott, J. (1984) *Conversations with Glenn Gould*. Chicago: University of Chicago Press.

Davies, S. (2001) *Musical Works and Performances: A Philosophical Exploration*. Oxford:
     Clarendon Press.

Dutton, D. (1983) 'Artistic Crimes', in D. Dutton (ed.) *The Forger's Art: Forgery and the Philosophy of Art*, pp.172–87. Berkeley: University of California Press.

Edidin, A. (1999) 'Three Kinds of Recording and the Metaphysics of Music', *British Journal of Aesthetics* 39 (1): 24–39.

Forfia, K. (1995) 'Rerecording the Goldberg Variations – Glenn Gould's Workshop', *Piano and Keyboard* 176: 34–8.

Friedrich, O. (1989) *Glenn Gould: A Life and Variations*. New York: Random House.

Gardner, H. (1982) *Art, Mind and Brain: A Cognitive Approach to Creativity*. New York: Basic Books.

Goehr, L. (1992) *The Imaginary Museum of Musical Works: An Essay in the Philosophy of Music*. Oxford: Clarendon Press.

Goodman, N. (1976) *Languages of Art: An Approach to a Theory of Symbols*. Indianapolis: Hackett.

———— (1984) *Of Mind and Other Matters*. Cambridge: Cambridge University Press.

———— (1986) 'A Note on Copies', *The Journal of Aesthetics and Art Criticism* 45 (3): 291–2.

Goodman, N. and Elgin, C.Z. (1988) *Reconceptions in Philosophy and Other Arts and Sciences*. London: Routledge.

Gould, G. (1964) 'Strauss and the Electronic Future', *Saturday Review* May 30: 58–9, 72.

———— (1965) 'A Word about the Piano', (liner notes of the LP *The Two and Three Part Inventions* (Inventions and Sinfonias) by J.S. Bach) CBS SBRG 72277.

———— (1966) 'The Prospects of Recording', *High Fidelity* 16 (4): 46–63.

———— (1983) 'What the Recording Process Means To Me', *High Fidelity* 33 (1): 56–7.

———— (1987a) 'The Grass is Always Greener in the Outtakes: An Experiment in Listening', in T. Page (ed.) *The Glenn Gould Reader*, pp.353–7. London: Faber and Faber.

———— (1987b) 'The Record of the Decade', in T. Page (ed.) *The Glenn Gould Reader*, pp.429–34. London: Faber and Faber.

Gould, G. and Davis, C. (1983) 'The Well-Tempered Listener', in J. McGreevy (ed.) *Glenn Gould by Himself and His Friends*, pp.275–94. Toronto: Doubleday Canada.

Gracyk, T. (1997) 'Listening to Music: Performances and Recordings', *The Journal of Aesthetics and Art Criticism* 55 (2): 139–50.

Kazdin, A. (1989) *Glenn Gould at Work: Creative Lying*. New York: E.P. Dutton.

Kenner, H. (1987) *The Mechanic Muse*. New York: Oxford University Press.

Kern, S. (1983) *The Nature of Time and Space 1880–1918*. Cambridge, Mass.: Harvard University Press.

Kivy, P. (1984) *Sound and Semblance: Reflections on Musical Representation*. Princeton: Princeton University Press.

———— (1997) *Philosophies of Art: An Essay in Differences*. Cambridge: Cambridge University Press.

Kostelanetz, R. and Cage, J. (1989) 'A Conversation About Radio in Twelve Parts', in R. Fleming and W. Duckworth (eds) *John Cage at Seventy Five*, pp.270–302. Lewisburg, Penn.: Buckwell University Press.

Levinson, J. (1990) *Music, Art and Metaphysics: Essays in Philosophical Aesthetics*. Ithaca, NY: Cornell University Press.

Mach, E. (1980) *Great Pianists Speak for Themselves*. New York: Dodd, Mead and Company.

Margolis, J. (1983) 'Art, Forgery and Inauthenticity', in D. Dutton (ed.) *The Forger's Art: Forgery and the Philosophy of Art*, pp.153–71. Berkeley: University of California Press.

Patke, R.S. (2005) 'Benjamin on Art and Reproducibility: The Case of Music', in A. Benjamin (ed.) *Walter Benjamin on Art*, pp.185–208. London: Continuum.

Payzant, G. (1992) *Glenn Gould: Music and Mind*. Toronto: Key Porter Books.

Rosen, C. (2005) *Piano Notes: The Hidden World of the Pianist*. London: Penguin.

Sagoff, M. (1978) 'On Restoring and Reproducing Art', *Journal of Philosophy* 75 (9): 453–70.

Said, E.W. (1983) 'The Music Itself: Glenn Gould's Contrapuntal Vision', in J. McGreevy (ed.) *Glenn Gould by Himself and His Friends*, pp.45–54. Toronto: Doubleday Canada.

Scott, H., Frost, T., Kazdin, A. and Carter, S. (1983) 'Recording Gould: a Retake Here, a Splice There, a Myth Everywhere', *High Fidelity* 33 (2): 55–60, 80.

Sessions, R. (1950) *The Musical Experience of Composer, Performer, Listener*. Princeton: Princeton University Press.

Smith, K. (2006) 'Mozart To Go', *Gramophone* 83 (1004): 10.

Sousa, J.P. (1906) 'The Menace of Mechanical Music', *Appleton's Magazine* 8 (3): 278–84.

Stanley, J. (2002) *Collecting Vinyl*. London: Octopus.

Steele, H. (1977) 'Fakes and Forgeries', *British Journal of Aesthetics* 17 (3): 254–8.

Sterne, J. (2003) *The Audible Past: Cultural Origins of Sound Reproduction*. Durham, NC.: Duke University Press.

Symes, C. (2004) *Setting the Record Straight: A Material History of Classical Recording*. Middletown, Conn.: Wesleyan University Press.

Théberge, P. (1997) *Any Sound You Can Imagine: Making Music/Consuming Technology*. Middletown, Conn.: Wesleyan University Press.

Tomes, S. (2004) *Beyond the Notes: Journeys with Chamber Music*. Woodbridge: Boydell Press.

Werness, H.B. (1983) 'Hans Van Meegeren *fecit*', in D. Dutton (ed.) *The Forger's Art: Forgery and the Philosophy of Art*, pp.1–53. Berkeley: University of California Press.

Zak A.J. III (2001) *The Poetics of Rock: Cutting Tracks, Making Records*. Berkeley: University of California Press.

Discography

Bach, J.S. (1965) The Two and Three Part Inventions (Inventions and Sinfonias). G. Gould. CBS LP SBRG 72277.

_____ (1968) *Electronic Realizations and Performances*. W. Carlos. CBS LP S63501.

Beethoven, L. van (1968) Symphony No. 5 arranged by F. Liszt. G. Gould. CBS LP SBRG 7094.

Evans, B. (1963) *Conversations With Myself*. Verve LP V/V6-8526.

Hallelujah (n.d) The Portsmouth Sinfonia. J. Farley. Transatlantic Records LP TRA-285.

Handel, G.F. (n.d) *Messiah*, Philharmonia Baroque Orchestra and UC Berkeley Chamber Chorus. N. McGegan. Harmonia Mundi HMU CD 907050.52.

Sibelius, J. (2004) Symphonies Nos. 3 and 7. London Symphony Orchestra. Sir C. Davis. LSO Live CD LS00051.

_____ (1977) *Kyllikki* and Three Sonatines. G. Gould. CBS LP SBR 235908.

Simpson, R. (1988) Symphonies Nos. 6 and 7. Royal Liverpool Philharmonic Orchestra. V. Handley. Hyperion CDA66280.

THEODORE GRACYK

Documentation and Transformation in Musical Recordings

The work of art in the machine age is a construction; it is built like the Parthenon.

Herbert Read (1961: 83)

The recording of a concert performance at the Albert Hall may be the same as a recording of a live stage play, but making a record in a studio is much more like making a film.

George Martin (1979: 77)

PHILOSOPHICAL speculation about music is as old as philosophy itself. However, philosophers have been slow to discuss what happens to music and to musical culture when the bulk of our musical experience stems from recorded music. Furthermore, many philosophers who discuss recorded music assume that recordings are mere documentations of the sonic dimension of musical performances.[1] Derived from an independent reality, recordings are thought to be 'of' or 'about' the sounds they reproduce. However, this characteristic does not distinguish recordings from telephones and radio broadcasts that carry sounds to listeners at remote sites. Rather, recordings are distinguished by the presence of technologies that allow for multiple playbacks of the same sounds: they provide repeatability without variation. Although music boxes and player pianos demonstrate that recordings are not unique in permitting such repeatability, it is recording technologies that made repeatable music available on a mass scale. This combination of repeatability and mass accessibility has emerged as a topic for philosophical scrutiny.

Among contemporary philosophers of music, Lydia Goehr (1992), Lee B. Brown (1996), and Stephen Davies (2001) suggest that the repeatability of recorded music changes the way people think about and listen to music.[2] Brown and Davies focus on unintended negative consequences of this repeatability. I will explore their prediction that listeners who spend a great deal of time with recorded music will become increasingly insensitive to music's interactive and performative aspects. I will also examine an important precursor to their analyses, namely Walter Benjamin's essay on art in the age of mechanical reproduction (1936). While Benjamin devotes much of his essay to the social effects of movies, I will consider his argument as it applies to recorded music.[3]

Two assumptions are at issue here. First, a particular technology is thought to have a favored use; in our case, sound recordings are supposedly used to document the sound of musical performances. Second, the widespread adoption of a particular technology and its favored use are thought to produce social transformations that would otherwise not occur. I will examine these assumptions in relation to sound recordings, and I will challenge the idea that *a* technology brings about *a* mode of consumption.[4]

I contend that these analyses underestimate the pragmatic dimension of technology (i.e. the ways that a single technology is adapted to different purposes by different users). In brief, the *recorded* nature of recorded music may be less significant for what it does to listeners than for the several things it does for them, as a platform for pursuing multiple and distinct ends of listening. Recordings are simultaneously documentations and stylized semblances, and it is, therefore, unlikely that recorded music would have a unitary, predictable social effect.[5]

Works of phonography and their social effects

For approximately two hundred years, Western musical aesthetics has emphasized the difference between musical works and their performances. Composers create music, as when Thomas Linley II composed the oratorio *The Song of Moses*. However, *The Song of Moses* does not cease to exist in those stretches of time when it is not being performed. What Linley created is a musical work, an abstract sound structure that can be distinguished from its instances, its performances. When a performance of the oratorio is recorded, it is only natural to think of that recording as an aural documentation of the performance or performances that generated the recording. This way of thinking about a recording reinforces the distinction between a musical work and the fleeting sounds that occasionally embody it. Recordings are essentially by-products of performances, which are, in turn, presentations of a musical work.[6]

Goehr, Brown, and Davies challenge standard ways of thinking about recordings. Borrowing Benjamin's famous phrase, Goehr suggests that the 'mechanical reproduction' of music has the potential to challenge our prevailing assumptions about the ontology of musical works and their performances (Goehr, 1992: 266–7), i.e. the assumptions that I outlined above in relation to Linley's oratorio. By eliminating subsequent performance variations, recorded music that exists only as recorded music might 'neutralize' the traditional concept of a musical work as a thing distinct from its embodiments. All music will be experienced differently if recordings alter our concepts about what constitutes a musical work. Goehr believes that this potential is largely unrealized (Goehr, 1992: 267).

Brown counters that significant changes have already taken place, for recordings no longer function as mere documentations of performances. According to him, once recordings of music abandon the documentary ideal, all sound recordings function differently. Drawing on Evan Eisenberg's notion of *phonography* as the art of studio production (Eisenberg, 1988: 110), Brown argues that sound recording has ushered in a new sort of musical work, namely works of phonography that are 'nothing but artifacts of phonography' (Brown, 2000: 113). Far from being documentations of performances, works of phonography are musical works in their own right.[7]

Obvious works of phonography include popular music recordings that do not aim to document how a particular performance sounded.[8] Speaking of the sonic constructions that are the legacy of the Beatles, their record producer George Martin noted that '[w]e have a different art form here' (Martin, 1979: 77). Many of the production techniques applied to John Lennon's vocals were there because Lennon disliked the sound of his own voice. In 1966, the Beatles stopped performing live for audiences. By 1967, it was less accurate to think of their recorded music as performed for purposes of recording than as constructed via recording. Engineering the illusion of documenting performances that never happened, Martin and the Beatles constructed virtual performances. This approach became the industry standard for recorded popular music, and thus for most recorded music. Because popular music has multiple playings without performances, it provides the challenge to modern tradition that Goehr imagines possible.[9] A musical culture that regards 'tracks' as musical works has already reconceptualized the possibilities for music.[10]

Brown identifies worrisome epistemic implications of recorded music's repeatability. Many recordings are works of phonography. However, many others, including many jazz recordings, are not. In a musical culture where works of phonography are the norm, audiences will come to think of all music in terms of tracks and playings. Consequently, audiences will apply inappropriate musical concepts to what they hear when they listen to records that are intended to serve as documentations of performances. As a result, recordings of live music will only serve to undermine the social practice of performing music, because listening repeatedly to a recording counterbalances its documentary aspect: 'the music stands in an adverse relationship with the calcifying medium with which we document it' (Brown, 2000: 122). The recording *At Newport* documents a stellar 1956 performance by the Duke Ellington orchestra, including tenor saxophonist Paul Gonsalves' extended improvisation during 'Diminuendo and Crescendo in Blue'. A good improvisation is a unique event, but the recording transforms Gonsalves' improvisation into a thing that can be heard again and again, until it ceases to surprise.[11] If there is one primary effect of recorded music, it is natural to infer that it is to alienate listeners from music's interactive and performative aspects (Brown, 2000: 123; Gracyk, 1997).

'The problem', Brown warns, 'concerns *repetition*, and its conceptual relative, reidentification' (Brown, 1996: 256).[12] He contends that improvisations are unique, and therefore not subject to reidentification. Recordings of improvisations have the unintended effect of teaching us to reidentify them. Generalizing, the technology of recording fundamentally reorients our listening habits, encouraging us to attend to all music with expectations that are only appropriate to works of phonography.

Within this line of thinking, more emphasis should be placed on the issue of decontextualization. Recordings present music without requiring immersion in the 'native' culture that informs proper appreciation of it. Hearing a jazz improvisation without understanding it to be an improvisation transforms it into something else, a composition. Think here of the vocalese arrangements done with some instrumental jazz solos. Ignorant of the true chronology of influence, I used to think that a certain recording of James Moody was an instrumental version of King Pleasure's 'Moody's Mood for Love'. The reverse is the truth. Moody was *improvising* on 'I'm in the Mood for Love'. King Pleasure derived his song from Moody, reifying the improvisation. Generalizing from such examples, it is tempting to conclude that recordings decontextualize sounds, thereby obscuring the creative processes that should influence our aesthetic responses. Art Garfunkel's vocal performance on Simon and Garfunkel's hit recording of 'Bridge Over Troubled Water' is extraordinarily angelic – an effect created, in large part, by constructing the vocal recording from small fragments of multiple performances. Much of the admiration that gets directed at Garfunkel's singing belongs to the engineering of Roy Hallee.

Once music is recorded, it becomes available to audiences who know it only as recorded music. Brown worries that such audiences will treat all recordings as works of phonography, as objects of aesthetic appraisal and evaluation in their own right. Documentary recordings are then appreciated without regard for their documentary function. Audiences feel free to listen to documentations of older or culturally foreign music without otherwise participating in the musical culture from which it arose. Thus, the spread of recorded music encourages listeners to apprehend music without concern for the cultural contexts that anchor our listening within a tradition. Isolated from formative social practices, all music is simultaneously understood as a fixed thing and as *l'art pour l'art*, art for art's sake. For Benjamin, music, when recorded, is reduced to its 'exhibition value' (1939/2003: 257). Unlike Brown, he regards this as a positive result. Although I question Benjamin's optimism, his ideas yield several insights that mitigate Brown's concerns.

Benjamin and the transformative mechanism

Benjamin's extended discussion of the effects of decontextualization occurs in his essay titled 'The Work of Art in the Age of Mechanical Reproduction' (1936).[13] There are many reasons to discuss this essay. First, its discussion of film has influenced most subsequent thinking about mass media. Since film and photography share fundamental features with recorded music, Benjamin's analysis is an obvious model for exploring the social effects of the increasing ubiquity of recorded music (Patke, 2005). Second, it is a paradigm of the general thesis that a new technology changes those who adopt it. Third, it inspired Theodor Adorno to produce a set of contrasting, more pessimistic essays on recorded music (Wolin, 1994: 163–212). Fourth, its central argument contains a curious but insightful equivocation concerning the features that generate the postulated social effects. I will exploit this aspect of the argument in my response to fears about the unintended consequences of recorded music. Finally, where many others are concerned about the negative social effects of 'mechanical reproduction', Benjamin is optimistic about them.

Setting the stage for his discussion of technology, Benjamin warns that '[j]ust as the entire mode of existence of human collectives changes over historical periods, so too does their mode of perception' (Benjamin, 2003: 255). Benjamin's discussion is not about the changes in our biological modes of perception, but rather about the changes that occur in our characteristic modes of perceptual attention and in associated habits of thought (Carroll, 1998: 130–2). When a society develops new ways of attending to and thinking about the world, social reorganization follows. Benjamin reasons that different artistic practices call for different 'modes of perception', so changes in art bring about changes in society.

Addressing the issue of which feature of technologically reproduced art alters our mode of perception, Benjamin points to its loss of 'aura'. He defines the aura of an artwork as 'the history to which the work has been subject' (Benjamin, 2003: 254). In other words, it is 'the sphere of tradition' surrounding a work. Awareness of this tradition includes consciousness of our cultural 'distance' from the work. Benjamin alleges that technological reproduction of a work destroys this aura (Benjamin, 2003: 255).

Benjamin derives the loss of aura from two other aspects of reproducibility that jointly encourage radical social effects (Benjamin, 2003: 253–4).[14] First, there is the iterability or repeatability that accompanies recording. Technological reproducibility provides decentralized access to the same sounds on multiple occasions, eliminating the necessity of organizing performances for audiences. Second, recording technology allows us to assemble a virtual performance by presenting a sound sequence that does not reflect any particular actual performance. Calling attention to early photography's lack of manipulability, Benjamin posits an essential difference between photography and film, and he identifies the evolution from documentary to non-documentary artifacts as the decisive source of desirable social effects (Benjamin, 2003: 257–9).

In response, I will argue that the opportunity to manipulate visual and auditory recordings on the *production* side of the reproduced artifact may be less significant for audience *reception* than he supposes. Different aspects of recording media facilitate different uses of recordings.

This result is not Benjamin's intended lesson. He claims that specific effects are 'inherent in the technology', minimizing differences in reception (Benjamin, 2003: 262). Once reception is indifferent to aura, Benjamin anticipates the widespread appearance of perceptual habits that will facilitate a progressive, critical viewpoint. More specifically, he predicts that reduced consumption of literature and painting in favor of photography and film will encourage the masses to reject capitalism. I will not explore the specific political consequences that he foresees. For my purposes, it is sufficient to note that in his view an anti-capitalist stance will emerge when increasing numbers of people adopt a generally more critical stance toward the ideologies supporting capitalism. His argument seems to be that a more critical stance towards our prevailing sources of information encourages criticism of the ideologies they reflect, destabilizing the power of those who control the media.[15] While I share Noël Carroll's view that Benjamin's argument requires too many unsupported assumptions (Carroll, 1998: 114–45), my purpose justifies ignoring this aspect of his argument in order to concentrate on the proposal that photography and film naturally facilitate one mode of audience response, a critical stance.

Benjamin's argument emphasizes the historical progression from photography to film. Like photography before the introduction of the photographic negative, pre-electronic sound recordings lacked manipulability. Every sound that reached the horn of the recording device was documented. Any variation was due to playback equipment. In contrast, electronic recording made it possible to filter sound and even to combine the input of multiple microphones; different inputs could be assigned different volumes, allowing engineers to mix and balance sound levels from different sources. Magnetic tape made it possible to go yet further. Sound recordings could be edited, permitting combinations of sounds that had originated in different events (e.g. in different performances at different times and places). Through collage techniques, the musical intentions of musicians and their engineering partners in the crime of aural deception could be more perfectly realized in a recording than in a live performance. Two sounds heard simultaneously during a playback no longer offered documentary evidence that they had simultaneous origins, nor could one suppose that two sounds heard in sequence documented two sounds made in the same sequence.

Sound recordings consequently transform any music they document. Audiences know that performers are mere 'props' for subsequent technological transformation (Benjamin, 2003: 260–1). Responding to a recorded performance at a remove and thus unable to interact with it, the audience 'takes the position of the camera' or recording device. 'This permits the audience to take the position of a critic, without experiencing any personal contact' with the performer (Benjamin, 2003: 260). The aura of the performance tradition is eliminated. So, once a certain stage arrives in the development of recording technology, recorded music encourages decontextualized listening. Around the middle of the twentieth century, all recordings become works of phonography. I will argue that aura is, nevertheless, not always eliminated.

Benjamin defends his developmental hypothesis in a long footnote found only in the second version of his essay. Accordingly, traditional works of art combine the 'tightly interfolded' yet distinct aspects of semblance and play (Benjamin, 1936/2002: 127, n. 22). Semblance is representational fidelity, and play is artistic freedom to experiment when crafting a semblance. Historically, art emphasized representations as focal points for social ritual. However, the process of creating a semblance always transformed whatever was represented. So, semblances exhibited play. To the degree that works of art displayed 'experimenting procedures' informing the construction of the semblance, they had exhibition value as objects of interest in their own right. But once we reached the historical stage dominated by technological reproducibility, 'the element of semblance has yielded its place to the element of play' (Benjamin, 2002: 127, n. 22). For Benjamin, this effect is most obvious with film. One can argue that sound recordings are also inherently technologies of play that treat musical performances as mere 'props' for recordings (Patke, 2005: 191–4).

Benjamin's thesis that technological reproducibility eliminates semblance and maximizes play assumes that recordings are neutral documentations of reality. In traditional art forms, audiences interact with semblances crafted by artists. The process of creating semblances is already infused with history and tradition, facilitating cult value. But Benjamin thinks that mechanical recording can depict reality without introducing a 'semblance'. Machines provide *'the most intensive interpenetration of reality with equipment'* (Benjamin, 2003: 264). Apparently, he believes that modern technology eliminates social interpretation during the production stage. Therefore, unedited documentation possesses neither cult nor exhibition value. Only the historical development of manipulability provides photographs, films and recordings with the element of play that provides exhibition value.

I see two problems with Benjamin's argument that all recording technology is inherently weighted toward the exhibition value of play.[16] First, although I grant that the editing of films and recordings can enhance our awareness of artifice and play, this result appears unrelated to the reduction of cult value (the loss of aura). Enhanced exhibition value seems primarily due to the complete separation of performance and audience. However, if decontextualization is due to iterability rather than manipulability, then our response to iterability might be different from our response to manipulability. Consequently, awareness of these distinct aspects of recording might affect audiences in competing ways. Therefore, I see no reason to agree that 'the element of semblance' is eradicated in favor of the 'element of play'.

Second, Benjamin's explanation of the loss of aura equivocates, and shifts back and forth between two distinct kinds of technological reproducibility. As a result, he thinks that the aura and cult value are doubly eliminated. First, mass reproduction obliterates any need for the original. Second, he denies that mechanical 'interpenetration of reality with [recording] equipment' is an interpretative intervention (Benjamin, 2003: 264). Only the manipulation of the recording can add 'art' value. This can only be the exhibition value that arises from human play during the transformative manipulation of the documentation. Claiming that films and recordings *inherently* divorce us from the human traditions they document, Benjamin concludes that they encourage a critical stance toward whatever they document. In the next section, I challenge Benjamin's claim that recordings are dominated by the element of play. My challenge undercuts his argument that technological reproducibility has an inherent tendency to produce a common audience response.

Challenging technological determinism

Approached as ideal categories, I understand Benjamin's distinction between semblance and documentation. I am not persuaded, however, that the technology of oil painting provides semblances while machine-assisted recording provides documentation without semblances. As demonstrated by any two movies adapted from the same literary source, very different perspectives have been taken on the fictional worlds of Charles Dickens and Jane Austen. Film adaptations have both cult value and exhibition value – and let's not forget that the less faithful version can make for the better movie. Similarly, different recordings of the same musical work can, as recordings, offer radically different interpretations of it, and the relevant differences are not restricted to differences in the performances and after-the-fact editing decisions. Against Benjamin, I think that the initial activity of recording documents two things: a source 'reality' and a human perspective on it. To the extent that movies and sound recordings are compared with their counterparts in the performing arts, we will observe just how complex those perspectives can be.

Different theater productions of a play and different musical performances of the same music vary in their treatment of the play or the musical work. Consequently, performances introduce an interpretative profile or viewing perspective to the work being performed.[17] Similarly, I propose that unedited film and sound recordings contribute an additional profile or listening perspective on a performance. Anyone who intentionally records music must decide how best to present the source material so that it represents a coherent performance. For example, the Grateful Dead allowed fans to make recordings from the concert hall soundboard used for adjusting volume levels; their fans have a long tradition of trading recordings of their concerts. The soundboard recordings capture the sounds generated by the stage microphones and electric feeds, but they lack the ambient sounds of the room and of the audience. Consequently, some fans prefer lower fidelity, non-soundboard recordings that muddy the music yet capture the 'feel' of being there, as when one fan praises one of these 'audience' recordings for letting them 'experience the experience'.[18] Each performance offers a profile of the music, and the two methods of recording the same performance produce distinctive documentary perspectives on it. Hence, each of these documentary recordings delivers a profile of a profile of the Grateful Dead's music.

The 'play' element of recordings becomes more pronounced with edited recordings. For instance, different production teams create very different versions of a single recording. Compare Bill Laswell's 1998 mix of 'In a Silent Way' and other tracks by Miles Davis with the releases Davis himself sanctioned from the same multi-track tapes during the period 1969–74. While it is tempting to think that the multi-track tapes are neutral documentations of performances, myriad production decisions have to be made when combining anywhere from two to two hundred independent tracks of sound into a monophonic, stereophonic, or even more complex presentation of the recorded sound.

Returning to the earlier discussion of phonography, we might assume that electronic music has no profile. Recordings of electronic music do not have to be recordings *of* a musical work that exists independently of the finished product. Here, it is tempting to think that there is no possibility of distinguishing between the performance profile and the recording's perspective on it. However, audible changes are introduced when converting an analogue recording to digital format, as has been done with tape compositions created at the Columbia-Princeton Electronic Music Center in the 1960s, revealing that even this kind of music permits of a distinction between the musical work and different profiles of it created during subsequent preparation for playback.

In the context of non-electronic music, phonography often obscures the difference between the performing and recording profiles. Just as a movie script is shot out of sequence in order to streamline production costs, most music is recorded piecemeal. The coherence of both the virtual performance and the listening perspective emerges in the production process itself; bits and pieces of music and sound are brought together by mixing various sources.[19] Even with non-electronic music, the recording process often collapses into the composing process. Many popular songs are composed on tape or digitally. The germinating idea is often a recorded chord sequence or rhythm. The 'composition' emerges gradually, through trial and error, as additions are recorded at different times and by multiple contributing musicians (Gracyk, 1996: 46–50).

In contrast, pre-electronic recordings are recordings of complete performances, arranged to make the best of the equipment's inherent limitations. Made by a stylus cutting a cylinder or master disc, no post-production was involved in translating the source material into a profile of a performance. As recordings *of* performances, it is tempting to think of pre-electronic recordings as similar to early photographs, which, according to Benjamin, have an exclusively documentary relationship to the reality they capture. Because pre-electronic technology does not permit any 'space for play' (Benjamin, 2002: 127, n. 22), only iterability and decontextualization are present to undermine our assumption that recordings merely document musical performances. Hence, unedited recordings of musical performances cannot be works of phonography. Nonetheless, Benjamin thinks that listening habits shaped by full-fledged phonography transform the status of all documentary recordings. The primitive stages of a technology 'strain' for effects that emerge only subsequently (Benjamin, 2003: 266).

But why should we agree that the later stage of the technology is already inherent in it? If audiences recognize differences among stages of recording technology, iterability might have very different social effects than manipulability. More to the point, why should we suppose that any of these stages encourages a distinctive mode of reception? Perhaps the human mind is insufficiently plastic to permit different technologies to affect us so profoundly (Carroll, 1998: 133). Let us set that point aside as an issue for neurobiologists and concentrate on Benjamin's account of documentation.

For Benjamin, a work's aura is a consequence partly of its uniqueness and partly of a social context. Prior to its technological reproduction, the audience could only encounter a work of art within 'the context of tradition' (Benjamin, 2003: 256). However, this analysis seems to focus on the visual arts at the expense of music. Adorno insightfully responds to Benjamin by noting that musical works are always already subject to endless reproduction. Every competent performance of a musical work provides access to the same work. The uncomprehending mass audience frequently responds by reintroducing a new aura, fetishizing selected elements of the music (Adorno, 1938/2002: 293–309; Patke, 2005: 197–200). Benjamin, therefore, makes too much of the idea that traditional art, as opposed to mechanically reproduced art, requires the audience to attend to it in its originating social context. Encountering Ludwig van Beethoven in live performance in the twentieth century – contrast Wilhelm Furtwängler conducting the Ninth Symphony in Berlin in 1942 with Leonard Bernstein conducting it there in 1989, following the fall of the Berlin Wall – is hardly Beethoven with an intact aura of nineteenth-century Vienna.

Although Benjamin's essay does not refer to Adorno by name, it is part of an ongoing exchange between them (Wolin, 1994: 163–97). In this context, Benjamin's response to Adorno is that technology furnishes the final step, uncoupling music from *any* tradition (Patke, 2005: 194–200). Without recordings, to hear music is to hear a performance, which always involves some exposure to its history. With recordings, one need not participate in Lutheran ritual in order to hear a cantata by Johann Sebastian Bach, nor join in the secular ritual of the concert hall in order to hear Beethoven. Benjamin thinks that this decontextualization – hearing without participating in any of the social trappings of the music's performance contexts – transforms listening into a genuinely critical activity.

The argument fails because it is false that audiences routinely become critical about the same aspects of every recording. Benjamin simply assumes that documentation can replace semblance without driving away the audience. However, not every documentary recording presents sufficient 'likeness' to its source to encourage critical listening, and many listeners are as critical of the documentary perspective as they are of whatever content is documented. Consider, for example, the performance by the Grateful Dead in Delhi, New York, on 8 May 1970. Fans trade an audience recording of that show. However, one Internet site that allows fans to post comments warns that this recording 'sounds horrifyingly bad. sounds like it was recorded from a mic[rophone] encased within a tin can, garbled and muffled to the point that its [sic] closer to noise than music'. Another posting states that listeners 'can BARELY make out the songs the sound is so bad', while yet another says about obtaining a copy, 'Thanks...But no thanks'.[20] Contrary to Benjamin's expectation, audiences who spend a great deal of time with recorded music do not expend all of their critical energy on the music that is recorded. Nor do they respond with admiration when the recording highlights its own enhanced 'sphere of play', for this often implies an undesirable corruption of the documentary function. Listening to recorded music does not encourage insensitivity to semblance. Analyzed according to Benjamin's categories, many Grateful Dead fans appear to experience no loss of interest in the music's aura.

Documentation

We need not pursue the chimera of perfect sound reproduction from a neutral perspective in order to judge recorded sound as offering better and worse presentations of musical sound.[21] Ironically, an increase in fidelity can subvert a recording's documentary function. A particular recording sounds 'like' an ideal performance of the music only by manipulating what would have been heard at a performance.

Were we genuinely insensitive to the 'distance' between what is documented and its engineered semblance, the manipulations that arise in the studio would strike us as strangely distorted, when, for instance, an acoustic instrument that has been carefully balanced against the volume of the other instruments emerges from the instrumental mix suddenly, increasing its relative volume, only to drop back into the mix when the solo ends.[22] But the practice of fluctuating volume persists on digital recordings, as does the artificial isolation of instrumental sounds, so that instruments can be made to selectively stand out from the total sound.

Listen to early recordings, such as the 1927 recordings of Dock Boggs, a coal miner and bootlegger from western Virginia who played banjo as he sang songs that trace back to the Child Ballads of England and Scotland. The engineers who recorded Boggs could not control volume and they could not isolate sounds coming from different sources. Whether accompanying his voice or soloing between the verses, Boggs' banjo remains at a constant volume. The sound of the banjo is, therefore, obscured whenever Boggs sings, his mouth closer than the banjo to the recording horn. As a result, the banjo, which serves as the primary musical voice, sounds oddly muted when Boggs stops singing. Boggs is also accompanied by guitar. Because the guitarist was located farther from the recording device than Boggs, however, the guitar barely registers on the recording. Because each sound source remains fixed in orientation toward a single recording horn or microphone, each musical voice is captured at a constant volume – relative to its distance from the recording instrument – and thus musical voices tend to interfere with one another.

Next, listen to any bluegrass recording of the 1940s. Once again, the arrangements are confined to acoustic instruments and human voices. Electronically recorded through a single microphone, the volume of the lead instrument definitely increases during its featured 'break'. This effect is achieved by the performance practice of co-ordinating the movements of the musicians toward and away from the single microphone as the piece is played.[23] On Bill Monroe's classic sides from the late 1940s, Earl Scruggs's banjo is barely audible until he steps forward for his solo. As Monroe steps back from the microphone to make room for Scruggs, the new clarity of the banjo means a loss of fidelity for Monroe's mandolin. In turn, the same holds for the fiddle and then the guitar. By the 1970s, Monroe's recordings utilized multiple microphones. The players no longer danced their dance to and from the microphone. While we hear volumes increase as each instrument or voice takes its turn, they do not blur into the ensemble when their featured turn is past and their volume drops. As balanced by a recording engineer, changes in volume are unrelated to anything done by the musicians. Decreased volume no longer means a sharp deterioration of timbre. One can easily hear similar differences among effects when comparing the early blues recordings of Bessie Smith with recent recordings of Cassandra Wilson.

My point is the obvious one that different eras of recording have distinctive styles. With the passing of time, all recorded music takes on a stylistic identity as a recording of a particular vintage. Each era of recording technology has a distinct aura. It is not simply that recordings never adequately capture the sounds we would hear if we were there in the room with these singers and their acoustic instruments. If we were there with Boggs, our relative distance from the performers and the acoustics of the performance space would combine to ensure that the guitar would be as clear as the banjo. Together, the two instruments might overpower the vocals. There is, therefore, an important sense in which later recordings replicate the *experience* of the music they document. Music is not merely a sequence of sounds. Music is an intentional object that knowledgeable listeners hear in the sounds. As a consequence, the effect of hearing a performance that we can see is not altogether different from the fluctuating volumes we hear on electronic recordings. If we know what to observe during an acoustic jazz or bluegrass performance, we can both *see* and *hear* each instrumentalist shift from a supporting to a leading voice, and our expectations will lead to a heightened interest in following a particular musical line, which will then stand out from the other voices. While Monroe's recordings beat out Boggs' by having better sound – for example, richer timbre – they also feature a greater fidelity to the experience of listening. Thanks to the manipulation of the sound at multiple stages of engineering and mixing, Monroe's later recordings 'play' with the sounds derived from the originating performances.

Contrary to Benjamin's prediction, the 'artistic function' does not disappear from successfully recorded music (Benjamin, 2003: 257). In his view, when we encounter so much technologically reproduced material, we become oblivious to its social origins. In response, I propose that recorded music bears witness to social origins that differ from those of 'the recipient in his or her own situation' (Benjamin, 2003: 254). Different sound recordings *sound* very different, and many listeners are aware of these differences and appreciate them as consequences of changing production practices. Recordings have their own aura, inviting reflection on their social origins.

As a consequence, recordings of Boggs – recordings that get so many details wrong from a perspective of fidelity – magnify the power of the documented performances. Responding to these recordings, knowing that they originate with a coal miner in 1927, is much like responding to photographs of past events that one has heard or read about. Nineteenth-century photographs of the battlefields of the American Civil War have a documentary power that no modern color photograph can have. It is one thing to read about the battle for Big and Little Round Top at Gettysburg and quite another to see Timothy O'Sullivan's photographs of the place taken two days after the battle. (Even the 'faked' ones, with the corpses repositioned for the best effect, seem more real than any modern photograph could.) Black and white, the old photographs are unfocused around the edges and wash out where the sky presents too much light. Maps and drawings are clearer sources of information about what happened at Gettysburg. Nonetheless, the photographs document the field of battle in a way that maps and drawing do not. Similarly, the more primitive recording equipment of the first half-century of recorded music provides those early recordings with an undeniable documentary power. However, this is not solely due to technology. As with photographs, recorded music's documentary value increases as it becomes sufficiently decontextualized so that the perceptual experience it supplies is otherwise rare or unavailable. At the same time, it must provide traces of its context of tradition to an audience interested in reconnecting to that context. Paradoxically, documentary power is magnified when we contextualize a decontextualized, but sufficiently informative, artifact. Anyone can purchase the Grateful Dead's *Anthem of the Sun* or the Beatles' *Revolver*. But now that Jerry Garcia and two Beatles are dead, any 'ruthless annihilation of the aura' that might arise from their technological reproduction encourages, rather than discourages, taking time 'for concentration and evaluation, as one can before a painting' (Benjamin, 2003: 266–7). The mimetic relationship that originally tempts us to substitute the decontextualized recording for the tradition-embedded music can later permit – perhaps even encourage – a documentary use of those same recorded sounds.

Because recordings are simultaneously documentations and stylized semblances, I do not believe that all recordings will eventually be conceived as works of phonography.

The multiple aims of recordings

Stepping back for a moment, what is the primary philosophical issue here? If we are merely speculating that various correlations indicate causality, it is not yet clear that we are dealing with a philosophical issue.

The primary philosophical issue concerns the nature of technology. Does an adequate understanding of the technology demand a teleological interpretation? Such a teleological perspective is a legacy of Immanuel Kant's thesis that there is no philosophy of art until we subsume our theorizing under the broader question of the legitimacy of teleological judgment (Kant, 1790/1987: 28–32). Prior to his recognition of the importance of the question of whether aesthetic judgment has an essential cognitive function, Kant denied that aesthetics is a philosophical topic (Kant, 1781/1965: 66). Recognizing that aesthetic judgment has a proper teleology invited inquiry into the essential ends of artistic activity. Similarly, the topic of recorded music takes on a distinctively philosophical character when we step back to ask whether various technologies imply distinctive ends.

With this background in mind, we are now positioned to explore Davies' sophisticated account of music and sound recording. He argues that the technologies that facilitate recorded music are inherently multifunctional, and the same technology, therefore, has different uses and different social consequences depending on its context of use. As a result, there are multiple kinds of recordings, categorized according to their pursuit of distinct values. Not every recording should be evaluated as a documentation of an independent event. A recording 'promotes different values' depending on the 'intended mode of presentation' (Davies, 2001: 317). Consequently, it is undesirable to employ a uniform critical perspective when listening to different kinds of recorded music.

Davies recognizes that recording technology can be used to generate musical works that cannot be separated from their recorded embodiments. In other words, one use of recording is generative: it allows composers to *construct* music by constructing recorded sound. The result is music 'created for playback, not for performance' (Davies, 2001: 25). Davies cites Pierre Schaeffer's *Étude Pathétique* of 1948 as an archetype. Popular music's most famous example is the Beatles' 'Revolution 9' (1968), assembled largely from pre-existing recordings that John Lennon found in the EMI tape library (Lewisohn, 1988: 138). These works are full-fledged cases of phonography, in which the recording process generates the musical work. The existence of such music does not imply, however, that it reflects an inherent, more advanced stage in the unfolding teleology of recording.

The generative function does not apply when recording a musical work conceived for live performance. We cannot evaluate a 1942 recording of Furtwängler conducting a Beethoven symphony, or a bootleg tape of the Grateful Dead performing in 1970, unless we understand the human intentions that directed the recording process. In these cases, the function of the recordings is primarily documentary. In other cases, a recording will aim, through studio manipulation, to create a representation of an ideal performance. There are, therefore, two distinct documentary aims: likeness and idealization. But since the two aims are at cross-purposes, when is one more appropriate than the other?

Because Davies recognizes that there are multiple kinds of musical works, we might expect him to say that the kind of musical work being recorded determines the proper documentary aim. We might suppose that recordings of works composed for concert performance (e.g. a Beethoven symphony) should concentrate on fidelity to actual performances, while all other recordings (including all recent works of popular music intended to be consumed primarily as music for playback) should concentrate on other values. Because they feature musical arrangements honed in live performance, the debut albums of the Beatles, the Rolling Stones, Bob Dylan, and the Grateful Dead should be judged as sonic representations of their early performances. As recordings, they should be evaluated in terms of the same values that apply to every recording of a Bach cantata or a Beethoven symphony.

Instead, Davies divides these recordings into two groups, i.e. live and studio recordings, according to the performance situation that generates the recorded sounds (Davies, 2001: 313–17). Live recordings capture performances given for an audience. Studio recordings are compiled from music performed in a studio specifically for the purpose of making a recording. Some recordings of Beethoven's Ninth Symphony, including both Bernstein's 1980 and 1989 versions, are recreations of a particular performance for an audience. In contrast, Bernstein's 1962 recording of Beethoven's Piano Concerto No. 5 with the New York Philharmonic features a studio performance undertaken for the purpose of making a record. In the former case, the recording should involve only enough sonic manipulation to simulate how the performance would have sounded to someone attending the performance. In the latter case, where a work for performance is performed in a recording studio, the controlling aim is a simulated performance emphasizing accuracy, consistency, and finish. These criteria for judging recordings are not restricted to 'serious' composed music. We should judge the Grateful Dead's various recordings of their composition 'St. Stephen' differently according to recording context. The 1969 studio recording, released as the first track of the album *Aoxomoxoa*, should not be compared to the powerful version on their first live album, *Live/Dead*. On this model, however, the Grateful Dead's album titled *Anthem of the Sun* seems to be a self-defeating project, because each track continuously mixes together multiple live and studio performances of the featured song (Lesh, 2005: 125–30).

Davies says little about the aims of a third category, i.e. recordings of musical works primarily intended for delivery to a mass audience *as* recorded music. Typically, these recordings feature songs that can also be performed live. However, the recordings emphasize arrangements tailored to exploit the available recording technology (Davies, 2001: 36). A clear example is the reversed guitars in 'I'm Only Sleeping' by the Beatles – musical passages that the group could not duplicate in live performance. Once recordings of works for studio performance become common, they establish the standard against which subsequent performances are measured. Should such recordings adopt the aims of 'studio performance', delivering a sonic representation of an ideal musical performance? Davies merely states that such recordings present a distinct case and should be judged 'in terms of other recordings, not live performances' (Davies, 2001: 317).

Because Davies' criteria for evaluating these three types of recordings involve a reconstruction of intentions, they leave us without direction for some other interesting cases. Consider two tracks, 'What's Become of the Baby?' and 'Rosemary', both of which appear on the Grateful Dead's third album, *Aoxomoxoa*. As two results of one recording project, could one be subject to the criteria for studio performance while the other is not? As a whole, the album bears witness to the fact that it was produced in a studio that had just acquired one of the world's first 16-track recorders. Although the melodies of the two songs suggest common origins in folk music (both have a notably Elizabethan flavor), the recordings involve prominent electronic alteration of Jerry Garcia's vocals. 'Rosemary' is the less radical of the pair. This delicate song features only Garcia's voice and acoustic guitar. The cleanly recorded guitar contrasts with the heavy filtering and bursts of simulated echo applied to his voice. The result sounds as if the guitar is two or three feet from the listener while the voice emanates from someone standing on a hill in the distance on a windy day. Musically similar yet simpler, 'What's Become of the Baby?' features Garcia again, this time singing *a cappella* for eight minutes. Much of the time, the heavy filtering of the voice, and random intrusions of echo and vocal reverberation render the words unintelligible. Here, the effect is that English sounds like a foreign language, as if a monk were singing in Latin in a cavern. What was obviously a song performed in a studio is transformed into something very close to an electronic composition.

Is 'What's Become of the Baby?' to be judged as an electronic work that is not for performance, like 'Revolution 9' by the Beatles? The historical record shows that it was never performed for an audience. The recording did serve as an electronic background for a live improvisation during a performance by the Grateful Dead on 26 April 1969. But 'What's Become of the Baby' was not itself performed. 'Rosemary' was performed for an audience exactly once, on 7 December 1968. Neither the strangeness of 'What's Become of the Baby' nor its lack of performance for an audience seem decisive in categorizing it, and neither provides sufficient reason to say that it is a different kind of musical work than 'Rosemary,' which it so closely resembles in process and result. Since the vocal effects on both songs could have occurred through electronic alteration during a live performance in 1969, neither qualifies as a work for studio performance according to Davies' criteria. Both must be studio idealizations of a work for performance, but as such both fail profoundly. My own response is that both tracks instantiate songs for performance while fitting none of Davies' recording categories. Like their predecessor, *Anthem of the Sun*, these two tracks have complex perspectives. Like a fictional film that sometimes adopts the point of view of a character, they are engineered to sound as if the listener is hearing a performance while her consciousness is hallucinogenically altered. The aim is to encourage an alternative perspective on relatively traditional-sounding music.

So how do I know that 'What's Become of the Baby' was not actually performed on 26 April 1969? I listened to a tape recording of the performance. The recording was made with a documentary aim and I listened with a documentary purpose, solely to find out whether 'What's Become of the Baby' was performed. I might listen again tomorrow, with a non-documentary purpose, in order to evaluate its semblance quality and rate the tape (but not the performance) on the website where I found warnings about the 'horrifyingly bad' quality of other circulating tapes. But I can also return to *Aoxomoxoa* and listen to 'Rosemary' with a documentary interest, in order to determine the chord progression that Garcia is playing. Then, I can listen to it once more as a constructed semblance.

Such cases suggest serious obstacles to anticipating or predicting the full range of aims that are compatible with either the production or reception of a piece of recorded music. I endorse Davies' position that there is no unifying function or aim inherent in recording technology. I recommend the additional step of denying that particular recordings can be assigned to one among a set of mutually exclusive categories.

The assumption that listeners treat all recordings as teleologically identical generates Benjamin's optimism. It generates Brown's concerns that listeners would evaluate jazz improvisations inappropriately, as if they were standard musical compositions. It also generates Davies' related concern that many listeners would confuse the idiosyncratic features of a particular performance interpretation with essential properties of the musical work. In response, I have suggested that the widespread practice of sharing unedited live recordings, some of poor quality, demonstrates that we have a long way to go before reproducibility and mutability destroy the aura of documentation. The decontextualizing element of recording has multiple consequences, including heightened interest in both the documentary and perspectival dimensions that provide recordings with their own aura of tradition.

Conclusion

A simplistic essentialism about sound recordings mistakenly reduces them to documentations of whatever is recorded. A more sophisticated stance recognizes that technological reproduction can interfere with this documentary function, and that recorded music might, therefore, transform our relationship to all music. Decontextualization is assigned an important role in this transformation. However, I have questioned common predictions about the effects of decontextualization. When we document music with recording technology, the result is a stylized representation of a performance or an ideal performance. Hence, recordings facilitate multiple aesthetic stances, reducing the likelihood that the technology will have a unitary social effect.

Notes

1   See, for example, Hernadi (1991: 53), Ingarden (1986: 157–8) and Wolterstorff (1980: 79). Important exceptions are Brown (1996) and Davies (2001).

2   I recommend Bimber's overview (1994) of the competing views on the relationship between technology and social organization. Like Goehr, Brown, and Davies, I endorse a 'soft' technological determinism: particular technologies influence social change without necessitating specific ones.

3   Because there is so much recorded sound besides recorded music, the issues that I
    explore are not confined to music. However, the most widespread use of sound recording
    technology has been the preservation and presentation of music. If the widespread adoption
    of recording technology alters society, it is likely that the initial effects of recording sound
    will appear in music and musical culture.

4   As a general position on technology, this thesis is known as technological determinism.
    According to so-called 'hard' determinists, '[a]s technology changes, so society follows.
    To change the social structure, one has to change technology' (Wise, 1997: 9). Attali
    (1977/1985) offers a controversial formulation of this thesis, arguing that the history of
    music divides into four distinct stages. In each stage, distinct technologies of musical
    reproduction facilitate distinct stages of social organization.

5   As such, I endorse Mark Katz's argument that 'the diversity of response to repeatability…
    demonstrate[s] that there can be no simple cause-effect relationship between recording
    technology and the activities of its users' (Katz, 2004: 31).

6   For a more detailed exposition of the thesis that recorded music documents performances,
    see Gracyk (1996: 38–46).

7   The distinction between documentary recordings and phonography invites comparison
    with the familiar distinction between documentary and non-documentary films in visual
    recordings. While some authors propose that there are two basic types of film (Bordwell and
    Thompson, 1997: 42–6), the realist tradition holds that films are inherently documentary
    (Kracauer, 1960).

8   Non-musical examples of phonography include Glenn Gould's sound constructs, available
    as *The Solitude Trilogy*.

9   The audience for a live musical performance hears sounds generated by someone's action
    of performing. We often refer to the sounds as the performance. The audience for recorded
    music hears sounds generated by someone's action of operating the machine. We can refer
    to these sounds as a 'playing' or 'playback' of the recorded sounds.

10 Zak (2001) adapts the term 'tracks' from the vernacular expression for the distinct musical
    sequences etched into a vinyl record, and I follow his lead.

11 Brown sympathetically quotes composer Roger Sessions' warning that recorded music
    offers a genuine experience of music 'just as long as it remains to a degree unfamiliar'
    (Sessions, 1950: 70–1). Brown correctly counters that Sessions does not take seriously the
    possibility that works of phonography should be judged differently than documentary
    recordings (Brown, 2000: 113).

12 Davies raises similar concerns about listeners who know the classical repertoire through
    recordings. These listeners are 'not in a strong position to appreciate either the work or the
    performance of it' (Davies, 2001: 328).

13 Benjamin prepared three different versions of the essay. The date here refers to the French
    translation of the second version, which was published during his lifetime. The first and
    third versions (1935 and 1939 respectively) were only published posthumously. Recent
    translations in Benjamin (2002: 101–33) and Benjamin (2003: 251–83) are more accurate.

14 Katz identifies the same cluster of features as potential sources of similar 'phonograph effects' (Katz, 2004: 189).

15 Benjamin's optimism arises from his assumption that collective viewing would destroy autonomous thinking (Benjamin, 2003: 264). He did not anticipate technological innovations that encourage private viewing, making film consumption more like reading.

16 Play includes shock effects. For more on Benjamin's assumptions, see Wolin (1994: 186–7).

17 My presentation of this topic is influenced by Ingarden (1986: 150).

18 Fan identified as Kevinguy789 at 'Grateful Dead Live at Boston Music Hall on 1971-12-01', URL (consulted August 2006): http://www.archive.org/details/gd71-12-01.aud.minchesvernon.24765.sbeok.shnf

19 Recordings of jazz tend to avoid overdubbing, and recordings of the classical repertoire generally limit the practice; but even here, there is variation in practice.

20 All postings from 'Grateful Dead Live at Farrell Hall (SUNY) on 1970-05-08', *Internet Archives*, URL (consulted August 2006): http://www.archive.org/details/gd70-05-08.aud.miller.32056.sbeok.flacf

21 For an extended discussion of the idea that fidelity is a social construct, see Sterne (2003: 241–6).

22 This effect was more pronounced during the era of long-playing vinyl since vinyl could not handle extreme variances of volume. Dynamics were flattened out, which meant that when one element seemed to get louder, it was generally because the other elements lost volume.

23 Bluegrass was not adapted for radio. It was invented for radio performance. Although the 'classic' bluegrass groups used acoustic instruments, every major bluegrass group of the 1940s and 1950s crafted its sound for the studio microphone and for the radio loudspeakers of the time. So the practice of choreographing the movements of the musicians was already part of the bluegrass 'sound' as it was normally heard, and cannot be dismissed as an artificial byproduct of the recording process.

References

Adorno, T. (2002) 'On the Fetish-Character in Music and the Regression of Listening', in R. Leppert (ed.) *Essays on Music*, pp.288–317. Berkeley: University of California Press. Original (1938) as 'Über den Fetischcharakter der Musik und die Regression des Hörens', *Zeitschrift für Sozialforschung* 7: 321–56.

Attali, J. (1985) *Noise: The Political Economy of Music*. Trans. B. Massumi. Minneapolis: University of Minnesota Press. Original (1977) as *Bruits: essai sur l'économie politique de la musique*. Paris: Presses Universitaires de France.

Benjamin, W. (1936) 'L'Oeuvre d'art à l'époque de sa reproduction mécanisée', *Zeitschrift für Sozialforschung* 5 (1): 40–68.

_____ (2002) 'The Work of Art in the Age of Its Technological Reproducibility', in H. Eiland and M.W. Jennings (eds) *Selected Writings, volume 3, 1935–1938*, pp.101–33. Cambridge,

MA: Belknap Press of Harvard University Press. Original (1936/1989 posthumous) as 'Das Kunstwerk im Zeitalter seiner technischen Reproduzierbarkeit', in R. Tiedemann and H. Schweppenhäuser (eds) *Walter Benjamin, Gesammelte Schriften, volume 7*, pp.350–84. Frankfurt am Main: Suhrkamp.

_____ (2003) 'The Work of Art in the Age of Its Technological Reproducibility', in H. Eiland and M.W. Jennings (eds) *Selected Writings, volume 4, 1938–1940*, pp.251–83. Cambridge, MA: Belknap Press of Harvard University Press. Original (1939/1974 posthumous) as 'Das Kunstwerk im Zeitalter seiner technischen Reproduzierbarkeit', in R. Tiedemann and H. Schweppenhäuser (eds) *Walter Benjamin, Gesammelte Schriften, volume 1*, pp.471–508. Frankfurt am Main: Suhrkamp.

Bimber, B. (1994) 'Three Faces of Technological Determinism', in M.R. Smith and L. Marx (eds) *Does Technology Drive History? The Dilemma of Technological Determinism*, pp.79–100. Cambridge, MA: The MIT Press.

Bordwell, D. and Thompson, K. (1997) *Film Art: An Introduction*. New York: McGraw-Hill.

Brown, L.B. (1996) 'Phonography', in L.B. Brown and D. Goldblatt (eds) *Aesthetics: A Reader in Philosophy of the Arts*, pp.252–7. Upper Saddle River, NJ: Prentice Hall.

_____ (2000) 'Phonography, Repetition and Spontaneity', *Philosophy and Literature* 24: 111–25.

Carroll, N. (1998) *A Philosophy of Mass Art*. Oxford: Clarendon Press.

Davies, S. (2001) *Musical Works and Performances*. Oxford: Clarendon Press.

Eisenberg, E. (1988) *The Recording Angel*. New York: Penguin Books.

Goehr, L. (1992) *The Imaginary Museum of Musical Works: An Essay in the Philosophy of Music*. Oxford: Clarendon Press.

Gracyk, T. (1996) *Rhythm and Noise: An Aesthetics of Rock*. Durham: Duke University Press.

_____ (1997) 'Listening to Music: Performances and Recordings', *The Journal of Aesthetics and Art Criticism* 55 (2): 139–50.

Hernadi, P. (1991) 'Reconceiving Notation and Performance', *Journal of Aesthetic Education* 25 (1): 47–56.

Ingarden, R. (1986) *The Work of Music and the Problem of Its Identity*. Trans. A. Czerniawski. Berkeley: University of California Press.

Kant, I. (1965) *Critique of Pure Reason*. Trans. N.K. Smith. New York: St. Martin's Press. Original (1781) as *Critik der reinen Vernunft*. Riga: Johann Friedrich Hartnoch.

_____ (1987) *The Critique of Judgment*. Trans. W.S. Pluhar. Indianapolis: Hackett Publishing. Original (1790) as *Critik der Urtheilskraft*. Berlin: Lagarde und Friedrich.

Katz, M. (2004) *Capturing Sound: How Technology Has Changed Music*. Berkeley: University of California Press.

Kracauer, S. (1960) *Theory of Film: The Redemption of Physical Reality*. Oxford: Oxford University Press.

Lesh, P. (2005) *Searching for the Sound: My Life with the Grateful Dead*. New York: Back Bay Books.

Lewisohn, M. (1988) *The Beatles Recording Sessions*. New York: Harmony Books.

Martin, G. (1979) *All You Need is Ears: The Inside Personal Story of the Genius Who Created the Beatles.* New York: St. Martin's Press.

Patke, R.S. (2005) 'Benjamin on Art and Reproducibility: The Case of Music', in A. Benjamin (ed.) *Walter Benjamin and Art*, pp.185–208. London: Continuum.

Read, H. (1961) *Art and Industry.* Bloomington: Indiana University Press.

Sessions, R. (1950) *The Musical Experience of Composer, Performer and Listener.* Princeton: Princeton University Press.

Sterne, J. (2003) *The Audible Past: Cultural Origins of Sound Reproduction.* Durham: Duke University Press.

Wise, J.M. (1997) *Exploring Technology and Social Space.* Thousand Oaks: Sage Publications.

Wolin, R. (1994) *Walter Benjamin: An Aesthetic of Redemption.* Berkeley: University of California Press.

Wolterstorff, N. (1980) *Works and Worlds of Art.* Oxford: Clarendon Press.

Zak, A.J. III (2001) *The Poetics of Rock: Cutting Tracks, Making Records.* Berkeley: University of California Press.

Discography

Beatles. (1966) *Revolver.* U.S. Capitol Records LP ST-2576 U.K. EMI Parlophone PCS 7009.

_____ (1968) 'Revolution 9' on *The Beatles.* Apple Records LP SWBO 101.

Beethoven, L. van. (1962) *'Emperor' Concerto.* L. Bernstein, conductor. Columbia LP MS 6366.

_____ (1980) *Ode to Freedom: Bernstein in Berlin.* L. Bernstein, conductor. DG CD 429861.

_____ (1989) *Classic Performances: Bernstein in Vienna. Beethoven Symphonies 4, 6 & 9.* L. Bernstein, conductor. DG CD 463468.

_____ (1999) *Furtwängler Conducts Beethoven.* W. Fürtwangler, conductor. Music & Arts Program CD 4049.

Boggs, D. (1997) *Country Blues: Complete Early Recordings.* Revenant Records CD 205.

Davis, M. (1969) *In a Silent Way.* Columbia LP CS 9875.

_____ (1972) *On the Corner.* Columbia LP KC 31906.

_____ (1998) *Panthalassa: The Music Of Miles Davis 1969–1974.* Reconstruction and mix translation by Bill Laswell. Sony CD 67909.

Duke Ellington. (1999) *Ellington At Newport 1956. Complete.* Columbia/Legacy CD 64932.

Gould, G. (1993) *Glenn Gould's Solitute Trilogy: Three Sound Documentaries.* CBC Records CD PSCD 2003-3.

Grateful Dead. (1968) *Anthem of the Sun.* Warner Bros. LP WS-1749.

_____ (1969) *Aoxomoxoa.* Warner Bros. LP WS-1790.

_____ (1969) *Live/Dead.* Warner Bros. LP WS-1830.

Monroe, B. (1992) *The Essential Bill Monroe & His Blue Grass Boys.* Sony CD C2K 52478.

Simon and Garfunkel. (1970) 'Bridge Over Troubled Water' on *Bridge Over Troubled Water* Columbia LP KCS 9914.

ANTHONY GRITTEN

Performing after Recording

The modern economy isn't about the redistribution of wealth –
it's about the redistribution of time.

Douglas Coupland (2004: 279)

WHEN and how are digital recordings useful to performers of Western classical music? This chapter on the relationship between today's performer and digital recordings (hereinafter 'recordings') explores these questions from the performer's perspective. Although the topic is recordings, the focus is on what the performer thinks she does and does not do live on stage.

In section I, I set up the standard – and still useful – conception of performing works, and note how recordings seem to challenge the performative singularity of aesthetic judgment involved in performing works live on stage, and to threaten, according to some, the uniqueness of the performing event through their repeatability. I ask whether we can distinguish live performing events from recorded performances in terms of singularity – which, on the face of it, constitutes the primary cultural value of the former – but leave open the question of whether this distinction can actually be sustained today in the wake of techno-scientific developments. In section II, I outline some contexts in which today's performer and performative set-up find themselves: digital technologies, virtual realities, and shifting societal formations and consumer patterns. In section III, I confront the paradox of recordings – their temporality is reliant upon, yet independent from, the temporality of performing live – and ask why performers naturally resist (or should resist, speaking pedagogically) the distraction offered by this paradox: why they do not generally take recordings as a panacea for their needs on stage.

I use the issue of recordings as a way of approaching singularity, and singularity as a way of framing contemporary aesthetic judgment. This essay follows the cultural displacement of the performer by recordings, hence my title: performing through and by means of – after, *d'après, nach, via* – recording.

I

The standard paradigm of performing concerns the representation of musical works. It uses terms like these: a performing event 'compliant with a score or notation is a sound object produced in accordance with the instructions for performing that are embodied in the score or notation' (Kivy, 2002: 225). Or these: 'expression comprises systematic patterns of deviation from the "neutral" information given in a score, which take the form of rule-based transformations of canonical values originating in the performer's internal representation of the musical structure' (Clarke, 1995: 22). Or these: 'our reasoned, stylistic, analytical assimilation of a score is (ideally) followed by the lightning intuition that releases a performance into living sound' (Howat, 1995: 19).

This set-up is not unique to performing music. We read similar messages in many non-artistic discourses. To wit: 'The information contained in this email [read: performing event] and any documents and files transmitted with it is intended only for the person, persons or entity to which it is addressed [read: listeners] and may contain confidential and/or privileged material [read: the work]' (Anonymous, 2006). Or: 'Marketing is the business function that identifies an organisation's customer needs and wants [read: performances of works], determines which target markets it can serve best [read: listeners] and designs appropriate products, services and programmes [read: performances] to serve those markets' (Kotler et al., 1996: xiii).

Common to most ways of framing performing in terms of representation is the concept of singularity. This drives the musical machine and is the *raison d'être* of its marketing strategy, for every performance must have a USP – a Unique Selling Point – in order to survive the marketplace. Think of qualities of performing, folk-psychological and/or empirical, that pursue it: liveness, artistry, integrity, authenticity, originality, unrepeatability, memorability, accuracy, efficiency, and musicianship. There are various 'best' ways of achieving and representing such qualities, according to context. Each could be used fairly interchangeably, but singularity allows me to contrast live and recorded performances. My use of singularity is obviously ideological (Auslander, 1999: 128–9); yet, my aim is not to discredit it, but to explore what it means for performers today. Singularity is associated with the ideology that, having left the green room, performing live occurs spontaneously and conjures its miracles without resort to predetermined principles. Some have phrased this as the quasi-improvisatory moment of performing (Benson, 2003; Evens, 2005; Gould and Keaton, 2000). More generally, the search for singularity during a live performing event involves reflective judgments. On stage, the performer's priority is to deal, consciously or otherwise, with what is happening physically there and then, even if – indeed, especially if – her intentions get subsumed in the heat of the moment by other imperatives not wholly in accordance with the variously pre-determined rules and representations underpinning her performing of the work. Such judgments on the spot are those that make the event a live performance rather than the replication of a recorded one, and they expand outwards into the rules and representations which in hindsight justify them. The performer's reflective judgments cannot exist in the absence of these same rules and representations, but her judgments relate to the live performing event as a birth does to the life of which it is the irruptive beginning. Each reflective judgment brings forth something musically new, even as its very newness is underpinned by principles and representations that lend it a potential structure. In its classic formulation, such reflective judgment is not the application of a concept to a sensuous intuition in order to file the particular under a representation, but a creative act: 'an ability to *reflect*, in terms of a certain principle, on a given presentation so as to [make] a concept possible' (Kant, 1790/1987: 399).

Recordings seem to oppose this set-up predicated upon singularity. Their inherent repetition seems to assimilate the rule-following of the performer, against which her judgments in live performance are set in relief – as a portrait's subject is against its background canvas – to paradigms congruent with the implied digital 'rules' of recordings – their fixities, stabilities, and repeatabilities. The question is whether the improvisatory, reflective elements of performing and the labour of live musical judgment are displaced by the rule of recordings, short-circuited by quicker and more efficient repetitive mechanisms (Godlovitch, 1998: 69; Rodowick, 2001: 38). For the nature of performing has been transformed by the repetitive and reproductive function of recordings. As recordings proliferate and new media spring up to replace yesterday's technologies, it is worth pausing to ask whether the standard set-up of performing is 'secure enough to withstand all the metaphysical challenges that recording sets in motion' (Bohlman, 1999: 31). Recordings, taking the challenge of synthesizers a stage further, also set in motion 'the disturbing message that the human skill, expertise, and dedication which go into the result are not special, and are just further mechanical functions' (Godlovitch, 1998: 69). The general implication here about the displacement of performing acknowledges that '[r]ight from the beginning, machines invented to counteract temporal erosion, to constitute a *speech* that would be indefinitely *reproducible*, to overcome the ravages of time by means of the construction of mechanical devices, were moving in the direction of a death blow to representation' (Attali, 1977/1985: 85). This is to say that it is unclear where the performer stands in the social totality, given that many of those who hear her interpretations will be used to an acousmatic life at the end of headphones or speakers. Once recovered from her initial reactions (perhaps 'astonishment and terror' (Katz, 2006), though hopefully also excitement at the opportunity for disseminating her work) to the prospect of a life saturated with recordings, mostly those of other performers and computers, the performer still has to work towards singularity, circumventing the problem of redundancy along the way: 'If the goal of a performance is to exactly mimic an *Urtext* recording, then why not simply play the *Urtext* recording and forget the concert? The point of live music is that it is always different' (Bowen, 1999: 441). Since the performer comes to know – sooner or later, by happy or sad coincidence – that her listeners sit elsewhere in the room and nowhere near her labyrinthine mind, it becomes clear to her, self-evident even, that '[t]he ability to convince the public in the concert hall is quite independent of absolute perfection' (Brendel, 1990: 201), and that '[p]resenting a performance is not "playing yourself back", like a recording in which you have somehow become entrapped, to be exhausted as the spectator of your own moving, but absent, self' (Cumming, 2000: 158–9). It is otherwise.

Changes in the elements and procedures of modern life have impacted upon how we apprehend cultural activities like performing music. The very quality of 'liveness' itself has become a minority interest economically and culturally, and 'whether defined in social or psychological terms, is [no longer]...essential to musical meaning' (Frith, 1996: 229). Similarly, the facts that technologically mediated 'repetition now constitutes the very threshold of music's social audibility' (Mowitt, 1987: 175) and that 'a concert is representation, but...[so is] a meal à la carte in a restaurant; a phonograph record or a can of food is repetition' (Attali, 1985: 41; cf. 128), indicate the general direction of the paradigm shift. There has been a transformation in the focus of attention in the capitalist machine: as John Mowitt wrote, reception now occludes production (the First World is a service economy), and the system occludes the subject (try surviving without a bank account!) (Mowitt, 1987: 176–7). Since the publication of retrospective collections *Rethinking Music* (Cook and Everist (eds), 1999) and *The Cultural Study of Music* (Clayton, Herbert and Middleton (eds), 2003), which considered cultures, markets and economies but spent little time on recordings *per se*, even musicology has witnessed a paradigm shift. Interpreting recordings with empirically grounded methods is now valued for engaging with the real world head-on. One scholar's website, for example, recently offered an additional option after the standard options of reading about biography, teaching activities and publications: it requested that the visitor 'do something really important' by signing a petition to oppose the extension of copyright on recordings (Leech-Wilkinson, 2006).

But recordings have not just changed the behaviour of musicologists. They have also changed how performers behave. For one thing, it is harder to be singled out from peers, since many performers sound like recordings (Attali, 1985: 85; Katz, 2004: 26; Philip, 1992: 231), and the performer is faced with the ideological residues of earlier performing generations ('Stop being imitators of your computers!' (Gitlis, 2007: liner notes)) and constantly bombarded with the desires of a media-controlled public that 'consumes in order to resemble and no longer, as in [the older regime of] representation, to distinguish oneself' (Attali, 1985: 110). Thus, the singularity of performing is often invested in factors other than 'just' the acoustic evidence: in interviews, in dress codes, in the body and facial movements conveying emotion and structure, and affording listeners interpretive opportunities, and more. Nelson Goodman's old maxim that the notated score enables the 'authoritative identification of a work from performance to performance' (Goodman, 1968: 128) may be true only for the performer, and then only partially (Butt, 2002: 113). For many listeners, recordings have taken over that role (François, 1992: 12), providing a point of constant, still fixity more efficiently than the silent score ever could.

In the light of these changes in behaviour, we should ask what happens while the performer is performing in the glare of the spotlights and microphones. Given that she is often being recorded as she performs (in private and public), given that being recorded is a promise and a threat (it can make and break careers), and given that what was once a singular event is now endlessly repeatable at the flick of a switch, what has happened to the singularity of performing live?

II

In this section, I expand the standard set-up described in section I, and ask if it remains valid for today's performer, given that recordings are omnipresent in her life, cementing friendships, narrating her life, helping her jog to work, and more. In preparation for section III, I shall examine two issues that illustrate the changes wrought on live performing by recordings: the ownership of interpretations, and the generation of interpretations by imitation.

The construction of a global market has tried to brush under the threshold of auditory perception the fact that, although recordings have deepened listeners' auditory abilities (after Freud we hear meaningful nuances in every sound), listeners generally do not, and do not need to, distinguish an interpretation *propre* from an imitated or forged interpretation – the real from the simulated; nor could they, since the acoustic evidence for both would be identical (Godlovitch, 1998: 57). The little parable Don DeLillo tells in *White Noise* about the resurrection of aura through the mass production of cameras makes the point well: 'We're not here to capture an image, we're here to maintain one. Every photograph reinforces the aura. Can you feel it, Jack? An accumulation of nameless energies' (DeLillo, 1984: 12–13). The case of Joyce Hatto also illustrates the fragility of interpretation (Cook and Sapp, 2007; Hurwitz 2007a, 2007b, 2007c; Inverne, 2007; Rose, 2007), though this says more about the industry and its supporting paraphernalia (critics and scholars) than about the work and worth of musical interpretation. Similarly, that Igor Stravinsky's recordings did not always bear out his written pronouncements is, dare one say it, not worth getting hot under the collar for.

'Sounds just like Alfred Brendel' is not the same as 'stole that from Brendel by trying to imitate it', even if it sounds the same, and listeners are unable to judge an interpretation reliably as being original or concocted from ideas that the performer has picked up from other performances, some live, some recorded: a bit of Brendel here, a bit of Wilhelm Kempff there; Brendel's pacing and Kempff's voicing; all Brendel. This is because interpretations are never private property in a strong sense and cannot be protected as such (Auslander, 1999: 135–9). Once embodied and set in motion in a particular way by a recording or live performance, they once again become common property and an exchangeable commodity; 'original' and 'concocted' are A and B sides of the same record. Similarly, the issue of whether or not an interpretation is original is a different issue from whether or not it has internal structural integrity and whether or not it can be identified as such according to appropriate stylistic criteria. The fact that an interpretation of a Schubert sonata seems to paste together characteristics of Brendel and Kempff, or of Brendel and the performer herself, does not mean that it is not an interpretation, even if its stylistic provenance or integrity raises eyebrows. The long and short of it is that recordings have no loyalty to the performer:

> Records are a kind of offspring of which one can't, unfortunately, say that one has to nurse them until they grow up and then forget them as soon as possible and let them lead their own lives. They lead their own lives at once, and are scarcely ever grown up! There's always something infantile about a record, at least as far as the artist is concerned.
>
> (Brendel, 1976: 147)

In a perverse way, this is the resurrection of aura post-Benjamin, as technology turns against its inventor:

> A manufactured product behaves as though nobody had created it, as though it exists by itself. The pure 'thingness' of the object appears to scorn all sign of it having been anything else. More still: it is not only that the subjective creator, that the process of creation is denied; the creation itself appears before the one who has produced it as an alien power and seeks to shape him, to influence his thinking and acting.
>
> (Mayer, cited in Hooper, 2006: 372)

Thus, we should conclude that '[w]hatever we hear on a recording is not itself sufficient to ground judgments of the player's real role and true merit. At most we can judge charitably that the player is as if creditworthy' (Godlovitch, 1998: 26; cf. Auslander, 1999: 86); other information about the performing event is always required, and this is what bow ties and pre-concert interviews do – they supplement what listeners believe, on the basis of acoustic evidence, about the performer's interpretation. The most efficient way to conceive the virtual reality of the interpretation inhabiting and hosted by the recorded track is that it is best heard 'as if' it were a live performance. Even if the performer, while performing, believes that she or her listeners can make reliable judgments of 'creditworthiness' and of the differences between original and forged interpretations, or between performing and recording *tout court*, she still faces a sensuous imperative to perform. She must still create a bodily intervention into a circumscribed time-space, a sense of occasion, an event.

It is natural, then, that many performers do not listen much to other performers' recordings, or live performances. For towards the end of practicing comparisons become invidious and imitations insidious; the interpretation finds its own way. Once the performer has reached this 'threshold' between green room and stage (Bakhtin, 1975/1981: 248; Bakhtin, 1963/1984: 61, 63, 73, 170–6, 287; Morson, 1994: 162–9, 201–6) and stepped over it into a performing event, she no longer hears herself the way she did in the practice room, nor hears what listeners hear while she is performing, nor indeed hears the sounds of her very own performance as listeners hear them elsewhere in the room, since she now attends to what she is required to do by the work she had been preparing and is now performing. As she will say, then, imitating the interpretations on recordings while performing is foolhardy at best (Frederickson, 1989: 199), if indeed it is possible, and can risk 'a break in concentration' if not something more, even when it is the recordings of expert performers that are taken as models (Howat, 1995: 10–12; Lisboa et al., 2005). It is hard to imagine how one might 'imitate' Mikhail Pletnev's or Claudio Arrau's interpretations of Balakirev's *Islamey*, even leaving aside issues of, say, acoustics in the former case (live in Carnegie Hall; Pletnev, 2001) and historical context in the latter (1928, after a year or so of Jungian counselling; Arrau, 2000). And what about the much more numerous less competent musicians? We do spend time learning how not to do things by watching others – on reality TV, masterclasses, swimming competitions, and so on – and we certainly learn something about performing from listening to recordings with bad intonation and fluffed entries as well as good practice. But listening to other performers and performing is dead easy, since they are waiting inertly; listening to oneself is something else, especially on stage. There is a fine line between imitation and exaggeration, and expert performing is valued for the ways in which it shows evidence of having assimilated and actively forgotten the imitated object in its striving for a singular interpretation – real or apparent. Forgetting takes place at the threshold between green room and stage, and beyond that, 'What did I do in rehearsal this afternoon?' and 'Whence this interpretation?' are questions that the performing musician lacks the time to answer.

III

Why is it, then, that performers generally do not imitate recordings, and that, despite acknowledging other performers' approaches ('She has a great way with Prokofiev') and their particular performances ('I'll never forget Lorenzo Ghielmi's recital in Haarlem'), they do not normally think in terms of patching together their interpretations from fragments of others' live or recorded interpretations? In what consists the performer's wisdom?

At this point we should turn outwards to digital technologies that support recordings. Here, the later writings of Jean-François Lyotard are useful, for they turn repeatedly to the relationship between technology and judgment. In this section, I explore the main challenge that recordings pose to the singularity of performing: what the performer (believes that she) gains in return for the affective temporal displacement of her activity set in motion by recordings. I focus on Lyotard at the expense of massive literatures in disciplines like Ergonomics and Management Studies for one reason: he was also specifically interested in aesthetic judgments.

According to Lyotard's classic definition of Postmodernism in terms of performativity, technology is 'a game, pertaining not to the true, the just, or the beautiful, etc., but to efficiency: a technical "move" is "good" when it does better and/or expends less energy than another' (Lyotard, 1979/1984: 44; cf. 51). In the wake of the paradigm shift wrought by this text and its acolytes, many have noted (negatively and positively) that technology saves time and increases efficiency (the same thing, it is often claimed) (e.g. Attali, 1985: 32, 41, 84–8, 90, 95, 101–2, 111, 124–6, 130–2, 141, 153; Auslander, 1999: 46; Bennington, 1988: 101, 127; Evens, 2005: 118; Harris, 2001: 131, 138–9, 143; Harvey, 2001: 116; Lyotard, 1983/1988: xiii, xiv, xv; Lyotard, 1984: xxiv, 11, 62; Lyotard, 1988/1991: 62; Lyotard, 1993/1997: 40, 46–7, 62–3). Through technological progress, they explain, we have developed a world of transparency, accountability, audit, efficiency, systemic optimisation, responsibility, relevance, and knowledge transfer: all procedures designed to increase productivity per unit time and for which 'the question (overt or implied) is no longer "Is it true?" but "What use is it?"'(Lyotard, 1984: 51; cf. Lane, 2000: 33, 86). This is a powerful claim indeed: the user can gain, accumulate, and stockpile time. Building upon the linguistic idea that the meanings of terms are to be found in their uses (Wittgenstein, 1953), the economic idea that machines 'are organs of the human brain, created by the human hand; the power of knowledge, objectified' (Marx, 1953/1973: 706), and the psychological idea that '[w]ith every tool man is perfecting his own organs, or he is removing the limits to their functioning' (Freud cited in Mowitt, 1987: 173), this ideology encompasses, *inter alia*, the predetermined fixities of Rational Choice Theory (e.g. Baert, 1998: 165–70), the belief that in 'an ethic of sheer performativity, human contact – face to face – has been rendered obsolete by interface' (Flieger, 1996: 90), and, perhaps in the extreme, Jean Baudrillard's infamous claim that 'the very definition of the real is *that of which it is possible to give an equivalent reproduction*' (Baudrillard, 1981/1983: 146: cf. Attali, 1985: 85; Auslander, 1999: 31; Connor, 1989: 153; Rodowick, 2001: 38).

It is certainly the case that technology ('ubiquitous computing') is making more decisions for us, and this is only just in medicine, warfare, space flight, and other ways of furthering human life: 'Divide and conquer, the strategy of the digital' (Evens, 2005: 70). For oil reserves as for the data on CDs, '[e]xtraction, distribution, and refinement are the most efficient path to a given end; they are modern technology's techniques, through which it institutes its *order*' (Evens, 2005: 64). Consider, too, a checklist of the properties of recordings – tangibility, portability, (in)visibility, repeatability, temporality, receptivity, and manipulability (Katz, 2004: 8–47) – alongside those of the digital domain – 'unique exactitude, robustness, repeatability, transportability, and applicability' (Evens, 2005, 69) – and those of the repetitive economy – scientism, imperial universality, depersonalisation, manipulation of power, and elitism (Attali, 1985: 113–16). The convergence of these three discourses around the drive to save time is an issue for the performer, since recordings make her a tempting offer based upon their digital properties.

According to Aden Evens, pursuing ideas of Stan Godlovitch, the dream of the digital is to arrive at 'a wholly virtual reality' in which we will be able to undo anything (Evens, 2005: 129, 183–4 n 22; cf. Godlovitch, 1998: 97–108, esp. 101).

This will come about because '[t]he digital implements an immaculate ordering that isolates desired properties and gives verifiable, repeatable, and measurable definitions' (Evens, 2005: 64); it 'captures the general, the representable, the repeatable, but leaves out the singular, the unique, the immediate: whatever is not formal' (Evens, 2005: 66). Indeed, 'the digital is entirely equal to its form, is nothing but its form...[and] holds nothing in reserve' (Evens, 2005: 69). In this regard, Evens, writing about digital computers, can be read as showing by extension how digital technologies help to 'save labour,...facilitate work,...help us to realize our desires' (Evens, 2005: 130). They 'extend our memory...extend our bodies...extend desire into expression... facilitate expression...effect the immediate presence of our desires in the world' (Evens, 2005: 164).

It would seem, then, extrapolating from the contexts of Evens' discussion, that within the new digital world the performing musician has 'all the time in the world to make aesthetic decisions' (Evens, 2005: 124), for technology has already cleared a path for her to follow. But Evens writes firmly that '[w]e must recognise the futility and self-defeat of striving to minimize effort' and that 'it would be a gross confusion to imagine that some sort of effort is saved thereby' (Evens, 2005: respectively 173, 190 n 36). Of the violence of recording technology, he explains that '[s]uddenly it became possible to isolate and control the musical work of art, to identify something as a work, and to re-present it to oneself under conditions of one's choosing' (Evens, 2005: 8–9); insofar as the performer is also a vicarious listener, one might believe that one no longer needs to get up from the proverbial armchair in order to expand the territory of one's musical knowledge. But he also notes that a recording is 'a reflux or distillation in which time is boiled off, for time must be added back in to get sound' (Evens, 2005: 54), and that the prosthetic interpolation of time is precisely the intervention of live performing events (Evens, 2005: 79, 80, 163). So, after the fact, recordings will have saved time but not stored it. They will not have gained surplus time, but displaced it from the physical world to the virtual, and demanded that the performer actively reinstate it. Indeed, the opposition cited above between 'face' and 'interface' is mistaken, because to separate them (historically or structurally) is to presuppose an underlying antagonism (to adopt an older Romantic ideology), when in fact they mutually dissimulate each other: the human is inhuman is human. The point is that technology (interfaces) is intimately related to human judgment (faces), particularly when today's performer performs.

Saving time, then, is not a simple matter of efficiency: even if every little helps, savings have costs. Lyotard writes of the 'streams of cultural capital' which hasten on like good citizens, that a good stream is 'one that gets there the quickest. An excellent one gets there almost right after it's left' (Lyotard, 1997: 4–5; cf. 45). Elsewhere he notes more generally that '[t]he principle of reason is the way of questioning which rushes to its goal, the reply' (Lyotard, 1991: 74), which generates 'impatient' discourses quickening after their solutions (Lyotard, 1981/1989: 273–4). All this worries his aesthetic sensibility: 'I do not like this haste. What it hurries, and crushes, is what after the fact I find that I have always tried, under diverse headings – work, figural, heterogeneity, dissensus, event, thing – to reserve: the unharmonisable' (Lyotard, 1991: 4; cf. 168). He responds with probity, gently 'delaying' and 'tarrying' with the feeling – *sensus* – from which reflective judgments emerge (Lyotard, 1987/1992: 5). His position is that of Critical Theory, which aims 'to disrupt the process through which "facts" become reified affirmations of "what is" at the expense of "what could be (otherwise)"' (Hooper, 2006: 17). The flipside of the technological drive identified by Lyotard is clearest when he comes to aesthetic judgment. With typical grace, he puts it efficiently *and* poetically: 'the aesthetic moment: a sigh, the provisional suspension of the principle of efficiency' (Lyotard, 1997: 58).

If this is the case – if, that is, after Lyotard, aesthetic judgments conflict with 'the principle of efficiency' and an emphasis on performativity – then we should ask whether recordings too conflict with musical judgment, given that, as a form of technology, they are bound up with the drive towards greater techno-scientific efficiency, whereas musical judgments are bound up in suspense – in 'intrigue' (Lyotard, 1997: 36). Consider their claims. Recordings not only ventriloquise and narrate a single continuous performance that can be apprehended synoptically, as often as not mythologising one that never actually happened or could not actually have happened except at the mixing desk (Frith, 1996: 211; Katz, 2004: 42). They also tempt the performer to believe that she can possess and replicate this virtual performance at will without mistakes or noise: after all, it is physically and virtually there on the CD player, and the mass media continually tempt her with dreams of achieving the 'X-Factor' by imitating recorded performances. Recordings also tempt her to believe that they speed up the learning process, the process of letting judgments emerge ('Why not articulate the bass like this?'; 'Surely Robert Craft's recording of *Agon* is too fast?'). And because this virtual acceleration is efficient and transparent, it appears to offer a tool to performers salaried by British Higher Education Institutions (HEIs) and destined for processing through the Research Assessment Exercise (RAE) machine. (The RAE makes quality judgments about research activity in UK HEIs, and the results determine the research income received by each HEI.) Recordings say jump, you say how high, depending on your auditors' needs.

The performer might be tempted to believe that recordings help her to find sufficient but not necessary shortcuts (Godlovitch, 1998: 53), to avoid the trial and error labour of pen and paper ('Emil Gilels did that, Vladimir Horowitz did that, but I don't especially like either; how about this?'; 'No need to think about that passage; I like what Stephen Hough does'). Like prosthetic limbs attached to music analysis, recordings claim to provide *a priori* answers to the questions of performing, but they also encourage the performer to leap to conclusions ('Given the respective recording conditions, and their choices of articulation, tempi, and use of pedaling, it is obvious what the contrasting historical-stylistic-ideological interpretations of Maria Yudina's, Marcelle Meyer's, and Martin Jones' recordings of Stravinsky's *Serenade en*

La are' (Yudina, 1995; Meyer, 1992; Jones, 1997)). We live, after all, in an acousmatic world where the 'remoteness of music *heard* from music *made* has become utterly commonplace' (Godlovitch, 1998: back cover; Katz, 2004: 14–18; Rodowick, 2001: 38). Given that the majority of listeners have been enculturated within this set-up and are accustomed to thinking of music as both 'remote' from its live performing event (mediated through iPods, say) and in terms of the ideology of perfection (another singularity) faked so easily by recordings, then (if she is aware of these circumstances) the performer might believe that recordings help to traverse the passage to and fro between performing and reception. Referring to another artistic medium, the point was phrased by Lyotard (in historical terms) thus: 'photographic and cinematographic processes can accomplish better, faster, and with a circulation a hundred thousand times larger than narrative or pictorial realism, the task which academicism had assigned to realism: to preserve various consciousnesses from doubt' (Lyotard, 1984: 74).

The notion that recordings might have therapeutic and utilitarian values (reducing doubt and speeding up the creation of musical singularity) panders to late capitalism's obsession with techno-science, saving time, improving efficiency, and raising productivity (Lane, 2000: 27–43). This is understandable. The performer has a job to do and many listeners are only interested in the end results, and not in how she practices privately and whether or not she employs a radically different body language on stage as opposed to when she relaxes in Starbucks with friends. Music, after all, has a difficult relation to other more easily commodifiable enterprises (of which, ironically, its own recording industry is one): 'There has been vast, labour-saving technical progress in [say,] watchmaking, which is still continuing. But live violin playing benefits from no labour (or capital)-saving innovations – it is still done the old-fashioned way' (Baumol and Bowen, cited in Laing, 2003: 314).

However, this buzz is just displacement activity and risks fetishising recordings for the wrong reasons, such that '[s]tockpiling [them] then becomes a substitute, not a preliminary condition, for [their] use' (Attali, 1985: 101). The issue, displaced behind techno-scientific rhetoric, is that '[r]ecordings are just traces or records of performances, and no more performances in their own right than photos are the objects photographed' (Godlovitch, 1998: 14). One could criticise, with Lyotard, that 'the monumentalised trace [of the art object in the museum, i.e. the recording] is not faithful to the event that has passed by. That it has lost the 'presence' and 'vigour' of the practice or the work when it emerged' (Lyotard, 1997: 167), but there would not be much point in being overly critical, since recordings are not just memorials to a possibly 'evanescent' performing event (Auslander, 1999: 45–6, 58, 112; Cook, 2003: 208; Katz, 2004: 5). They are also generators of new expressions (Clarke, 2002: 187; Clarke, 2004: 88; Davies, 2001: 295; Evens, 2005: 23; Frith, 1996: 232; Godlovitch, 1998: 97; Katz, 2004: 15; Philip, 2004: 47–9). This is hardly surprising, since for the performer it is self-evident acoustically and physically that '[t]he recording process imposes its own time on the recorded object, one having very little to do with the external, real-time of performance, of the internal musical-time of the composition' (Dellaira, 1995: 196).

Nevertheless, despite their multiplicity, distributability, and portability, recordings do fix the work in an uncanny way. Like television, and like analyses both musical and psychoanalytical, they claim to give the performer an immediacy and intimacy with the work (Auslander, 1999: 16, 35) – she can dissect it (pause, rewind, adjust the volume) – and provide a shortcut between practising and performing. In part, this follows the cultural paradox that has built up around recordings, namely, that their 'innate' authority and authenticity is 'invested' in them by their users: 'We know that recording and event are different and yet, because the event can only happen once but the recording can be played back again and again, the recording seems invested with some kind of authority, something we can go back to, to consult, verify, or analyse' (Dellaira, 1995: 194). It is not that the potential beliefs described above are necessarily indolent or false, despite claims that listening to recordings 'is a lazy shortcut, the musical equivalent of looking up the answer in the back of the book' (Hill, 2002: 133). Indeed, they may work for the performer time after time and not even be conscious, let alone articulated verbally for essays like this. Not many performers bother to analyse musical works in the Schenkerian manner of Mannes-trained performers like Murray Perahia (Rink, 2001), but not many performers are inarticulate. It is that these folk-psychological beliefs are efficacious only insofar as they provide a way for her to step over the threshold of judgment separating practising from performing. However, there are no shortcuts; performing is not management consultancy. As Kant said, judgment is 'understanding which comes only with the passage of time' (Kant, 1798/1978: 93). As we say, time passes judgment.

Recordings, then, do not give the performer surplus time. Shirking the work of performing, displacing and delaying the moment of judgment – the step over the threshold – they fake performing, as the extreme case of Music-Minus-One recordings illustrates, where one makes the purchase in the belief that one can go home and 'play along with' the Berlin Philharmonic in the lounge (Davies, 2003: 94–107). They tempt the performer with an easy alibi: alongside the standard set-up in which 'one listens to a recording with the expectation of hearing it again – with an awareness of the reproducibility of its content' (Davies, 2001: 304; cf. Mowitt, 1987: 175) – we could pause here on the cultural value invested in 'live' and 'authentic' recordings precisely because they have resisted the temptation of the fragmentary splice. After Philip Auslander, recordings offer templates for replication rather than scripts for performing (and definitely not texts for representation) (Attali, 1985: 118–19, 128; Auslander, 1999: 50, 104, 136), but this is still not enough for the performer. After she has switched off the CD player, the threshold between green room and stage awaits, and she must judge and act. As one sociologist puts it, music

allow[s] us to understand taste not as a recording of fixed properties of an object, not as a stable attribute of a person, and not as a game played between existing identities, but as an accomplishment...It relies closely upon moments, places, opportunities: taste is not only an activity, it is an event, oversensitive to the problematic relationship between – as they nicely say – a combination of circumstances.

(Hennion, 2003: 90)

Recordings do not make the performer's job on stage quicker, insofar as she remains bound by the obligations of performing live, and they do not remove any of its challenges: it is still an open-ended 'combination of circumstances'. While composers and recordings tell stories, the performer has to live through one as well, both while listening to and after having listened to those of composers and recordings (Evens, 2005: 159, 189 n 28; Winner, 1977: 202). Beyond the threshold, recordings become less important in the search for 'a little something *live* and unexpected. A good loophole' (Lyotard, 1997: 11). There, the performer has nothing and must perform in a 'suspended sigh'. This performative suspense can be conceived in terms of the analogous relation between everyday and literary languages:

> If the literary text [read: recording] reveals itself to be a staged discourse, asking only that the world it represents should be taken *as if* it were a real world, then the recipient [read: performer] has to suspend his or her natural attitude to the thing represented (i.e. the real world [read: musical work]). This does not mean that his or her natural attitude is transcended, for it is still present as a virtualized background, against which comparisons may be made and new attitudes may take shape.

(Iser, 1993: 220)

Beyond the threshold, in the sigh of performing, the impossible happens, quite inefficiently: epistemology gives way to ethics, language to utterance; everything the performer knew (note the tense) is supplanted by everything she does (must do).

IV

In this essay, I have explored four propositions. First, recordings are useful up to the threshold of performing, the door between green room and stage. Secondly, they sometimes save time by speeding up the process of preparation. Thirdly, they falsely tempt the performer to believe that she may not only save time, but gain and stockpile surplus time, that she may accumulate a virtual credit against which live musical judgments made on stage, whether prepared beforehand or spontaneously, can be cashed in as representative, cross-referenced judgments, rather than made properly for themselves on the spot. And fourthly, the virtual time of the performance imagined and prepared by the performer prior to going on stage (and indeed while performing) counts for nothing until actualised there and then on the spot.

I have also tried to give credence to the idea that '[t]he place of technology in the history of aesthetic judgment has always been a curious one' (Rodowick, 2001: 37). Technology is a tool used to accomplish things – ironing, driving, writing, waiting, eating, and of course performing. This is as true for recordings as it is for other technologies – instruments, fingers, lungs, notations, bow ties, and so on. However, we can also conclude that live performing and non-live recordings have a mutually implicating relationship: for the performer *qua* performer (and probably listeners too), to entertain the possibility of one is, *ipso facto*, to engage with the necessary co-presence of the other, with their 'relation of dependence and imbrication rather then opposition' (Auslander, 1999: 53). This may be more along the lines of Baudrillard than of Lyotard, but it is clear that just as it is by definition ambiguous from acoustic evidence alone whether the reality TV show playing now is live or a repeat (Auslander, 1999: 44), so today the performer cannot perform without recording. And this is as true of Arnold Schönberg, whose own conducted performances of *Pierrot Lunaire* assumed (or at least show) different interpretative strategies according to whether it was a live radio broadcast or a studio performance (Byron, 2006–7), as it is for the latest conservatoire graduate in search of listeners.

Yet it is also the case that alongside this intimacy between performer and recording, recordings are nevertheless a distraction from the issue of singular live musical judgments, and performers are thus usually uneasy about embracing recordings as a panacea for performing-related problems. This is because a still small voice echoes in the performer's ear every time she makes a decision, every time she commits her body to a certain gesture, every time she judges her own playing in need of immediate change, every time she simply listens: as one virtuoso has remarked, albeit metaphorically as befits its context, '[l]et the ear carry you, and it will carry the sound' (Goerner, 2006). On stage, this voice persists in asking the performer as she searches at each moment for the most appropriate way to do her job, 'Why do we have to save...time to the point where this imperative seems like the law of our lives?' (Lyotard, 1991: 67). Her performing answers for her, 'you don't.'

References

Anonymous (2006) [Email Signature]. Email read 31 August, London.

Attali, J. (1985) *Noise: The Political Economy of Music*. Trans. B. Massumi. Minneapolis: University of Minnesota Press. Original (1977) as *Bruits: essai sur l'économie politique de la musique*. Paris: Presses Universitaires de France.

Auslander, P. (1999) *Liveness*. New York: Routledge.

Baert, P. (1998) *Social Theory in the Twentieth Century*. Cambridge: Polity Press.

Bakhtin, M.M. (1981) *The Dialogic Imagination: Four Essays*. Trans. C. Emerson and M. Holquist. Austin: University of Texas Press. Original (1975) as *Voprosy literatury i estetiki*. Moscow: Khudozh.

_____ (1984) *Problems of Dostoevsky's Poetics*. Trans. C. Emerson. Minneapolis: Minnesota University Press. Original (1963, rev. edn) as *Problemy poetiki Dostoevskogo*. Moscow: Khudozh.

Baudrillard, J. (1983) *Simulations*. Trans. P. Foss, P. Patton and P. Beitchman. New York: Semiotext(e). Original (1981) as *Simulacres et simulation*. Paris: Galilée.

Bennington, G. (1988) *Lyotard*. New York: Columbia University Press.

Benson, B. (2003) *The Improvisation of Musical Dialogue*. Cambridge: Cambridge University Press.

Bohlman, P. (1999) 'Ontologies of Music', in N. Cook and M. Everist (eds) *Rethinking Music*, pp.17–34. Oxford: Oxford University Press.

Bowen, J.A. (1999) 'Finding the Music in Musicology: Performance History and Musical Works', in N. Cook and M. Everist (eds) *Rethinking Music*, pp.424–51. Oxford: Oxford University Press.

Brendel, A. (1976) *Musical Thoughts and Afterthoughts*. London: Robson Books.

_____ (1990) *Music Sounded Out*. New York: Farrar Straus Giroux.

Butt, J. (2002) *Playing with History*. Cambridge: Cambridge University Press.

Byron, A. (2006–7) '*Pierrot Lunaire* in Studio and in Broadcast: *Sprechstimme*, Tempo and Character', *Journal of the Society for Musicology in Ireland* 2: 69–91.

Clarke, E. (1995) 'Expression in Performance: Generativity, Perception and Semiosis', in J. Rink (ed.) *The Practice of Performance*, pp.21–54. Cambridge: Cambridge University Press.

_____ (2002) 'Listening to Performance', in J. Rink (ed.) *Musical Performance*, pp.185–96. Cambridge: Cambridge University Press.

_____ (2004) 'Empirical Methods in the Study of Performance', in E. Clarke and N. Cook (eds) *Empirical Musicology*, pp.77–102. New York: Oxford University Press.

Clayton, M., Herbert, T., and Middleton, R. (eds) (2003) *The Cultural Study of Music*. New York: Routledge.

Connor, S. (1989) *Postmodernist Culture*. Oxford: Blackwell.

Cook, N. and Everist, M. (eds) (1999) *Rethinking Music*. Oxford: Oxford University Press.

Cook, N. (2003) 'Music as Performance', in M. Clayton, T. Herbert and R. Middleton (eds) *The Cultural Study of Music*, pp.204–14. New York: Routledge.

Cook, N. and Sapp, C. (2007) 'Purely Coincidental? Joyce Hatto and Chopin's Mazurkas', URL (consulted March 2007): http://www.charm.rhul.ac.uk/content/contact/hatto_article.html

Coupland, D. (2004) *Microserfs*. London: Harper Perennial.

Cumming, N. (2000) *The Sonic Self*. Bloomington: Indiana University Press.

Davies, S. (2001) *Musical Works and Performances*. Oxford: Oxford University Press.

_____ (2003) *Themes in the Philosophy of Music*. Oxford: Oxford University Press.

DeLillo, D. (1984) *White Noise*. New York: Penguin.

Dellaira, M. (1995) 'Some Recorded Thoughts on Recorded Objects', *Perspectives of New Music* 33(1)–2: 192–207.

Evens, A. (2005) *Sound Ideas*. Minneapolis: University of Minnesota Press.

Flieger, J. (1996) 'The Listening Eye: Postmodernism, Paranoia, and the Hypervisible', *Diacritics* 26 (1): 90–107.

François, J.-C. (1992) 'Writing Without Representation, and Unreadable Notation', *Perspectives of New Music* 30 (1): 6–20.

Frederickson, J. (1989) 'Technology and Music Performance in the Age of Mechanical Reproduction', *International Review of the Aesthetics and Sociology of Music* 20 (2): 193–220.

Frith, S. (1996) *Performing Rites*. Cambridge, Mass.: Harvard University Press.

Godlovitch, S. (1998) *Musical Performance*. New York: Routledge.

Goerner, N. (2006) Masterclass on F. Chopin's Sonata Op.35 in B♭ Minor. RNCM, Manchester, 14 May.

Goodman, N. (1968) *Languages of Art*. Indianapolis: Bobbs-Merrill.

Gould, C. and Keaton, K. (2000) 'The Essential Role of Improvisation in Musical Performance', *The Journal of Aesthetics and Art Criticism* 58 (2): 143–8.

Harris, P. (2001) 'Thinking @ the Speed of Time: Globalisation and its Dis-Contents or, Can Lyotard's Thought Go on Without a Body?', *Yale French Studies* 99: 129–48.

Harvey, R. (2001) 'Telltale at the Passages', *Yale French Studies* 99: 102–16.

Hennion, A. (2003) 'Music and Mediation: Toward a New Sociology of Music', in M. Clayton, T. Herbert and R. Middleton (eds) *The Cultural Study of Music*, pp.80–91. New York: Routledge.

Hill, P. (2002) 'From Score to Sound', in J. Rink (ed.) *Musical Performance*, pp.129–43. Cambridge: Cambridge University Press.

Hooper, G. (2006) *The Discourse of Musicology*. Aldershot: Ashgate.

Howat, R. (1995) 'What Do We Perform?', in J. Rink (ed.) *The Practice of Performance*, pp.3–20. Cambridge: Cambridge University Press.

Hurwitz, D. (2007a) 'Will the Real Joyce Hatto Please Stand Up!', URL (consulted March 2007): http://www.classicstoday.com/features/021807-joycehatto.asp

———— (2007b) 'The Hatto Affair: A Victimless Crime?', URL (consulted March 2007): http://www.classicstoday.com/features/022607-hattoaffair.asp

———— (2007c) 'The Hatto Affair: I Did it For My Wife', URL (consulted March 2007): http://www.classicstoday.com/features/022607-mywife.asp

Inverne, J. (2007) 'Masterpieces or Fakes? The Joyce Hatto Scandal', URL (consulted March 2007): http://www.gramophone.co.uk/newsMainTemplate.asp?storyID=2759&newssectionID=1

Iser, W. (1993) 'Representation: A Performative Act', in M. Krieger (ed.) *The Aims of Representation*, pp.217–32. Stanford: Stanford University Press.

Kant, I. (1978) *Anthropology from a Pragmatic Point of View*. Trans. V. Dowdell. Carbondale: Southern Illinois University Press. Original (1798) as *Anthropologie in pragmatischer Hinsicht*.

———— (1987) *Critique of Judgment*. Trans. W.S. Pluhar. Indianapolis: Hackett Publishing. Original (1790) as *Critik der Urtheilskraft*. Berlin: Lagarde und Friedrich.

Katz, M. (2004) *Capturing Sound*. Berkeley: University of California Press.

_____ (2006) "'Astonished and Somewhat Terrified'": Learning to Live with Recordings', paper presented at the British Library, London.

Kivy, P. (2002) *Introduction to a Philosophy of Music*. Oxford: Oxford University Press.

Kotler, P., Armstrong, G., Saunders, J. and Wong, V. (1996) *Principles of Marketing*. Hemel Hempstead: Prentice Hall.

Laing, D. (2003) 'Music and the Market', in M. Clayton, T. Herbert and R. Middleton (eds) *The Cultural Study of Music*, pp.309–20. New York: Routledge.

Lane, R. (2000) *Jean Baudrillard*. London: Routledge.

Leech-Wilkinson, D. (2006) URL (consulted August 2006): http://www.kcl.ac.uk/kis/schools/hums/music/dlw/

Lisboa, T., Williamon, A., Zicari, M. and Eiholzer, H. (2005) 'Mastery through Imitation: A Preliminary Study', *Musicae Scientiae* 9 (1): 75–110.

Lyotard, J.-F. (1984) *The Postmodern Condition: A Report on Knowledge*. Trans. G. Bennington and B. Massumi. Minneapolis: University of Minnesota Press. Original (1979) as *La Condition postmoderne: rapport sur le savoir*. Paris: Éditions de Minuit.

_____ (1988) *The Differend: Phrases in Dispute*. Trans. G.V.D. Abbeele. Minneapolis: University of Minnesota Press. Original (1983) as *Le Différend*. Paris: Éditions de Minuit.

_____ (1989) 'Analysing Speculative Discourse as Language-Game' (trans. G. Bennington), in A. Benjamin (ed.) *The Lyotard Reader*, pp.265–74. Oxford: Blackwell. Original (1981) as 'Essai d'analyse du dispositif spéculatif', *Degrés* 9: 26–7.

_____ (1991) *The Inhuman: Reflections on Time*. Trans. G. Bennington and R. Bowlby. Stanford: Stanford University Press. Original (1988) as *L'Inhumain: causeries sur le temps*. Paris: Galilée.

_____ (1992) 'Sensus Communis', in A. Benjamin (ed.) *Judging Lyotard*, pp.1–25. London: Routledge. Original (1987) as 'Sensus Communis', *Le Cahier (du Collège International de Philosophie)* 3: 67–87.

_____ (1997) *Postmodern Fables*. Trans. G.V.D. Abbeele. Minneapolis: University of Minnesota Press. Original (1993) as *Moralités Postmodernes*. Paris: Galilée.

Marx, K. (1973) *Grundrisse. Foundations of the Critique of Political Economy*. Trans. M. Nicolaus. Harmondsworth: Penguin. Original (1953) as *Grundrisse der Kritik der Politischen Ökonomie*. Berlin: Dietz.

Morson, G. (1994) *Narrative and Freedom*. Evanston: Northwestern University Press.

Mowitt, J. (1987) 'The Sound of Music in the Era of its Electronic Reproducibility', in R. Leppert and S. McClary (eds) *Music and Society*, pp.173–97. Cambridge: Cambridge University Press.

Philip, R. (1992) *Early Recordings and Musical Style. Changing Tastes in Instrumental Performance 1900–1950*. Cambridge: Cambridge University Press.

_____ (2004) *Performing Music in the Age of Recording*. New Haven: Yale University Press.

Rink, J. (2001) 'Perahia's Musical Dialogue', *The Musical Times* 142 (1877): 9–15.

Rodowick, D. (2001) *Reading the Figural, or, Philosophy after the New Media.* Durham, NC: Duke University Press.

Rose, A. (2007) 'Joyce Hatto: The Ultimate Recording Hoax', URL (consulted March 2007): http://www.pristineclassical.com/HattoHoax.html

Winner, L. (1977) *Autonomous Technology.* Cambridge, Mass.: MIT Press.

Wittgenstein, L. *(1953) Philosophical Investigations.* Posth. Trans. G.E.M. Anscombe. Oxford: Blackwell.

Discography

Arrau, C. (2000) *The Early Years.* Marston CD 52023-2.

Craft, R. (1993) *Stravinsky: The Composer Volume IV. 'American Stravinsky'.* Music Master Classics CD 01612-67113-2.

Gitlis, I. (2007) *Nicolò Paganini: 24 Caprices pour Violon Seul.* Philips 4428960.

Jones, M. (1997) *Stravinsky: Music for Piano.* Nimbus CD 5519-20.

Meyer, M. (1992) *Les Introuvables de Marcelle Meyer.* EMI CD 7-67405-2.

Pletnev, M. (2001) *Pletnev Live at Carnegie Hall.* DG CD 471157-2.

Yudina, M. (1995) *Russian Piano School vol. 4.* Melodiya CD 74321-25176-2.

MARC BATTIER

Phonography and the Invention of Sound

Introduction

DURING the last decade of the nineteenth century and the first decade of
the twentieth, several inventions including the telephone, phonograph and
radio, completely changed the way sound appears in culture, leading to the
emergence of an awareness of different kinds of aural perception. The development
of new forms of art and the birth of cinema were also among the factors that led to
unprecedented changes in how people think about sound. One of the most interesting
historical facts is that musicians were not the only agents in this process: poets,
writers, film makers, art critics, music critics and visual artists were equally involved
in bringing about momentous changes in sound culture. Their testimonies indicate the
extent to which they all contributed to the search for new ways of transforming art,
poetry and music while putting the question of sound – and noise – at the centre of
their preoccupation. In a certain sense, they were part of an artistic trend involving the
invention of new contexts for sound, or, simply, the invention of sound.

This trend touched upon various aspects of sound: while noise was very much
at the centre, there was also an epiphany of the voice and its new uses. Poetry, for
instance, invented new vocal sounds, using syllables with no meaning. Musical
instruments were also scrutinised and at times deemed unable to cope with the quest
for new sounds; the need to involve technology for this purpose was a frequently
mentioned theme. However, one cannot expect clear and well-defined ideas on
sound technologies in this period. Technology was often considered a means to
go beyond existing resources, while how this could be achieved was not always
obvious. French poets Guillaume Apollinaire and Henri-Martin Barzun turned to
the phonograph as early as 1911 in their search for new forms of poetry, departing
from the path of the Italian Futurists, but this never led to actual experiments. Their
writings, however, mark the onset of a reinvention of the phonograph. Originally
intended as a machine of reproduction, it became in the imagination of the two
poets an instrument of creation. Phonography played a major role in these attempts
to redefine sound and any form of art that uses sound, including music and poetry.
The term 'phonography' in this context does not refer to a particular definition by
a particular artist, but is used in the same way as, for instance, 'photography' or
'cinematography', i.e. a general term coined to encompass a specific technological
environment in which capturing what our senses perceive is the main factor.

The first artistic path in connection with phonography appeared in literature just after the first sound technologies became available. The most influential in this respect has been the phonograph (1877), although the telephone (1876) and, to some extent, the radio (c.1900) also had great influence. In literature, sound technologies were the instrument of telepresence, prosopopeia or recreation of the dead, and artificial human beings, the best-known examples appearing in Jules Vernes (*Le Château des Carpathes*, 1892), Guillaume Apollinaire (*Le Roi-Lune*, written c.1908, published in 1916), Raymond Roussel (*Locus Solus*, 1913), and James Joyce (*Ulysses*, 1922). A striking example of this trend can be found in a novel by Villiers de l'Isle-Adam titled *L'Ève future* (1886), in which an artificial woman is able to speak through a machine, thus putting the technology into applications for which it was not intended, albeit in a phantasmagorical manner.

Another artistic path appeared in the writings of poets and musicians, in connection with the desire to embrace all that is audible, including sounds from nature, industry, urban life, new technological inventions, exotic cultures, and speech as well as noise. This path represented a holistic aspiration, a driving force born from the way artists lived through the urban revolution at the turn of the century, bringing along an acute awareness of sound as such. In a short novel called *Le Roi-Lune*, Apollinaire described the extraordinary events involving his protagonist, who happened to be King Ludwig II of Bavaria. In the following passage, sounds from the outside world are gathered in the king's chamber by means of a sampling technique of some sort:

[The Moon-King] was seated in front of a keyboard, one key of which he was applying with a weary air; and it remained stuck, so that there came from one of the pavilions a murmur both strange and continual. At first I was unable to discern its meaning. The well-developed microphones which the king had at his disposal were regulated in such a manner as to bring into the cellar noises of life on earth from the most far away places...Now it is murmurs from the Japanese countryside...Then, through another depressed key, we are transported in midmorning, the king hails the socialist hard work in New Zealand, I can hear the whistling of geysers...Doum, doum, boum, doum, doum, boum, doum, doum, boum, it is Peking, the gongs and drums of the patrols...The king's fingers run over the keys, haphazardly, raising them up, in some fashion simultaneously, all the murmurs of the world have just been made for us, as we remain stationary, a tour by ear.

(Apollinaire, 1916/1977: 316)[1]

This very phenomenon of capturing and gathering sounds from the globe was called by Apollinaire 'symphonie du monde' (Apollinaire, 1977: 316).

Futurist artists Francesco Balilla Pratella and Luigi Russolo, especially the latter in his 1913 manifesto *L'Art des bruit*, wrote eloquently about using sounds from outside the realm of musical instruments, sounds from the street, the city, and machines. While their aim was to replace conventional musical instruments by sound machines that did not involve sound technology, a holistic approach to sound, which can be traced back to the idea of 'symphonie du monde' in the writings of Apollinaire and of the Russian Futurists, later became the basis for various early electroacoustic experiments, as in Walter Ruttmann's film without pictures (1930) and Pierre Schaeffer's 'Symphony of Noises' (1948). The holistic approach was but one answer to the need to widen the resources for the art of music so that all kinds of sounds around us could become material for it. For example, all that is audible could be gathered and turned into a symphony: this is what motivated Schaeffer to start in 1948 his first experiments leading to the invention of *musique concrète*. In fact, the concept of 'Symphonie de bruits' is the bedrock on which he developed his musical ideas. It is important to note that there is no piece with this title: it is an idea, an intention, an inspiration. By the same token, there is no piece called 'Concert de bruits' – a name given to the 1948 radio program – and no piece called 'Etude de bruits' – a name later used to designate the first five studies as distinct from other experiments. Yet, these terms are important in that they refer to ideas that identify distinct stages in the development of *musique concrète*. This is what Schaeffer wrote in 1948 to the Director of the French national broadcasting company, Radiodiffusion Française:[2]

```
                             - I -
         OBJET DES RECHERCHES ENTREPRISES AU CLUB D'ESSAI
                  en avril, mai, et juin 1948
               en vue d'une production intitulée :

              " SYMPHONIE DE BRUITS "

                        -----------

     Mon premier propos était, en collaboration avec un musicien,
de réaliser une "Symphonie de bruits" c'est-à-dire une composition
où un grand orchestre eût donné la réplique à une suite de bruits
concertants. En réalité, ce propos a été progressivement abandonné
et remplacé par une suite de recherches moins directement efficaces
qui peuvent être classées sous plusieurs rubriques :

         a) production de bruits musicaux ou non,
         b) composition de ces bruits en vue d'oeuvres musicales ou non
```

Similar ideas are expressed in Schaeffer's seminal book, *A la recherche d'une musique concrète*, published in 1952, where he wrote: 'De retour à Paris, j'ai commencé à collectionner les objets. J'ai en vue une "Symphonie de bruits"'[3] (Schaeffer, 1952: 12). This idea resonates with the *Roi-Lune* of Apollinaire, written at the turn of the twentieth century: capturing sounds outside of the panoply of conventional instruments was indeed the first step in enlarging musical resources and inventing new musical sounds.

Capturing sounds, recording sounds

In 1936, having taken refuge in England, Rudolf Arnheim wrote a book about radio as a new medium, simply titled *Radio*. In this influential text, first published in London by Faber and Faber and recently made available in German and French, Arnheim, who is mostly known for his theories on visual art perception, approached the radio from the perspective of the microphone, considered to be an instrument. He emphasised that the act of applying a microphone to a sound source deforms and modifies our perception of the original. In other words, the way the microphone captures sounds is unlike the way the ear does so, and the former, therefore, reveals behaviours, colours and textures that would otherwise remain hidden from the human ear. Most of what Arnheim wrote in 1936 could easily be applied to the phonograph.

The same remark is true about Futurists' ideas on radio. In 1933, two Futurists, Filippo Tommaso Marinetti and Pino Masnata, wrote a manifesto in which they invented a new use for the medium called 'La Radia'. What transpires from their writing is the fact that microphones can reveal new sounds. Other radio experiments of the time, such as the ones by Ezra Pound at the BBC in 1931 (Fisher, 2002), insist on the creative use of the microphone. Mexican–American composer Carlos Chavez, in his 1937 book *Toward a New Music*, in which radio has a central place, mentions how sound technology could serve musically creative aims, while Igor Stravinsky, Carol-Bérard, Theodor Adorno and László Moholy-Nagy, amongst others, saw early on how phonography could become an instrument of musical creation. Schaeffer also wrote extensively on the creative use of the microphone when recording theatre plays with Jacques Copeau (Schaeffer, 1989).

Radio, then, was seen by many artists as a creative tool, particularly because of the possibilities offered by the microphone: while the radio could be described as a trajectory of sound from the moment of capture by microphones to the broadcast through electromagnetic waves, it is the microphone that captured the imagination of artists. Radiophony and phonography – the latter referring to the use of the phonograph as a medium – have precisely one thing in common, and that is the microphone. Many of the ideas that were behind the first experiments on electroacoustic music came from the realisation that capturing sounds with the microphone yielded new perceptions of them and thus should be at the centre of research on sound. While phonography cannot be regarded as the sole technology at play in the birth of electroacoustic music, through its reinvention in the imagination and in the hands of artists it became the device through which aspiration for new sounds could at last be realised. Phonography had profound effects on the evolution of musical creation, but there is still much to explore in order to understand how this came about.

In a recent book titled *Capturing Sound* (2004), musicologist Mark Katz studied the uses of the phonograph in a wide variety of settings and intentions, and introduced a number of categories aimed at defining these different contexts. The properties retained by Katz are: tangibility, portability, invisibility, repeatability, temporality, receptivity, and manipulability. Because I am more focused on the role played by phonography in the creation of music during the twentieth century, I will propose an altogether different typology.

Conservation

Although the two operations accomplished by a phonograph – to record and to restore – can easily be considered as a unified feature, they nevertheless should be distinguished. The principle of conservation is the first criterion to be extracted from the possibilities of the phonograph.

Charles Cros, French poet and the unfortunate inventor of the paleophone (1877), wrote in his poem titled 'Inscription' (1908) that time flees, but thanks to the inscription of sound, it is held back:

> Comme les traits dans les camées
> J'ai voulu que les voix aimées
> Soient un bien, qu'on garde à jamais,
> Et puissent répéter le rêve
> Musical de l'heure trop brève;
> Le temps veut fuir, je le soumets.[4]

Cros identified the essence of sound recording as the capacity to retain and reproduce sounds whose waves are inscribed in a groove. For him, the phonograph, as it was for Thomas Edison and Emile Berliner, was first and foremost a device conceived for reproduction. While this is but one of the possibilities offered by the phonograph, it is one that composers took advantage of in the very process of realising electroacoustic music. The second electronic music synthesiser developed by the Radio Corporation of America in New Jersey over the second half of the 1950s is an example. It had its output signal socket connected to an electric phonograph capable of recording the live performance of the synthesiser driven by the input of the punched paper. More to the point, one consequence of the disc as a storage medium has been the composition of electroacoustic pieces of music tailored to fit the length of a long-playing record. This approach was put to use by such prominent composers as Morton Subotnick or Karlheinz Stockhausen.

Conservation has another function, which has become a familiar one, but when phonography was new it had yet to be discovered: the phonograph can allow the dead to speak to us. Writers, in particular, were the first to put forward the prosopopeia function of the phonograph. In *Ulysses*, James Joyce evoked this idea, suggesting that the dead are still communicating with us:

> Besides how could you remember everybody? Eyes, walk, voice. Well, the voice, yes: gramophone. Have a gramophone in every grave or keep it in the house. After

dinner on a Sunday. Put on poor old greatgrandfather. Kraahraark! Hellohellohello amawfullyglad kraark awfullygladaseeagain hellohello amawf krpthsth. Remind you of the voice like the photograph reminds you of the face.

(Joyce, 1922: II, 6, Hades)

Whether the phonograph repeats or creates words remains to be seen. When Jacques Derrida discussed some sonic aspects relevant to Joyce's texts, he coined a new French verb: 'gramophoner' (Derrida, 1987: 79). For Derrida, the use of the telephone in Joyce's texts, particularly in *Ulysses*, is similar to a distant, invisible voice, which is nevertheless incapable of recreating the past (Derrida, 1987: *passim*; see in particular note 1, p. 79). While the telephone is a way to mediate the vocal expression, the phonograph recreates the voice.

Artificial life

Early on, various kinds of commercial exploitation of the capacity for conservation have led the phonograph to be regarded as a source of artificial life. This aspect belongs to the phenomenon of synthetic creatures born of the imagination of nineteenth- and early twentieth-century writers.

Landmarks of this trend can be found in Jules Vernes' *Le Château des Carpathes* (1892), in which a deceased Italian opera soprano continues to perform in a remote castle. Vernes, curious of all kinds of innovations, combined the technologies of the telephone and the phonograph to conceptualise the recreation of the voice of the singer, Stella: her appearance is rendered by a technology named the telephote, which, while richly described, was never realised and remained imaginary. The telephote was for images what the telephone is for sound (du Moncel, 1882). In the novel, the name of the main character, Télek, reminds us of the new telecommunication technology and, furthermore, how various sound and visual devices can effectively be combined to produce the extraordinary and the unthinkable.

When it came to creating an artificial being, the phonograph was often called upon to produce a realistic rendition of the speaking or singing voice. However, unlike a doll or a machine, an artificial being is capable of expression, and there ought to be some way in which it can create the semblance of life. This led Villiers de l'Isle-Adam in *L'Eve future* (1885–86) to imagine that a very gifted scientist would equip an artificial woman with a device in order to create an appearance of realistic conversation. The scientist, named Thomas Alva Edison in the novel, applied the technology of the phonograph to this effect, and this is how Miss Hadaly was able to speak. Even if the phonograph is, technically speaking, a device that was conceived and built for reproduction, it did not require much effort to turn it into a production machine of some sort.

A few years later, Raymond Roussel went on to imagine that it would be possible, with some considerable technology and careful reflection, to engrave on the surface of a disc a groove that would, in effect, be the synthesis of a long-gone natural model. In his novel *Locus Solus* (1914), a madman, Lucius, succeeds in recreating the voice of a dead person, of his savagely murdered daughter, by using the voice of another woman as a model for the conception of the groove, and, when completed, he could play the voice of his daughter, 'O Rébecca'. Before musicians could even consider it, the question of artificial life provided the context in which the phonograph became an instrument of production.

The capture

On one side of the recording phonograph lies a microphone, capturing the acoustical waves and turning them into an electrical signal appropriate for recording, while the horn or the loudspeaker does the reverse operation. The phonograph is a network of functions, states, processes and operations. Each of these can be studied separately.

Although the microphone, in the words of Boris de Schloezer, 'is nothing more than a copying apparatus, it may nonetheless become an essential instrument of musical innovation, as perhaps tomorrow it will enrich our lives by giving us a new means of expression' (de Schloezer, 1931: 9). Undoubtedly, many would disagree with de Schloezer since the microphone is the actual capturing device, providing the phonograph with a signal to record. As a transduction tool it has its own qualities which can easily be studied in themselves.

Marinetti and Masnata published in 1933 a Futurist manifesto in the *Gazzetta del Popolo*, titled 'La Radia'. Even though the aim of the text at first appears to be a call for the creative use of radiophony, the Radia manifesto is, in reality, an hymn to the yet untapped power of the capture. In many of the 28 clauses, the microphone is seen as a lever that would stir the imagination of the artists, as is clear from these excerpts: the Radia, they wrote, will be the 'reception, amplification and transfiguration of vibrations emitted by matter. Just as today we listen to the song of the forest and the sea, so tomorrow shall we be seduced by the vibrations of a diamond or a flower'; they wrote of 'the characteristic life of every noise and the infinite variety of concrete/abstract and real/dreamt through the agency of a people of noises' and even 'struggles of noises and of various distances, that is, spatial drama joined with temporal drama'. The particular role played by the microphone was to be studied in depth in a seminal text by Arnheim, *Radio*, published in 1936.

Authenticity

For the German critic Hans Heinz Stuckenschmidt, phonography was an essential factor in the mechanisation of music. One of his early observations, seemingly innocuous, was based on an evaluation of the machine-like precision of the recording technology: 'Music stamped directly on the record is produced with ideal precision and without individual interpretation' (Stuckenschmidt, 1927: 10). Stuckenschmidt was also responsible for introducing a term to describe this music 'stamped directly on the record', which was subsequently used to name a new form of music born of the recording technology. This is how he evokes it: 'But the advantages of such authentic records are immediately apparent. The composer can make use of any tone-colour he chooses, even those non-existent in our modern orchestra' (Stuckenschmidt, 1927: 11). The key idea of authenticity is linked to the autographic capability of the phonograph, to use a term and classification introduced by philosopher Nelson Goodman (Goodman, 1968). Creating music for the disc is to depart from the assertion that music is allographic, since it means that the phonographic process is used creatively: it is not the result of the recording of a live, external performance. This new music cannot exist outside of the disc medium, as is implied by the expression 'authentic records'. In the same way that a work of art exists in its concrete substance, the disc is the piece of music: there is no intermediary form of representation, such as a score, for instance.

Stuckenschmidt's ideas found their realisation in a dedicated studio at the Cologne radio, which was conceived in 1951. Indeed, the reference to the theme of authenticity can be noted in the foundation text of the studio, broadcast on radio on 18 October 1951: 'It will be possible to tackle the problem of a "music specific to the radio" and supply the hörspiel[5] with acoustical effects made of previously unheard sounds. Means for the fabrication of such music and authentic sounds are already present in each [radio] studio' (Morawska-Büngeler, 1988: 8).[6]

Materials for composition

Awareness of the holistic capabilities of phonography was also apparent among composers. One of the first to express this view was Carol-Bérard, a French composer much interested in the use of noise, as well as, incidentally, in music from East Asia. In an article titled 'Recorded music – Tomorrow's instrumentation', which appeared in a 1929 issue of *Modern Music*, the composer envisioned a clear and effective use of the record as material for composition. This is quite remarkable at a time when no such experiments, at least in this way, are known to have been conducted, save for a few short-lived ones by Futurist artist Tziga Vertov around 1916 in Russia. For Carol-Bérard, the wealth of sounds and noises offered by nature as well as by industrial machines constitute an environment suitable for musical creation, provided it is possible to gather and use them:

> Why, and I have been asking this for fifteen years, are phonograph records not taken of noises such as those of a city at work, at play, even asleep? Of forests, whose utterance varies according to their trees – a grove of pines in the Mediterranean mistral has a murmur unlike the rustle of poplars in a breeze from the Loire? Of the tumult of the crowds, a factory in action, a moving train, a railway terminal, engines, showers, cries, rumblings?

(Carol-Bérard, 1929: 28)

After having identified the types of sounds to be collected, what remained for Carol-Bérard was to find a way of using them in composing, and he revealed a powerful insight in the following statement, even if one can find some innocence in its expression:

> If noises were registered, they could be grouped, associated and carefully combined as are the timbres of various instruments in the routine orchestra, although with a different technique. We could then create symphonies of noise that would be grateful to the ear. There are plenty of symphonies today which are anything but agreeable, while there are at large and unregistered, a myriad of delightful sounds – the voices of the waves and trees, the moving cry of a sailing vessel's rigging, an airplane gliding down, the nocturnal choruses of frogs around a pool.

> (Carol-Bérard, 1929: 28)

In this passage, the composer mentions two of the main propositions later emphasised by Schaeffer in the process of building a theory of *musique concrète*, i.e. a symphony of noise and a taxonomy of sound objects. In the poetic evocation of various categories of recorded sounds, ranging from the natural to the industrial, Carol-Bérard states clearly the need to work upon them in an orderly fashion. This necessity would become one of the foundations of *musique concrète* and Schaeffer would devote a considerable part of his research to the question of sound taxonomy, with the aim, already underlined by Carol-Bérard, of organising the sounds collected from the outside world by categories of timbre and, in the end, using the musical ear as the ultimate tool for this task. This is the idea Carol-Bérard introduced later in the same 1929 article, in which he hinted at a shift from sound object to musical object. To move from the former to the latter meant that the anecdotal content of natural sounds is replaced by a musically charged sound material, which would later be called *objets musicaux* by Schaeffer:

> Once registered, naturally no significance other than that of sound can attach to individual noises. They will cease to be the creaking of a bus axle, the rumbling of a cauldron, the roaring of a cataract. They will have become merely noise factor, as saxophones, clarinets, violas or oboes are factors of musical sound. A new field will open up for an art not imitative but truly creative, intriguing and difficult. To the sonorous material already at the artist's command a wealth of unforeseen riches will be added.

> (Carol-Bérard, 1929: 29)

Disc as medium

Stuckenschmidt further developed this remark by Carol-Bérard when he evoked the question of inscribing on the medium. This led him to discuss the notation of artificial sounds intended to be used for audio devices, which he described as the family of phonographs:

> The problem now is to find as adequate a system for instruments of the phonograph type. Here the tone is not transformed into graphic signs easily recognisable, but into short, wavy lines so minute as to be extremely difficult to study. This obstacle, however, might be overcome with a microscope; the lines could be divided into definite rubrics and a fixed scheme established embracing all shades of tone-colour, pitch and dynamic intensity. With this new script definitive sounds could be transcribed. Sound waves would be shown in highly magnified form; in order to be transferred to the record they would need to be reduced by a photo-mechanical process.
>
> (Stuckenschmidt, 1927: 11)

The reversal of the function of the phonograph came early on from a visual artist, Moholy-Nagy, who in 1923 published an article in the art review *Der Sturm* developing an entirely new approach to phonography. The text introduced two ideas, which stand out as a breakthrough in the approach to sound technology and creation. The first one, clearly stated, is that the phonograph can play a role that is entirely the opposite of what it had been designed for: rather than capturing live performances and recording existing sounds, the machine is capable of playing back sounds which had no prior existence as they result from the grooves engraved directly unto the surface of the disc. As a visual artist and experimenter, Moholy-Nagy was able to focus on the shape of the groove; it is from this observation that the artist reinvented the phonograph:

> I had suggested to change the gramophone from a reproductive instrument to a productive one, so that on a record without prior acoustic information, the acoustic phenomenon itself originates from engraving the necessary etched grooves.
>
> (Moholy-Nagy, 1923/1989: 54–6)

The second idea derived from the first as a necessary condition: to establish an alphabet of visual signs 'which renders all former instruments unnecessary' (Moholy-Nagy, 1989: 56). Furthermore, the artist looked for a new form of harmony between the shape of the visual signs and the sounds they produce. The signs, which could be termed 'phonograms', could be ordered according to specific proportions in order to create 'a new mechanical harmony'. With these lines, Moholy-Nagy saw the phonograph as a device that would permit sound synthesis to come into existence. When the sound is 'written' directly unto the surface of the disc, the phonograph becomes a musical device, which can do without acoustical sources, and particularly without musical instruments.

Fig. 460. — Le phonographe. Vue extérieure.

The phonograph, Louis Figuier, *Merveilles de la science*, Supplément, vol. II, 1891, p.643

The physicality of the groove was, of course, the object of Moholy-Nagy's observation. Other attempts to create graphical shapes from acoustical waves had been successfully realised, such as the famous resonance shapes by Ernst Chladni published in 1787. While the artist may have been the first to draw such a dramatic conclusion that does away with pre-existing acoustical performance and to choose to sculpt new sounds directly on the disc, the fact that grooves were an exact image of the vibrations had been observed quite early on, with the invention of an apparatus to record acoustical vibration on a prepared surface. The device was called a 'phonautograph' by its inventor, Léon Scott de Martinville, and was presented in 1856. Léon Scott worked as a typographer in Paris and later opened a print shop. It is through the approach of a visual rendering that the device came about. Two years later, Louis Figuier, a remarkable writer on scientific matters, noted that it is possible to identify certain qualities of sound by looking at the shape engraved on the recorded surface. From this observation, Figuier concluded that a new science was now possible, and that it would be based on sound stenography: sound representation, as brought

about by the phonautograph, enabled a type of writing not previously possible, and so the alphabet, with which words and sentences are notated, would be complemented by the visual shapes of a living person. One could then read a play and, by looking at the sound stenography, imagine how a famous actor rendered the text. On many ways, this is different from sound stenography as defined by Sir Isaac Pitman around 1837, for instance, as it aimed at reception and reconstruction of a performance and not merely a simple notation.

Fig. 466. — Le phonautographe.

Louis Figuier, *Merveilles de la science*, Supplement, vol. II, 1891, p.639

Phonography as a medium of exploration

Edgard Varèse may have been the first to call for a meeting with scientists, but he was not the only one. Russian émigré Arthur Lourié talked about the problem in a well-known panel discussion, organised and published in Paris in 1930 by the art review of Georges Ribemont-Dessaignes, *Bifur*, with Edgard Varèse, Alejandro Carpentier, Robert Desnos, Arthur Lourié, and Vincent Huidobro. The editor, Ribemont-Dessaignes, asked the participants about their views on 'the music of the future, or, rather, the future of music' (Varèse, 1930: 121). Interestingly, this article appeared in the summary of the issue under the name of Varèse; and indeed it was Varèse who started the discussion, but Lourié made a strong point of defending the need of new technological tools, which could only be, at that time, the phonograph. After having stated that the conventional orchestra, which is 'archaic, is preventing musical thought from developing', Lourié declared:

> To explore in depth this problem [mechanisation], a sort of Congress should convene in which musicians and physicists would meet and discuss the aspects of creation and production, while eliminating the so-called 'normal' music from the past and the present. In particular, the congress should come up with a programme, which would study 'the elimination of current musical instruments[7] that should be replaced, to great advantage, by new means'.
>
> (Varèse, 1930: 127)[8]

This statement echoed Varèse, who had previously mentioned the need for such collaboration, and again in *Bifur*, he emphasised the need for improved recording equipment:

> One thing I would like to see happen is the establishment of acoustics laboratories where composers and physicists would collaborate. This would be useful even in the domain of recording instruments.
>
> (Varèse, 1930: 127)[9]

Other sound technologies were available at that time, albeit few could actually be used to experiment with new music. Alongside the phonograph were the radio, which Carlos Chavez discussed, and the cinema; in fact, in the same issue of *Bifur*, Benjamin Fondane discussed the new possibilities of sound reproduction in films and evoked the German experimental director, Walter Ruttmann, who invented sound experimentation on sound track with his film without image, *Week-End* (1930).

Chavez shared a similar view on the question of establishing a scientific collaboration process to search for new means of creating music. While his famous essay, published in 1937, addressed the question of adapting new music for the radio, he expressed ideas that promote the same kind of approach with the hope that certain specific musical qualities will evolve:

> The collaboration of engineers and musicians should produce, in a few years, a material appropriate and practical for huge electric musical performances.

> (Chavez, 1937: 178)

Among the musical properties such collaboration would affect were:

> The incredible harmony of timbres, in which the perfect gradation of colouring is obtained; the evaluating of the intensity of the planes which produce an effective perspective of sound; the articulation of the most complex rhythms; the most delicate and varied melodisation – all this will be achieved through the electric media of sound production.

> (Chavez, 1937: 178)

Music without instruments

'Can we compose special music for the phonograph and the radio and thus create a new art?' (de Schloezer, 1931: 9) asked French essayist de Schloezer in 1931, hinting at a music composed without instruments. Schaeffer drew the distance between the electroacoustic process where phonography was a prominent actor, and the world of musical instruments, hence emphasising the unique role played by the capture of concrete sounds. There lies an approach that, as we have seen, was foreseen by many; but no-one had expressed it better than John Cage, or quite as early on. In 1937, Cage wrote:

> Most inventors of electrical musical instruments have attempted to imitate 18th- and 19th-century instruments, just as early automobile designers copied the carriage...Given four phonographs, we can compose and perform a quartet for explosive motors, wind, heartbeat, and landslide.

> (Cage, 1937: 3)

Indeed, the inventor of *musique concrète*, Schaeffer, wrote the following in giving an account of his early experiments: 'There is no instrument to play *musique concrète*'[10] (Schaeffer, 1952: 26). Being in the early stages of his experiments, he realised that this posed a problem, and added: 'That is the main difficulty.'[11] While dealing with machines to create music at first appeared to be a problem for him, Schaeffer soon realised that there was a considerable number of procedures that could be applied to affect the way a disc was played by a phonograph: changing the speed, creating a closed loop, playing backwards, taking a fragment of sound off a larger section, mixing and blending. In other words, *musique concrète* was invented in 1948 because the phonograph offered quite a few modes of sound transformation. In addition, the technology available at a radio studio of the time, with its amplifiers, filters and rudimentary mixing consoles, created further possibilities; but the disc was the main agent from which Schaeffer developed a whole theory, which he pursued even when phonographs were replaced by tape recorders in the early 1950s. In many ways, composing *musique concrète* was equivalent to putting a performer in the position of a composer, in charge of the form and the sequence of events, as well as a conductor who controls the overall shape of the music. Later, Schaeffer came to express the process of creating music without instrument by introducing the idea of a virtual instrument: 'In a given work where the author, concrete or electronic, is incapable of saying by what causal process a certain series of sounds has been produced, it will seem as if these sounds originated from a specific instrument. What can be the timbre of an instrument that does not exist?' (Schaeffer, 1966: 68)[12]

The disc as work of art

Taxonomy of the phonograph in the realm of artistic creation would not be complete without a mention of a new form of art practice, born from the disc as an object. Visual artists, sound artists, sound poets, and installation artists were some of the practitioners who used the disc as an art object.

Although the phenomenon of the 'record as artwork', as Germano Celant put it, has not yet been thoroughly studied, the field has led to interesting distortions of phonography. In a catalogue published in 1977, Celant reviewed a wide diversity of approaches. Discs by artists pose a new kind of problem. There are, at least, two classes of objects realised by artists whose practice takes place usually outside of music or even audio art. These are, most frequently, painters, sculptors, conceptual artists, filmmakers or video artists. Their production can be divided in two categories: sound art and discs as plastic objects. In the first instance, the artist creates a sound-based piece or set of pieces, as with Michael Snow's *The Last LP* (1987); in the second, there might be silent discs, or discs turned into visual objects, such as with Marcel Duchamp's *Rotoreliefs* (1935), which are silent discs based on the technology of the phonograph but are conceived (and, in this case, patented) to be looked at rather than to be heard. The moving images appeared in time on a silent phonograph.

Conclusion

In this historical evocation of musical creation through sound technology, the phonograph can be seen as a complex model that serves many different purposes. The term phonograph is suited to encapsulate all these aspects. As such, the phonograph has been a major tool for both conceptual and material approaches to musical thought and enabled a wide variety of new perspectives on sound to come about during the twentieth century. If the notion of sound has become a fulcrum in that century, it is largely due to the possibilities offered by the phonograph.

Notes

1   Translation from the French original by the author.
2   Unpublished document (1948) kindly provided by François Bayle: 'Aim of research carried out at the Club d'Essai in April, May, June 1948 for a work entitled "Symphonie de bruits" [Symphony of Noises]. My original idea was to compose a "Symphonie de bruits" in collaboration with a musician, i.e. a work in which a large orchestra would be in dialogue with a sequence of noises in concert. In fact, this idea has been gradually abandoned, and replaced by a series of less immediately effective research projects, which can be classified under several headings: a) a production of musical or non-musical noises; b) composition or not of these noises for musical works'. English translation of all passages quoted from Schaeffer in the text are by Christine North.
3   'Back in Paris, I have started to collect objects. I have a "Symphony of Noises" in mind'.
4   Fifth stanza of the poem titled 'Inscription':
      As in cameo the faces,
      I wished to make beloved voices
      Treasures kept for ever more,
      That can recapture music's dream
      Child of all too fleeting time,
      Time flies, I am its conqueror.
      (Translation from the original French by Christine North)
5   The German word *Hörspiel* can be rendered by 'Radio play'. Note that it is usually kept in its original form.
6   Translation from the German original by the author. *Nachtprogramm*, NWDR, Cologne, 18 October 1951. The tape of this broadcast is available from the WDR Archives in Cologne. It is on this radio program that Eimert et al. played some electronic experiments, prepared in Bonn by Meyer-Eppler.
7   'timbres instrumentaux "vivants"'.
8   Translation from the French original by the author.
9   Translation from the French original by the author.
10   'Il n'y a pas d'instrument à jouer de la musique concrète'.
11   'Telle est la difficulté majeure.'
12   'Dans telle oeuvre, dont l'auteur, concret ou électronique, est bien incapable de dire par quel processus causal a été réalisée une certaine succession de sons, tout se passé comme si ces sons provenaient d'un instrûment déterminé'.

References

Apollinaire, G. (1977) 'Le Roi-Lune', in M. Décaudin (ed.) *Œuvres en prose complètes vol. I.* Paris: Gallimard, pp.303–19. Originally (1916) in *Le Poète assassiné.* Paris: Bibliothèque des Curieux.

Arnheim, R. (1936) *Radio.* London: Faber and Faber.

Cage, J. (1973) 'The Future of Music: Credo', in *Silence,* pp.3–6. Middletown: Wesleyan University Press. Originally (1937) delivered as a lecture in Seattle.

Carol-Bérard (1929) 'Recorded Noises – Tomorrow's Instrumentation', *Modern Music* 6 (2): 26–9.

Celant, G. (1977) *The Record as Artwork from Futurism to Conceptual Art: The Collection of Germano Celant.* Fort Worth: The Fort Worth Art Museum.

Chavez, C. (1937) *Toward a New Music: Music and Electricity.* New York: W.W. Norton.

Chladni, E. (1787) *Entdeckungen über die Theorie des Klanges.* Leipzig: Weidmanns Erben. French translation (1809) as *Traité d'acoustique.* Paris: Courcier.

de Schloezer, B. (1931) 'Man, Music and the Machine', *Modern Music* 8 (3): 3–9.

Derrida, J. (1987) *Ulysse gramophone. Deux mots pour Joyce.* Paris: Galilée.

du Moncel, Th. (1882) 'Le téléphote', in *Le microphone, le radiophone et le phonographe,* pp.289–319. Paris: Librairie Hachette.

Fisher, M. (2002) *Ezra Pound's Radio Operas: The BBC Experiments, 1931–1933.* Cambridge, Mass.: MIT Press.

Goodman, N. (1968) *Languages of Art: An Approach to a Theory of Symbols.* Indianapolis: Bobbs-Merrill.

Joyce, J. (1922) *Ulysses.* Paris: Shakespeare and Co.

Katz, M. (2004) *Capturing Sound: How Technology Has Changed Music.* Berkeley: University of California Press.

Marinetti, F.T. and Masnata, P. (1933) 'La Radia', *Gazzetta del Popolo,* Oct.

Moholy-Nagy, L. (1923) 'Neue Gestaltung in der Musik. Möglichkeiten des Grammophons', *Der Sturm* 7. Reprint (1989) in U. Block and M. Glasmeier (eds) *Broken Music,* pp.54–6. Berlin: Daadgalerie, Berliner Künstlerprogramm des DAAD and gelbe Musik.

Morawska-Büngeler, M. (1988) *Schwingende Elektronen. Eine Dokumentation über das Studio für Elektronische Musik des Westdeutschen Rundfunks in Köln 1951–1986.* Köln-Rodenkirchen: Tonger.

Roussel, R. (1914) *Locus Solus.* Paris, Librairie Alphonse Lemerre.

Schaeffer, P. (1952) *A la recherche d'une musique concrète.* Paris: Seuil.

———— (1966) *Traité des objets musicaux.* Paris: Seuil.

———— (1990) *Propos sur la Coquille.* Arles: Phonurgia Nova.

———— (1989) *Dix ans d'essais radiophoniques: du Studio au Club d'Essai, 1942–1952.* Arles: Phonurgia Nova. With 4 CDs.

Stuckenschmidt, H.H. (1927) 'Machines – a Vision of the Future', *Modern Music* 4 (3): 8–14.

Varèse, E. et al. (1930) 'La mécanisation de la musique', *Bifur* 5: 121–9.

Vernes, J.G. (1892) 'Le Château de Carpathes', *Magasin* 55 (649) and 56 (672).

Villiers de l'Isle-Adam (1886) 'L'Eve future', *La vie moderne* 18 July 1885 – 27 March 1886.

II
Genre-specific Studies

MICHAEL FRITH

'Donner l'Illusion de la Chose Ecrite'[1]: Reflections on Recordings of Organ Improvisations

Introduction

'To give the illusion of a written work' was, according to Charles Tournemire (Tournemire, 1931: 49), the intention of César Franck when improvising at the organ, as it was for Tournemire himself and for many since.[2] Indeed, the relationship between improvised music and fully notated 'works' is somewhat ambiguous and has always been contested, but the advent of recording introduced new complications and issues of identity, which this chapter will explore. Recording may come to be seen as the most important and revolutionary development in the history of music since the refinement of those forms of notation which facilitated repeat performances. Such notations allowed the musical event to be subsequently replicated in more or less its original form – or at least with an identical 'sound structure' (see Davies, 2001: 47–98) – by people who had not heard the original; it led to the concept of 'musical composition' as we know it and facilitated the development of complex techniques – of polyphony, of extended structures, of the use of large performing forces. By the mid-eighteenth century, it had led to the solidification of the 'work' concept, which, as Lydia Goehr and others have pointed out, exercised a regulative role in musical production in the nineteenth and twentieth centuries, though it was present to varying degrees long before (Davies, 2001; Goehr, 1992; Samson, 2000, 2002, 2003; Talbot, 2000). The whole European 'classical' tradition in music is founded upon a pantheon of great composers and canonic works; all details sufficient to the identity of each work are encoded in a score (though music composed before the *Werktreue* era may require considerable input from the performer), which makes it available for a theoretically infinite number of interpretations in performance. The question of whether or not a score is essential to the identity of a 'work' is a matter of some debate among philosophers (Ingarden, 1966/1986: 38–40).

The complexities of the work–performer relationship and of work-character in the Western classical tradition seem far removed from spontaneous music making, 'music making *simpliciter*' as Stephen Davies calls it (Davies, 2001:11), however necessary and successful the illusion of spontaneity may be for a 'good' performance of a 'work'. In any case, the score remains fixed and cannot encode all the subtle details that make one performance different from another and allow the performer the illusion of freedom (see Goehr, 1998: 148). For many centuries the relationship between improvised and notated music was fruitful and symbiotic. If improvisation has become a less prominent component of classical music in the last two centuries, it is not simply that we have become too dependent on notated scores (though, undeniably, we have) but that, as performers and listeners – and probably composers, too – we place excessive emphasis on our canon of received 'classics', a trend to which our use of recordings as a staple form of musical experience has further contributed. While it is the unique performance that any particular recording encodes (even if many modern recorded performances are synthetic products of a number of separate takes and patches), allowing the experience of that single performance to be infinitely repeated, within the 'classical' sphere, recording has contributed to the ontological separation of works and performances: the 'work' is potentially available in multiple performances and exists independently of any instantiation of it, for it is essentially 'supratemporal', albeit characterised by 'an internal, immanent, quasi-temporal structure', whereas a performance takes place 'in the real world here and now' (Ingarden, 1986: 67). Even though recordings have undeniably made a wider repertoire available than ever before and stimulated intense connoisseurship among ordinary listeners into the niceties of different interpretations, they are largely conceived, produced and marketed as recordings of performances of *works*.

However, not all live performances in the Western classical tradition have been, or are, of works. There is a widely held assumption that within this tradition the practice of public improvisation died out during the nineteenth century, apart from a limited and short-lived revival in the aleatory techniques of the *avant garde* of the 1950s and '60s. This certainly seems to be the assumption made by Davies in an otherwise comprehensive exploration of the field (Davies, 2001: 11–19). Organists, however, have continued to this day to practise and develop the art in the concert hall, in competitions and examinations, and within the church's ceremonial. Many of the most celebrated organ virtuosi have been, and are, not only interpreters but also improvisers and composers; much composition for the organ has grown out of traditions of improvisation and bears traces of improvisatory practice.

Historical background: before recording

Since 1930 various organists have recorded improvisations. In this chapter, I discuss some 'classic' recorded improvisations, in particular those by Tournemire, which were subsequently transcribed by Maurice Duruflé (1958). My concentration on the modern French school should not be taken to imply that there are no worthwhile schools of organ playing and improvisation elsewhere; but recordings of French organ music and organists are particularly widely known and available, as are, to only a slightly lesser extent, recordings of their improvisations. First, however, a brief discussion of improvisation before the age of recording is appropriate, not only to explain how the art survived into and continued to flourish during the twentieth century, but in order to provide a basis for the discussion of philosophical issues in connection with recordings of improvisations, in particular those that are relevant to current speculations concerning the ontology of works and performances, and their relationships to notation and sound recording.

While increasing dependence on notation and notated works may have been partly responsible in accelerating the general decline of improvisation within the classical tradition, the study of compositional techniques on paper has been a fertile stimulus and discipline for improvisation just as much as for written composition. It was largely as a result of the compositional complexities facilitated by notation that it became possible for performers to improvise sophisticated counterpoint and formal structures. And, equally, serendipitous discoveries in the course of improvisation have inspired and enriched written works. Much of the organ's inherited repertoire has resulted from improvisations – either as an initial stimulus in the conception and inspiration of the work, or as the remembered basis for the work itself, newly rethought and tightened up in the compositional process.

During the seventeenth and eighteenth centuries many publications of organ music were intended, ostensibly, as models of good improvisatory practice, and often produced as guides for students, or as substitutes for improvisation for the organist of 'une science médiocre' as he is described in the preface to the second *Livre d'Orgue* of Antoine-Nicolas Lebègue (c.1631–1702) (Higginbottom, 2001). Indeed, many such 'Organ Books' produced in France during this period contained short versets of stereotyped character and longer interludes such as *Offertoires*, as were demanded in the church's ceremonial. The same function may be assumed for the numerous sets of variations on popular *Noëls*, similar to those improvised in the more prestigious churches before Christmas Midnight Mass. A latter-day recorded example of such an improvisation may be heard on *L'Art de l'Improvisation* by Pierre Cochereau (1977, Face 2).

It is likely that Johann Sebastian Bach originally had similar intentions for a compilation such as the unfinished *Orgelbüchlein*. The didactic intentions given on the title page[3] may not have been limited to performing techniques and written composition, for as Peter Williams has suggested:

> [a]s long as improvisation was pursued as a serious musical aim (i.e. until the twentieth century) it was generally assumed that the highest form of extemporising was that which was also most intricate on paper, e.g. fugue. Tightly organised motivic harmonisations of the kind found in the *Orgelbüchlein* must represent another extempore ideal.

> (Williams, 1980: II, 3n)

Bach's facility in improvisation is legendary and well documented. His obituary (C.P.E. Bach and Agricola 1750–4; in David and Mendel, 1998: 297–307) recounts the famous visit to Johann Adam Reinken for whom he performed a half-hour improvisation on the chorale *An Wasserflüssen Babylon* to the old man's surprise and delight; it also mentions Bach's ability to understand instantaneously the possibilities of any theme he was given.

Drawing on both Johann Nikolaus Forkel's biography (in David and Mendel, 1998: 417–82) and the obituary, Albert Schweitzer summarises:

> If he improvised for as long as two hours together, the theme remained the same from the beginning to the end. First he made a prelude and fugue out of it on the full organ. Then he showed his skill in registration in a trio or a four-part movement; then, as a rule, came a chorale-prelude. Finally, he developed a new fugue upon the old theme. So at least we are told by Forkel, who also says that, according to Emmanuel, the organ compositions that we have give no adequate idea of the magnificence of Bach's improvisations on the organ.
>
> (Schweitzer, 1908/1911: I, 209–10)

Compositional techniques learnt and mastered on paper provided a foundation for the highest forms of improvisation, enabling the organist spontaneously to invent intricate motivic counterpoint. Conversely, the notated work could embody an idealised realisation of a conception executed only imperfectly in the prior act of improvisation. The case of the *Musical Offering* is, in all probability, not an isolated instance of Bach's 'improving' a previously improvised piece when writing it down. Nevertheless, Forkel's view of the magnificence of Bach's improvisations as opposed to the composed works may be taken at face value; an improvisation, simply by virtue of being an improvisation and known to be such by the listener, can often engender a greater degree of excitement and make a vivid impression of a different type from that of a composed work. Those works which embody 'improved improvisations' are, in the absence of recordings, the nearest we can get to an appreciation of the improvisational skills of organists of the pre-recording era. Organ music surviving from the Baroque era must surely be 'only the notational tip of an enormous improvisational iceberg' (Butt, 2002: 113).

Just over a century after Forkel's reminiscences, Vincent d'Indy recalled Franck's organ improvisations in similar terms:

> Here [Sainte-Clotilde], in the dusk of this organ loft, of which I can never think without emotion, he spent the best part of his life. Here he came every Sunday and feast-day – and towards the end of his life every Friday morning too – fanning the fire of his genius by pouring out his spirit in wonderful improvisations which were often far more lofty in thought than many skilfully elaborated compositions... [f]or César Franck has, or rather *was* the genius of improvisation, and no other modern organist, not excepting the most renowned executants, would bear the most distant comparison with him in this respect.
>
> (d'Indy 1906/1909: 42–3)

Franck was one of the founding fathers of the modern French organ school, and his importance for the present study lies in his influence on the next generation of organists, which included those who were the first to make recordings of improvisations. From 1872 until his death in 1890 Franck was Organ Professor at the Paris Conservatoire. Only a small proportion of his curriculum was devoted to repertoire or technique; at least five of the six hours every week were regularly given to improvisation, and his class became, in effect, an alternative composition course for students of a progressive turn of mind.[4] Improvisation continued to be a major part of the liturgical organist's skills, for almost all of the next generation of French organ virtuosi were church musicians as well as composers. They featured prominently as improvisers and as performers of their own compositions in secular performances involving demonstrations of new instruments, and in the recitals that proliferated in France after 1878.[5]

Improvisation in the age of recording

The twentieth century produced a great flowering of the art of improvisation, particularly in France. The pupils of Franck, Charles Marie Widor and Alexandre Guilmant – among them Tournemire and Louis Vierne and the rather younger Marcel Dupré – all came to hold posts in the major organ lofts of Paris and most pursued international careers as virtuoso performers and composers for the organ. Their works nearly all bear traces of improvisatory practice, and some notable contributions to the organ repertoire originated, as in earlier times, in improvisations. Dupré's first major concert improvisation in the United States in 1921, for example, resulted three years later in his *Symphonie-Passion*. He recalls that at the end of his recital on the famous organ in the Wannamaker store in Philadelphia, he was given four liturgical themes:

> I decided, in a flash, to improvise an organ symphony in four movements which depicted the life of Jesus: 'The World Awaiting the Saviour', 'Nativity', 'Crucifixion', and 'Resurrection'...As Dr. Russell announced my scheme to the audience, everyone in the Grand Court stood up. Encouraged by this enthusiasm, I improvised, feeling as I never felt before.

> (Dupré 1972/1975: 80–2)

The relationship of the published work to the original improvisation may be slight; judging from his recordings, Dupré's improvisations tended to be more conservative in idiom than his written compositions. The same may be true of *Le Chemin de la Croix*, which was originally improvised as a series of reflections between a reading of poems by Paul Claudel in February 1931 (Dupré, 1975: 97).

A generation later, Olivier Messiaen wrote his *Messe de la Pentecôte* (1950) as a summation of his improvisatory practice to that date (Samuel, 1967: 17), and his monumental *Méditations sur le Mystère de la Sainte-Trinité* (1970/2) resulted directly from the experience of a series of improvisations between sermons on the doctrine of the Holy Trinity, given at the centenary of the Trinité church in Paris where he had been organist since 1931. At least one feature – the concluding of several movements with the song of the yellowhammer – was carried over from the original improvisations (Hill and Simeone, 2005: 275–6); there are also significant thematic links with some of his recorded improvisations, which are discussed below.

Vierne and Tournemire were the first to make recordings of improvisations (1929 and 1930 respectively) followed by others including Dupré, Jean Langlais, Cochereau, Jean Guillou and, in some recently discovered material, Messiaen – the most celebrated figure to have emerged from the modern French organ school.

Broadly, three types of recordings are represented: those recorded in 'studio' sessions (even though these are almost inevitably 'on location' in church or concert hall); improvisations in concerts; and those recorded during church services. The second and third categories obviously involve 'live' performances in the presence of an audience. Improvisations in concerts and competitions usually entail the ritual presentation (often in a sealed envelope) of previously unseen and often specially composed themes; those recorded under 'studio' conditions require the trust of the listener in accepting that they are truly improvisations. There is naturally some overlap between these categories: Cochereau, for example, included a demonstration of the liturgical organist's art in a *Messe Dominicale* in his *L'Art de L'Improvisation* (1977, Face 4), and three of Tournemire's recordings discussed below are based on liturgical plainsong melodies. Some of these recordings have been transcribed by enterprising pupils and admirers, and subsequently published. Among recent examples are transcriptions by David Briggs – a former student of Langlais, and one of the finest improvisers of his generation – of several improvisations by Cochereau (1992), including the famous variations on 'Alouette, Gentille Alouette' (originally recorded on Phillips 6521 008 and published by United Music Publishers).

Tournemire's recorded improvisations

The most famous of all recordings of improvisations were those made in 1930 and 1931 by Tournemire on the Cavaillé-Coll organ in Sainte-Clotilde, Paris, where he had been *Organiste Titulaire* since 1898, a post previously held by his erstwhile teacher, Franck.[6] He was not the first to make such recordings: his colleague at Notre-Dame, Vierne, had recorded three improvisations in October 1929 and January 1930. Tournemire's recordings, however, soon became the better known. The period of their recording coincided with his engagement in his greatest compositional enterprise – *L'Orgue Mystique*, a cycle of 51 liturgical suites for the Sunday and festival Masses of the church's year, each consisting of *Entrée, Offertoire, Elevation, Communion* and *Sortie*; these could be played instead of improvisations at the appropriate points if desired, for they were almost entirely based on the plainsong chants and hymns proper to each occasion. The numbers given in parentheses below correspond to the order in which they appear in Duruflé's published versions of his transcriptions (1958):

1. *Cantilène*: recorded 30 April 1930; issued September 1930 (vol.1, No.2).
2. *Choral-Improvisation sur le 'Victimae Paschali'*: recorded 30 April 1930; issued October 1930 (vol.2, No.5).
3. *Fantasie sur l''Ave Maris Stella'*: recorded 30 April 1930; issued October 1930 (vol.2, No.4).
4. *Petite Rhapsodie Improvisée*: recorded 1931; issued November 1931 (vol.1, No.1).
5. *Improvisation sur le 'Te Deum'*: recorded 1931; issued March 1932 (vol.1, No.3).

Three of the improvisations (2, 3 and 5) are based on well-known plainsong tunes that have formed the basis for countless written works over the centuries (not only for organ); they are also among the most frequently used themes for improvisations by liturgical organists. Tournemire was, therefore, calling upon a familiar tradition and a vast reservoir of personal experience. We do not demand that what we hear in any improvised performance is unprepared or completely *ab ovo*; there are numerous structural strategies as well as harmonic and textural possibilities that the player has used before. Throughout *L'Orgue Mystique* the plainsong themes used in the improvisations occur in several suites, and there is much use of similar rhetorical and formal devices. Comparisons between the recorded improvisations, which are now available on CD, and the notated works are often instructive.

Tournemire's own advice to Langlais on how to improvise in concert sounds, perhaps, a little tongue-in-cheek:

First, you create an atmosphere...Then you introduce a theme. This is followed by a massive crescendo, reaching a climax on a large, dissonant chord, followed by a long silence, followed by a second dissonant chord (all to frighten the audience!). Then one concludes quietly on the Voix Célestes.

(quoted in Frazier, 2002: 9)

In practice he was nothing like as formulaic as this, though there are residual traces of such thinking. Whilst each of the three improvisations based on plainsong begins not with an atmospheric introduction but with part of the theme, there are several 'massive crescendos', and the two dissonant chords (of an intervallic structure beloved of the composer which is to be found in similar contexts in several of the suites of *L'Orgue Mystique*) feature prominently in the *Choral-Improvisation sur le 'Victimae Paschali'* (p.27), with cadenza-like flourishes emanating from them and dissolving into dramatic silences. *Fantasie sur l''Ave Maris Stella'* is the only one of the three to end quietly – a well-known feature of Tournemire's postludes, whether written or improvised. *Fantasie sur l''Ave Maris Stella'* is perhaps the most successful in approximating the character of 'the written thing', but it is by no means the most frequently performed. It has a high degree of internal coherence and formal unity, though it necessarily suffers when compared to those pieces from *L'Orgue Mystique* that use the same theme, such as the final pieces from suite No.2 (*Immaculata Conceptio B. Maria Virginis*) and suite No.35 (*In Assumptione B.V.M.*), the latter being the celebrated *Paraphrase-Carillon*. As an improvisation it has a remarkable coherence and continuity, helped by the distinctive contours of the theme and its pervasively Dorian-mode flavour.

The *Choral-Improvisation sur le 'Victimae Paschali'* is deservedly the best known of the set, though it is less consistent and coherent than the *Fantasie sur l''Ave Maris Stella'*; perhaps it relies a little too heavily on virtuoso rhetoric and conventional 'topics' and gestures[7] but it is certainly more exciting to listen to and play. It will serve well as an example for more detailed consideration, containing as it does many features common in improvisations and illustrating the inherent problems arising from their recording. As with the *Fantasie sur l''Ave Maris Stella'*, its overall duration is a little over eight minutes, and this, in the original nocturnal recording session, necessitated a break about halfway through while the recording engineers prepared a second wax master-disc. Tournemire, therefore, had to freeze the music in his head for about 20 minutes until they were ready. This might have created problems, but in fact there were benefits. In the former piece, the pause comes at a natural point in the structure; in the latter, shortly before the break a new development starts – in a march-like rhythm over an ostinato in E minor (page 27, *piu animato*) – which promises more than it delivers, for it has to be terminated prematurely; but it does so with a magical, Phrygian-flavoured cadence. The break serves more than its utilitarian purpose, for after a pause for thought Tournemire resumes with a new chorale-like version of the theme (*Voix Humaine, Trémolo*), which forms the tranquil heart of the piece – twelve bars of inspired mystical meditation.

The piece begins and ends virtuosically. At the beginning, the first strain of the theme is presented as a fanfare in free rhythm. Tournemire, as a true disciple of Franck, played with very broad style, very freely and with much *rubato*: 'Let us throw the metronome away' was his advice[8] (Tournemire, 1931: 33; see also Jaquet, 1978: 6). Duruflé's score shows a *ritenuto* halfway through the first bar, *largo* at the beginning of the second, and *rallentando* in the third and fourth. However, there are further refinements in the detail, such as the triplet dotted quaver-semiquaver-quaver of the anacrusis and the crotchet-within-a-triplet chord on the fourth beat of bar two. Is this precision a further result of the player's freedom? Has Duruflé, the transcriber, been over-literal and, in attempting to preserve the original freedom, created excessive precision? How exactly should the player of the notated work attempt to replicate these passages? Should she accept their precision literally, or treat them freely? We will return to this issue.

The matter is further complicated by the fact that the transcriber has 'cleaned up', or at least regularised, some moments in the piece where the player's freedom became virtually un-notatable. On page 30, for example, the first four bars of *animato* contain rhythmic irregularity amounting to about an extra half beat, which sounds suspiciously like unintended instability; Duruflé seems to have thought so, because in the score it is ironed out into regular bars of 4/4. It is not unknown, even among the most accomplished improvisers, for rhythmic consistency to suffer slightly when the excitement takes over; it is of little consequence in live performance and hardly noticed. In return, the flow of adrenalin brings compensations. Tournemire himself wrote of how the subconscious assists in improvised contrapuntal invention – the visitation of the 'angel of inspiration' (Tournemire, 1931: 50) – though counterpoint is not a prominent feature of these recordings. As Joël-Marie Fauquet has pointed out, he was equally aware of the effect of inspiration in making possible technical feats that would otherwise have required much practice (Fauquet, 1981: 19). The two bars of pedal solo that precede the triumphant return of the theme (*presto* at the foot of page 30) are surely such a case. Extreme agility of the ankles is demanded, and the passage is often awkward even for those with the finest pedal technique; few players can match the sheer élan and apparently nonchalant brilliance of the original.

The piece ends with a full organ presentation of the plainsong theme harmonised in 'chorale' style (*Grand Choeur*, in French terms), its four phrases punctuated by cadenza-like flourishes. The harmonic colouring of G minor seasoned with E minor, which has been a characteristic of the piece, including its overall key-structure, is present to the end. This is a far more inventive and convincing example of the grand, rhetorical style of French organ music than the *Improvisation sur le 'Te Deum'*, the last of the five improvisations, in which there seems to be somewhat excessive reliance on conventional, stereotyped gestures. But this is the reaction of a listener and performer long acquainted with it; as a live improvisation it would, in all probability, not have elicited any adverse comment. It affords a useful illustration of the potential dangers of recording improvisations. By their nature, improvisations are ephemeral and do not necessarily lend themselves to the detailed scrutiny given to 'works', which are composed at leisure and intended for repeated listening; but the excitement they can sometimes generate explains why C.P.E. Bach found his father's improvisations more magnificent in effect than his written works.

Are recorded improvisations works?

Ways in which the performance-as-work culture of early nineteenth-century piano music gradually evolved into a work-dominated ethos have been traced and exhaustively discussed by Jim Samson in various studies (Samson, 2000, 2002, 2003). With that change in emphasis, there was also a decline in the importance of improvisation and in the value placed on the improvisatory techniques that nourished the compositions of the virtuosi. By the end of the century, almost all virtuoso pianists, many of whom were significant composers, performed 'works', including their own, in their recitals, but rarely improvisations. In organ recitals, however, which became increasingly common in the early twentieth century, improvisation retained its importance, particularly in those given by French organists (Beechey, 1970). Many concert improvisations were given generic titles (*Symphonie, Prélude et Fugue*, etc.), which barely distinguished them from the works on the programme; indeed, they often succeeded in sounding like written music. To be sure, audiences were always informed of their status as improvisations; enjoyment and admiration were enhanced by the knowledge that what sounded so well thought-out and accomplished was truly the product of the moment and would never be heard again in that form. The recording of an improvisation automatically confers on it a different nature; because it is available for repeated listening and study, it aspires to 'work-status'. Transcription exacerbates the confusion: the 'written thing' is no longer an illusion.

Tournemire clearly appreciated this distinction. On several occasions the late Felix Aprahamian urged him to have his recorded improvisations transcribed and published, but he always objected that 'they were intended as improvisations, not as pieces to be learned and performed by other organists' (in Frazier, 2002: 37). After their posthumous publication, Aprahamian wrote that they were 'now available to players, and have been made available contrary to the composer's expectations and probably contrary to his wishes as well' (in Frazier, 2002: 37).

Thus, in the apparently innocent processes of recording and transcription a profound ontological change has taken place. We may well observe that merely to record an improvisation is quite innocuous; after all, jazz musicians have been doing exactly that for almost a century, and not only is it accepted practice, it is also the chief means of disseminating their products – their 'works'; the historical canons of jazz consist entirely of such recordings. Unlike the classical tradition, however, jazz has no 'imaginary museum of musical works' in score form, nor does a *Werketreue* concept regulate practice (Goehr, 1992). The classical composer has the opportunity to reflect at leisure, to eliminate the unnecessary and inferior, and to refine and improve the best in his work in order to make it fit for repeated listening and contemplation. The discrepancy is all the clearer when the written-down improvisation is published and others reinterpret it. Tournemire's improvisations are inferior *as works* to the best of his written compositions, and his reputation as a composer is not well served by too frequent performances of the transcriptions as works. There is much fine music in his *L'Orgue Mystique* (as well as his many other works, including his orchestral and chamber music), which deserves to be better known; many of the organ works bear traces of improvisatory practice, often quasi-improvisatory in style, but which have been thought out and composed at leisure. Tournemire's mature musical language was largely inherited from that of Claude Debussy, which was itself improvisatory in character, always carefully concealing a fundamentally formalistic approach. As Pierre Boulez has written of Debussy's *Ibéria* (Boulez, 1981/1986: 319): 'everything suggests a superior, polished kind of improvisation', no doubt referring to a letter from Debussy himself to André Caplet on the subject of the transition between the second and third movements: 'Ce n'a pas l'air d'être écrit'[9] (in Simeone, 2003: 113). Thus, written composition draws close in its effect to improvisation, and improvisation gives the illusion of being written; but each remains conceptually different and separate.

Davies (*pace* Ingarden, 1986) asserts confidently that '[i]mprovisations are not musical works' (Davies, 2001: 15). He discusses the ontological status of an improvisation written down at leisure by its own performer–composer, and also C.P.E. Bach's transcription of one of his father's improvisations, which became thereby a 'description of a work' rather than a prescription 'addressed by the composer to potential performers' (for Davies, it is little more than a possibility that a recorded improvisation might later be transcribed by another person and published as a 'prescription').[10] Once an improvisation is recorded it becomes trapped within its own unique interpretation. Problems begin to arise when transcription further reifies the work/performance by encoding any features of the interpretation that could be considered not to be part of the essential sound-structure: written-out *rubato* comes into this category. We might assume that any other performer of the notated 'work' would feel duty-bound to perform these original interpretational characteristics, even if, having asked herself the question 'Would the composer have notated these passages more straightforwardly if he had been writing a "work"?', her answer is affirmative. Further, is it open to additional 'interpretation', in a way similar to that in which we may take note of a composer's own recording of one of his conventionally composed works – of its boundaries and acceptable limits of freedom – without feeling obliged slavishly to replicate it? Possibly; but the issue is not altogether straightforward, for the composer has created and notated a 'sound-structure' that is by its nature and intention open to multiple interpretations, in a way that the improviser has not. If Tournemire had transcribed the improvisations himself, how would he have notated some of these details and how might he have performed them subsequently? Or if he had had the opportunity to play the pieces again from Duruflé's transcriptions, would he have been bound by these interpretative details embedded in the sound-structure? Probably not, for, as the composer, he might well have felt at liberty to make changes in pitch and rhythm, the core of the 'sound-structure' itself (which is no more than what many nineteenth-century pianists did with previously published versions of their compositions). Few organists, who have themselves re-recorded these pieces, have entirely succeeded in recapturing the excitement and spontaneity of the originals, and there is often something slightly studied, if not stilted, in their approaches to the notated *rubato*. Certainly, the notorious pedal solo in the *Choral-Improvisation sur le 'Victimae Paschali'* is often played with more caution than in Tournemire's flamboyant original.

But not always. If a performer approaches the score of the transcribed improvisations like any other work to be newly thought out and interpreted afresh, entertaining in the process the possibility that Tournemire might not necessarily have been the ideal performer of his own music (as is not altogether uncommon among composers), might he actually succeed in making the 'work' as he performs it an 'improvement' on the 'work' as we know it from Tournemire's recording? The *Choral-Improvisation sur le 'Victimae Paschali'* might possibly benefit from a more spacious approach to certain passages, while at the same time reducing the length of some of the pauses. This might reveal the 'work' to have a more compelling dramatic structure than might have been previously thought. This is conceivably the ultimate stage, the final consequence, of recording an improvisation: the 'illusion of the written thing' has been surpassed; the *actual* written thing that it has become must now, in its re-performance and possibly its re-recording, give the illusion of a spontaneous interpretation, surpassing the qualities of the original.

Problems for the performer may arise in any work that is a result of the composer's having notated his improvisatory ideas prescriptively, or with a misleading degree of precision. John Butt (Butt, 2002: 121) discusses a particularly interesting case in the *Entrée* from Messiaen's *Messe de la Pentecôte*, which as we have already seen was the fruit of many years of improvisation in church. Butt comments that the esoteric complexity of the irrational rhythms was important for its 'look' on paper and not to be followed literally in performance; in his own recording (1957) the composer reverts to 'improvisational mode, largely ignoring the letter of the rhythmic notation' (Butt, 2002: 121). This is confusing in a work in which passages of cerebral rhythmic organisation so characteristic of Messiaen at this period are to be found side by side and often combined with improvisatory freedom (as in the *Sortie: le Vent de l'Esprit*). It also seems to conflict to some extent with the view of Messiaen's confidante and interpreter Almut Rössler, who states with specific reference to this same passage in the Introit that '[i]t can generally be said that Messiaen wants a rhythmically exact rendition of his music' (Rössler, 1986/1986: 148). She goes on to add: 'After the text has been completely mastered, here and there there arises the possibility of imperceptibly making the music supple by agogic means corresponding with the accents and developments of melodic tension – just as in classical music'. But that is far from 'ignoring the letter' (Rössler, 1986: 148).

The value of recorded improvisations

Whatever our reservations about re-listening to musical performances that were intended to be ephemeral, the considerable number of such recordings now extant are a valuable resource for the understanding of twentieth-century organ music and its practice. They not only reveal the immense skill and mastery of the great improvisers but shed light on the whole practice of organ composition and performance. For French organ music is rooted and grounded in improvisatory practice, and the vast written repertory reveals countless traces of improvisation. To a non-organist, such music often seems merely 'organists' music' and has been much maligned. For example, Martin Cooper writes:

There is no other branch of music, except the liturgical, in which all musicians would admit the inferiority of everything written in the last two hundred years, of organ music written after 1750, to that written before. In fact organ music has, for at least a century, interested nobody but organists. Nevertheless, within this rather doubtfully musical sphere, the names of Guilmant, Gigout, Widor, Tournemire, Vierne and Dupré have become world-famous, and the distinctive features of the French school – skilled improvisation and great brilliance of effect – are universally recognized even in those circles where they are not valued highly.

(Cooper, 1951: 170)

That was more than fifty years ago, before the music of Messiaen became widely known and brought to the organ and its music a new respect from the wider musical public. A new generation of organists who understood the tradition has emerged, with a knowledge and awareness of improvisatory practice that enables us to approach the repertoire with a more sympathetic and informed ear. Thus, works such as the well-known *Te Deum* paraphrases by Langlais and Jeanne Demessieux are revealed in relation to their roots; Tournemire's recorded improvisation on the same theme is but one of their many immediate progenitors.

Likewise, the recently issued recordings of Messiaen's improvisations during Masses and other ceremonies at La Trinité reveal the composer – at the time of the recordings in his late 70s – experimenting and re-using ideas from some of his published works in a sort of composition workshop. Here, we encounter the ageing master in a mostly relaxed and mellow frame of mind; there is little of the fearlessly radical approach that in earlier years had made him the object of hatred and protest from some of the older worshippers (Messiaen and Samuel, 1986/1994: 118) nor of the 'monstrous beauty, opening up immense caverns where rivers flow, where piles of precious stones glitter...the impression that hell was opening, suddenly gaping wide' (Julien Green in a diary entry from 1949, given in Hill and Simeone 2005: 185). Perhaps what was shocking in 1931, and even in 1949, had become familiar and acceptable by 1984–7 when these recordings were made. Nevertheless, early in his tenure of the post he had realised the necessity of compromising by improvising in a variety of styles, not only to suit the tastes of the congregations at the different services but to take account of the liturgical context:

When circumstances constrained me, it was sometimes very classical. For instance I came up with pastiche voluntaries – faux Bach, faux Mozart, faux Schumann, and faux Debussy – in order to continue in the same key and in the same style as the piece just sung. Even so, I improvised in my own style, living off my old harmonic and rhythmic 'fat'.

(Messiaen and Samuel, 1994: 25)

The recordings, collectively entitled *Improvisations Inédites* (La Praye, DLP 0209), contain no pastiche 'classical' music, but they sometimes resemble Tournemire (as in the arabesques of the dialogue in Improvisation 7 on CD1, based on the plainsong *Viderunt Omnes*), while in Improvisation 6 Messiaen comes close to the spirit of the Toccata from Widor's Fifth Symphony. The greatest interest, however, seems to lie in their similarity to passages in his later organ works, particularly when he is meditating on one of his favourite plainsong themes, such as the Alleluia for All Saints' Day (*Alléluia de la Toussaint*). This makes several appearances, the most significant of which is in Improvisation 4 on CD2, where the treatment is strikingly similar to that in Meditation VIII from the *Méditations sur le Mystère de la Sainte Trinité* (pages 72–3 in the score), composed at least fifteen years earlier (passages in the *Méditations* such as this elicited some surprise, when the work was first heard in 1972, in those unfamiliar with Messiaen's liturgical practice). More frequently, however, we hear music similar to passages from his last organ work, *Livre du Saint Sacrement*, which was written in 1984. Not unexpectedly, the two communion prayers, *Prière avant la Communion* and *Prière après la Communion* furnish the most frequent correspondences and references, particularly the dialogue of a short motif between *Grand Orgue* and *Positif* with 16ft. and 2 2/3ft. stops, to the accompaniment of *gambe et voix céleste* on the *Récit*, a feature which occurs several times.

It is a cause for regret that on these valuable and revelatory discs, which were not originally professionally recorded,[11] the different improvisations are not identified by date or liturgical function (e.g. hour/type of mass, whether *Offertoire, Communion, Sortie*, etc.), though some informed guesswork is possible in many cases. This contrasts, for example, with the CD *Pierre Cochereau – l'Organiste Liturgique* (Solstice SOCD 226), which is exemplary in this respect; it gives an excellent sample of the great organist of Notre-Dame at work in four composite Sunday masses; he was a musical personality diametrically different from Messiaen, but equally representative of the French tradition. Recordings of improvisations, therefore, allow the listener to experience a living tradition of a musical practice rather than of objects, i.e. works. They are not permanent artefacts to be contemplated and revisited – in Goehr's terms, musical works to be given perfect performances; rather, they tend towards an aspiration to 'the perfect musical performance' (Goehr, 1998: 150). This distinction differentiates between a work-based practice, in which the performer is subservient to the demands of the score, the work becoming an idealised abstraction, and a practice which emphasises the cultural, social and physical aspects of performance itself. A recording by its very nature tends to eliminate the social and renders the physical merely implicit, as the performer cannot be seen – a condition that similarly obtains in many live organ performances. However, a perfect musical performance 'suitably adapts an age-old purpose of secular and sacred drama to transform and transport the audience through transfiguration' (Goehr, 1998: 150), an apt description of the ethos of many organ improvisations. Improvisations are slices from temporal successions – many of them liturgical observances, which themselves are in endless rotation, eternally repeated, yet never the same. They are not essentially aspirations toward 'works' but have an independent ontology, even when recorded; in listening to them we should ideally resist the temptation to hear them as works, and experience them in the same way as we may listen to recorded jazz improvisations, as highly developed and often far-from-simple examples of 'music making simpliciter', as possibly the most essentially musical form of music there can be. Thus, in experiencing a recorded improvisation we must readjust our whole musical epistemology: we must allow the recorded improvisation to take prior place to the written and/or recorded work, and the written work to become an epiphenomenon of the primary musical act of improvisation.

Of course, we may hear in improvisations and their recordings the genesis of musical ideas which eventually coalesce into permanent works, and also the after-life of those ideas; more than in any other musical context the boundaries of the 'work' here become porous and permeable. I suggest that another valuable aspect of recorded improvisations lies not in the possibility of notation and re-performance by others, nor yet as examples and objects for study by would-be improvisers (after all, the traditional source for that discipline is written works and the composition exercises derived from them), but as a source of insight into a musical practice that must by its very essence change and evolve. So much of the improvisatory practice of the past is lost and can never be recovered, to the detriment of our understanding of the works that have been left to us. In their recorded improvisations no less than in their written works, the great organists of the twentieth century have bequeathed to the world a priceless archive for future understanding of an important aspect of the culture and practice of our age.

Notes

1　Literally 'To give the illusion of the written thing'.

2　In this connection, see also Dupré (1972/1975: 45); Vierne recounts Widor's comment after having heard the young Dupré improvise: 'Are you sure he improvised? It seemed written'. Frazier (2002: 9–11) quotes both Vierne and Tournemire giving detailed advice as to how to give the illusion of written composition.

3　'Little Organ Book, in which guidance is given to an inquiring organist in how to implement a chorale in all kinds of ways, and at the same time to become practised in the study of pedalling, since in the chorales found therein the pedal is treated completely obbligato' (in Williams, 1980: II, 3).

4　See Vierne, 'Mes Souvenirs' in *Cahiers et Mémoires de l'Orgue*, 134 bis III 1970: 23 (cited in Fauquet, 1999: 479): 'Sur les six heures de classe faites chaque semaine, le Maître en consacrait au moins cinq à l'improvisation'. Fauquet devotes a whole chapter (XX) to Franck's organ class, summarising many written testimonies by students. It should be noted, however, that Widor, Franck's successor as Organ Professor, deplored this almost exclusive emphasis on improvisation, preferring to concentrate on technique and repertoire (Ochse, 1994: 183–5).

5 1878 was the date of the inauguration of the Cavaillé-Coll organ in the Salle des Fêtes of the Palais du Trocadéro; this was Paris' first concert hall organ and the initial series of recitals, given by almost all the leading organists in Paris, provided an enormous stimulus to the prestige of the organ in French musical culture.

6 It is worth pointing out that these and some other recordings made at the time are the only evidence we have of the sound of the instrument in its original form, as Franck knew it. It was enlarged and rebuilt in 1933.

7 'Topics' have been defined as 'subjects for musical discourse' by Ratner (1980: 9–29). The theory has proved very influential in recent years and has been further developed by semioticians such as Agawu (1991: 6, 26–50)

8 'Jetons le metronome loin de nous'.

9 Simeone's translation is: 'It sounds as though it's improvised'.

10 Davies is aware that there have been such instances: 'the original attains a new ontological standing...an improvisation can become transmuted into a work' (Davies, 2001: 14, footnote 8). He does not agree that the original concept (in the improviser's mind at the time of its spontaneous realisation) might be given 'work' status by virtue of its being an imagined 'sound-structure', because by its nature there is only one performance/interpretation.

11 We have Olivier Glandaz, from the organ-building firm of Beuchet-Debierre, who maintained the organ at the time, to thank for having the foresight to initiate this series of recordings (information from the liner notes of the CD set by Maxime Patel).

References

Agawu, V.K. (1991) *Playing with Signs*. Princeton, NJ: Princeton University Press.

Beechey, G. (1970) 'Organ Recitals by French Organists in England', *The Organ* 49: 108–17.

Boulez, P. (1986) *Orientations: Collected Writings*. Trans. J-J. Nattiez. London: Faber and Faber. Original (1981) as *Point de Repère*. Paris: Christian Bourgois.

Butt, J. (2002) *Playing with History*. Cambridge: Cambridge University Press.

Cochereau, P. (1992) *Variations sur 'Alouette, Gentille Alouette'*. Transcribed by D. Briggs. London: United Music Publishers.

Cooper, M. (1951) *French Music from the Death of Berlioz to the Death of Fauré*. Oxford: Oxford University Press.

David, H.T. and Mendel, A. (eds) (1998) *The New Bach Reader*. Rev. C. Wolff. New York: Norton.

Davies, S. (2001) *Musical Works and Performances: A Philosophical Exploration*. Oxford: Oxford University Press.

Dupré, M. (1975) *Recollections*. Trans. R. Knearearm. New York: Belwyn Mills. Original (1972) as *Marcel Dupré Raconte*. Paris: Editions Bournemann.

Fauquet, J.-M. (1981) 'Charles Tournemire et l'Orgue' in *Orgues et Organistes Français en 1930* (booklet insert with EMI 2 C 153-16411/5).

_____ (1999) *César Franck*. Paris: Fayard.

Frazier, J. (2002) 'In Gregorian Mode', in R. Ebrecht (ed.) *Maurice Duruflé – the Last Impressionist*, pp.1–64. Lanham, Maryland: The Scarecrow Press.

Goehr, L. (1992) *The Imaginary Museum of Musical Works: An Essay in the Philosophy of Music*. Oxford: Oxford University Press.

_____ (1998) *The Quest for Voice: Music, Politics and the Limits of Philosophy*. Oxford: Oxford University Press.

Higginbottom, E. (2001) 'Lebègue', in S. Sadie and J. Tyrrell (eds) *The New Grove Dictionary of Music and Musicians*, vol. xiv, p.430. London: Macmillan.

Hill, P. and Simeone, N. (2005) *Messiaen*. New Haven: Yale University Press.

d'Indy, V. (1909) *César Franck*. Trans. R. Newmarch. London: The Bodley Head. Original (1906) as *César Franck*. Paris: Félix Alcan.

Ingarden, R. (1986) *The Work of Music and the Problem of its Identity*. Trans. A. Czerniawski. Berkeley: University of California Press. Original (1966) as *Utwór muzyczny i sprawa jego tozsamosci*. Warszawa: Panstwowe Wydawnictwo Naukowe.

Jaquet, M.-L. (1978) 'L'oeuvre d'Orgue de César Franck et notre temps', *L'Orgue* 167: 5–42.

Messiaen, O. and Samuel, C. (1994) *Olivier Messiaen: Music and Colour. Conversations with Claude Samuel*. Trans. E.T. Glasow. Portland, Oregon: Amadeus Press. Original (1986) as *Olivier Messiaen: Musique et couleur*. Paris: Editions Belfond.

Ochse, O. (1994) *Organists and Organ Playing in Nineteenth-Century France and Belgium*. Bloomington: Indiana University Press.

Ratner, L. (1980) *Classic Music: Expression, Form and Style*. New York: Schirmer.

Rössler, A. (1986) *Contributions to the Spiritual World of Olivier Messiaen*. Trans. B. Dagg and N. Poland. Duisberg: Gilles & Francke Verlag. Original (1986) as *Beitrage zur geistigen Welt Olivier Messiaens*. Duisberg: Gilles & Francke Verlag.

Samson, J. (2000) 'The Practice of Early-Nineteenth-Century Pianism', in M. Talbot (ed.) *The Musical Work: Reality or Invention?*, pp.110–27. Liverpool: Liverpool University Press.

_____ (2002) 'The Musical Work and Nineteenth-Century History', in J. Samson (ed.) *The Cambridge History of Nineteenth-Century Music*, pp.3–28. Cambridge: Cambridge University Press.

_____ (2003) *Virtuosity and the Musical Work: The Transcendental Studies of Liszt*. Cambridge: Cambridge University Press.

Samuel, C. (1967) *Entretiens avec Olivier Messiaen*. Paris: Belfond.

Schweitzer, A. (1911) *JS Bach*. Two vols. Trans. E. Newman. London: Breitkopf & Härtel. Original (1908) as *JS Bach*. Berlin: Breitkopf & Härtel.

Simeone, N. (2003) 'Debussy and Expression', in S. Trezise (ed.) *The Cambridge Companion to Debussy*, pp.101–16. Cambridge: Cambridge University Press.

Talbot, M. (2000) 'The Work-Concept and Composer-Centredness', in M. Talbot (ed.) *The Musical Work: Reality or Invention?*, pp.168–86. Liverpool: Liverpool University Press.

Tournemire, C. (1931) *César Franck*. Paris: Delagrave.

_____ (1958) *Cinq Improvisations pour Orgue (reconstituées par Maurice Duruflé)*. Two vols. Paris: Durand.

Williams, P. (1980) *The Organ Music of JS Bach*. Three vols. Cambridge: Cambridge University Press.

Discography

Cochereau, P. (n.d.) *L'extraordinaire Pierre Cochereau aux grande Orgues de Notre-Dame de Paris* (including *Improvisations sur 'Alouette, Gentille Alouette'*). Philips 6521 008.

_____ (1977) *L'Art de l'Improvisation*. FY records: FY059/60 (2 LPs of improvisations recorded on the organ of Notre-Dame, Paris). Reissued on CD Solstice FYCD 059.

_____ (2005) *L'organiste liturgique* (4 messes dominicales en improvisations) Solstice SOCD 226.

Messiaen, O. (1992) 'Messe de la Pentecôte', CD 4 in *Messiaen par lui-même*. EMI CZS 7 67400 2 (original Ducretet-Thomson, 1957).

_____ (2002) *Improvisations Inédites*. 2 CDs, La Praye DLP 0209.

Tournemire, C. (2002) 'Petite rhapsodie improvisée'; 'Improvisation sur le "Te Deum"'; 'Cantilène'; 'Choral sur le "Victimae paschali [laudes]"'; 'Fantasie sur l'"Ave Maris Stella"'. CD 1, in *Orgues et organistes français du XX siècle*. 5 CDs, EMI 7243 574866 2 0. (Originals Polydor, 1931).

BRUCE ELLIS BENSON

Stealing Licks: Recording and Identity in Jazz

T HERE are few forms of music – at least in the West – more fluid than jazz. By its very nature, it is constantly in improvisational motion. There are many implications of recording for a musical art that is so dependent upon improvisatory practices. In this chapter, I wish to focus on the issue of identity of what jazz musicians call 'licks', and their relationship to recording. Defining the term 'lick' is actually rather tricky: a lick can consist of a short melodic motif or a more extended unit; it may end in a full cadence, but most likely it is part of a larger melodic/harmonic scheme.[1] The fact that licks are ubiquitous in jazz improvisations is precisely the reason that the term 'lick' can mean almost any musical pattern that is in some way recognizable and that is not, strictly speaking, part of what we might call the 'tune itself'.[2] As an improvisatory practice, jazz has always incorporated borrowing or stealing of licks. Precisely because we have no recordings of early jazz, there is no way of being sure that improvised licks were part of jazz practice from the beginning. But there is every reason to think that such was the case.

Yet, how exactly does recording affect the practice of borrowing licks and the licks themselves? I shall argue that recording affects the identity of licks in two seemingly paradoxical ways. On the one hand, the identity of a lick is determined by the act of recording in a way that a performance – or even a long series of repeated performances that included the same lick – simply could not do. A recording is, therefore, a kind of documentation of a particular lick, one that both fixes it and associates it with a particular performer. On the other hand, the fixing of the lick by way of recording opens up new possibilities of transforming the lick. In other words, recording both fixes a lick (in a way and to a degree that simply playing it would not do) and helps facilitate its transformation. Although this double movement might seem strange, it is in practice what recordings serve to do. As a result, recorded licks still retain an element of common property about them at the very same time they become someone's property. By being recorded (and by recordings being disseminated), licks inevitably become part of the common jazz vernacular. This is partly due to budding and senior jazz musicians intentionally picking up licks from other players. It is also partly due to the fact that hearing jazz played a certain way simply influences how one plays. In other words, jazz licks get picked up even unintentionally.

In this chapter, I analyze this simultaneous 'fixing' and 'making available' that recordings bring about, by considering how jazz licks come into existence and what kind of life they lead. Accordingly, the first section concerns the emergence of a lick, while the second section focuses on the question of its continued existence. Finally, in the third section, I turn to the first jazz recordings as illustrative of the complications the identity and ownership of a jazz lick involve. Although such creative borrowing is certainly to be found in our day, it is remarkable that the very first two jazz recordings, made by the Original Dixieland Jass Band, proved problematic from the standpoint of both identity and ownership, and involved lawsuits. Ironically enough, even though we have considerably stronger conceptions of intellectual property rights and stricter enforcement today, the fact that jazz musicians borrow from one another has –over the decades – become recognized as simply the way jazz functions. Thus, we would be less likely to have such lawsuits brought about today, despite this being a far more litigious era.

The birth of a lick

Edmund Husserl's essay 'The Origin of Geometry' (1939/1970) is an interesting backdrop against which to consider the origin of a lick. For Husserl provides us with an account of what it takes for something (in his case, a geometric idea) to come into existence, to lead a life, and to take on a kind of permanence. Since these are exactly our questions – regarding licks rather than geometric theorems – his account proves helpful in unpacking the questions of genesis, constitution, identity, and ownership of jazz licks.

Before we begin to examine the birth of a lick, a more explicit definition is in order. Robert Witmer defines a lick as follows:

> A term used in jazz, blues and pop music to describe a short recognizable melodic motif, formula or phrase. Improvising jazz and blues musicians have at their disposal a repertory of licks, some of their own invention by which they can be identified, some borrowed from other players, and a solo may be little more than the stringing together of a number of such fragments. In some styles (e.g. slow blues) and for some ubiquitous chord progressions (e.g. I–II–V–I in major or minor keys) a common stock of licks is in circulation.

> (Witmer, 2006)

Each of these characteristics is important. First, a lick is some kind of motif or phrase that has some kind and degree of identity. It need not be a commonly known motif (such as a Wagnerian motif associated with a particular character in a Wagnerian opera), but it must have enough of an identity such that one can hear it and identify it. However, that identity must *simultaneously* be sufficiently fluid so that the lick retains its identity even when being repeated with variation. We will consider examples of such fluid identity shortly. Second, Witmer is right that jazz musicians operate with a 'repertory' of licks, and that these may be of one's own making or borrowed from others. How one puts licks together is very much part of how one generates an improvisation. Third, from that bag of licks, one pulls out the elements for a solo (or else a backup vamp). One's bag of licks forms the basis for one's improvising.

When, though, is a lick? In other words, at what point can we say that 'it' has come into existence? Here, we come to a much more difficult question than that of simply defining a lick. For, if licks can be both products of one's own invention and borrowed from others, then they may not have a definite identity. The question is one of both ontology and ownership. Given that licks usually have a kind of history, they are often both in motion, i.e. changing in terms of identity, and 'owned' by more than one person. And if licks could be neatly separated into the categories of 'one's own invention' and 'borrowed', then we would have two sharply defined groups. Such is not the improvisational reality, however. Consider, for example, an actual text composed of jazz licks and titled *1001 Jazz Licks: A Complete Jazz Vocabulary for the Improvising Musician* (Schneidman, 2000). Exactly where these licks come from is unclear. Jack Schneidman claims they are 'based on the idiomatic traits of different eras in jazz history. For example, the licks from the swing era resemble the work of master tenor saxophonists Lester Young, Coleman Hawkins, as well as the great guitarist Charlie Christian' (Shneidman, 2000: 2). In addition to the language of 'resemblance', Shneidman describes some licks as paying 'homage' to other musicians, while the last group of licks in the collection 'demonstrates some of the intervallic and harmonic concepts of today's greatest contemporary jazz musicians' (Shneidman, 2000: 2). Perhaps we can say that licks occupy a space somewhere between simple repetition and complete innovation. A helpful way of explaining this sense of origin is provided by Mikhail Bakhtin[3], who argued that:

> [t]he word in language is half someone else's. It becomes 'one's own' only when the speaker populates it with his own intention, his own accent, when he appropriates the word, adapting it to his own semantic and expressive intention...[The word] exists in other people's mouths, in other people's contexts, serving other people's intentions; it is from there that one must take the word, and make it one's own.

(Bakhtin 1975/1991: 293–4)

Although Bakhtin is speaking of language here, the same holds for licks. One puts licks together in much the same way as one takes words and makes them into phrases. In one sense, they are now 'one's own', but there is still the sense that they are borrowed from others. If such a conception is correct, then the birth of a lick is not easy to pinpoint; indeed, a lick may even be the sort of entity that does not necessarily have a clear moment of conception *per se*.

Consider how this explanation of the genesis of a lick compares with Husserl's conception of origin. On Husserl's account, there is some original geometer somewhere who first comes up with certain geometric ideas. In fact, Husserl's goal in 'The Origin of Geometry' is to 'inquire into that sense in which [the geometric idea] appeared in history for the first time' (Husserl, 1970: 354). Yet, interestingly enough, Husserl does admit that this moment of 'the first time' was necessarily preceded by something else. As he puts it, 'a more primitive formation of meaning necessarily went before it as a preliminary stage' (Husserl, 1970: 356). In other words, even on Husserl's account, the first time was not really the first time. Indeed, given the idea of 'a more primitive formation' as the precedent, it becomes difficult to know what would count as the 'first time'. Should such a 'primitive formation' or a more developed one be regarded as 'the first time'? Husserl leaves such a question unanswered. Shifting back from geometry to jazz licks, it is likewise difficult to know what counts as the first appearance of a lick. Let me work this out in two ways. First, if jazz is (as history shows) the result or confluence of various factors – European band music, African-American rhythms, church music of various traditions, etc. – then it is difficult to speak of an origin of jazz in general.[4] Second, if jazz is indeed the outgrowth of all of these musical influences, each of which would have had (most likely) its own collection of licks, then it is difficult to speak of the 'origin' of a jazz lick. *When* does a lick first appear? Here, there can be no easy answer; instead, one must be content with a somewhat paradoxical solution. On the one hand, to say simply that jazz licks have *no* origin (what Husserl would call their *Erstmaligkeit*, or 'first time') would be to deny the possibility of innovation. Surely, there are licks in jazz that at least seem to appear – or appear to some degree – at a particular point in time. Indeed, we can point to particular famous recordings that pinpoint the identity of a particular lick. On the other hand, if licks are like linguistic phrases that get interchanged, and in the process change and develop, then we may not be able to speak of an origin that can be pinpointed in time. Jacques Derrida speaks of the 'living present' as being 'always already' a trace of the past (Derrida, 1967/1973: 85). His point is that the present is never simply a new moment. Instead, it contains traces of the past that live on into the present, even in new forms. In other words, the 'now moment' of the present is partially composed of 'past moments'.

In effect, a jazz lick is a musical idea. Like any kind of idea, one gets musical ideas in various ways – in a flash of insight, from listening to others, by putting two or more elements together, or reworking an old idea (or perhaps some combination of the above). Further, in the same way intellectual ideas can be both different and yet have a commonality, so musical ideas may not be exactly the same and yet still exhibit a commonality. This also explains how a lick can display a certain continuity amidst change: for instance, a modified version of a lick may have the same four pitches as the original version, but with added notes. Such an example well illustrates Derrida's idea of the present containing traces of the past. The past 'lives on', but it takes on a different form.

If jazz licks live on in the present, and are likewise in constant motion, then what gives them their identity?

The shifting identity of a lick

Returning to Husserl's account of a geometrical idea is once again helpful. Put simply, Husserl thinks that once a geometric idea is formed, it is first of all retained in the geometer's immediate memory and then passes on to long-term memory. At this point, though, the idea is purely *intra*subjective – that is, within the subject. This point raises some interesting questions that Husserl does not answer. What does it mean for something to be simply 'in one's mind'? Husserl can only appeal to something like an interior language, in which one speaks to oneself.[5] In order for it to become *inter*subjective – or one could say *objective* – it must be expressed in speech. Furthermore, it only reaches the highest level of objectivity, in the sense of being objectively available to all, once it is written down. While *1001 Jazz Licks* is an example of such writing, fulfilling Husserl's criterion of ultimate objectivity, it is nevertheless highly unusual. In general, licks are not written down (or, if they are, likely as not it's on a napkin or piece of scrap paper). And here is where we must come back to recording. For there is every reason to think that *1001 Jazz Licks* is actually the result of recording, i.e. that the text reflects various licks as preserved by recording. Along these lines, most of what we have of notated jazz is the result of transcriptions of recordings. Of course, jazz musicians often use fake books or lead sheets that contain melodies and chord progressions, and sometimes licks. It is, nevertheless, recording much more than notation that preserves jazz licks.[6]

Given that jazz licks are like a vocabulary of building blocks that one uses to constitute a solo, it follows that any collection of licks constantly grows and changes. A lick borrowed from a musical great might stay just the same, but much more likely it will morph into something different. In this respect, it is interesting that – in an entirely different context – the classical rhetorician Quintilian noted that pure repetition is impossible. While Quintilian might seem an odd source to cite in a discussion of jazz improvisation, his work on *inventio* (which could be literally translated as 'invention', but also quite plausibly as 'improvisation', precisely because invention for him *is* in effect a kind of improvisation, in which one builds upon what already exists) is perhaps the finest work we have regarding how one 'invents' rhetoric.[7] According to Quintilian, 'there is nothing harder than to produce an exact likeness, and nature herself has so far failed in this endeavour that there is always some difference which enables us to distinguish even the things which seem most like and most equal to one another' (Quintilian, 1922: 10.2.10). Put into jazz terms, it is difficult to reproduce a lick *exactly*. The tendency in copying is to introduce something of one's own (some extra notes, a change in tempo, a different emphasis, etc.). Hence, there is every reason to think that, due to the fluidity of jazz improvisation and the difficulty of exact repetition, jazz licks are constantly being developed and changed. It is hard to imagine, for instance, any jazz musician learning all or even just some of the 1001 licks, and then playing them exactly as written over their entire improvising career. One might begin with such licks as a kind of basis for improvising, but one would naturally progress beyond them.

Paul Berliner provides a number of excellent examples of the remarkable balance of identity and fluidity of jazz licks. In his book titled *Thinking in Jazz: The Infinite Art of Improvisation*, Berliner follows the development of a lick in fifteen different solos over forty-six years (Berliner, 1994: 576–8).[8] He begins with the two-bar lick from a recording of 'Baby, Won't You Make Up Your Mind?' (18 October 1946) by the Billy Eckstine band, with Miles Davis in the trumpet section. He then moves to a two-bar revamping of it in a solo by Davis in 'Rifftide' (8–11 May 1949), and an eight-bar elaboration by Bud Powell in 'The Street Beat' (30 June 1950). Returning to Davis, Berliner cites an eleven-bar sequence from 'The Serpent's Tooth' (30 January 1953). He concludes with more contemporary recordings, which include four- and three-bar versions by John Scofield in 'You Bet' (December 1991), and Benny Green and Christian McBride in 'Billy Boy' (1992) respectively. If one casually looked at these various solos as transcribed, the identity of the lick would not necessarily be immediately apparent, since they represent rather significant variations on it in terms of key signature, length, phrase expansion, etc. Yet, if one takes the time to analyze these seemingly quite different licks, one can see a basic structure that unifies them. The simplest and most elegant of these is found in Davis' recording of 'Rifftide', in which the lick simply consists of the pitch-classes A F A F E-flat C. The kind of fluid identity displayed by this series of jazz licks – and by licks in general – might perhaps be best described in terms of the fluid identity that results from combinations of DNA that we call 'children'. Ludwig Wittgenstein's notion of 'family resemblance' is often invoked to explain this kind of identity. Instead of a strict sort of identity, similarities between licks are like family resemblances in which there are common features combined with differences (Wittgenstein, 1953/2002: no.67). Just as certain features may be found in certain family members but are not necessarily present in all, so licks can share some features with some licks and other features with other licks.

Naturally, licks had identities long before recording. As long as there is a consciousness that can identify a series of notes *as* a lick, that lick exists. One need not even *play* such a series of notes for it to exist. To exist, then, a lick – just like a musical phrase or a melody – requires a consciousness that hears the series of notes *as* a lick. Here, returning to Husserl is once again helpful. In attempting to explain our experience of time, Husserl uses the example of a melody. Were we to hear tones sounded simultaneously, we would not be able to hear them as forming a melody. On the other hand, hearing them simply as discrete tones would not result in an experience of melody either. Instead, 'in each moment we would have a tone, or perhaps an empty pause in the interval between the two sounding tones, but never the representation of a melody' (Husserl, 1928/1991: 11). In other words, we must hear those tones as constituting a melody in order for them to be constituted as a melody. Obviously, the existence of a melody (or of a lick) is most evident when it is being played. As Georg Wilhelm Friedrich Hegel reminds us:

[u]nlike buildings, statues, and paintings, the notes have in themselves no permanent subsistence as objects; on the contrary, with their fleeting passage they vanish again and therefore the musical composition needs a continually repeated reproduction, just because of this momentary existence of its notes.

(Hegel, 1842–3/1975: II, 909)

Nevertheless, a melody or lick can be retained in short-term memory, which 'holds in consciousness what has been produced and stamps on it the character of the "just past"' (Husserl, 1991: 88). From there, it can pass on to long-term memory and continue its existence by being transmitted to others through performances, including the simple humming of the tune. Hans-Georg Gadamer claims that all art begins in 'play,' which results in a *'transformation into structure'* (Gadamer, 1960/1989: 110). Exactly what form this 'structure' takes depends upon the musical genre. No doubt, there are cultures in which melodies have been preserved by way of memory and performance over centuries or even millennia. Indeed, there are musical genres in which such preservation is still the norm. Conversely, Western art music depends upon the score.

But what about the case of jazz licks? How are they transformed from a mere spontaneous one-time appearance to somehow having a lasting existence? In the early days of jazz, they were likely preserved by way of memory (and, perhaps in some cases, by being written down). However, given both that (i) jazz came of age precisely when recording technology came of age, and (ii) jazz licks were generally not preserved by way of writing, recording technology became, in effect, the default mode of both preservation and dissemination of jazz licks. While there is no question that jazz licks could (and did) survive and at the same time have an identity simply by way of memory and performance, in the contingency of jazz history it just so happens that recording proved to be a particularly powerful way of documenting and providing an identity to jazz licks. My argument, then, is that the degree of documentation and identity provided by recording for jazz licks is unmatched by memory and live performance alone.

On the other hand, as Berliner's example above shows, recordings of a lick make it possible for others to take that lick and modify it to suit a different context. Quite paradoxically, recording means that any given text – or lick – that is identified as *mine* effectively escapes from my control. This second claim is hardly new; it is already anticipated by Plato, who wrote extensively on the difference between writing and speaking (which, for our purposes here, I read as the difference between playing and recording). In *Phaedrus*, Socrates considers the respective positions of speaking and writing. Speech is held up as superior to writing, for in the spoken word the speaker is immanently present. Indeed, the spoken word cannot exist without my – or at least *someone's* – voice. That voice and the speech it produces have an unbroken continuity. My voice is connected to what I say, which means that *I* am connected to what I say. In contrast, Socrates identifies writing as a *pharmakon*, which can be both a cure and a poison (Plato, 1961: 274e–275a).[9] One aspect of this 'poisonous' effect is that of forgetfulness. For our purposes here, though, a much more important aspect is that writing creates a distance between the one who writes and the written word; it is as if one has almost no control over the word once it is written down. Derrida takes up precisely this last point (Derrida, 1972/1981: 63–171). According to him, one does lose control over that which one writes. Indeed, structurally, writing entails one's death (Derrida, 1973: 96f). Once my thoughts are committed to paper, I am no longer necessary for their continued existence.

Recording produces a similar, though not identical, effect. On the one hand, precisely because my improvisation can be played even when I am dead, it gives me a kind of immortality. Furthermore, recording something – as opposed to merely playing it – provides one far greater control over the finished product. It is no coincidence that Igor Stravinsky, for example, took great pains to record many of his works: he wanted to provide the definitive way of playing them as a kind of musical imperative for all future performers (Benson, 2003: 151). On the other hand, a recording of my improvisation means that it can be heard without my presence, without even me being alive. Even after my death, my improvisation lives on. Moreover, recording takes control away from me and hands it to the listeners, who can now have command performances any time and place they like. If I am improvising in a particular place (i.e. a geographical space), one must be in proximity to hear that improvisation. Once that improvisation is committed to some recording medium – a vinyl cylinder, a CD, or an MP3 file – the recording can go just about anywhere. Space, at least, is no longer a restriction. Nor, for that matter, is time. *My* recording can be disseminated on the Internet infinitely. Moreover, that dissemination can take place without anything (such as a title or inscription) connecting it to me. These considerations might be seen as simply having practical implications. Not doubt, there are those too. My point is much deeper than that, however: *ontologically*, the status of my improvisation – once recorded – has changed. What was once an ephemeral sound has been caught, so to speak, in a permanent medium, and exists not just as a one-time occurrence, but also as a fully repeatable one. As a recording, my improvisation has a *virtual* existence, and can be turned into an actual one by being played over and over again. A recording can be taken into all sorts of locations I could never have imagined and played before audiences in very different circumstances. All of those aspects have to do with my loss of control over an improvisation that comes about by way of recording.

Of course, it is easy to make the case regarding loss of control too strongly. Jazz recordings do indeed make jazz improvisations available to a wide and new audience, meaning that many young jazz musicians (from early on in jazz history) listened to recordings to learn improvisations. Whether it was Jimmy McPartland and friends in Chicago learning the improvisations of the New Orleans Rhythm Kings by going through them measure by measure, or his wife Marian McPartland in England learning by listening to jazz on the radio, many jazz musicians got their start by little more than sheer imitation of what they heard on recordings. Is this, then, more a matter of contingency than of ontology or logic? In one sense, it just so happened that jazz and recording technology came of age roughly together, so that the latter significantly shaped the former.[10] But, in another sense, that contingent feature becomes – if not *de jure* at least *de facto* – a part of the history of jazz, and thus a part of jazz improvisation *as we know it*.

The effects of recording – immortality coupled with loss of control – are indeed real. Turning to a specific case shows just how much both are true.

The remarkable case of the Original Dixieland Jass Band

That the first two recordings in jazz were *both* the subject of lawsuits is, to say the least, remarkable. Given that defining intellectual property is becoming increasingly important, we would most likely assume that litigation over such property – in this instance, jazz licks – would be the norm today.[11] Yet, precisely the opposite is the case. While those first two recordings were contested, the history of jazz recordings since then has been relatively calm. As far as I can tell, the main reason for this lack of contestation is that jazz improvisers came to realize that borrowing is simply part of the way the game of jazz is played. However, these early recordings do remarkably illustrate the points regarding identity that we have already explored.

Before we consider the recordings themselves, it is worth noting that the first jazz recordings were made by a band of white – rather than *black* or *Creole* – musicians such as Bunk Johnson or Jelly Roll Morton (both of whom made recordings much later). Since jazz has long been considered an African-American musical genre, one would not expect white musicians to be the first to record.[12] The usual explanation has been that, once again, whites were the first to capitalize on something distinctly African-American. One problem with that explanation is that everything we know about jazz in turn-of-the-century New Orleans leads us to believe that white musicians were playing jazz quite actively from the very beginning. Exactly what role the ODJB played in creating jazz is difficult to determine. Ted Giola writes: 'No evidence exists to support the claim that the ODJB initiated the jazz tradition – indeed, it is even doubtful that the band was the first white group of New Orleans musicians to play jazz...But smug dismissals are equally off the mark' (Giola, 1997: 38). There is no question that the ODJB was one of the most important groups playing jazz (or 'jass' or 'jas' as it was first spelled). More importantly, there is good reason to think that the ODJB was the first group (or at least one of the first) that actually *wanted* to record. As it turns out, Freddie Keppard, a black musician who led the Original Creole Band, actually refused an offer to record from the Victor Talking Machine Company in 1916. That refusal in itself would not be particularly interesting, but the reason given is very much connected to the way in which we have seen recordings take on their own lives. For Keppard did not want to record out of fear that his band's improvisations would be copied: 'Nothin' doin', boys. We won't put our stuff on records for everybody to steal' (in Leonard, 1962: 96). Not surprisingly, the ODJB evidently needed to be persuaded to record because of the same fear. Of course, it turns out that this fear was well placed, for the recordings of the ODJB were ones that numerous jazz musicians – including Bix Beiderbecke – listened to intently with precisely the goal of copying. In the early years of jazz, the ODJB may well have been the most copied of all bands. Although speaking of copying another band, Jimmy McPartland's account gets at exactly what these early bands feared: stealing lock, stock, and barrel.

> What we used to do was put the record on – one of the Rhythm Kings', naturally – play a few bars and then all get our notes. We'd have to tune our instruments up to the record machine, to the pitch, and go ahead with a few notes. Then Stop! A few more bars of the record, each guy would pick up his notes and boom! We would go on and play it. Two bars, or four, or eight – we would get in on each phrase and then all play it.
>
> (in Shapiro and Hentoff, 1955: 120)

The fact that white musicians were the first to record has little to do with race and much to do with the fear of losing one's licks.

Indeed, losing one's licks, in one sense or another, turns out to be the main issue in both of the lawsuits that resulted from these first recordings. The first of the suits is not only the more famous but also the more interesting one in terms of identity. The ODJB played a tune called 'Livery Stable Blues'.[13] However, such a title was considered far too vulgar for The Victor Talking Machine Company, which had in its catalogue refined classical music. The solution to this problem was simply renaming the song as 'Barnyard Blues'.[14] While that was the name under which the band's agent Max Hart copyrighted it (incidentally, under his own name), it was listed on the cylinder as 'Livery Stable Blues'. That mistake would have probably gone unnoticed had it not been that a former band member, Alcide 'Yellow' Nunez, realized that the tune that he recognized as 'Livery Stable Blues' was not copyrighted. In a clearly retaliatory move, he brought out the sheet music version of 'Livery Stable Blues' with a publisher in Chicago, Ray Graham, using his name and that of Ray Lopez as the composers. This immediately resulted in a lawsuit on multiple fronts, with Nick LaRocca, the band's leader, filing both against the Chicago publisher and against Victor, for copyrighting the wrong song, and also bringing out his own version of the tune under the title 'Barnyard Blues'.

While there are many details to this story, what is particularly interesting and relevant for our concern here is what happened in the trial of the ODJB members against the Chicago publisher. On LaRocca's account, he had composed the song in 1912. However, given that there was neither a sheet music version nor a recording of this song up until 1917, it was a claim that turned out to be hard to maintain. In effect, the problem was two-fold: i) to sort out whether LaRocca or Nunez was the composer of the tune, and ii) whether there was any clear identity to 'Livery Stable Blues' against not only 'Barnyard Blues' but also any blues at all. Of course, these problems are intimately intertwined. For, if there is no stability of identity to any particular blues tune, then neither LaRocca nor Nunez would be in a position to claim 'ownership'.

Regarding the second question, Theodore F. Morse, a composer of hundreds of popular songs, was brought in as an expert for the defense. He stated that there was no substantive difference between the two tunes. Then, a music critic named May Hill was brought in to argue for the much larger claim: that there simply is no difference between blues tunes in general. She went so far as to claim that such tunes as 'Chicago Blues', 'Alabama Blues', and 'Livery Stable Blues' could all be played at the same time without any harmonic discord at all.

The most interesting of the testimonies, however, was that of Nunez, who said: 'Jedge, blues is blues.' In effect, Nunez was to make two remarkable claims. One was similar to Hill's point, namely that 'all blues is alike.' The other was that the composition of the 'Livery Stable Blues' was so much a group effort – and so strongly related to other compositions – that no-one could take credit for it. As he (rather memorably) put it:

> You see...nobody wrote the 'Livery Stable Blues'. Naw. Nobody writes any of that stuff. I invented the pony cry in the Blues, and LaRocca, he puts in the horse neigh. We was in the Schiller cafe, rehearsin', see? And I suggests that we take the 'More Power Blues' and hash 'em up a bit. My friend, Ray Lopez, he wrote the 'More Power Blues'. All blues is alike.
>
> (Brunn, 1960: 81)

These claims alone would have been more than enough to complicate thoroughly the authorship of 'Livery Stable Blues', but that was not the end. The pianist Ernie Erdman, who used to play with the band, claimed that he (as admitted by LaRocca) came up with the title for the tune.

Untangling all these claims simply proved too much for the judge. He concluded:

> No claim is made by either side for the barnyard calls that are interpolated in the music, no claim is made for the harmony. The only claim appears to be for the melody...The only question is, has there been a conceived idea of the melody that runs through this so-called 'Livery Stable Blues'...The Court is satisfied, from having looked over the manuscripts, that there is a very decided resemblance between the aria – the melody of 'More Power Blues' and the 'Livery Stable Blues'. The finding of the Court is therefore that neither Mr LaRocca and his associates nor Mr Nunez and his associates conceived the idea of this melody. They were a strolling band of players and like – take the Hungarian orchestras, if you will, but with no technical musical education, having a natural musical ear – quick ear and above all a retentive ear, and no human being could determine where

that aria came from that they now claim was produced at the Schiller Cafe for the first time.

(Brunn, 1960: 84–5)

As far as the judge was concerned, there simply was not enough of a clear identity for 'Livery Stable Blues' to distinguish it from other blues. Of course, the judge made this ruling on the basis of never having heard either blues. Moreover, the judge does not give us any idea of exactly what the differences are between the two blues, so it is difficult to know how to evaluate his ruling. What further complicates this account is that, if Nunez was right, the piece was a combined effort. Finally, the various animal calls, which might arguably be termed licks, were not even considered by the court.

Before drawing any conclusions from this particular case, it is worth noting two further developments that raise significant problems and questions. First, the music on the A-side of the recording, 'Dixieland Jass Band One-Step', likewise became the source of controversy.[15] The publisher, Joseph B. Stern and Company, noted a similarity between one of the pieces on this recording and 'That Teasin' Rag', one of the pieces it published. Exactly where the similarity lies is not fully clear. Harry Otis Brunn claims that the similarity concerns only 'the rather weak coincidence that two bars of the trio were similar' (Brunn, 1960: 86), whereas Tim Gracyk makes the more substantial claim that the ODJB had actually borrowed 'a strain' from the piece (Gracyk, 2000: 256). Having consulted the sheet music for 'That Teasin' Rag' (Jordan, 1909), and listened to the 'Dixieland Jass Band One-Step', my own account is that the chorus of 'Dixieland Jass Band One-Step' is remarkably similar to the chorus from 'That Teasin' Rag' in terms of melodic structure. The resemblance is hardly exact, but it is clearly there. In any case, Victor dealt swiftly with this problem by reissuing the tune with the phrase 'Introducing "That Teasin' Rag"' added to the title. Second, in an effort to see whether – at least *legally* – 'all blues is blues', the ODJB took the audacious step of recording 'More Power Blues' (with minor changes) under the title 'Mournin' Blues'.[16] Interestingly enough, as Brunn notes, 'no one ever challenged the theft' (Brunn, 1960: 86).

These cases prove illustrative regarding the identity of jazz licks in a number of ways. That the judge was unable to come to any conclusion about the identity of the two pieces ('Livery Stable Blues', as found in sheet music form published by Ray Graham, and 'Barnyard Blues', as recorded by the ODJB) is not particularly instructive. There is every reason to think that the two pieces *were* more or less identical. In contrast, two specific features of the first case stand out. First, even if Nunez's claim that 'nobody wrote the "Livery Stable Blues"' is far too strong to take seriously, the less forceful claim that its formation had been due to a collaborative effort appears relatively believable. Exactly what had been needed to hash up the 'More Power Blues' is unknowable at this point. Yet, it likewise seems implausible to think that 'Livery Stable Blues' was *simply* a product of LaRocca's own creation. Instead, something along the lines of the collaborative story as told by Nunez is much more likely to have been the case. Here, it is important to note that the *recording* is, by necessity, much more than a simple melody and chords. Instead, it reflects the collaborative improvising that a group like the ODJB did as a matter of course. And the difference between the tune as performed and in its simplest form (i.e. melody and chords) would necessarily be quite significant.

Second, the recognition of this complexity leads to an interesting point regarding the recording. While it might be thought that a recording would serve to *establish* the identity of a song, the case of the 'Livery Stable Blues' would lead one to think otherwise. Or, to put it another way, the kind of ideality that implies a stable identity, which according to Husserl can be provided by writing, is not guaranteed by a recording. What Husserl means by 'ideality' is the potential for an entity to remain exactly the same despite being manifested in various tokens or instances (on his account, *Pride and Prejudice* remains the same whether printed in an inexpensive paperback edition or bound in leather). This is not to say that recording in no way serves to provide a degree of identity. Rather, it is to note that this identity is still not fully 'ideal' (in Husserl's sense of being completely unchanging).[17] At most, a recording captures a moment in time. That moment, at least in this case, is neither simple nor discrete. It is, instead, a moment that is the product of many and varied pasts. Moreover, it is the gateway to many and varied futures. For, even though many jazz musicians no doubt tried to duplicate such pieces as 'Livery Stable Blues', those duplications would almost certainly have varied from the original.

Third, the borrowing that forced the Victor company to add 'Introducing "That Teasin' Rag"' to the 'Dixieland Jass Band One-Step' is so much a part of jazz today that such complaints about stealing licks are few and far between. In contrast to what Harold Bloom calls 'the anxiety of influence' (Bloom, 1973), i.e. the desire to be an independent creator, John P. Murphy has spoken of the 'joy of influence' that characterizes most jazz musicians (Murphy, 1990). One of the examples Murphy uses is what in jazz is known as 'quotation'. Quoting another jazz musician is considered a way of *honoring* that musician. In other words, jazz musicians simply expect such borrowing to take place – and are honored when it does.

That 'Mournin' Blues' went unchallenged is, I think, significant. One could argue, of course, that the ODJB members, past and present, were simply tired of lawsuits, and therefore unwilling to take up the challenge. But just as plausible an explanation would be that jazz musicians were beginning to recognize that what they were doing was in effect borrowing from one another in a collaborative effort. Certainly that has become a common assumption in jazz performance practice over the past century. That these lawsuits happened at the beginning of jazz – rather than more recently, in an age in which lawsuits are generally much more common – tells us that jazz musicians had to work through the implications of an improvisatory craft in which borrowing was fundamental. It also tells us something about recording, namely that it was simply not powerful enough to 'fix' the identity of any improvisation so firmly that it would not be susceptible to being appropriated and reworked by other jazz musicians.

All of this has significant implications for both the identity and the dissemination of jazz licks. Returning to Husserl's account of how writing serves to fix an ideal object, which can be anything that is repeatable and has an identity that transcends any particular instantiation, we can see that recording of licks both documents those licks, thus making them 'someone's' property, and simultaneously makes them available for others. At least in jazz, recording has from the beginning played this dual role. Of course, this is understandable, given that in Husserl's view an ideal object (in this case, a lick) is not fully ideal until it becomes fixed by way of writing (in this case, recording). The result is that recording is both powerful and impotent. It is powerful enough to give identity to a lick and connect it to a particular performer, but it is powerless to keep that lick from being appropriated by someone else. Or perhaps, we should put this more strongly: in effect, recording serves as a remarkable medium for making just such borrowing of licks possible. Rather than shut that jazz interaction down, it has instead opened it up. As we noted earlier, this is precisely what had worried Plato about writing. Once something is written – or recorded – one loses control over it. The problem with writing is that it both documents and creates the possibility of something taking on a life of its own, which can lead to its meaning either being fixed or morphing into something that the author never intended. Translating this into jazz performance practice, the lick that gets recorded is no longer directly (but only indirectly) connected to its author. Moreover, it is much more susceptible to being co-opted and re-worked by any other jazz player.

Consider how Derrida describes the difference between speaking and writing, comparing the latter to an orphan:

> The status of this orphan, whose welfare cannot be assured by any attendance or assistance, coincides with that of a *graphein* which, being nobody's son at the instant it reaches inscription, scarcely remains a son at all and no longer *recognizes* its origins, whether legally or morally. In contrast to writing, living *logos* is alive in that it has a living father (whereas the orphan is already half dead), a father that is *present, standing* near it, behind it, sustaining it with his rectitude, attending it in person in his own name.
>
> (Derrida, 1981: 77)

Although Derrida overstates the case here, the point is clear enough. Writing – or, *mutatis mutandis*, recording – makes something into an orphan by removing its clear connection to its author. However, it strikes me that this claim is only half true. Most jazz recordings are rather closely connected to their authors, i.e. the performers who make them. Indeed, one could argue exactly the opposite (as I have above), namely that recordings serve to *establish* the identity of licks with particular performers. Yet Derrida's point that writing allows for a disconnection is likewise valid. Recordings can disseminate licks so that they become common property. Rather than being orphans, we might say that they become children of the entire jazz village. Of course, one can argue that it is precisely this ability of licks to become common property that has enabled jazz to flourish. Stealing licks, then, is central to the health of jazz performance. Rather than being something over which to sue, it is something to be celebrated.

Notes

1   Whether a 'riff' is similar to a 'lick' is a question I shall not tackle here. Instead, I will confine my attention to what jazz musicians call 'licks'.

2   Of course, licks *can* become part of the tune itself and, in some famous cases, have indeed done so. Probably the best-known example is Thelonious Monk's 'Round Midnight'. Although Monk wrote the tune, some accounts would have it that when Cootie Williams recorded it in 1944, he added some embellishments. In any case, the official copyright for the tune included both Monk and Williams. Then, when Dizzy Gillespie recorded it in 1946, he added an eight-measure introduction and a coda. The result was a change in the copyright to include Gillespie as another of the composers of the tune. In 1955, Miles Davis added a three-measure interlude. Although Davis did not get included in the copyright, jazz musicians generally play the tune with all of these embellishments. For a short history of 'Round Midnight', see Berliner (1994: 88). A much more detailed account (with sheet music examples) is found in Bowen (1993: 151–7).

3   Here, I follow the lead of Bowen (1993: 143–5).

4   The problematic nature of the origins of jazz is universally recognized. See, for example, the discussions in Floyd (2000), Taylor (2000) and Youngren (2000). Also see Ake (2002: 10–41).

5   See Derrida's critique of this interior conversation in 'The Voice that Keeps Silence', Derrida (1973: 70–87).

6   One might consider an interesting counterfactual question: if recording technology had not been invented, would jazz have the array of licks that it has available today? While no real answer can be given to counterfactual questions, one can only speculate that the stock of jazz licks would be infinitely poorer.

7   *Merriam–Webster's Collegiate Dictionary* (2003) includes the following under the definition for 'improvisation': 'to make or fabricate out of what is conveniently on hand.' For jazz musicians, chords, melodies, and lick are 'what is conveniently on hand'.

8   One interesting question that Berliner sidesteps is whether there is any *earlier* instantiation of this lick. Is the 'first' example really the first? Or does it build on some other improvisatory lick? Given the fact that licks are traces of the past, such a genealogy could conceivably go back quite far. Moreover, it might turn out to be difficult to arrive at an agreement as to whether an earlier lick really was related to a later one.

9   That writing is a *pharmakon* comes out particularly clearly in the following section of *Phaedrus*, as translated in Derrida (1972/1981: 96–7): 'Here, O King, says Theuth, is a

discipline (*mathêma*) [i.e. writing] that will make the Egyptians wiser (*sophôterous*) and will improve their memories (*mnêmonikôterous*): both memory (*mnêmê*) and instruction (*sophia*) have found their remedy (*pharmakon*)'.

10 Mark Katz makes this point as well as any (2004: 48–84). Of course, there is a famous example (or at least an urban legend) of this working the other way around. So the story goes, the length of the CD was chosen by Sony president Norio Ohga, who found that seventy-four minutes perfectly accommodated his beloved Beethoven's Ninth Symphony. In any case, sometimes technology dictates; sometimes it is the music (or movies or some other art form) that dictates technology's contours. For more on this story, see http://www. snopes.com/music/media/cdlength.htm

11 There are many examples of contemporary concern for intellectual property rights and control thereof. Two books that consider such questions are McLeod (2001), and McSherry (2001).

12 The question of race and jazz is one that I have addressed elsewhere. It is an important, even if highly controversial, discussion. See Benson (2006).

13 For this account, I am dependent on what is assuredly the most extensive study of this case, i.e. the one by Brunn (1960).

14 It is unclear to me why the term 'barnyard' was more acceptable than 'livery stable'. Perhaps this is simply a feature of the English language changing over time in such a way that the connotations of these two terms have morphed, and we can no longer detect a significant difference between the two.

15 'Livery Stable Blues' and 'Dixie Jass Band One-Step' first appeared as two sides of a 78rpm by Victor with issue number 18255. Both were recorded on 26 February 1917.

16 'Mournin' Blues' was first issued by Victor in 1918 (#18513). Modern reproductions of these recordings can be found on *The Original Dixieland Jazz Band: First Jazz Recordings 1917/1923*, vol.2 (Jazz Archives #82; 158492).

17 There is a similarity between Husserl's sense of ideality and Platonic 'ideas'. Once an entity comes into existence, it is like a Platonic idea. But, for Husserl, entities have an origin. For Plato, 'ideas' are eternal.

References

Ake, D. (2002) *Jazz Cultures*. Berkeley: University of California Press.

Bakhtin, M.M. (1991) *The Dialogic Imagination: Four Essays*. Trans. C. Emerson and M. Holquist. Austin: University of Texas Press. Original (1975) as *Voprosy literatury i estetiki*. Moscow: Khudozh.

Benson, B.E. (2003) *The Improvisation of Musical Dialogue: A Phenomenology of Music*. Cambridge: Cambridge University Press.

_____ (2006) 'The Fundamental Heteronomy of Jazz Improvisation', *Revue internationale de philosophie* 4: 453–67.

Berliner, P.F. (1994) *Thinking in Jazz: The Infinite Art of Improvisation*. Chicago: University of Chicago Press.

Bowen, J.A. (1993) 'The History of Remembered Innovation: Tradition and Its Role in the Relationship between Musical Works and Their Performances', *The Journal of Musicology* 11: 139–73.

Bloom, H. (1973) *The Anxiety of Influence*. New York: Oxford University Press.

Brunn, H.O. (1960) *The Story of the Original Dixieland Jazz Band*. Baton Rouge: Louisiana State University Press.

Derrida, J. (1973) *Speech and Phenomena and Other Essays on Husserl's Theory of Signs*. Trans. D.B. Allison. Evanston: Northwestern University Press. Original (1967) as *La voix et le phénomène: Introduction au problème du signe dans la phénoménologie de Husserl*. Paris: Presses Universitaires de France.

_____ (1981) *Dissemination*. Trans. B. Johnson. Chicago: University of Chicago Press. Original (1972) as *La Dissémination*. Paris: Seuil.

Floyd, S.A. Jr. (2000) 'African Roots of Jazz', in B. Kirchner (ed.) *The Oxford Companion to Jazz*, pp.7–16. Oxford: Oxford University Press.

Gadamer, H.-G. (1989) *Truth and Method*, second rev. edn. Trans. J. Weinsheimer and D. G. Marshall. New York: Crossroad. Original (1960) as *Warheit und Methode*. Tübingen: Mohr.

Giola, T. (1997) *The History of Jazz*. New York: Oxford University Press.

Gracyk, T. (2000) *Popular American Recording Pioneers, 1895–1925*. Binghamton, NY: Haworth.

Hegel, G.F.W. (1975) *Aesthetics: Lectures on Fine Art*. Trans. T.M. Knox. Oxford: Oxford University Press. Original (1842–3) as *Vorlesungen über die Aesthetik*. Berlin: Duncker und Humblot.

Husserl, E. (1970) 'The Origin of Geometry', in D. Carr (trans) *The Crisis of European Sciences and Transcendental Phenomenology: An Introduction to Phenomenological Philosophy*, pp.353–78. Evanston: Northwestern University Press. Original (1939) as 'Der Ursprung der Geometrie als intentional-historisches Problem', *Revue internationale de philosophie* 1: 207–25.

_____ (1991) *On the Phenomenology of the Consciousness of Internal Time*. Trans. J. Brough. Dordrecht: Kluwer. Original (1928) as *Vorlesungen zur Phänomenologie des inneren Zeitbewusstseins*. Tübingen: Niemeyer.

Jordan, J. (1909) 'That Teasin' Rag'. Chicago: Joseph B. Stern and Co.

Katz, M. (2004) *Capturing Sound: How Technology Has Changed Music*. Berkeley: University of California Press.

Leonard, N. (1962) *Jazz and the White Americans: The Acceptance of a New Art Form*. Chicago: University of Chicago Press.

McLeod, K. (2001) Owning *Culture: Authorship, Ownership, and Intellectual Property Law*. New York: Peter Lang.

McSherry, C. (2001) *Who Owns Academic Work? Battling for Control of Intellectual Property*. Cambridge, MA: Harvard University Press.

Mish, F.C. (ed.) (2003) *Merriam–Webster's Collegiate Dictionary*, eleventh edn. Springfield, MA: Merriam–Webster.

Murphy, J.P. (1990) 'Jazz Improvisation: The Joy of Influence', *The Black Perspective in Music* 18: 7–19.

Plato (1961) 'Phaedrus', in E.Hamilton and H.Cairns (eds) *The Collected Dialogues*, pp.476–525. Princeton, NJ: Princeton University Press.

Quintilian (1922) *Institutio Oratio*, vol. 4. Trans. H.E. Butler. Cambridge, Mass: Harvard University Press.

Shapiro, N. and Hentoff, N. (eds) (1955) *Hear Me Talkin' To Ya: The Story of Jazz As Told By the Men Who Made It*. New York: Dover.

Schneidman, J. (2000) *1001 Jazz Licks: A Complete Jazz Vocabulary for the Improvising Musician*. New York: Cherry Lane.

Taylor, J. (2000) 'The Early Origins of Jazz', in B. Kirchner (ed.) *The Oxford Companion to Jazz*, pp.39–52. Oxford: Oxford University Press.

Witmer, R. 'Lick', *Grove Music Online*, URL (consulted June 2006): http://www.grovemusic.com/shared/views/article.html?section=music.49259

Wittgenstein, L. (2002) *Philosophical Investigations: The German Text, with a Revised English Translation*. Trans. G.E.M. Anscombe. Oxford: Blackwell. First published posthumously (1953) in a German–English edition.

Youngren, W.H. (2000) 'European Roots of Jazz', in B. Kirchner (ed.) *The Oxford Companion to Jazz*, pp.17–28. Oxford: Oxford University Press.

Discography

Original Dixieland Jazz Band, vol. 2: First Jazz Recordings 1917/1923. (1995) Jazz Archives #82 CD 158492.

TONY WHYTON

Acting on Impulse!: Recordings and the Reification of Jazz

Introduction

I N his article 'Rock 'n' Recording: the Ontological Complexity of Rock Music'
(1998), John Andrew Fisher argues for a reconceptualisation of rock music and its
relationship to recordings. Fisher suggests that in rock the recording should be
understood as the primary text and that the relationship between the music and the
recording is unique, especially when compared to score-based classical music and
performance-oriented jazz (Fisher, 1998: 110). As a researcher concerned with the
cultural study of jazz, I am interested in exploring how such common understandings
of the music can be challenged and, more importantly, how – following the promotion
of jazz as a canonical art form – the ontological status of the music is changing.
Echoing Fisher's philosophical take on rock music, I argue for a reconceptualisation
of jazz where the recording takes centre stage, not only by transforming experiences
and understanding of the music but also by embodying the values, aspirations and
myth-making tendencies of its listeners. Through a discussion of the proliferation
of historical reissues, I suggest that the power and influence of recording over jazz
discourse is widely underestimated, even if its central role in the development of the
music is acknowledged. The relationship between jazz performance and recording
has moved from one of synergy to a form of hegemony, with the historical recording
dominating current jazz practices by stealth.

In this context, I conceptualise historical jazz as a reified object rather than a
sonic experience, and develop an intertextual reading of John Coltrane's studio
recordings on the Impulse! label, exploring how reissues appeal to jazz listeners
and have the ability to influence behaviour. I suggest that historical recordings are
used as vehicles to instil jazz with heightened aesthetic status, helping to promote
the music as an autonomous art form. This process creates an ontological shift that
moves the music away from its social context towards a celebration of it as mysterious
and transcendent of the everyday world. In exploring this concept, I discuss
the ideological motivations behind the promotion of historical jazz recordings as
canonical artefacts and use Christopher Small's (1998) theory of 'musicking' to
examine the ways in which recordings reflect the desires for myth-making and icon
worship amongst present-day jazz audiences.

Recordings and the jazz canon

The status of jazz as a canonical art form is very much dependent on the legacy of its recorded history; the recording offers itself as the primary vehicle for the canonisation of jazz, and the history of jazz recordings is most often used as the benchmark for standards and quality of performances. This reliance on a mass-produced document – the recording – differentiates jazz from other art forms, such as Renaissance painting, where the appreciation of an original remains central to the discourse. In the context of jazz music, notions of the 'original' artwork and the singularity of authorship can prove problematic in terms of analysis, as the canonicity of jazz is built upon a number of divergences from more established canonical discourses. For example, unlike most Western art music, where a relatively fixed score forms the basis for numerous interpretations and recordings, the jazz performance stands alone as an independent, unrepeatable event, shaped by the improvisatory skills of the performer. As soon as it is frozen in time the fleeting creative idea becomes a permanent artefact for subsequent generations to explore and replay. This raises interesting issues in relation to the meaning, value and context of jazz performances. I suggest below that jazz on record presents a number of historical and cultural challenges that differentiate it from, say, classical music or rock, and this complexity feeds back into our relationship with the music itself. In jazz, the distinction between the composer and the performer is often blurred; whether a performer is performing his own original material or adapting and improvising on the music of others, the recording solidifies each improvisation, turning it into a permanent composition. Furthermore, although jazz is often discussed and described as an art form that celebrates group dynamic and interaction, the recording encourages the listener to engage in a focused relationship with a solo artist. The conflation of performer and composer only serves to intensify this relationship, which privileges the iconic solo artist at the expense of other group members. Finally, while the issues surrounding jazz on record may be similar to those surrounding rock music as far as its iconic recordings and obsessive record collectors are concerned, jazz is increasingly discussed in terms that are used to evaluate and understand classical music.[1]

Perhaps due to a lack of distinction between live and recorded jazz (Rasula, 1995) and the myth that jazz is somehow an unmediated experience (Gabbard, 2004a; Whyton, 2006), jazz recordings are often celebrated as having ephemeral qualities that promote the music as improvisatory or 'in the moment'. Gary Tomlinson (1992) and Georgina Born (2005), for example, have examined how jazz records can be used to undermine the concept of the 'musical work' in Western classical music, their improvisatory quality challenging the idea of fixed interpretations of music. In contrast to this dominant understanding of jazz as performative 'text', I argue that the growing trend of reissuing historical jazz recordings transforms the music from a radical, fleeting and communal practice into a conformist, reified and autonomous art form. This shift in ontological status parallels the development of classical music, as discussed by Small (1998) and Lydia Goehr (1992), who suggest that at a certain historical moment Western society became obsessed with the interpretation of works rather than with performance events themselves, and that music started to be discussed as a reified object instead of a social activity. In effect, by treating jazz recordings as canonical artefacts, we transform the music from an action to an abstraction, from verb to noun, text to work.[2]

The recorded legacy of jazz also gains a heightened significance as the desire for a definitive jazz canon develops. Through the documentation the recording provides, jazz is legitimised; musicians, writers and jazz enthusiasts use the recording and its history to construct a lineage of significant historical milestones. In this respect, recordings are not only essential to the study of jazz history but also problematic for writers wishing to develop an objective picture of the music's past. For example, Jed Rasula describes recordings as a 'seductive menace' (Rasula, 1995: 134), accounting for the fact that while records are essential to historians in constructing a definable and legitimate history for jazz, through their cultural dominance, they at the same time skew understandings of the past and limit our perspective on jazz history. Frank Kermode (1988) suggests that canonised artworks are complex and contradictory in that they can be understood as being at the same time firmly locked in time, and as having the ability to transcend time. I suggest that when viewed as permanent artefacts canonical records not only unlock doors into the historical environment within which they were born, but can also embody a romanticised view of history such that nothing in the present can compete with the past. Ironically, this point is further complicated by the fact that jazz recordings dating from the 1970s onwards are detached from established landmarks of the music's past and often described in diverse and fragmented terms linked to the breakdown of the genealogical framework of jazz history.[3] Canonised recordings are promoted as having inherent value; they are considered to be 'great' since they have supposedly stood the test of time. Simultaneously, and paradoxically, the canonised recording is set free of time and place; it is presented as autonomous, divorced from its original context and transcendent of social forces.[4] The canonised recording serves to reinforce myths of universality and transcendence; freed from the constraints of the everyday world, it is deemed to have a fixed worth, regardless of context. Additionally, new meanings are assigned to canonised works over time, their status gaining an enhanced significance as history is rewritten. What was originally an ordinary, average-selling release can come to be regarded as a seminal work of masterpiece status when constructing history from the present.

When new meanings are created and canonical status is achieved, it becomes ever less likely that the recording is received as an object of negative criticism. For example, in his book *Satchmo*, Gary Giddins describes Louis Armstrong's LP of Disney songs – previously not regarded as a great work of the jazz canon – as 'a masterpiece of its kind...the ultimate test of his alchemical powers' (Giddins, 2001: 147). Furthermore, canonical reverence is seen throughout the jazz community on a regular basis. Take, for example, Pat Metheny's outburst at Kenny G for daring to create a track overdubbing a performance of jazz legend Armstrong (Washburne and Derno, 2004: 123), which ironically followed Metheny's previous desire to throw off the shackles of jazz convention. Similarly, people rarely discuss the music of the living jazz 'great' Sonny Rollins in the same way as iconic Coltrane, the 'spiritual master' of jazz. This point is unwittingly alluded to in an article on Rollins published in 2001 and titled 'Approaching Enlightenment', which discusses the spiritual side of Rollins and his status as a jazz legend (Panken, 2001). However, as the title of the article suggests, the performer has not yet achieved the iconic status of Coltrane – perhaps death is the only thing that divides the two artists?[5] Here, jazz mirrors the world of classical music through reverence for bygone artists; as Small has maintained, for most people, 'a great composer is almost by definition a dead composer' (Small, 1998: 87).

As major players in the construction of the jazz canon, record companies have a vested interest in promoting the legacy of 'great' music, not only because reissues, bonus tracks and master editions feed the consumer desire for the 'authentic' experience, but also because a relatively small promotional budget will help sell a back catalogue reliably and consistently. I argue that record companies promote historical recordings as reified masterpieces, and present each jazz recording not only as representing a snapshot of a historic period but, despite its mass production, also as a unique creation. Indeed, the proliferation of transcriptions of recorded improvisations, and even re-recordings of historic recorded performances, are testament to the power and effects of reification.[6] Within the context of canon building, record companies set out to distinguish between everyday releases and the established 'classics' of jazz history. This has led certain companies to rationalise their output, and designate specific labels for reissues. For example, in the case of Universal Music, Verve has taken on the role of the main label for newly recorded jazz in recent years, whilst Impulse! – the label historically associated with the jazz vanguard – has produced mainly historic reissues. The promotion of the recorded legacy of jazz has reached new heights, not only in the technological advances of digital re-mastering and editing, but also in the repackaging of original and 'authentic' products. Given this background, it is difficult at times to know where the contemporary artist fits in, as new artists are at risk of not recouping valuable investment capital. Indeed, in promoting the value of reissues, producers such as Michael Cuscuna have commented on the fragmented relationship between contemporary jazz artists and major recording companies, as major labels are committed to promoting back catalogues and celebrating jazz's iconic legacy (Cuscuna, 2005). The problems faced by record companies are echoed in the nature of contemporary jazz music; there is a conflict between innovation and the subservience to a defined tradition. Once again, the canon thrusts artists into a position of feeling that they need to either 'pay their dues' or reject convention in search of the innovative or eclectic. Either way, the music's historical legacy provides the basis from which to proceed.

Case study: John Coltrane,
The Complete Impulse! Studio Recordings

The following case study demonstrates the problems inherent in the promotion and reception of jazz recordings as mystical and transcendent artworks. These problems are exacerbated by recording companies devoted both to promoting a legacy of great recordings and supporting contemporary artists who perform 'new' works. Using the Impulse! label as a case study, I explore the company's strategies in promoting iconic jazz recordings through an analysis of Coltrane's *The Complete Impulse! Studio Recordings* released in 1998, and demonstrate how political issues, by means of affirming the implicit ideology, and philosophical concepts, such as the shifting cultural aesthetic of jazz, permeate everyday situations. I discuss the significance of historical recordings and the consumer desire for icon worship, and go on to examine the implications and effects of canonisation on the current jazz scene. The Impulse! record label has always been heavily associated with cutting-edge marketing and design, recognising from the outset the potential for collectability in jazz recordings. The label is also particularly interesting because of its integral links to the later career of Coltrane, arguably the most revered icon in jazz, and his Classic Quartet, celebrated as one of the most creative ensembles in the music's history.[7] When exploring the relationship between recordings and the jazz canon, the label also provides an interesting case study for analysis as many of their releases – most notably, Coltrane's *A Love Supreme*, featured as part of the complete collection – were self-consciously promoted as canonical at the time of their release. In this respect, the label not only comments on current tastes and values, but has also played an explicit part in the historical construction of the jazz canon.

(1)   Acquiring culture

Scott DeVeaux discusses the widespread desire of the mainstream jazz community to elevate jazz to the status of 'America's Classical Music', instilling the music with a degree of cultural capital (DeVeaux, 1999). Echoing this phenomenon, I would suggest that the Coltrane collection demonstrates an extreme example of the record company's (and the consumer's) desire to elevate recordings to a higher aesthetic status. The product is designed to be a definitive collection of recordings from a significant period in jazz history. The iconic status of Coltrane is also emphasised within the physical material of the product; the single word 'COLTRANE' is displayed on both spine and outer and inner covers, an acknowledgement that the surname itself has become a cultural institution. Accompanying the name on the outer cover is an image of Coltrane in a typically reflective, spiritual and non-performative pose. Coltrane has become the embodiment of both the physical and spiritual quests of jazz; he represents the complete physical and emotive jazz icon whilst transcending the physicality of his art through his spirituality. The Coltrane collection feeds the consumer's multi-faceted desire to collect. In his book *The Recording Angel* (2005), Eisenberg discusses the impact of recordings on Western culture and draws some insights into the human desire to collect, and his ideas feed directly into the issues at play in the Coltrane release. Eisenberg suggests that recording represents the historical imperative to capture fleeting musical events in a physical form; this recording, as a supposedly definitive collection, encourages consumers to believe that they own a slice of history – a passing musical event is reified and captured for eternity.

In the Coltrane collection, several devices are used to give the consumer a sense of owning a special part of history. The sleeve notes are packed with accounts and testimonies of the period and the recordings themselves are presented to the listener as if in a pure, unadulterated form, outside the rigours of the standard post-production process. The following quotation is embossed on the inside cover of the collection:

> It felt like a perfect blend, a joy. It was always a joy, in a recording studio or a nightclub. It was the same feeling, in front of a large audience or no one at all. Music was our sole purpose.

> (Elvin Jones)

Here, the sentiment – considered authentic as it is spoken by one of the quartet members – reiterates the fact that these recordings were made at a special moment in Coltrane's career. Therefore, the release is presented as though it is an act of witnessing; as consumers, we are encouraged to accept that it is not about money, audiences, fame or product, but is art for art's sake. Delving deeper into this idea, Impulse! uses every means necessary to construct a sense of a priceless, authentic and original artefact within the release. In the past, a jazz recording might well be accompanied by a third party endorsement – a critic or musician – or some stylish photography, but essentially the recorded sound would speak for itself; in the majority of cases, the supporting material would remain implicit and subordinate to the recorded material. However, I would argue that *ownership* of the Coltrane recording engenders a sense of value as well as perceived authenticity as a tactile experience. Unusually, the collection is bound in imitation leather and encased in metal; permanent materials that not only age well but also retain a timeless quality. When compared to a conventional plastic CD jewel case, this presentation commands both a distinct material value as well as a physical sense of permanence. The timeless quality of the outer casing is reinforced on the inside, where the sleeve notes are printed in the format of an original recording log sheet. The chosen font is evocative of the period and the text is printed askew, as if the daily recording schedules have been pieced together for this occasion only.

This set of recordings fuels our desire for collection whilst promoting itself as an exclusive object. The metal casing shrouding the collection is deliberately aged with imitation rust and the design of the sleeve is such that opening the case requires a sense of determined effort. We are thus encouraged to receive this CD as if it has been taken directly from the vaults of the Impulse! archive. From this perspective, the definitive, imitation leather-bound collection is released for the discerning jazz connoisseur as a genuine and authentic artefact of history, a trophy within the world of record collecting. Whereas record collecting as trophy hunting is perhaps more synonymous with the world of vinyl releases, many current CD releases are designed to appeal to consumers who wish to continue to set themselves apart from the everyday collector. In this way, the Coltrane collection appeals to the jazz collector on a number of levels; not only does the set have a certain high cost – obvious in its presentation – it also presents itself as something unique, not appealing to every taste.

Although the product conveys a sense of 'worth', the recording privileges content above commercial value; it defines itself as having almost archival status. This non-commercial view of the work can be seen in the quotation from Jones given above and is also demonstrated by the way in which the recordings are taken out of their original commercial context. Each track and recording in this set is identified firstly by name and secondly by date and catalogue number. This factual archivist information is then interspersed with either technical or aesthetic reasons as to why some recordings were chosen over others for general commercial release. The release of previously unacceptable material in a commercial context would perhaps be something to frown upon, with record companies seen as 'cashing in' on substandard material. For contemporary artists, the release of previously rejected works would signify both a lack of ability and poor judgement, and would undermine the quality of their musicianship. By contrast, Coltrane and his Classic Quartet have now reached a status where all their material is *worth* something.

(2)   The quest for enlightenment

The significance of Coltrane's spiritual iconic status should not be underestimated. Arguably, the artist commands the most intense spiritual persona of all jazz 'masters'. David Ake comments on how the spiritual dimension of Coltrane has been taken to extremes:

> [T]he existence of San Francisco's St John's African Orthodox Church, where parishioners revere the late saxophonist John Coltrane as 'the divine sound Baptist', reveals the degree to which many listeners (and not just church members) view the musician as one deeply and singularly attuned to a 'higher power'.
>
> (Ake, 2002b: 257)

Here, Coltrane is worshipped as a saint, his recorded music performed as part of weekly religious rituals. This is obviously an extreme form of reverence; however, this example demonstrates the potential of jazz icons to inspire their fans to associate spiritual adoration and the quest for enlightenment with their favourite recordings and related paraphernalia.

The Coltrane collection features an altruistic commentary from executive producer Cuscuna in which he discusses the previously undiscovered material of this release. Throughout his accompanying testimony, Cuscuna talks of the 'endless hours' spent listening to the quartet and the way in which they provided him with 'ecstatic' and 'formative' experiences. As collectors, we are encouraged not only to delve into the recordings but also to devote time and energy to listening. Here, another jazz mythology is reiterated; only through time and effort will the listener be able to gain access to the hidden secrets of the recording and the musicians at play – in this world even listeners have to 'pay their dues'. The collector's quest for understanding has a deep resonance with the world of jazz scholarship, as those with the biggest and most comprehensive collections are often considered, albeit misguidedly, as the ones with the most knowledge. Within this context, definitive recordings can have the paradoxical effect of not only promoting devoted listening but also encouraging collectors to have a love of culture without having an interest in it – a love that is satisfied by ownership rather than listening.[8]

This resonates throughout the presentation of the Coltrane collection; the difficulty of accessing the individual recordings gives the collector a heightened sense of reward when consuming the material. Works are not presented to the listener for their convenience or user-friendliness; this differs entirely from the world of commercial pop music, where releases are designed for immediate consumption.[9] The determined effort required to access the individual recordings also taps into the collector's desire for displaying cultural objects. The stunning presentation of the collection serves almost as status symbol or a piece of interior design; the encased CDs are easier to display than to play. As a cultural object, the collection echoes Roland Barthes' concept of 'the work', which leads the owner into a position of worship rather than active, critical consumption (Barthes, 1977). Barthes' writings on the idea of 'the work' help to uncover the dangers involved in the process of canon formation. Within a work-like state, the artwork is a definable entity bound up with a single-strand 'authentic' history, the iconic author figure represented as a conduit for divine inspiration.

In his study, titled 'Free, Single and Disengaged', John Corbett describes the quest for an enlightened experience within recordings as a form of 'fetishistic audiophilia' (Corbett, 1994: 42). For Corbett, the alleviation of surface noise, scratching and hissing on contemporary recordings instils in the consumer the belief that music is detached from the everyday world; in effect, there is a purity of experience bound up through recordings. Corbett states:

> To render music free of noise is to grant it its proper musical status as sonically autonomous...Surface noise indicates the surface, a reminder of the visible topography of recorded musical objects.

(Corbett, 1994: 41)

According to Corbett, the recording presents consumers with an interesting dichotomy: the conflict between wanting to restore the visual dimension of the disembodied voice, and wanting to create a 'natural' autonomous sonic experience. Corbett suggests that rather than being in opposition to each other, these two fetishistic tendencies co-exist. The Coltrane collection is a good example, encouraging the consumer to get closer to the artist either in physical terms, through the wealth of supporting documentary materials, or metaphysical terms, through its simultaneous heightening of the mystery of the sonic experience.

(3) Nostalgia

Recent studies of advertising and consumption have commented on the significance of nostalgia within consumer practices. In his study of nostalgia in contemporary advertising, for example, Andrew Wernick (1997) relates nostalgia both to a desire for a home-coming – born out of dissatisfaction with the contemporary world – and the need to belong. The Coltrane collection reinforces this interpretation of nostalgia through promoting a sense of belonging, a feeling of completeness and a return to the values of the past. Not only does the collection comment on the historicising process, it also reflects Coltrane's iconic significance today. With its retro-packaging, photographs, musical out-takes, and testimonies, the work presents itself as a direct link to history, offering a window into a bygone era. It appeals not only to the nostalgic tendencies of consumers, but also to the fetishistic nature of record collectors. Corbett describes the contradictions at play within this process – the desire for identification on the one hand, and the need for individuality on the other – as the two modes of commodity fetishism; both fetishes remain mutually supportive within the development of the capitalist marketplace (Corbett, 1994: 34). Indeed, the Coltrane collection gains its own cult status and value that set it apart from the everyday consumable object; to use Eisenberg's description, 'the true hero of consumption is a rebel against consumption' (Eisenberg, 2005: 15). In turn, the owner of the work is made to feel part of a unique set of collectors, a part of a discrete and distinguished jazz community.

The futility of the fetishistic collector's nostalgic quest for the definitive recording was demonstrated four years after the release of the *Complete Impulse! Studio Recordings* when Impulse! issued additional 'new' material as part of a subsequent Coltrane release. Ashley Kahn described the situation:

> Yet there are times when the best music and best intentions are simply not enough to make the reissue business an easy one. Take, for example, the recent 'Deluxe Editions' of the 1962 albums *Coltrane* and *Ballads*, which include the original released material plus a wealth of unused takes and false starts. 'In '98, we put out the popular *Classic Quartet* box with a great booklet and eight discs,' reports Ken Druker, Verve's head of catalog development, 'and called it *The Complete Impulse! Studio Recordings*.' Meanwhile, [Bob] Thiele, who passed away

two years previously, had donated his collection of recordings and LPs to his New
Jersey high school, which eventually passed the reel-to-reel tapes on to Rutgers
University's Institute for Jazz Studies. There, Institute head Dan Morgenstern
auditioned the tapes in 2000 and, realizing that some were never-heard Coltrane
session masters, returned them to Verve. Adds Druker: 'So we immediately began
working on them for release in 2002. They came out and of course the e-mails
started – "Why did we hold these back in '98?"; "Do we know what the word
complete means?" [*laughs*]. You can't win.'

(Kahn, 2006: 276)

This account neatly articulates both the consumer desire to own the definitive
collection and the simultaneous futility of searching for the complete recorded
experience. However, rather than viewing this type of situation as a product
of circumstance, some commentators question the motives of record companies
who decide to release additional material after issuing 'complete' collections. For
example, historian and broadcaster Phil Schapp examined the strategies of record
companies at the IAJE jazz convention in 2003, discussing both the repackaging
and the 'holding back' of recordings by Armstrong and Ella Fitzgerald as a means of
further stimulating consumer desire to collect. As part of his presentation, Schapp
read out an extensive list of Armstrong/Fitzgerald album releases, all of which were
marketed as 'new material'. However, on closer inspection, all albums consisted of
the same (very limited) recording material, albeit in different presentations, with the
exception of one track, which did not appear on any recording (Schapp, 2003).

Whilst it is often stated that great music speaks for itself, there is no denying
the importance of the visual appeal of recorded products. Historically, the Impulse!
label was at the forefront of album cover design; its gatefolded LPs all displayed the
distinctive black and orange spine, the company's trade exclamation mark designed
to emphasise the impact of the label on the scene.[10] Indeed, many of the company's
early titles were designed to build on the distinctiveness of its visual identity, carving
out a unique place within the jazz recording market and embodying the values of
jazz as 'art'.[11] Arguably, the arrival of Coltrane in 1961 cemented Impulse!'s identity
as an innovative and progressive label, as well as confirming its status in the jazz
market. Coltrane's *Africa Brass* was only the sixth release under the new label's
banner; however, the work of the artist has defined the marketing strategy for
Impulse!, even up to the present day. Creed Taylor, the brainchild behind the identity
of the newly-formed Impulse!, commented on these innovations:

> The gatefold was not being used except on very special albums, but all of the
> Impulse titles were to be gatefolds…I tried to juxtapose the visual on the album
> cover with the title itself, like Gil [Evans]'s *Out of the Cool* or Oliver Nelson's *Blues
> and the Abstract Truth*. They're all words that grab you. I mean, there's nothing
> really abstract about the blues but it's a truth…At first there was this 'who the
> heck is Oliver Nelson and what is *Blues and the Abstract Truth*?' kind of thing.

Soon enough there was a thread of 'What do you mean? It's on Impulse. It's good-looking, great-sounding stuff.'

(in Kahn, 2002: 53–4)

The visual impact of Impulse! recordings not only proved popular with collectors, they also provided inspiration to a host of other companies trying to develop a cutting-edge image. The Black Saint label, for example, was inspired by the Charles Mingus LP *The Black Saint and the Sinner Lady* released on Impulse!, and its spines in turn clearly paid homage to the Impulse! brand.

Within this framework, the Impulse! label offers a useful example of the paradox that exists within today's jazz marketplace, where back catalogues tend to dominate the contemporary marketing agenda. Indeed, since 1999 Impulse! has focused their output on reissues, with notable exceptions: *McCoy Tyner Plays John Coltrane* in 2001 and Alice Coltrane's *Translinear Light* in 2004, for example, show the continuing indebtedness to the Coltrane brand. Here, the dominance of the iconic Coltrane signals the demise of the label's investment in contemporary releases, with new releases such as Tyner's having to cite Coltrane in the album title.[12] Ironically, the figurehead of Coltrane, associated with cementing the vision of Impulse! label as a forward-looking and at times politically charged label, can now be seen to represent the downfall of the label as a promoter of contemporary jazz. Coltrane's legacy is something which overpowers the marketplace, affecting Impulse!'s commitment to contemporary releases.

This situation sums up the problems faced both by record companies and jazz musicians in an age where the construction of a jazz canon has a significant impact on contemporary music and the marketing of products. Artists face the problem of conforming to constructed benchmarks whilst simultaneously aspiring to be original. Advertisers feel a real need to establish the longevity of their jazz product; unlike the understood usage and immediacy of pop music, jazz has to cede its contemporaneity in order to achieve 'classic' status. Tradition, lineage and musical autonomy are essential requirements for an artwork to enter into the musical canon, and contemporary jazz artists are thrust into a world where they feel the need to age instantly in order to be accepted. The pressures on contemporary artists to conform to established benchmarks, and the paradox this creates impact upon jazz at many levels. Indeed, writings on jazz often reinforce the position of revering canonised works whilst criticising contemporary artists for doing the same. Take the following two quotations from the supporting essay to Geoff Dyer's literary jazz work *But Beautiful*:

> In the five years it was together the classic quartet of Coltrane, Elvin Jones, Jimmy Garrison, and McCoy Tyner – the greatest creative relationship between four men there has ever been – hauled jazz to a pitch of expressivity that has rarely been exceeded by any other artform.

(Dyer, 2000: 202)

> The long shadow of Coltrane and the question of what can still be said in the bebop idiom are part of a larger doubt facing contemporary jazz players: does any new and important work remain to be done?...Since its tradition is one of innovation and improvisation, jazz, it could be argued, is never more traditional than when it is boldly iconoclastic.

(Dyer, 2000: 207)

Here, we have an example of overly romanticised icon worship on the one hand, celebrating the unassailable achievements of the Coltrane quartet, and a criticism of contemporary music for not being able to escape the overwhelming influence of historical works, on the other. Within this context, it is easy to understand how contemporary artists can feel the need to live up to the masters of the past or are confused at the prospect of challenging established convention.

This situation feeds directly into the dominance of nostalgia within today's production and consumption of jazz. The two common definitions of nostalgia revolve around being separated from home or longing for the past; consumption of the Coltrane collection might, therefore, lead us to long for a home-coming, to desire a return to a magical age in jazz history, when the music was considered cutting edge, progressive and political. It is an irony that the nostalgia marketing of the Coltrane collection today is so at odds with the label's original aspirations in the 1960s, a perceived utopian moment of radicalism when art was created not by looking backwards but by looking forwards. When taken to their logical conclusion, nostalgic references in products such as these lead to a crisis in culture, by pointing to a bygone age that can never be recovered.[13] Once this is realised, the consumer (and contemporary artist) is placed in a vacuum where there is no way back and no straightforward means of progression. The result of this crisis leads to a cocooning where the consumer can only find solace in the 'natural' values of the past. In this sense, the nostalgic impulse says as much about our relationship to the present and the future as it does to the past, representing either current dissatisfaction or fear of the future.

From reification to deification

The Impulse! case study has shown that the issues surrounding jazz recordings are complex and relate to key themes of iconicity, collection, nostalgia, community and cultural value. I suggest that we can account for the appeal and impact of reissues such as the Coltrane collection on a number of levels. First, we could view these products as part of a wider cultural sea-change, where the jazz market now demands retro-imagery and nostalgia, but what is presented to consumers is far from the technological optimism seen in products and advertisements of the 1950s and 1960s. For example, during its formative years, the Impulse! label promoted the technological aspects of its recordings, stressing the mediated nature of the listening experience: 'And this IMPULSE promises: inspired performances given every advanced technical aid to insure supreme clarity and authenticity.'[14] Within this context, technology is something that cleanses rather than clouds, whereas today's consumers have come to expect 'fidelity' as a matter of course and are seeking an intimate and direct audio experience, devoid or transparent of technological mediation. Second, consumer desire to build musical icons could be seen as the result of the postmodern condition, the decline of contemporary belief systems and a crisis of identity. Andreas Huyssen (1986: 178–221), for example, discusses the general dissatisfaction with modernity; the resultant postmodernity finds solace either in looking back (nostalgia) or looking sideways (eclecticism). Third, we could view 'spiritual' and iconic products such as the Coltrane collection as a mode of industry manipulation; as Berger (1990) suggests, products are instilled with a sense of bogus religiosity to mask their mass-produced and mechanically-reproduced status. Although I would agree that recording companies promote certain modes of consumption through the choice, presentation and packaging of their products, the overall situation is more complex than pure industry manipulation. To view the relationship as one-sided would be to deny the complex exchanges and interactions between producers and consumers.

Finally, I would suggest that these types of recording comment on the cultural capital of jazz as an art form and its artistic value. Canonical recordings are not only promoted by opportunistic recording companies wishing to reissue their back catalogues by any, manipulative, means necessary. Iconic recordings are prevalent for a reason, as they appeal to, and reflect current tastes and consumer desires. Arguably, jazz needs recording icons to help enhance the status of the art form and to further separate it from the everyday world; these icons enable jazz to be raised to the level of an autonomous art. Equally, jazz consumers need the inherent order and focus of a select band of canonical recordings.

For example, Small has commented on the way in which people both need and draw on 'great' composers as mythological heroes of culture, using them to assert values and to provide models for behaviour and relationships (Small, 1998: 87–9). He suggests that, arguably, audiences need myths more than the individual figures themselves when celebrating iconic works; artists within the musical pantheon exist outside historical time. This goes some way to explain why living artists cannot be considered 'great', as the realities of their live 'presence' subjugate the mythologies of the past. Although Small does not focus on recording in any significant detail, I would argue that recordings play an essential part in the 'musicking' of people, i.e. the way in which they engage with music on all levels, from performing and listening to dancing. I would also stress that, in relation to the construction of mythologies, recordings offer themselves as a two-way channel of influence, both affecting and being affected by the tastes and values of listeners.[15] In this respect, mythologies are constructed and preserved to serve the needs and desires of the present day; they say as much about current society as they explain the values of the past.

The reification of jazz fundamentally changed its development; indeed, the history of jazz is so deeply entwined with the history of its significant recordings that one is often written as a history of the other. Equally, the issues surrounding jazz recordings are unique to the music, and serve to amplify its distinct values, codes, conventions and mythologies. It is perhaps surprising that this close and complex relationship so often goes unspoken in jazz musicology. If, as musicians and listeners, we delve a little deeper and explore our individual relationships to jazz recordings, we can uncover the critical significance of our own impulsive behaviour.

Notes

1   José A. Bowen (1993), for example, discusses the canonisation of jazz largely through a discussion of musical performances and their relationship to lead sheets or 'real' books. Bowen acknowledges the differences and complexities of jazz performance in comparison to classical music performances; however, when discussing the concept of the musical work, he compares jazz to the notated forms of classical music and underplays the significance of recordings in jazz. Within this context, Robert Walser (1995) has demonstrated how analytical writings in jazz that mirror methodologies established in classical music are problematic in that they both undermine the value of jazz as an art form with its own discernable history and fail to capture its signifyin(g) and intertextual qualities.

2   For an overview of the contextual and political issues surrounding the canonisation of jazz, see DeVeaux (1999) and Gabbard (1995).

3   The most notable recent example of the symbiotic relationship between jazz history and recording is Ken Burns' PBS documentary series *Jazz* (Burns, 2001), which was accompanied by its own collection of 'essential' jazz recordings (*Ken Burns Jazz*, 2000). In his recent study of this documentary, DeVeaux suggests that the five-CD package accompanying the series concludes with an example of non-descript fusion, demonstrating that Burns adheres to the belief that jazz died in the 1970s (DeVeaux, 2001–2).

4   For a detailed study of the ideology of autonomous art in jazz, see Ake (2002a) and DeVeaux (1999).

5   In the introduction to *Jazz and Death* (2002), Frederick J. Spencer examines the fascination in jazz discourse with dead artists, and how their portrayal differs from that of the living.

6   A good illustration of this is the way in which almost every solo of Coltrane or Charlie Parker has been transcribed for performance and analysis. See, for example, Owens (1995) and Porter (1998).

7   Coltrane's move to the Impulse! label coincided with his most experimental and spiritual phase, and he was still signed to the label at the time of his death in 1967. This relationship has been the making of the label, and Impulse! has continued to trade both on the success and the spirituality of Coltrane in its other recordings.

8   Eisenberg elaborates on the ownership of records in his chapter 'Music Becomes a Thing' in *The Recording Angel* (2005: 9–28).

9   The current proliferation of complete recordings and boxed sets is particularly interesting,

given the rise of the download. Arguably, the divergence between the immediacy of MP3s and the longevity of the boxed set is becoming greater, with each occupying their own space in the market.

10 The Impulse! label made an exception for Coltrane's *A Love Supreme* (1965), which carried a white and black spine, symbolising its otherness and explicit spirituality.

11 Whereas Blue Note Records have become associated with quintessential jazz imagery – for example, see Marsh and Callingham (2002) – Impulse! records provide an ideal model for comparative analysis as they have adopted an explicit visual strategy as part of their marketing activities since the company's inception. For examples of the visual impact of Impulse! see album covers for Coltrane's *A Love Supreme* (1965) and Oliver Nelson's *Blues and The Abstract Truth* (1961).

12 This pattern of new releases does not include the vocal music of Diana Krall, who continued to produce albums for Impulse! around and beyond this period.

13 I focus here on the specifics of the Impulse! label; however, several texts deal with the conservative and nostalgic tendencies of current jazz culture. My conclusions should, therefore, be read in the context of works such as Gabbard (2004b), Hall and du Gay (2000), Stanbridge (2004) and Walser (2002).

14 From an Impulse! advert in *Downbeat* magazine, April 1961.

15 See, for example, Eisenberg (2005) and Katz (2004) for detailed analyses of the impact and influence of recordings on society.

References

Ake, D. (2002a) *Jazz Cultures*. Berkeley: University of California Press.

_____ (2002b) 'Learning Jazz, Teaching Jazz', in M. Cooke and D. Horn (eds) *The Cambridge Companion to Jazz*, pp.255–69. Cambridge: Cambridge University Press.

Barthes, R. (1977) *Image-Music-Text*. London: Fontana Press.

Berger, J. (1990) *Ways of Seeing*. London: Penguin.

Born, G. (2005) 'On Musical Mediation: Ontology, Technology and Creativity', *Twentieth-Century Music* 2 (1): 7–36.

Bowen, J.A. (1993) 'The History of Remembered Innovation: Tradition and its Role in the Relationship Between Musical Works and Their Performances', *The Journal of Musicology* 11 (2): 139–73.

Burns, K. (2001) *Jazz: A Film by Ken Burns*. The Jazz Film Project Inc. DD4721.

Corbett, J. (1994) *Extended Play: Sounding Off from John Cage to Dr. Funkenstein*. Durham, NC: Duke University Press.

Cuscuna, M. (2005) 'Strictly on the Record: The Art of Jazz and the Recording Industry', *The Source: Challenging Jazz Criticism* 2: 63–70.

DeVeaux, S. (1999) 'Constructing the Jazz Tradition', in R. Walser (ed.) *Keeping Time: Readings in Jazz History*, pp.416–26. New York: Oxford University Press.

_____ (2001–2) 'Struggling with Jazz'. *Current Musicology* 71–73: 353–74.

Dyer, G. (2000) *But Beautiful*. London: Abacus.

Eisenberg, E. (2005) *The Recording Angel: Music, Records and Culture from Aristotle to Zappa*. New Haven: Yale University Press.

Fisher, J.A. (1998) 'Rock 'n' Recording: the Ontological Complexity of Rock Music', in P. Alperson (ed.) *Musical Worlds: New Directions in the Philosophy of Music*, pp.109–23. Pennsylvania: Pennsylvania State University Press.

Gabbard, K. (1995) 'The Jazz Canon and its Consequences', in K. Gabbard (ed.) *Jazz Among the Discourses*, pp.1–28. Durham, NC: Duke University Press.

_____ (2004a) *Black Magic: White Hollywood and African American Culture*. New Jersey: Rutgers University Press.

_____ (2004b) 'Miles from Home: Miles Davis and the Movies', *The Source: Challenging Jazz Criticism* 1: 27–41.

Goehr, L. (1992) *The Imaginary Museum of Musical Works. An Essay in the Philosophy of Music*. Oxford: Clarendon Press.

Giddins, G. (2001) *Satchmo: The Genius of Louis Armstrong*. New York: Da Capo Press.

Huyssen, A. (1986) *After the Great Divide: Modernism, Mass Culture and Postmodernism*. London: Routledge.

Hall, S. and du Gay, P. (eds) (2000) *Questions of Cultural Identity*. London: Routledge.

Kahn, A. (2002) *A Love Supreme: The Creation of John Coltrane's Classic Album*. London: Granta Books.

_____ (2006) *The House That Trane Built*. London: Granta Books.

Katz, M. (2004) *Capturing Sound: How Technology Has Changed Music*. California: University of California Press.

Kermode, F. (1988) *Canon and Period*. Oxford: Oxford University Press.

Marsh, G. and Callingham, G. (2002) *The Cover Art of Blue Note Records*. London: Collins and Brown.

Owens, T. (1995) *Bebop: the Music and Its Players*. New York: Oxford University Press.

Panken, T. (2001) 'Approaching Enlightenment', *Downbeat* 68 (2): 22–7.

Porter, L. (1998) *John Coltrane: His Life and Music*. Ann Arbor, MI: University of Michigan Press.

Rasula, J. (1995) 'The Media of Memory: The Seductive Menace of Records in Jazz History', in K. Gabbard (ed.) *Jazz Among the Discourses*, pp.134–62. Durham, NC: Duke University Press.

Schapp, P. (2003) 'Jazz Records Are Our Books!', paper presented at the International Association for Jazz Education Convention, Toronto, Canada.

Small, C. (1998) *Musicking: The Meanings of Performing and Listening*. Middletown: Wesleyan University Press.

Spencer, F.J. (2002) *Jazz and Death*. Mississippi: University of Mississippi Press.

Stanbridge, A. (2004) 'Burns, Baby, Burns: Jazz History as a Contested Cultural Site', *The Source: Challenging Jazz Criticism* 1: 81–99.

Tomlinson, G. (1992) 'Cultural Dialogics and Jazz: A White Historian Signifies', in K. Bergeron and P.V. Bohlman (eds) *Disciplining Music: Musicology and its Canons*, pp.64–94. Chicago and London: Chicago University Press.

Walser, R. (1995) '"Out of Notes": Signification, Interpretation, and the Problem of Miles Davis', in K. Gabbard (ed.) *Jazz Among the Discourses*, pp.165–88. Durham, NC: Duke University Press.

_____ (2002) 'Valuing Jazz', in M. Cooke and D. Horn (eds) *The Cambridge Companion to Jazz*, pp.301–20. Cambridge: Cambridge University Press.

Washburne, C. and Derno, M. (eds) (2004) *Bad Music: The Music We Love to Hate*. New York: Routledge.

Wernick, A. (1997) 'Resort to Nostalgia: Mountains, Memories and Myths of Time', in M. Nava, B. Richards and I. Macrury (eds) *Buy This Book: Studies in Advertising and Consumption*, pp.207–23. London: Routledge.

Whyton, T. (2006) 'Birth of the School: Discursive Methodologies in Jazz Education', *Music Education Research* 8 (2): 65–82.

Discography

Burns, K. (2000) *Ken Burns Jazz: The Story of America's Music*. Verve CD [box set] B0000525QL.

Coltrane, A. (2004) *Translinear Light*. Impulse! CD B000219102.

Coltrane, J. (1998) *The Classic Quartet: Complete Impulse! Studio Recordings*. Impulse! CD IMPD8-280.

_____ (2003) *A Love Supreme*. Impulse! CD B000061002.

Mingus, C. (1995) *The Black Saint and the Sinner Lady*. Impulse! CD IMPD174.

Nelson, O. (1995) *Blues and the Abstract Truth*. Impulse! CD IMPD154.

Tyner, M. (2001) *McCoy Tyner Plays John Coltrane – Live at the Village Vanguard*. Impulse! CD 3145891832.

TONY GIBBS AND JOHN DACK

A Sense of Place:
A Sense of Space

Introduction

I T is self-evident that since its invention in 1878, the recording and subsequent reproduction of sound by mechanical and other means has had many profound consequences for music. Both the actual techniques of recording sounds and the ways in which the products – the recorded artefacts – are used have changed music's commercial status and the manner in which it facilitates social interchange. The dissemination and distribution of recorded music resulted in a process of commodification, which continues today as digital downloads become increasingly commonplace. It has even been suggested that downloads threaten the existence of the compact disc and other fixed media. Such effects on market forces must be acknowledged, but with the rapid development of technology all predictions are at best only provisional.

In addition to these changes in the market place, composers and producers have also been active in using the actual medium of recording to creatively intervene in how sounds can be preserved, modified and, most important of all, subsequently used as 'musical' material. Musicians now have access to any sound that can be recorded. But this statement needs to be examined: what is meant by a 'recorded' sound? Few would claim that recordings 'simply' preserve sounds in a neutral manner. Sound events are either captured within the controlled acoustic setting of a studio or are subject to the fixed characteristics of a location. Examples of this might be the reverberation of a concert hall or, in the case of an outdoor location, the reflections from buildings and other acoustically significant objects. These acoustic characteristics might be considered secondary features, subservient to other aspects of music such as pitch, spectral constitution or duration. Nevertheless, they are integral aspects of the recording and thus crucial to the way sounds can be used and perceived. Subsequent (usually digital) processing can manipulate these acoustic qualities, and environments with characteristics that are entirely artificial but 'realistic', or impossible to create in the real world can be suggested. Thus, the acoustic properties of locations (real or virtual) are now part of both the record producer's and the electroacoustic composer's palette of possibilities.

Our concern in this chapter is the interaction between the act of recording and the way such acoustic environments are preserved and communicated. Three subject areas have been selected for particular attention: recording techniques in classical, popular and electroacoustic music. Though these genres are often regarded as irreconcilable examples of low- and high-art, issues of place and space are, in fact, common to all of them. For example, even the most basic recording of music in a popular genre demands a complex series of decisions regarding the placement of microphones and instruments/voices. In so doing, record producers and engineers create a mixture of discrete sonic locations by means of studio techniques. The individual components of the drum kit are placed in one or more discrete positions (and possibly different acoustics) within the stereo image, the lead guitar in another and the voices often in other, different ambiences. Even though the recognition of such complex environments is not the primary purpose of the final product, a unique 'sound' is created and the clarity of the individual instruments' positions is necessary to the commercial success of the record.[1] The electroacoustic composer is also acutely conscious of how locating sounds can result in complex interactions that may create acoustic environments and thereby enhance meaning and clarify intention – though financial success in this latter genre is rarely an issue.

We will address some of the ways in which various genre-specific approaches to the compositional and recording processes utilise these various possibilities. In so doing, we seek to examine our experience of sound in relation to space and how the resulting sensibilities inform and are themselves informed by those places that we perceive, experience or imagine. We also highlight certain areas of apparent contradiction in the reassignment of nominally spatial criteria to other functions such as, for example, timbre and examine how the transition may be made between compositional and performance spaces.

In his 1945 study *Phénoménologie de la perception*, the French philosopher Maurice Merleau-Ponty (1908–61) discussed how we become aware of the space in which we find ourselves and how we experience its contents. 'Space', he said, 'is not the setting (real or logical) in which things are arranged but the means whereby the position of things becomes possible' (Merleau-Ponty, 1945/2002: 284). Here, Merleau-Ponty identifies the inseparable and vitally important relationship between object and context: in our case between sound object and the acoustic context in which it is set. With a little imagination, we can extend this initial relationship to include the idea – very much a part of popular music recording practice – that the sonic qualities of the space not only contribute to the sound's position in the stereo image, but also, potentially, to the final timbre of the sound object which results from this interaction.

We experience music in particular places, be they concert halls, living rooms or cars. With the obvious exception of the Walkman (or, more currently, iPod) approach to listening, the acoustic qualities of these places influence what we hear. We may not appreciate their qualities or impact in detail at a conscious level but their influence is nonetheless substantial. A space may be described or to some extent defined by its acoustics and, as Merleau-Ponty observes, once defined we can begin to populate it with sound objects. In the case of the record producer or electroacoustic composer, these may include only those objects 'fit for purpose' whereas in a more natural setting, they will be objects that are part of the local sound environment. Once populated, the sound space passes into a more specific realm. It is no longer just an undefined space with certain qualities: it has become a *place*, somewhere that we can go to. It is, if you like, the Albert Hall with its legendary echoes, Wembley Arena with its alarming reflection from the rear wall, the Festival Hall with (until recently) its very neutral and 'dead' acoustic. In the following sections, we will consider the impact and application of this basic idea and its derivatives with particular reference to our three nominated subject areas.

Classical recording

The techniques and procedures of classical music recording are well established and, with relatively minor changes, are of long standing. Essentially, most variants confer both temporal and locational identities upon the recorded work in question. Emphasis is placed on the when and the where of the recording, perhaps to subtly reinforce its credibility as a 'real' product made by real creative people rather than the result of some technical sleight of hand.

Critics and writers of sleeve notes typically refer to and comment upon 'the performance' whereas, as we all know, there is very often, in reality, no single complete performance upon which to comment at all, but rather an assemblage of partial ones designed to appear as if contiguous. The temporal identity is therefore often illusory, but nonetheless broadly consensual: we accept what we know to be anomalous if not downright untrue and thereby enter into a conspiracy of sorts, one that is designed to confirm temporal identity and continuity and hence to enhance credibility.

The classical recording engineer has at his or her disposal a set of technical tools no less diverse and capable than those available to those who work in other musical genres. In general, however, and with the obvious exception of editing, these are used to a far lesser extent than is the norm in the recording of pop/rock music or in the technical realisation of electroacoustic works. Most particularly, this applies to the synthesis of spaces by means of artificially generated delays and reverberations, which are used very rarely indeed. Their virtual absence from the armoury of the classical recordist contrasts significantly with their hugely important usage in the other genres, and we may speculate that this is in some way connected with the establishment of the previously mentioned senses of temporal and locational identity and, by implication, credibility. It is far easier and more comfortable to believe that a particular work was recorded at a specific time in a specific place than to be forced to accept that it is the product of innumerable edits and the synthesis of artificial acoustics or, if you prefer, a collage of no particular temporal or locational provenance.

Why should this be so? If we are to be cynical, the issue appears, in part at least, to be one of credibility and the maintenance of elitist status; but the insistence on these criteria may go further. By establishing and reinforcing the view that a particular recording was made at a particular time and in a particular place, the opportunity is presented for the identification and indeed the celebration of an *event*. That event is, of course, the performance and it is this – be it real or illusory – that is presented for critical appraisal. We are invited by the writers of sleeve notes to acknowledge the achievements – real or created by editing – of the performers and, by our acquiescence, we acknowledge the acceptability of this fiction.

It follows that, if, by means of judicious editing, we can create the temporal illusion of a contiguous performance, there should logically be a locational equivalent whereby we can, to put it crudely, 'fake the space' by technological means. For example, there are generally agreed parameters such as reverberation time that may be adjusted to suit chamber or symphonic music. Surely by such means we can create a believable virtual place in which our performance can take place?

Recent technological developments, particularly in respect of acoustic sampling can not only do this, but can also offer the opportunity for a performance to be rendered into the environment of choice, be it the Concertgebouw Hall of Amsterdam, or Carnegie Hall in New York. This most recent approach is dramatic in both implication and technical quality but is nonetheless hardly more than a carefully structured and specific rendition of a technology that has been available for some time. Starting with the advent of electronic sound processing in the 1920s, it has become increasingly possible to create virtual acoustic environments of sufficient credibility to render them acceptable as actual places; yet practitioners of classical recording (almost invariably) choose not to do so. Indeed, they may go further and eschew many other techniques that are readily available. Perhaps the most notable of these is that mainstay of pop/rock recording, the overdub. There is a general reluctance on the part of classical recordists to adopt this approach. Better, it would seem, to be constrained to assemble the finished work by a multiplicity of edits than to record a soloist performing to a previously recorded orchestral part. Again we must ask why.

Here perhaps the answer may be a little more complex. We can of course restate the celebration of the event of performance as a major factor, but is it not possible, indeed probable that the coexistence of all audible components of the work in the same space, at the same time, leads to a subtle and perhaps synergistic interaction with the acoustic environment of the location of recording? Hence, an otherwise identical recording will sound substantially different in different locations and this cannot readily be replicated by the simple expedient of 'adding some reverb'. Some extra, seemingly intangible and certainly non-duplicable factor has entered the equation.

Technical models may provide some help here: the existence of significant energy at ultrasonic frequencies in the 'output' of an orchestra is clearly possible, if not inevitable, and the possible interactions of these very high pitches with each other and the acoustic properties of the space may create difference tones, which – despite being at quite low energy levels – would fall within the audible spectrum and hence become a part of the heard experience. Clearly, unless all components are present simultaneously, this potentially significant interaction cannot take place.

In choosing a location for classical recording, the issue of optimal acoustics is obviously of utmost importance and, if successfully addressed, can minimise the requirement for additional technical intervention. This leads in turn to a short and potentially 'clean' programme chain with the result that not only are the performance aspects of the work optimised but their recording has the potential to be of the highest quality. Compare if you will any number of recordings made in appropriate locations using single or simple microphone systems with those made in the artificial environment of the studio using multitrack technology. The results, we suggest, speak for themselves.[2]

Recording in pop and rock

Turning now to the second of our genres – pop/rock – we find a wholly different perspective. In these styles, there is often an apparently paradoxical situation insofar as a single recording may, on careful analysis, appear to have been created in a multiplicity of locations and, by implication, in an asynchronous fashion. Here, we should perhaps redefine 'locations' as 'environments' since the ambiences associated with the various components of current recording practice will typically combine synthetic and real acoustic environments. This state of affairs represents a hybrid of a number of approaches, by no means the least significant being the complete artificiality of location within a given space implied by the universal use of the pan pot.

Born largely of technological and economic necessity, the early practices of the rock 'n' roll studio were technically simple and carried thereby much of the locational identity found in classical recording. One might cite the characteristic and readily identifiable 'sounds' of, for example, Sun Studios[3] in Memphis where Elvis Presley created his early works or Norman Petty's Clovis Studios in which Buddy Holly[4] worked. Perhaps one of the best-known examples in this context is Brian Wilson's work on the *Pet Sounds*[5] album. In this, he sought to emulate the sound of his great idol, Phil Spector. Apart from using many of the same musicians, Wilson carefully sought out and worked in the same studios that Spector had used to create his famous 'Wall of Sound',[6] believing (largely correctly as it turned out) that their acoustic qualities were the key to the successful reproduction of this style. In this respect at least, Wilson approached his work in much the same way as a classical producer might.

Although Wilson used multitrack recording, he did so in a way that seems somewhat limited by modern standards. Backing tracks were typically mixed live to one or two tracks and the remainder used for multi-layered vocals. The fuller exploitation of the multitrack recorder, at this stage still to come, had enormous impact upon these approaches. Now there was no requirement for simultaneity of performance at any level. Removed from the need for temporal consistency, the logical extension of this approach was similarly to dispense with any sense of place or at least with any sense of a *single* place. Now each component could be recorded separately at the best time and in the 'best' location. This implied the use of different acoustic spaces – real or simulated – for different instruments, each being chosen for optimal effect. By optimising each component, it was reasoned, the best possible collective product would be an almost inevitable result. Careful examination of many recordings of the late 1960s, '70s and '80s often shows the simultaneous existence of multiple acoustic spaces and this reinforces a perceived lack of most of the qualities deemed desirable in classical practice: the multiplicity of acoustics is paradoxical, and often confusing, and it undermines the credibility of the finished product as a single 'event' that takes place in real time in a single place.

This creates a central issue: the concept of simple locational identity is dismissed to be replaced by a synthesis of diverse components which do not necessarily point, so to speak, in a common direction. By implication, therefore, unlike the consequences of classical recording practice, in this discipline the component parts (voices and instruments) that make up the work do not interact to any substantial extent. Whether or not this is an issue of substance is for debate: in respect of classical practice, as mentioned previously, some argument has been advanced in support of the creation of audible content by acoustic interaction between component instruments. As has been noted, this involves the contentious issue of difference tones – one that is beyond the scope of this chapter.

An early attempt to address the implications of multitrack technology was to adopt the polar opposite to the classical approach – to record each component separately with as much isolation and as little 'natural' acoustic as possible. Command Studios in London took this approach to the ultimate: a series of areas were provided, each of which was as acoustically dead and isolated from the others as could be achieved. The thinking behind this was that acoustics could and should be created and imposed as appropriate and in isolation. The consequences of performing in what was, to all intents and purposes, an anechoic and atemporal environment were, to say the least, not happy ones and this practice was readily discarded.

One response to this unsuccessful approach was epitomised in the practices of the 1970s in which successful bands would opt to record in certain studios in part at least because of the drum (or brass, or string, etc.) sound for which they were particularly known. Studio designers would vie with each other to create spaces with a range of instrument-specific acoustic qualities. In no sense did this design philosophy seek to integrate the sound of the individual components; rather it sought to optimise them on an individual basis with little regard to the quality of the final product as assembled from the (necessarily separated) multitrack tape. One must observe, however, that acoustic considerations were by no means the only factors in the choice of recording environment. Nonetheless, indulgence invaded acoustic design too for a time: for example, expensive Hawaiian lava rock enjoyed a brief popularity as the wall lining of choice for drum booths in the practice of at least one highly successful designer of the period.[7]

The accepted practice that has finally emerged for this genre is a hybrid of natural acoustics – most notably of conspicuously live drum booths – and artificially (that is to say digitally) generated environments. Oddly, some presets of digital reverberation units (for example, the Lexicon 'warm room') have themselves acquired the acoustically iconic status of actual venues: perhaps a nod in the direction of the classical tradition. The perceived need for a sense of place may, perhaps, be harder to dismiss or at least more tenacious than we might expect.

Electroacoustic realisation

The technologies available to the pioneers of electroacoustic composition and realisation were conspicuously poor in respect of their ability to synthesise spaces and places as readily as they could create what we might call 'tonalities'.[8] This situation has changed dramatically in recent times and yet, its availability notwithstanding, the use of synthetic spaces is largely rejected by practitioners in this genre.

The electroacoustic practitioner, we suggest, eschews (in this respect at least) the concept of a single performance event and, by focussing to an ultimate extent upon the qualities of components, removes them from any existence in either time or space save for the duration of specific events and their possible diffusion to components of a specialised sound system. Sounds may be placed in specific positions in space for compositional purposes but, with rare exceptions, there is no attempt to create, by means of technological intervention, a believable place in the sense that the classical recording practitioner might wish to create the simulation or representation of a particular concert hall. By implication, the electroacoustic composer in general does not seek to create the sense of a performance, or indeed of an actual event or occasion.

Component sounds are typically created and assembled in accordance with compositional intentions. These rarely include the creation of a single event, located unambiguously in a single time and place: indeed the inclusion of information that could indicate, describe or identify a specific location is highly unusual. The placing of sounds in spatial locations is, however, a common practice, which is further supported by the use of sound diffusion as a presentation technique. This relies upon the qualities of the place in which the presentation takes place and, with some exceptions, does not imply the encoding of place identity within the programme material.

There are, of course, important exceptions to this approach. Perhaps the best known is Jonathan Harvey's 1980 work *Mortuos plango, vivos voco* in which the audience is invited to consider themselves inside a giant bell. The other main component of the piece is a boy's voice, which flies around within this space (itself established by processed bell sounds) in dramatic fashion. Here Harvey defines both location and its qualities very precisely indeed. In general, however, where such techniques as reverberation are used by electroacoustic practitioners, they function as timbral modifiers rather than as indicators or descriptors for acoustic environments. There is perhaps an unconscious intent to reinforce the synthetic and often analytical nature of much electroacoustic music by presenting it outside the standard issues of time, space and location. Nevertheless, the acoustic characteristics of real or virtual spaces and locations are exploited by various electroacoustic composers to create musical signification.

Location and place in electroacoustic music

The recording medium and the electroacoustic studio are inextricably linked. From the earliest examples of *musique concrète*, techniques of recording had consequences, not only for the sounds that composers could use but also for the implied spatial settings of such sounds. The studio and recorded sounds encouraged an extensive reappraisal of many traditional musical concepts. Practices of electroacoustic composers increasingly demanded that subject areas such as 'expression', 'performance' and the 'instrument' be examined and perhaps even clarified in the light of these new conditions. Space and location play particularly important roles in such fundamental re-evaluations of music. Theoreticians and philosophers have always used spatial metaphors when discussing music: electroacoustic musicians can participate in, and contribute to this discourse. If we examine instrumental music there is no shortage of examples of explicitly spatial references. The antiphonal music of Giovanni Gabrieli in St Mark's Cathedral in Venice is frequently cited for its use of specific locations from which sounds emerged. Many other composers also used spatial distribution in their compositions. Sounds coming from various directions and heights can be heard in Hector Berlioz's *Grande Messe des Morts* from 1837 and its theatrical (in the best sense of the word) performance in the church of les Invalides – if ever there was a site-specific work it is surely this one. Moreover, Gustav Mahler often required off-stage musicians to play in his symphonies to create a sense of 'distance' ('wie aus der Ferne' is indicated in the score). Hearing music being played literally 'at a distance' in a concert hall by an invisible group of musicians is relatively commonplace today. It is nevertheless an impressive and often moving effect and demonstrates unequivocally what all musicians know: distant sounds are not just quieter, but their spectral constitution is qualitatively different as high frequency components are absorbed by the air. In these works, if sounds are not perceived as coming from different directions or distances, the music is undeniably impoverished. An increasing sensitivity to space and location is evident in post-war composers – a fact doubtless stimulated by studio experiences. Composers such as Luciano Berio, Iannis Xenakis and Henry Brant composed works that demand the placing of instrumentalists in precise locations on stage or amongst the audience. With the increased importance of sound diffusion in electroacoustic 'performance', issues of spatial distribution are now central to many composers' musical thinking.

Electroacoustic musicians might benefit from an increased awareness of these practices which can be deliberately appropriated to form part of their own repository of compositional strategies. One electroacoustic genre is particularly concerned with the acoustic characteristics of specific locations. 'Soundscape' compositions frequently rely on the recognition of real-world sound events. Furthermore, a general sense of the actual location of a sound recording can be important to the composition's network of meanings. Many composers who use sounds in this way are actively involved in the World Forum for Acoustic Ecology which originated in the World Soundscape Project in the early 1970s. Many approaches can be subsumed within the WFAE, but a common feature is the composer's desire to promote a sensitivity to our sound environment via artworks such as compositions and sound installations.[9] In addition, we can often identify an archival agenda as these composers alert us to the fact that certain sounds are disappearing and their use in compositions does at least preserve them in a more permanent form. This is exemplified by one of the WFAE's founders, R. Murray Schafer, and his projects such as the *Vancouver Soundscape* (1973) and the *Five Village Soundscapes* (1975). In both these cases the actual provenance of the recorded sounds is important. Some will be designated 'soundmarks', a term 'derived from landmark and refer[ring] to a community sound which is unique or possesses qualities which make it specially regarded or noticed by the people in that community' (Schafer, 1977: 10). Thus, the sound's origin, its specific location with particular, perhaps even unique characteristics is emphasised and in so doing a network of cultural and social relationships is implied.

Two electroacoustic composers whose work can be examined in reference to such practices are Thomas Gerwin (1955–) and Luc Ferrari (1929–2005). Both composers have produced works in which acoustic settings contribute to how the piece is perceived. Examples of the importance of specific locations can be cited in Gerwin's CD *Karlsruhe: Klangbilder einer Stadt*. This collection of ten 'acoustic portraits'[10] was initially used as part of an installation called *Klangstatt*, and only subsequently released on CD. Such interdisciplinary practices are common in the electroacoustic medium and often blur the distinction between the roles of composer and sound artist. Gerwin collected the sounds for these works from August 1994 to March 1995. The quality of the recordings confirms the scrupulous care with which Gerwin approached this task. There is no intervention in the recordings other than editing. All other characteristics remain faithful to the original place and time of recording.

The first piece in the collection is entitled 'Hauptbahnhof und Zoo' (Main Station and Zoo) and the listener is taken on a short 'sound walk' from the confines of the main railway station in Karlsruhe to the nearby zoological gardens. There is, of course, a certain amount of trust involved. Can we be sure that all the sounds do indeed come from the locations specified? Gerwin assures us this is so and we have no reason to doubt him. There is no information regarding the times of recording – Gerwin might have visited the station and zoo on different days and selected the most appropriate recording. All these decisions remain within the control of the composer. Nevertheless, he must also work with 'given' material which remains a fixed aspect of the composition. These are the cavernous environments of the station concourse and the platforms with the resonant sounds of trains, trolleys rattling, announcements and people conversing. Such sounds are replaced briefly with the more open, non-reflective ambience of urban streets. Traffic and other urban sounds are supplanted by animal cries in the distance which gradually become louder as we approach the zoo. Then, we are taken into the zoo where human interaction intermingles with what are clearly the sounds of animals. Once again, some places in the zoo are interior others exterior, but the different stages of the 'journey' are never in doubt. Gerwin does not mix, for example, trains with elephants to encourage the listeners' imagination of unreal or impossible worlds. Instead, we are taken around specific environments, which, even if we do not know them, communicate by the way the composer arranges different acoustic spaces. These are explicit examples of sounds occurring in certain places and the spatial cues by which they can be located are of utmost importance. Gerwin's work alerts us to the fact that we should never underestimate the remarkable sensitivity of humans to such aurally perceptible details. Certain structural features are apparent. The resonant characteristics of the station are repeated in the zoo section as we enter a building with similar acoustic features. The aforementioned progression from 'outside' to 'inside' (and vice versa) is also repeated. By contrast, the sounds of the busy social interaction within a station where people generally stay only as long as required and are always waiting – indeed wanting – to leave are replaced by those of the zoo where people choose to linger for extended periods of time. This work by Gerwin, therefore, encourages us to move from one real location to another purely by the use of locational sound cues. In keeping with the sense of progression between individual locations, most scenes follow in sequence with only discrete mixing.

Another piece in the collection is called 'Universität' (University). 'Universität' begins with old bicycles arriving, their brakes squeaking. Gerwin's subsequent sounds depict the various parts of the institution of a university in subtle ways. However, he does not resort to a banal recording of a lecture or interchanges in a seminar. Rather, the sounds relate to human activities which can only be construed as intellectual within the context of the location from which the sounds originate. The air conditioning whines, we hear the action of writing (the text, of course, can never be known to us), a dot matrix printer spins out more unknown texts in the dead, flat acoustic space of offices and libraries. In the social space of (perhaps) the canteen we can hear human voices, though if we listen carefully the human voice is often present in the background – the 'human' is never eliminated from this 'acoustic portrait'. In this way, Gerwin's sound world conjures up the atmosphere of quiet thought and intellectual activity which is emphasised rather than diminished by the suppression of human speech. In this work, the continuity of space and, by implication, time is presented in a clear, linear narrative.

By contrast with Gerwin's work, Ferrari's *Music Promenade 1* (1967–9) consists of sounds recorded in various locations from 1964 to 1967 followed by another two years of compositional activity.[11] If Gerwin's use of locations emphasises the local and – to the residents of Karlsruhe at least – the familiar, then Ferrari draws on a much broader range of sounds and their acoustic qualities. The original intention was to have different materials recorded on four tapes replayed simultaneously on four tape-recorders. The version on CD is one realisation. Unlike Gerwin, Ferrari frequently disrupts recordings of certain locations by suddenly interposing bursts of sounds from other sources. The effect is dreamlike and occasionally unsettling as different times and places are folded into each other. Nevertheless, in one section Ferrari also contrasts 'indoor' sounds (the sounds of traditional instruments, creaking doors and other similar noises) with 'outdoor' sounds (a military parade) thereby creating not only a witty, playful juxtaposition of acoustic qualities but positing the concept that the characteristics of spaces are as important (in this case perhaps more important) than the sounds which were recorded within those spaces. As listeners, we hear the 'progression' in Ferrari's composition from one acoustic space to another. The close proximity of the instruments is imposed in a surrealistic manner on the broad acoustic spaces within which the military parade takes place. There is an element of dramatic conflict as spatial contrasts are emphasised by placing the irregular rhythms and atonal melodic vocabulary of the former with the all-too-regular military rhythms of the latter. The different acoustic spaces support the sense of disruption and musical anarchy: just as the soldiers begin to establish their marching patterns it is subverted by the avant-garde musicians.

These contrasts comprise the first half of the work on CD. Thereafter, we hear several dramatic productions in various languages and the emphasis is on the human voice even though interruptions occur as before. We are spectators to the intensity of the dramatic voice and the section concludes with fading repetitions of 'Sleep no more' (*Macbeth*, Act 2). Thus, this work by Ferrari also makes use of not only recognisable sounds but their original location of recording. The perceived acoustic settings are exploited to create contrast or continuity.

In addition to the interplay arising from clearly recognisable sounds and their possible settings, the electroacoustic musician must also consider the relationship between the composer's space and the venue in which the composition will be presented. This is rarely an issue for pop/rock musicians as recordings that display sophisticated use of different discrete acoustic spaces are not generally played for communal listening in a large concert hall – the 'live' concert serves that purpose. However, unless a work is intended solely for replay via headphones, the concert venue and the playback system will have an effect on a 'performance' of a composition. If the composer has made use of various types of acoustic setting, the role of sound diffusion will be crucial. Whether a work is recorded in a stereo or in a multi-channel format, the way the sounds are distributed in the venue will reproduce (or not) the original recordings. The spaces created so carefully by the composer – the 'composer's space' – are now placed within the space of the concert hall – the 'listener's space'. The way these spaces interact can be consonant or dissonant and we realise that sounds in space, like words in a language, begin to assert themselves in ways we might not be able to predict. The composer Denis Smalley has written about these issues and we would recommend the interested reader to consult his text on the 'indicative field of space' (Smalley, 1992).

Conclusion

We have argued that different genres approach the issue of acoustic space and, by implication, the creation of place, of a sense of 'whereness', in very different ways. For the classical tradition, the intention is to create a believable simulation of a real-time performance, one that is located in a single physical location at a specific time. It is, by implication, an event that is of significance and that is to be celebrated.

The pop/rock sensibility disregards this approach, preferring the optimisation of component parts, arguably (the cynic might suggest) in the pursuit of ever-increasing spectacle. Even so, an element of performance and its inherent impressiveness remains and this at least implies (if not demands) a degree of continuity and consistency. The single 'celebratable' event is perhaps implied but its virtuality is at least partially acknowledged. The focus is upon spectacle (which we might uncharitably describe as 'sound and fury') and this is, in part, established and reinforced by dramatic – not to say melodramatic – acoustic contrasts and paradoxes.

By contrast, electroacoustic composers seem, in most cases, to retain a remarkable degree of detachment from these considerations. Where classical recording practitioners seek to reinforce and exploit conventional perceptions of time, space and place, and rock and pop engineers and producers manipulate these perceptions to amplify scale and enhance spectacle, electroacoustic composers frequently adopt an almost ascetic approach such that a sound object is to be appreciated as a pure entity, often divorced from any relationship. Yet, we find within this genre a whole spectrum of degrees of site-specificity ranging from what we might call 'pure' soundscape pieces to those which invoke a creative use of space such as in Ferrari's work. There is perhaps a case to be made for the creation of another distinct genre for such works since, in some respects at least, they seem informed by a quite different sensibility from the electroacoustic 'mainstream'.

Furthermore, the issue of electroacoustic performance – which we take to imply the practice of diffusion – by virtue of occurring at a specific time and in a specific place implies a degree of commonality with the classical approach, which leads, as we have suggested, to a celebratable event. Given that all such events, by their nature, acquire much of their experiential qualities from the particular place in which they happen, we may find ourselves in paradoxical spaces wherein, for example, a highly reverberant sound may be experienced in a relatively 'dead' environment and vice versa. We may need to ask whether the acoustic of the recording or of the space in which it is heard should be accorded precedence or whether, in permitting such contradictions, we may be tacitly agreeing that a property that we normally associate with space can be transformed into one of timbre and hence become a compositional tool in a quite conventional sense.

We must ask, therefore, how much importance should be accorded to objective 'accuracy' or whether there are simply differences that respond to what are perceived as genre-specific needs. There may be a case to be made for believability: human nature likes the idea that whatever it is that we hear was created at a particular time and in a particular place. This is, perhaps, something that our logical sensibilities demand and something that classical recording practice has grasped with some success. That electroacoustic practice has not done so – or at least not in the 'conventional' way – may possibly suggest that this is one reason for its continuing marginalisation from the mainstream. That rock and pop have embraced the exploitation of acoustic space with almost excessive enthusiasm may be seen as evidence of their reliance upon spectacular qualities and indeed their ephemerality.

It seems clear that both the qualities of space as evidenced by acoustic dimensions and the way in which these feed into the creation of a sense of a real actual physical place or location are highly significant in how we respond to composed, performed and realised works. There is significant diversity in approach and this diversity appears, to a large extent, to be specific to each genre. There is, however, a transcendent consideration: that of the human need to believe in a specific space, a particular place.

Another French philosopher, Gaston Bachelard (1884–1962), wrote of how accurately one must hear in order to hear the geometry of echoes in an old house (Bachelard, 1958/1994: 60–1). Bachelard wrote of domestic spaces whereas we have discussed those of recorded musical styles; but it is surely no surprise that it is these very echoes, upon which our sense of both space and place is founded, that contribute so much to the validation of our listening experience.

Notes

1   A good example of this may be found in 'Dreaming while you sleep' from the 1991 album *We Can't Dance* by Genesis. Virtually every sound component is placed in its own acoustic environment or is accompanied by a different time-based process (e.g. slapback echo), which suggests a distinct acoustic ambience.

2   Excellent examples of the successful application of a single microphone approach may be found in a number of Nimbus recordings that have used the Calrec Soundfield microphone

system. See, for instance Swierczewski (1992). A good example of the use of two pairs of stereo microphones may be found in Zinman (1992).

3   See, for example, *The Legendary Sun Records Story* (2000).

4   See, for example, Holly (2008).

5   See The Beach Boys (1990).

6   Excellent examples of this can be found on Spector (1991).

7   See, in particular, the design work of Tom Hidley, founder of Westlake (and later Eastlake) Audio.

8   A term coined by composers Louis and Bebe Barron (best known for their work on the soundtrack of the 1956 film *Forbidden Planet*) to distinguish their work from 'conventional' approaches to musical composition. The term is used here to refer to considerations of timbre and pitch, two aspects of electroacoustic sound that are relatively easy to control and modify.

9   A variety of different approaches can be read in Järvilluoma and Wagstaff (2002), LaBelle (2006), Truax (2001).

10   There are twelve tracks on the CD: tracks 11 and 12 are disregarded for the purposes of the present discussion. Track 11, 'Stimmfächer', consists of the polyphonic layering of voices and track 12, 'Karlsruh'-musik', starts with a radio presenter referring to Gerwin's activities in recording sounds in Karlsruhe, and then continues with a piece consisting of sounds from Karlsruhe in general. In addition, track 10, 'Durlacher Turmberg', is exceptional in that it reprises many of the sounds used in the previous nine tracks.

11   For more information on Ferrari's works, see Castanet et al. (2001) and Caux (2002).

References

Bachelard, G. (1994) *The Poetics of Space.* Trans. M. Jolas. Boston. Beacon Press. Original (1958) as *La poétique de l'espace.* Paris: Presses Universitaires de France.

Castanet, P.-A., Gayou, E. and Teruggi, D. (eds) (2001) *Luc Ferrari: Portraits Polychromes.* Paris: Ina-GRM / Cdmc.

Caux, J. (2002) *Presque Rien Avec Luc Ferrari.* Editions Main d'Œuvre.

Järvilluoma, H. and Wagstaff, G. (2002) *Soundscape Studies and Methods.* Helsinki: Finnish Society for Ethnomusicology.

LaBelle, B. (2006) *Background Noise: Perspectives on Sound Art.* New York: Continuum.

Merleau-Ponty, M (2002) *The Phenomenology of Perception.* Trans C. Smith. London: Routledge. Original (1945) as *Phénoménologie de la perception.* Paris: Gallimard.

Schafer, R.M. (1977) *The Soundscape.* Rochester: Destiny Books.

Smalley, D. (1992) 'The Listening Imagination: Listening in the Electroacoustic Era', in J. Paynter, T. Howell, R. Orton and P. Seymour (eds) *Companion to Contemporary Musical Thought*, vol.1, pp.514–54. London: Routledge.

Truax, B. (2001) *Acoustic Communication.* Westport: Ablex Publishing.

Discography

Ferrari, L. (2008) *Presque Rien.* Ina-GRM 275 482.

Genesis (1991) *We Can't Dance.* Virgin GEN CD3.

Gerwin, T. (1995) *Karlsruhe: Klangbilder einer Stadt.* Edition Modern – Tre Media.

Holly, B. (2008) *Not Fade Away: Buddy Holly 1957 – The Complete Recordings.* El Toro B000X23KA2 (3-CD set).

Spector, P. (1991) *Phil Spector – Back to Mono 1958–1969.* Phil Spector Records 7118-2.

Swierczewski, M. (1992) *Charles Ives.* With the Gulbenkian Orchestra. Nimbus Records NI 5316.

The Beach Boys (1990) *Pet Sounds.* Capitol Records CDP 7 48421 2.

The Legendary Sun Records Story (2000) Pulse PBX CD 336.

Zinman, D. (1992) *Henryk Górecki Symphony No. 3 Op. 36.* With London Sinfonietta and Dawn Upshaw. Elektra Nonesuch 7559-79282-2.

III
An Ethnomusicological Interlude

ROBERT REIGLE

Humanistic Motivations in Ethnomusicological Recordings

T HE aims and uses of ethnomusicological recordings are philosophical in that term's most basic sense: they constitute actions undertaken with a view to love and pursue wisdom. This chapter presents an initial foray into the ideas behind ethnomusicological recordings, the history of their dissemination, and their broadening effect on concepts of music and musical aesthetics.[1] The work of the recordists discussed below reveals ethnomusicology's humanistic intentions, which have increasingly born fruit via the exponential growth of technological change.[2] While this chapter introduces some of the salient concepts motivating ethnomusicologists to publish sound recordings, future work should relate these ideas to the full scope of meanings associated with ethnomusicological recordings, including not only their ethnographic, but also cognitive and humanistic aspects and emphasizing their aesthetic reception outside the music's original culture. That project would entail extracting overtly philosophical topics such as meaning, ontology, and aesthetics from within the more general ethnomusicological writings, and evaluating the concept of ethnomusicology itself.

Recordings and recordists' philosophies

This section consists of three parts. First, I consider some of the general assumptions that shaped both the scholarly and public use of ethnomusicological sound recordings. Secondly, I present a chronology of milestones in the history of ethnomusicological recordings in order to provide a context for a discussion of their role in the dissemination of international ideas. Finally, I identify some of the purposes of a small but carefully chosen selection of prominent ethnomusicologists and record companies, along with a consideration of the music anthology sent into outer space on Voyager.

When Walter Fewkes made the first ethnomusicological field recordings in 1890 (DeVale, 2001), he could not have imagined that sound recordings would one day be digitized at rates exceeding 44,100 samples per second. Nor would Noel Josephs, the Passamaquoddy singer Fewkes recorded, have guessed that his voice would reach listeners as a found object in a modern composition, a century later.[3] Now marketed on compact disc or available on the Internet, early ethnomusicological cylinder recordings mark both an end of innocence and a portal to new worlds of cultural exchange. Fewkes' aim nevertheless remains consonant with the motivations of present-day ethnomusicological recordists and producers: to gain (or permit access to) a better understanding of a previously unknown music by experiencing its sound.

Beginning with Fewkes' recordings, comparative musicologists embraced recording technology as the opportunity to scientize their work, and validate it with objective analyses of sounds and images. There was (and is) a pressure to legitimate ethnomusicological work with the stamp of science – a pressure symptomatic of the remarkable tenacity and dominance of positivism.[4] What philosophical assumptions supported such an agenda? While it is difficult to ascertain a comprehensive set of predispositions, we can nonetheless identify some of the general views held in Europe and America, and consider the extent to which musicological writings followed, questioned, or opposed such notions. The literature of the late nineteenth and early twentieth centuries suggests that many people felt that music was a universal language and that the world's musics would follow an evolutionary path towards European harmony and aesthetics (Nettl, 2005: 42). Today, many people around the world feel that pan-European musics or styles are superior: witness the role of European music in conservatories around the world;[5] the adoption of European forms by international music institutions;[6] the harmonization of national anthems; and the use of pan-European rhythms, harmonies, instruments, song forms, and production techniques in world popular genres (Nettl, 2005: 160). Aesthetics, education, market pressures, social experience, racism, or xenophobia may play a role in shaping this view.

Among the basic assumptions regarding the purpose of ethnomusicological studies, we can cite four that have changed during the last decades of the twentieth century due to insights gained through the study of recordings. Before the 1960s, some scholars felt that: (1) studying the structures of 'primitive musics' could reveal the sound of pre-historic European music (Sachs, 1938); that (2) the aesthetic response of the ethnomusicologist was unimportant (or rather, must be kept in check); or that (3) music can be apprehended through its sound. Furthermore, in the early years of comparative musicology, (4) many scholars regarded the music of 'low' technology cultures as unchanging, as opposed to the rapidly changing pan-European musics (Nettl, 2005: 272). It required a substantial body of sound recordings for scholars to question these assumptions and propose alternative views. It is important to note that ethnomusicologists have not simply adopted the opposites of these four assumptions. Rather, access to recordings has made an essential contribution towards broader, more sophisticated, and more nuanced stances on those ideas.

Before the advent of sound recordings, scholars had to rely on written texts to represent music. The first 'recordings' of 'exotic' musics were the transcribed notations made by missionaries, government officers, and explorers around the sixteenth century (Bohlman, 1988; Ellingson, 1992: 110–2). A few major ethnomusicological studies in European languages appeared during the eighteenth and early nineteenth centuries. In the first decades of the twentieth century, some of the assumptions mentioned above motivated scholars to select particular musics as worthy of study. For example, the idea of isolated groups as living specimens of cultural 'missing links' or as examples of European lifestyles from several thousand years ago, encouraged researchers to select groups such as Australian aborigines and remote African cultures for intensive studies (Sachs, 1965; Waterman, 1963).

Comparative musicologists typically studied musics of the 'other' rather than of their own tradition, though in some countries scholars studied musics of their own country, often under the rubric of folklore. After World War II, ethnomusicologists per se began to study their own musics. The musics of the other still constitute the majority of pan-European ethnomusicological research topics; ethnomusicologists focus largely on the musics outside the purview of the musicological mainstream, and direct much of their writing primarily towards readers outside the geographic location of their research. Recordings made in various nations for local markets function as ethnomusicological recordings when taken to an 'other' culture for study.[7] Starting in the 1930s, however, companies began to market cross-cultural recordings with the dual intention of providing study materials and introducing listeners to foreign sounds for aesthetic appreciation.

Tracing the history of the cross-cultural dissemination of ethnomusicological recordings contextualizes the parallel spread of the philosophical ideas associated with them, such as the growing awareness of Asian philosophies in the West and South. In addition to philosophies, musical ideas crossed stylistic borders via recordings. For example, some of the sounds used by the pan-European composer Giacinto Scelsi in pieces such as *I Presagi*, *Hurqualia*, and *Uaxuctum*, bear likeness to Tibetan Buddhist music. By the end of the twentieth century, most pan-European composers had heard Indian classical music (but not the diverse and seldom-recorded Indian tribal [*adivasi*] musics), gamelan, didjeridu, central Asian overtone singing, and quite probably many others. Jazz composers also demonstrated great interest in world musics; saxophonist Albert Ayler composed a piece, 'Bells', with the same melody as 'Pfeni Nengoma', a song from what is now Zimbabwe, that appeared on *The Columbia World Library of Folk and Primitive Music, volume X* (Tracey, 1954).

Given the limited accessibility of sound archives during the twentieth century, commercial recordings provided the primary access to the world's musics. Many of the companies producing the largest series of world music recordings had been established by 1970; several began converting their catalogues to compact disc in the late 1980s. The following is a list of some of the milestones in the history of ethnomusicological recordings:

1922 – The first sale was made of *Die Demonstrations-Sammlung von Erich M. von Hornbostel* [The Demonstration Collection of Erich M. von Hornbostel], the first anthology of traditional music recordings. Drawing from the University of Berlin's Phonogramm-Archiv, Hornbostel produced the set of 120 cylinders, intending it for institutional buyers (Reinhard, 1963: 12). By the time the collection appeared, its format was rapidly becoming obsolete; Columbia gramophone company, for example, had stopped publishing cylinders in 1912 (Weber, 2001: 1). The anthology formed the basis of important studies by comparative musicologists who did work at the Berlin Archiv, including Erich Fischer, George Herzog, Mieczyslaw Kolinski, Fritz Bose, Henry Cowell, and Marius Schneider (Reinhard, 1963: 10). In 1963, Folkways Records issued 42 of the recordings on a set of two LPs (Reinhard and List, 1963), and in 2000, Wergo issued some recordings from the cylinder period as part of a four-CD set, *Music! The Berlin Phonogramm-Archiv 1900–2000* (Simon and Wegner, 2000).

Circa 1929 – Arthur Miles made the first recording of overtone singing in the United States: 'Lonely Cowboy' (Miles, 2000).

1931 – Hornbostel released *Musik des Orients*, twelve 78-rpm records on the Odeon and Parlophone labels marketed to the European general public (Reinhard, 1963: 12), and reviewed in a 1934 issue of *Gramophone* ('Hindsight', 2004: 142). The set contains 76 minutes of musics from Japan, China, Java, Bali, Siam, lower India (classical *raga*s), Persia, Egypt, and Tunis, and includes a 24-page booklet. Note that 'the Orient' included North Africa. Several labels issued the recordings, including HMV (78s), and Decca and Folkways (LPs) (Hornbostel, 1979). Until the 1950s, *Music of the Orient* was the only anthology of Asian musics (indeed, of world musics) widely available (Waterman et al., 1951: 683).

1932 – Robert Lachmann chaired the Recording Committee of the Congress of Arab Music, held in Cairo, 14 March – 3 April. The committee recorded more than 175 discs, which it 'considered the first step toward reconstructing Arab music in its presumably ancient, uncontaminated, and distinctive form' (Racy, 1991: 73).

1944 – The Archives Internationales de Musique Populaire, Geneva, began issuing its three collections of 78s, including *The World Collection of Recorded Folk Music* (1951–8), the first series of recordings published in co-operation with the United Nations Educational, Scientific, and Cultural Organization (UNESCO) (Van Peer, 1999: 377). VDE-Gallo reissued *The World Collection* on six LPs: one disc of African, one of Asian and Eskimo, and four of European musics (Brailoiu, 1984).

1946 – The Musée de l'Homme in Paris began issuing ethnomusicological recordings on its in-house imprint, Musée de l'Homme. For the first two years, the pressings were intended only for museums and sound archives. In 1948, the museum began sponsoring publications on the Boîte à Musique (BAM) label, aimed at the general public; the first three discs contained field recordings from the Congo (Van Peer, 1999: 377). The museum later sponsored publications on the Contrepoint, Vogue, and Le Chant du Monde labels.

1948 – Moses Asch and Marian Distler founded Folkways Records, eventually issuing 2,168 albums from over 130 countries (Olmsted, 2003).

1950 – Peter Fritsch founded Lyrichord Records. They have issued recordings of music from around the world, including seminal albums recorded by leading researchers. More recently, Lyrichord has produced a series of 'traditional world music' DVDs.

1955 – The first full albums of Indian classical music that achieved wide distribution in the West were published (Daniélou, 1955; Khan, 1995; see Crossley-Holland, 1959: 60). Indian folk music albums and shorter classical examples had preceded them, including *Music of India: Traditional & Classical*, on Folkways (album duration: 29:23) (Singh, 1951).

1955 – *The Columbia World Library of Folk and Primitive Music*, edited by Alan Lomax, began publication. Seventeen volumes were published through 1963: Scotland, Ireland, England, France, Spain, Northern and Central Italy, Southern Italy, Romania, Bulgaria, Yugoslavia, India, East Asia, Indonesia, Australia and New Guinea, British East Africa, French West and Equatorial Africa, Venezuela (Kaye and Barton, 2003: 105, n. 4). Rounder Records has reissued eight of these on CD, often with additional tracks, and plans to reissue the entire series, including volumes for Canada and Mexico that Columbia never released.

1955 – The first album of Tibetan music to be marketed in the West appeared: *Musique tibétaine du Sikkim* (Rouget, 1955).

1956 – The Library of Congress began issuing LPs of American folk music.

1957 – The *History of Music in Sound, v. 1: Ancient and Oriental Music* was published (Wellesz, 1957).

1957 – Charles Duvelle founded the OCORA (Office de Coopération Radiophonique) collection published by Radio France. OCORA-Radio France has issued approximately 86 vinyl albums and more than 300 compact discs of ethnographic recordings from around the world.

1961 – The first recording of overtone singing marketed in Europe appeared on *Musique religieuse chinoise et tibétaine* (Migot, 1961). (Peter Crossley-Holland (1974), however, suggested that side B of his 1965 LP *The Music of Tibetan Buddhism III* (Kassel: Bärenreiter-Musicaphon BM-30L-2011), was the first). Migot's album drew the attention of ethnomusicologist Laurence Picken, who pointed out that '[t]he voice quality of these Tibetan *bassi profundi* is remarkable for its jew's-harp-like richness in overtones, inviting comparison with the "double-voice" of the Tuva, for example' (Picken, 1963).

1961 – UNESCO began sponsoring the *UNESCO Collection of Traditional Music of the World*. Several important LP series were published in collaboration with different record companies, including *A Musical Anthology of the Orient* (26 titles), *An Anthology of African Music* (14 titles), *Musical Sources* with

Philips, *Musical Atlas* with EMI, plus additional titles from Southeast Asia and Oceania with Bärenreiter-Musicaphon. In 1988, UNESCO formed an arrangement with Naïve/Auvidis, subsequently releasing 115 titles of new or reissued recordings. In 1998, Rounder records also began reissuing titles from these series. As a result of 'the large number of superb documentary audio recordings appearing almost everywhere in the world', UNESCO stopped sponsoring publications in the *UNESCO Collection of World Music* series in 2005, and canceled its distribution contract with Naïve/Auvidis (Van Zanten and Seeger, 2005).

1960s – The Berlin Phonogram Archiv began publishing its *Museum Collection* series (Van Peer, 1999: 377); the series continued on CD, and reissues along with new titles are being issued by Wergo. Topic Records began issuing world music recordings. The International Library of African Music issued a 210-LP series, *Sound of Africa*, and produced a 25-LP series for Decca, *Music of Africa*; both are available on CD, along with a new series of discs.

1967 – The Nonesuch Explorer Series of LPs began, continuing until 1984.

1969 – The Vogue label began issuing LPs from the Musée de l'Homme (Van Peer, 1999: 377).

1974 – Alain Normand started the Playasound label, producing more than 300 recordings of world music.

1977 – The Voyager spacecraft carried a Golden Record into space (see discussion below).

1980 – Publication of Elizabeth May's edited volume *Musics of Many Cultures: An Introduction*, the first world-music appreciation textbook to include ethnomusicological recordings.

1980s – The Music of the World label was founded.

1987 – The Smithsonian Institution acquired Folkways Records, eventually making the whole catalogue available on CDR, and continuing the Folkways legacy with new releases on the Smithsonian Folkways label.

1988 – The Victor Company of Japan (JVC) issued *The JVC Video Anthology of World Music and Dance*, consisting of 30 video tapes and 9 books (Fujii, 1988).

1990s onward – Companies including JVC, PAN, Inedit, Buda Musique, Ellipsis Arts, Philips/Universal/Kora Sons (Prophet series), and Traditional Crossroads issued important series of world music recordings. Internet delivery of recordings expanded.

1992 – Eckart Rahn began issuing world music recordings on his Celestial Harmonies label, emphasizing multiple-CD sets of world classical traditions.

1992 – MP2 files appeared on the Internet, followed by MP3s in 1995.

2006 – The closure of Tower Records' international chain of stores (but continuing online), marking the end of an era in world-music retailing, was emblematic of the change from retail store to Internet shopping.

This chronology delineates the interface between the sound recordists, who extend a long tradition of representing music, and the organizations that sponsor, publish, and market their recordings. Based on their own accounts in liner notes (discussed below) and on the low sales figures for ethnomusicological recordings,[8] one can argue that the recordists' motivations are largely philosophical (in the sense of pursuing wisdom) or educational rather than financial. Ethnomusicological recordings reflect the three intimately interconnected concerns of knowledge, aesthetics, and/or preservation. For example, one may wish to preserve music that has aesthetic appeal; in order to gain knowledge of a repertoire, it must exist (be preserved) in some form – in other words, it must be commodified. Ethnomusicologists must mediate such concerns through the realities of publishing and distributing sound recordings (Zemp, 1996).

Access to the world's musics through commercial sound recordings expands the palette of potential analytical methods to include, for example, those dependant upon the repeatability of the sound event and those involving comparison across cultures. Each method is underpinned by the philosophical assumptions that supported its development. For example, being able to play a recording many times facilitates the identification of structural devices in the sound; structuralism has its own set of strengths and weaknesses that may or may not be appropriate in a given instance. While the uses of technology for analyzing recorded sound have grown increasingly more sophisticated (such as the advances in timbral analysis), the use of recordings as social texts has led to a reduction in sonic analysis in the ethnomusicological literature, as evidenced by the diminishing importance of transcriptions in publications (Marian-Bălaşa, 2005).

Originating before the advent of recordings, the use of transcription as a documentary technique lasted into the 1970s, when ethnomusicological recordings reached sufficient amounts, quality, and affordability for sounds (rather than music notation) to represent repertoires, thus shifting transcription largely to the domain of analysis. When ethnomusicology began, no ethnomusicological recordings were being marketed; the twentieth century saw a steady increase in the accessibility of musics outside one's own culture. Austrian ethnomusicologist Erich M. von Hornbostel (1877–1935) produced the first two sets of commercial recordings representing the world's musics (see above). His foreword to the *Musik des Orients* reveals an interest in the 'Exotic':

> Widely varying interests – among the musical and educational, no less than the general public – are calling for examples of Exotic Music. The materials collected for scientific purposes in the various phonographic archives, though most valuable for research work, does not always come up to the present-day high standards of recording and artistic reproduction...Not only have the interests of musical science been considered, but also historical, cultural, and ethnographical aspects, so that the collection provides valuable help in the teaching of history and geography in schools and colleges.

> (Hornbostel, 1979: 1)

Hornbostel was clearly concerned with the aesthetic reception of the music, as indicated by his comment about 'artistic reproduction' and the quality of the selections themselves. The brief but substantial annotations, including the 'tonal structure' of each selection in staff notation, confirm that he prepared the set as an educational tool, an ethnomusicological document, and an aesthetic demonstration of inaccessible yet worthy repertoires.

The loss of some of Hornbostel's collected recordings to the Allied bombing of Berlin was one of the reasons Moses Asch (1905–86), along with Marian Distler (1919–64), founded Folkways Records in 1948 (Bluestein, 1987: 298). Consistent with the work of many ethnomusicologists, Asch felt it was important to preserve traditions – including national musics suppressed through political and social actions – and lamented the loss of ethnomusicological sound recordings, which he viewed as vital historical documents. With the aim of producing a sonic history of culture, Asch took the name for his company from sociologist William Graham Sumner's 1906 book *Folkways: A Study of the Sociological Importance of Usages, Manners, Customs, Mores, and Morals* (Bluestein, 1987: 298). Asch recounted that he had been inspired by Theodore Roosevelt's introduction to John Lomax's book of *Cowboy Songs and Other Frontier Ballads*, 'which guided me through life because he said that folklore and songs are the cultural expression of a people.' (Young, 1977: 3, cited in Olmsted, 2003: 12) For Asch, sound recordings of folk music functioned as vessels of truth:

> I became conscious of history and that folk music always gave you a sense of something that happened before that someone set down for us to remember, for they always felt that there is a moral, a universality, a truth to something that people pick up and sing and talk about and bring back from generation to generation.

> (Young, 1977: 6, cited in Olmsted, 2003: 16)

By creating an 'encyclopedia of sound', Asch sought to ensure the permanent availability of 'sound as meaning and content, the elements so dear to the individuals and groups that identify with the cultural relevance of their aural expression' (Olmsted, 2003: 7, 15).

Henry Cowell (1897–1965) produced and annotated many albums for Folkways Records in keeping with his commitment to teaching. These include a series of five double albums entitled *Music of the World's Peoples* (1951–5), which share the name of a course he taught at Columbia University (Mitchell, 1966: 78). Rather than organizing the recordings 'by races, by styles, by history, or by geography', he 'presented instead a sampling of widely contrasted musics from many levels of culture and many parts of the world' (Cowell, 1951: 1). This random ordering of the world's musics demonstrates the Chinese concept of yang/yin (as unity in diversity) with which Cowell was familiar, and encourages a non-hierarchical hearing (free from group associations) of the individual components of the whole, thus enabling the serendipitous discovery of new sounds.[9] The purpose of the series was to introduce new aesthetics, and concomitantly, promote intercultural understanding: 'That which may seem raucous at first may come to sound beautiful on further hearing; and at the very least, it will be found to be full of meaning and feeling. There is no better way to know a people than to enter with them into their musical life' (Cowell, 1951: 1). Furthermore, recordings are necessary because written transcriptions alone cannot convey the full range of pitch and rhythm subtleties, and thus music's 'real feeling' (Cowell, 1951: 1).

Cowell's humanistic stance is emblematic of the widely held view that music has extraordinary value as a social, cultural, aesthetic, and historic force. Nowhere is this concept better propagated than through the work of the United Nations Educational, Cultural, and Scientific Organization (UNESCO). That organization sponsored a series of published recordings from 1951 to 1958, and then started anew in 1961 under the direction of ethnomusicologist Alain Daniélou (1907–94). Intended to provide 'a source of invaluable inspiration for today's creators, musicologists, and traditional music lovers', the recordings were selected with both documentary and aesthetic concerns in mind ('Traditional Music', n.d.: 1). Daniélou emphasized the latter, seeing his purpose as promoting East-West understanding by presenting

> to a large music-minded audience the higher forms of art-music – the music Orientals call 'classical' by opposition to folk music – so as to prepare its place as a full and equal partner in the international musical life...The present anthology does not aim at being ethnomusicological...Our purpose has been to record *music*, the best music available, performed by the best professional musicians, and as far as possible unstained by modern trends and influences.
>
> (Daniélou, 1963: 162)

These remarks reveal two long-standing though not universally held assumptions, namely the superior status of art music and a characterization of modernity in negative terms. Daniélou's third assumption, however, is currently salient in ethnomusicological research: the potential for recordings to play an important role in developing cultural equity.

Anthropologist/ethnomusicologist Anthony Seeger has helped the Suyá of the Brazilian Amazon protect their culture, while at the same time 'translating' their music to a wider audience. He has written widely on humanistic, anthropological, and ethnomusicological topics. One of the most prominent thinkers about the use of ethnomusicological recordings, he wrote:

> Music is much more than just the sounds captured on a tape recorder. Music is an intention to make something called music (or structured similarly to what *we* call music) as opposed to other kinds of sounds...Music is also, of course, the sounds themselves after they are produced. Yet it is intention as well as realization; it is emotion and value as well as structure and form.
>
> (Seeger, 2004: xiv)

Seeger's paramount concern regarding recordings is the rights of the performers/
creators/owners. These rights, however, function in the real world of consumers,
businesses, academics, and dynamic music communities (such as the Suyá
themselves).

Ownership rights are extraordinarily complex in the case of the Voyager Golden
Record, the album made out of gold and sent to outer space on the Voyager spacecraft
in 1977. The contents, assembled under the direction of scientist Carl Sagan,
included 27 music selections, totaling nearly 90 minutes ('Golden Record', 2003).
The representation of the world's musics included examples from all six inhabited
continents: Africa (3'), Australia/Oceania (4'), Latin America (5'), North America
(9'), Asia (23'), and Europe (42'). The selections on the Voyager Golden Record, well
chosen in terms of quality, show a hierarchical thinking along conventional lines:
that art music (especially that of Western Europe's Baroque and Classical eras)
should take prominence in representing the achievement of humanity. As one of the
stated goals was to represent musics of all time periods, it appears that the editors
intended African and Oceanic examples to represent very ancient times – before
the art musics of Asia and Europe appeared. The view that musics of low-technology
cultures represent very old forms had been dismissed or assumed untenable among
ethnomusicologists around the 1970s, but recent work by Victor Grauer[10] has created
a renewed interest in the topic.

The Voyager Golden Record constitutes an important anthologizing of the world's
musics, as does Hornbostel's *Music of the Orient*. The ideas leading to these works,
along with the motivations in evidence from the recordists discussed above, point
to one basic goal: to promote intercultural understanding through the appreciation
of the diversity of the world's musics. This purpose is evident in the work of most
ethnomusicologists (including those not trained in the discipline, such as Moses
Asch), though the means to achieve the goal include a vast array of approaches,
methodologies, and emphases. Those means are shaped by the particularities of the
different musics studied around the world, and thus as a group, ethnomusicologists
indirectly represent all of the world's philosophies through their work.

Broadening horizons

Academic systems necessarily develop out of the philosophical milieu of their own
locale, and the assumptions, biases, and limitations of the indigenous setting tend
to be revealed when knowledge, particularly cross-cultural knowledge, increases
and becomes absorbed into the mainstream. As cross-cultural exchanges grew
in speed and depth during the nineteenth century, topics of study expanded to
include all of the world's cultures (at least nominally), and Sumner coined the
term 'ethnocentrism' in his 1906 book, *Folkways*, mentioned above. The world's
philosophies and the study of the forms in which they manifest themselves have
not, however, been fully integrated into academic discourse (see below). In the case

of music, the task of broadening academic horizons to bridge pan-European views with the wider palette logically falls to musicians trained in exploring diversity: ethnomusicologists. Recordings played, and continue to play, a central role in this project, first as the mechanism that made analysis possible and, after World War II, more importantly as the medium through which listeners could access new vistas of sound. With the advent of recordings, ethnomusicologists could select a repertoire to study based on its sound, without having to first attend a performance *in situ*. The new access to diverse music systems led to changes in basic concepts of music, and world-music appreciation textbooks accompanied by ethnomusicological recordings began to appear in 1980.

Musics

One of the most important issues concerning recordings is how they have affected the idea of music itself. Surprisingly omitted from standard reference works such as *The Concise Oxford Dictionary of Music* and the various editions of *The Grove Dictionary of Music and Musicians* (until 2001), the term 'music' has been increasingly pluralized to 'musics' as concrete examples (recorded sounds) of the diversity of the world's music cultures began to make their appearance.[11] How have the philosophies of ethnomusicologists and ethnomusicological record companies contributed to the 'discovery' of particular musics, and to the recognition of musical diversity itself?

Comparative musicologists, scientists studying music, and anthropologists were often forward thinking in terms of moral behavior, and some early writings reveal a respect for otherness not shared by the majority. For example, Alexander Ellis (1885) forcefully challenged the preeminence of major and minor scales, and in the nineteenth century, Adolf Bastian used participant observation techniques that did not gain widespread currency until after World War I (Köpping, 2005). Although one of their original motivations was a desire to understand music evolution under the assumption that harmony was a pinnacle (Ames, 2003), Carl Stumpf and Hornbostel's founding of the Berlin Phonogram Archive at the turn of the twentieth century led to an international broadening of musical understanding.

During the twentieth century, musical relativism gained importance in two ways, both of them made possible via the mechanism of sound recordings. First, through increasing knowledge, rapidly communicated, the cultural diversity of humankind across the dimensions of space (geography) and time (history) became better known. Entrenched hierarchies of musical quality (such as the supremacy of polyphony) were thrown in question, and economic hegemony as arbiter of musical style came under attack. The United Nations, emblematic of the growing sense of international community and responsibility, established its educational, scientific, and cultural organization (UNESCO), sponsoring world music recordings (1951–2005) and encouraging nations to establish 'Living Human Treasure' systems modeled after those of Japan (1950) and Korea (1964). In the last decade, UNESCO began three new initiatives concerned with ethnomusicological recordings: The Proclamation of Masterpieces of the Oral and Intangible Heritage of Humanity (1997–2006), UNESCO Cities of Music, and the Convention for the Safeguarding of the Intangible Cultural Heritage.

Second, the intersection of local and international aesthetics led to the development of increasingly global music preferences and understanding. Geographically disparate cultures could share in the aesthetic appreciation of a particular musical repertoire through the medium of sound recordings. Musically, this produces both diversification and homogenization. As the world's population increases, the size of listening communities becomes large enough to sustain special interests, thus allowing for increasing diversity. On the other hand, the international availability of such diversity produces commercial pressures, and sameness of difference. The multinational record companies, which began in the early years of sound recording, have now made possible or caused an extraordinary homogenization of popular musics. Meanwhile, exposure to such a great diversity of musics through entertainment, marketing, and educational media, may contribute to a reduction in difference (rather than its discovery) via the mechanism of continual newness; that is, listeners group diverse musics together into the homogeneous category of 'new' or 'different'.

As the aesthetic scope of musics broadened via the medium of recordings, so did the conceptual. The view that 'the music' is an autonomous printed score, or a sound, has given way to the idea that music is inseparable from its creators and hearers. Although recordings capture the sound in an object, and 'performers' 'play' the sound (set that complex waveform into motion), that sound has significance only as an experience of listeners. In other words, the idea of a piece of music as an objective entity that may be analyzed strictly according to the arbiters of quality has given way to a concept of the musical work that is more fluid, dependent upon human action, and changeable through the interface between group and individual experience. While recorded sound constitutes an object the human origins of which can only be imagined rather than visually observed, it is not until one hears a recording that it becomes music; experience is the locus of music. John Blacking, one of the most influential ethnomusicologists of the twentieth century, summed up this view in a seminal lecture: '[t]he value of music is, I believe, to be found in terms of the human experiences involved in its creation.' (Blacking, 1974: 50) Blacking used the term 'creation', I believe, not only in the sense of composer and performer actions, but also in the sense of 'causing to sound', as in playing a recording.

Educational recordings

Music education typically focuses on local genres – local in the sense that a significant portion of the regional populace appreciates, participates in, or knows them. For example, pan-European classical music originated in Europe, but it may be considered local in Seoul, where it is commonly taught to all age groups. The North American volume of *The Garland Encyclopedia of World Music* (Koskoff, 2001) provoked some controversy by devoting a great deal of space to musics from around the world that are performed there, rather than concentrating solely on the music of the first inhabitants, descendants of European settlers, and musics of local origin. Composer and ethnomusicologist Cowell, who sang Japanese and Chinese songs with his friends while growing up in San Francisco, held an internationalist view of American music long before such ideas gained common currency: 'the music of Japan, as well as that of China and other oriental countries, is part of American music' (Cowell, 1963: 25). Many people in the United States, however, did not share Cowell's view, nor were similar views typical in other countries. Historically, each cultural group is more or less open to syncretism and change according to temperament, access, and experience; and their openness itself changes over time, as in the case of Japan, whose political policy switched from isolationism to internationalism.

During the last decades of the twentieth century, philosophies of music education have placed greater emphasis on diversity. Partly as a result of the globalization of knowledge and the availability of resources, educators have incorporated a wider range of musics in their teaching. At the primary school level in the United States, for example, the incorporation of world musics was formerly typical only of specialized educational strategies such as those of Rudolf Steiner (Waldorf), Maria Montessori, Carl Orff, Zoltán Kodály, and so on, but gradually became more widespread. World music courses, now common in college music departments around the world, contribute to the general level of awareness of the world's musical diversity. Exposure to world musics may come via sound recordings (purchased or heard in libraries), or through teachers.

Perhaps the most common first exposure to ethnomusicological recordings, however, is the few tracks appended to the anthologies prepared for music appreciation courses. In the English language, the standard was set in the 1950s with the publication of *The New Oxford History of Music*, a series of ten books written by leading scholars. To accompany the books, Oxford University Press separately published ten boxed-sets with booklets (originally on 78-rpm discs, then reissued on two LPs) (Wellesz, 1957). The first book of the series, *Ancient and Oriental Music*, contains articles on 'primitive', Asian, ancient, and Islamic musics. No modern anthology has replaced this important work, and the book remains in print half a century after its first publication, while the accompanying sound recordings, unfortunately, went out of print long ago. The placement of the volume as the initial one in the series, followed by the others in chronological order, beginning with *Early Medieval Music up to 1300*, reflects the idea that 'Oriental' and 'primitive' musics were ancient and in some sense predecessors of European classical music. Indeed, the theory that humans originated in Africa lends a historic/genetic basis to the possibility of a musical link between Europe and Africa.[12] Transcriptions alone were not enough to convince scholars of the parity of different musics, and it was not until the availability (which

I would date to the 1960s) of a substantial range of world music recordings that a significant portion of musicologists accepted alternatives to the view that European harmony was the pinnacle of world music development (Stewart, 1980).

Authors of music appreciation texts began to include ethnomusicological recordings around the 1960s, and by the 1990s it was unusual for a general text to leave out such music. For example, the eighth edition of *The Norton Recordings*, which accompanies the book titled *The Enjoyment of Music*, includes one American jazz, one European folk, one African traditional, and one Chinese traditional track among its 47 examples (Machlis and Forney, 1999). As colleges began teaching more world music classes, the need for textbooks increased. Although beginning in the 1930s a number of record companies had issued series anthologizing world musics, only a few books that surveyed this repertoire appeared during the mid-twentieth century. Marian Cotton and Adelaide Bradburn published a book without sound recordings, *Music Throughout the World: A Course in Understanding and Appreciation Based on the Music of Many Countries*, in 1953. In 1971, Mantle Hood published a book with sound sheets, *The Ethnomusicologist*, intended for ethnomusicologists; and David Reck's remarkable *Music of the Whole Earth* appeared in 1977, but without sound recordings. Surprisingly, however, the first world-music appreciation textbook with sound recordings did not appear until 1980: Elizabeth May's edited volume, *Musics of Many Cultures: An Introduction*, which included three 7-inch sound sheets. This was followed in 1984 with Jeff Todd Titon's edited collection, *Worlds of Music: An Introduction to the Music of the World's Peoples* (1984), and the multi-authored book co-ordinated by Bruno Nettl (with Philip Bohlman, Charles Capwell, Isabel Wong, and Thomas Turino), *Excursions in World Music* (1992), both of which included two cassettes. A number of similar texts appeared after 1992, including works by John Kaemmer (1993), Jonathan Stock (1996), Dorothea E. Hast, James R. Cowdery, and Stanley Scott (1999), Kay Shelemay (2001), William Alves (2006), Terry E. Miller and Andrew Shahriari (2006), and Michael Bakan (2007). Several of the texts have appeared in revised editions. Sound and video recordings play an increasingly important role in such materials, and new forms of recording and distribution shape the ideas that students and teachers have regarding what constitutes a proper representation of a musical culture.

Conclusion

While the disciplines of linguistics and literature enjoy accepted and extensive subdivisions dealing with cross-cultural comparison, most universities consign the parallel sub-discipline in philosophy to the field of comparative religion (Littlejohn, 2006), and thus bracket it from mainstream philosophical inquiry (hence not challenging positivism/scientism). Likewise, what began as comparative musicology was replaced by ethnomusicology over the decades of the 1950s, '60s, and '70s, as its mainstream shifted towards social science. The global disciplines of anthropology and ethnomusicology can contribute to a broadening of the philosophical mainstream, by making accessible the spectrum of human thought and behavior. As a microcosm of meaning and feeling, music is especially potent, and when mediated through recordings, can transcend geographic, temporal, and cultural barriers, to effect substantial, cumulative change in world philosophy and culture. For example, appreciating ethnomusicological recordings may help establish understanding- and aesthetic-bases for combating the ills of ethnocentrism, nationalism, religious fundamentalism, fascism, and racism, while simultaneously celebrating the connectedness and integrity of musical and philosophical diversity (Feld, 2002; Seeger, 2003).

The twentieth-century shift from global understanding of music based on hearsay, ethnocentrism, and belief in music's evolution towards European harmony, to one based on knowledge of its sounds, cultures, and underlying philosophies, resulted from the adoption of relativistic views. Such views, in turn, came about through many causes, one of the most important being the dissemination of ethnomusicological and world music recordings. The pan-European notion of music (the one most documented in international languages) among musicians and a growing proportion of the general public, has changed from the concept of a single (and agreed-upon) 'music' to the idea that the world has many 'musics.'

Motivations shaping the work of world-music sound recordists include preservation of diversity, aesthetic appreciation, advancing human understanding, cultural advocacy, economic gain, and promoting a philosophical or political agenda. This chapter presented representative statements regarding the purposes of ethnomusicological recordings and suggested that the twin humanistic goals of cross-cultural understanding and aesthetic appreciation underlie the efforts towards their production.[13] Understanding the history of world music availability is prerequisite to tracing the flow of philosophical ideas across geographic, temporal, cultural, linguistic, and academic/public frontiers. Ethnomusicological sound recordings and their dissemination via commercial recordings comprise the foundation of that history.

New recording formats were among the advances in technology and communications that made possible the rapid growth of international popular culture, which took place after World War II. Although cross-cultural music exchange has occurred since before recorded history, the advent of sound recordings dramatically increased the quantity and quality of sonic difference that listeners might hear. Thus, the late twentieth century saw extensive studies of exoticism, Orientalism, and cross-cultural aesthetics, in response to the greatly expanded palette of sonic experience that became the societal norm. Under the influence of ethnomusicological recordings, the monolith of mainstream music aesthetics (good music = common practice harmony→chromatic harmony→serialism→post-serialism) is giving way to the many possible worlds of 'ugly beauty' (to borrow a term from Thelonious Monk (1968)).

Musics from around the world entered pan-European primary school education long ago, but often via simplified transcriptions that omitted or distorted culturally salient features such as timbre, rhythmic flexibility, tuning systems, duration, performance context, and so on. The advent of new recording media, especially 78s, LPs, floppy sound sheets, cassettes, video, compact discs, and MP3s, allowed increasingly accurate sound models. The expansion of college courses on world music has deepened the music appreciation skills of many listeners.

Through the medium of sound recordings, the introduction of increasingly sophisticated representations of the world's musics into all levels of education has paralleled and fueled a concurrent use of the same in broadcast and Internet media. The resulting expanded range of sounds experienced by the public has dramatically increased the complexity of the meanings of ethnomusicological recordings, thus advancing cross-cultural awareness through aesthetic appreciation of the world's musics and bringing to fruition the humanistic purposes of ethnomusicological recordings.

Notes

1   This chapter concerns all of the world's musics, but the discussion revolves around pan-European ethnomusicology and philosophy as a result of the inaccessibility of more in-depth information from around the world (for a view of Asian music studies, see Witzleben (1997)). Following current practice in ethnomusicology, I use the plural 'musics' when referring to a group of individual genres, and the singular 'music' to mean the undifferentiated concept of organized sound (for further elaboration, see below, under 'Musics'). I use the term pan-European in the sense of wholeness of the group or style (not as the idea of a contiguous Europe), to signify European ideas and their diaspora, including the European art-music tradition. This term, brought to my attention by George Emanuel Lewis (1996: 91), provides a less hegemonic/hierarchical alternative to 'Western', while avoiding the negativity of 'non-Eastern', which I had suggested in Reigle (1996).

  Ethnomusicologists regard their discipline as beginning in the late nineteenth century, though Jaap Kunst did not coin the term 'ethnomusicology' until 1950. I use the term 'ethnomusicological recordings' to denote recordings made at least partially for the purpose of documentation or study; aesthetic, economic, and other motivations also play a role, but not an exclusive one (though the distinction is not always clear-cut). In this chapter, I occasionally refer to, but do not focus on, recordings made largely for economic profit, though they are certainly essential to the discipline of ethnomusicology. I have not covered video recordings, due to space limitations.

2   The term 'recordist' entered common vocabulary circa 1925–30. Its use in this chapter is generic: one who records (in this case) music.

3   American composer John Schott incorporated Fewkes' recording of Passamaquoddy Indian Noel Josephs (Josephs, 1977) into a composition issued on compact disc (Schott, 2000).

4 Musicologist Hans Keller's incisive comment on this matter still holds true, I believe: 'This refusal to face the metaphysical problem one way or the other is – and I mean no offence – the supreme (if unpremeditated) critical cowardice of our age.' (Keller, 1957: 38)

5 Celia Applegate and Pamela Potter write, '[f]or musical audiences today, the words "German" and "music" merge so easily into a single concept that their connection is hardly ever questioned.' (Applegate and Potter, 2002: 1)

6 See, for example, Racy (1991).

7 For a discussion of the international sales of recordings from Eastern vendors to Western buyers and vice versa in the first decades of the twentieth century, see Gronow (1981). For a seven-volume discography of ethnic recordings in the United States (marketed towards national, linguistic, racial, or religious groups), see Spottswood (1990).

8 See, for example, Olmsted (2003: 190): 'a very long time to sell enough copies to break even'; Seeger (1995: 340): 'usually have to be subsidized to be published at all'; Zemp (1996: 54 n.9): 'sold less than 50 copies a year'.

9 Perhaps prompted by the idea of unity in diversity, Cowell used the plural 'musics' within his notes for the series, despite the singular form in the title.

10 Victor Grauer worked with Alan Lomax in 1961 to create the Cantometrics coding system, and in subsequent research. Recently, he has revived some of the concerns that ethnomusicologists had neglected during the last three decades, especially the evolution of music, comparison, and universals. Jonathan Stock edited two issues of *The World of Music* devoted to discussions of, or spawned by Grauer's work (Stock, 2006a and 2006b).

11 Some of the early uses of the plural occur in composer Vincent d'Indy's article 'Old and Young Musics' (1901), and in a bibliography/discography of Asian musics (Waterman et al., 1947). During the second half of the 1970s, British musicians published a journal called *Musics*, covering improvised, composed, and indigenous musics. For a European discussion of this terminology, see Dahlhaus (1998).

12 For an interactive presentation by a leading geneticist of the migrations out of Africa, see Oppenheimer (n.d.). See also note 10, above.

13 For a discussion of the purposes of ethnomusicology in general, see Nettl (2005: 12–15).

References

Alves, W. (2006) *Music of the Peoples of the World*. Belmont, CA: Thomson Schirmer. Book and two CDs.

Ames, E. (2003) 'The Sound of Evolution', *Modernism/Modernity* 10 (2): 297–325.

Applegate, C. and Potter, P. (2002) 'Germans as the "People of Music": Genealogy of an Identity', in C. Applegate and P. Potter (eds) *Music and German National Identity*, pp.1–35. Chicago: The University of Chicago Press.

Bakan, M.B. (2007) *World Music: Traditions and Transformations*. Boston: McGraw-Hill. Book and three CDs.

Blacking, J. (1974) *How Musical Is Man?* Seattle: University of Washington Press.

Bluestein, G. (1987) 'Moses Asch, Documentor', *American Music* 5 (3): 291–304.

Bohlman, P. (1988) 'Missionaries, Magical Muses, and Magnificent Menageries: Image and Imagination in the Early History of Ethnomusicology', *The World of Music* 30 (3): 5–27.

Cotton, M. and Bradburn, A. (1953) *Music Throughout the World: A Course in Understanding and Appreciation Based on the Music of Many Countries*. Boston: C.C. Birchard.

Cowell, H. (1951) Liner notes to *Music of the World's Peoples*. New York: Folkways Records. FE-4504. Two LPs and eight-page booklet.

_____ (1963) 'Music of the Orient', *Music Journal* 21 (6): 25–6, 74.

Crossley-Holland, P. (1959) 'Oriental Music on the Gramophone', *Music and Letters* 40 (1): 56–71.

_____ (1974) Review of *Tibetan Buddhism, Tantras of Gyütö* (Recordings and notes by David Lewiston (1973). One LP, Nonesuch H-72055), *Ethnomusicology* 18 (1): 339–41.

Dahlhaus, C. (1998) 'Music – or Musics?', in O. Strunk, R.P. Morgan and L. Treitler (eds) *Source Readings in Music History, volume 7*, pp.239–44. New York: W.W. Norton.

Daniélou, A. (1963) 'Some Remarks on the Review of the Musical Anthology of the Orient in the Journal of the International Folk Music Council', *Journal of the International Folk Music Council* 15: 162–5.

DeVale, S.C. (2001) 'Fewkes, Jesse Walter', in S. Sadie and J. Tyrrell (eds) *Grove Music Online*, URL (consulted November 2007): http://www.grovemusic.com

Ellingson, T. (1992) 'Transcription', in H. Myers (ed.) *Ethnomusicology: An Introduction*, pp.110–52. New York: W.W. Norton.

Ellis, A. (1885) 'On the Musical Scales of Various Nations', *Journal of the Royal Society of Arts* 33: 485–527.

Feld, S. (2002) 'Sound Recording as Cultural Advocacy: A Brief Case History from Bosavi, Papua New Guinea', in G. Berlin and A. Simon (eds) *Music Archiving in the World: Papers Presented at the Conference on the Occasion of the 100th Anniversary of the Berlin Phonogramm-Archiv*, pp.59–65. Berlin: VWB, Verlag für Wissenschaft und Bildung.

'Golden Record' (2003) Pasadena: NASA Jet Propulsion Laboratory, California Institute of Technology, URL (consulted November 2007): http://voyager.jpl.nasa.gov/spacecraft/goldenrec.html

Gronow, P. (1981) 'The Record Industry Comes to the Orient', *Ethnomusicology* 25 (2): 251–84.

Hast, D.E., Cowdery, J.R. and Scott, S. (1999) *Exploring the World of Music*. Dubuque, IA: Kendall/Hunt Publishing. Book, Faculty Guide, Preview Guide, three compact discs or audio cassettes, 12 half-hour programs on three DVDs or 12 VHS tapes. Videos available free online, from Annenberg CPB, URL: http://www.learner.org/resources/series105.html

'Hindsight' (2004) *Gramophone* 82 (980): 142.

Hood, M. (1971) *The Ethnomusicologist*. New York: McGraw-Hill. Book with three 33 1/3 rpm, seven-inch sound sheets.

Hornbostel, E.M. von (1979) [1931] Liner notes to *Music of the Orient*. New York: Folkways Records. FE-4157. Two LPs and notes.

d'Indy, V. (1901) 'Old and Young Musics', *Music* 20: 22.

Kaemmer, J.E. (1993) *Music in Human Life: Anthropological Perspectives on Music*. Austin: University of Texas Press. Book and audio cassette.

Kaye, A.L. and Barton, M. (2003) 'The 1950s: World Music. Introduction', in R.D. Cohen (ed.) *Alan Lomax: Selected Writings 1934–1997*, pp.97–106. New York: Routledge.

Keller, H. (1957) 'Schoenberg's "Moses and Aron"', *The Score* 21: 30–45.

Köpping, K.-P. (2005) *Adolf Bastian and the Psychic Unity of Man: The Foundations of Anthropology in Nineteenth-Century Germany*. Münster: Lit Verlag.

Koskoff, E. (ed.) (2001) *The Garland Encyclopedia of World Music, volume 3: The United States and Canada*. New York: Garland Publishing. Book and CD.

Lewis, G.E. (1996) 'Improvised Music after 1950: Afrological and Eurological Perspectives', *Black Music Research Journal* 16 (1): 91–122.

Littlejohn, R. (2006) 'Comparative Philosophy', in J. Fieser and B. Dowden (eds) *The Internet Encyclopedia of Philosophy*, URL (consulted November 2007): http://www.iep.utm.edu/

Machlis, J. and Forney, K. (1999) *The Enjoyment of Music: An Introduction to Perceptive Listening*. New York: W.W. Norton. Book and four enhanced multimedia discs. The CDs bear the title, *The Norton Recordings, Eighth Edition, Shorter Version*.

Marian-Bălaşa, M. (2005) 'Who Actually Needs Transcription? Notes on the Modern Rise of Method and the Postmodern Fall of an Ideology', *World of Music* 47 (2): 5–29.

May, E. (ed.) (1980) *Musics of Many Cultures: An Introduction*. Berkeley: University of California Press. Book with three 33 1/3 rpm, 7-inch, mono sound sheets.

Miller, T.E. and Shahriari, A. (2006) *World Music: A Global Journey*. Book and two CDs.

Mitchell, W.J. (1966) 'Henry Dixon Cowell. March 11th, 1897. December 10th, 1965', *Journal of the International Folk Music Council* 18: 77–8.

Nettl, B. (2005) *The Study of Ethnomusicology: Thirty-one Issues and Concepts*. Urbana: University of Illinois Press.

Nettl, B., Bohlman, P., Capwell, C., Wong, I. and Turino, T. (1992) *Excursions in World Music*. Upper Saddle River, NJ: Prentice-Hall. Book with two cassettes.

Olmsted, T. (2003) *Folkways Records: Moses Asch and His Encyclopedia of Sound*. New York: Routledge.

Oppenheimer, S. (n.d.) 'Journey of Mankind: The Peopling of the World', URL (consulted November 2007): http://www.bradshawfoundation.com/stehpenoppenheimer/main.html

Picken, L. (1963) Review of *Musique religieuse chinoise et tibétaine*, edited by André Migot (1961). Seven-inch EP, Boite à Musique LD-383. *Journal of the International Folk Music Council* 15: 158.

Racy, A.J. (1991) 'Historical Worldviews of Early Ethnomusicologists: An East-West Encounter in Cairo, 1932', in S. Blum, P.V. Bohlman and D.M. Neuman (eds) *Ethnomusicology and Modern Music History*, pp.68–91. Urbana: University of Illinois Press.

Reck, D. (1977) *Music of the Whole Earth*. New York: Scribner.

Reigle, R. (1996) 'A Comparison of Human and Spirit Voices', *Pacific Review of Ethnomusicology* 8 (1): 51–66, and CD tracks 3–4.

Reinhard, K. (1963) 'History of the Berlin Phonogramm-Archiv'; 'The Demonstration Collection', in K. Reinhard and G. List (eds) *The Demonstration Collection of E.M. von Hornbostel*, pp. 6–12. New York: Folkways Records and Service Corporation.

Sachs, C. (1938) 'Towards a Prehistory of Occidental Music', *The Musical Quarterly* 24 (2): 147–52.

_____ (1965) *The Wellsprings of Music*. New York: McGraw-Hill.

Seeger, A. (1995) 'Singing Other Peoples' Songs', in R. Sakolsky and F. Wei-Han Ho (eds) *Sounding Off! Music as Subversion/Resistance/Revolution*, pp.339–44. Brooklyn: Autonomedia.

_____ (2003) 'Changing Lives with Recorded Sound: Recordings and Profound Musical Experiences, The CMS Robert M. Trotter Lecture 2001 (Unabridged)', *College Music Symposium* 42: 1–8.

_____ (2004) *Why Suyá Sing: A Musical Anthropology of an Amazonian People*. Urbana: University of Illinois Press. Book and CD.

Shelemay, K.K. (2001) *Soundscapes: Exploring Music in a Changing World*. New York: W.W. Norton. Book and three CDs.

Spottswood, R. (1990) *Ethnic Music on Records: A Discography of Ethnic Recordings Produced in the United States, 1893 to 1942*. Urbana: University of Illinois Press.

Stewart, M. (1980) 'The Echoing Corridor: An Introduction to Field Recordings of Ethnic Music', *Early Music* 8: 339–57.

Stock, J. (ed.) (1996) *World Sound Matters: An Anthology of Music from Around the World*. London: Schott. Three volumes: Transcriptions, Teachers' Manual, Pupils' Questions; and two compact discs.

_____ (guest ed.) (2006a) *Echoes of Our Forgotten Ancestors. The World of Music* 48 (2).

_____ (guest ed.) (2006b) *Echoes of Our Forgotten Ancestors II. The World of Music* 48 (3).

Sumner, W.G. (1911) [1906] *Folkways: A Study of the Sociological Importance of Usages, Manners, Customs, Mores, and Morals*. Boston: Ginn and Co.

Titon, J.T. (ed.) (1984) *Worlds of Music: An Introduction to the Music of the World's Peoples*. New York: Schirmer Books. Book and two audio cassettes.

'Traditional Music.' (n.d.) URL (Consulted November 2007): http://www.unesco.org/culture/en/

Van Peer, R. (1999) 'Taking the World for a Spin in Europe: An Insider's Look at the World Music Recording Business', *Ethnomusicology* 43 (2): 374–84.

Van Zanten, W. and Seeger, A. (2005) 'UNESCO Collection Terminated (UNESCO Records/CD Series)', *Bulletin of the International Council for Traditional Music* 107: 19.

Waterman, R.A. (1963) 'On Flogging a Dead Horse: Lessons Learned from the Africanisms Controversy', *Ethnomusicology* 7 (2): 83–7.

Waterman, R.A., Lichtenwanger, W., Herrmann, V.H., Poleman, H.I. and Hobbs, C. (1947) 'Bibliography of Asiatic Musics', *Notes*, 2nd Series, 5 (1): 21–35.

_____ (1951) 'Survey of Recordings of Asiatic Music in the United States, 1950–51', *Notes*, 2nd Series, 8 (4): 683–91.

Weber, J. (2001) 'Recorded Sound, I.2 Acoustic Recording', in S. Sadie and J. Tyrrell (eds) *Grove Music Online*, URL (consulted November 2007): http://www.grovemusic.com

Witzleben, J.L. (1997) 'Whose Ethnomusicology? Western Ethnomusicology and the Study of Asian Music', *Ethnomusicology* 41 (2): 220–42.

Young, I. (1977) 'Moses Asch: Twentieth Century Man', *Sing Out!* 26 (1): 2–6.

Zemp, H. (1996) 'The/An Ethnomusicologist and the Record Business', *Yearbook for Traditional Music* 28: 36–56.

Discography/Videography

Brailoiu, C. (ed.) (1984) [1951–8] *Collection universelle de musique populaire enregistrée/The World Collection of Recorded Folk Music*. Geneva: VDE-Gallo VDE 30–25 to VDE 30–30. Six LPs with notes. Originally published by the International Archives of Folk Music, C.I.A.P., Ethnographical Museum on 40 sound discs, 78 rpm, 10", with notes.

Crossley-Holland, P. (1965) *The Music of Tibetan Buddhism III*. Kassel Bärenreiter-Musicaphon BM-30L-2011.

Daniélou, A. (ed.) (1955) *Anthologie de la Musique Classique de l'Indie*. Paris?: Ducretet-Thomson 320 C 096-8. Three LPs with 31-page booklet.

Fujii, T. (ed.) (1988) *The JVC Video Anthology of World Music and Dance*. Tokyo: Victor Company of Japan, Ltd. 30 VHS tapes and nine books.

Hornbostel, E.M. von (ed.) (1979) [1931] *Music of the Orient*. New York: Folkways Records FE-4157. Two LPs and notes. Previously issued on Odeon/Lindstroem (*Musik des Orients*, 1931), Parlophone/HMV (1934), and Decca (1951).

Josephs, N. (1977) [recorded 1890] 'Snake Dance Song', in R. Spottswood (ed.) *Religious Music: Solo & Performance*, track 17. Washington: Library of Congress. LBC-15. LP with ten-page brochure.

Khan, A.A. (1995) *Then and Now: The Music of the Great Master Continues*. Alam Madina Music Productions. Two CDs, the first is a reissue of the 1955 Capitol recording, *Music of India: Morning and Evening Ragas*.

Migot, A. (ed.) (1961) *Musique religieuse chinoise et tibétaine*. Paris: Boite à Musique LD-383. Seven-inch EP with notes.

Miles, A. (2000) [~1929] 'Lonely Cowboy', in *When I Was a Cowboy, vol. 1*. Newton, NJ: Yazoo Records 2022. CD and liner notes.

Monk, T. (1968?) *Underground*. New York: Columbia Records, CS-9632. LP recorded 14 December 1967. Includes 'Ugly Beauty' by T. Monk.

Reinhard, K. and List, G. (eds) (1963) *The Demonstration Collection of E.M. von Hornbostel*. New York: Folkways Records and Service Corporation. FE-4175. Two LPs and 40-page booklet.

Rouget, G. (ed.) (1955) *Musique tibétaine du Sikkim*. Paris: Contrepoint MC 20.119. LP and notes. Also issued on Museé de l'Homme LD-11 and Vogue LVLX-187.

Schott, J. (2000) 'Elegy: Noel Josephs and Jesse Walter Fewkes', in J. Schott, *Shuffle Play: Elegies for the Recording Angel*, track 21. New York: New World Records. CD 80548.

Simon, A. and Wegner, U. (eds) (2000) *Music! 100 Recordings – 100 Years of The Berlin Phonogramm-Archiv, 1900–2000*. Mainz, Germany: Wergo. SM-1701-2. Four CDs and 284-page booklet.

Singh, W.W. (ed.) (1951) *Music of India: Traditional and Classical*. New York: Folkways Records FW-4422. One LP and notes.

Tracey, H. (ed.) (1954) *Bantu Music from British East Africa. The Columbia World Library of Folk and Primitive Music, volume X*. New York: Columbia. KL-213. One LP with extensive notes.

Wellesz, E. (ed.) (1957) *History of Music in Sound, vol. 1: Ancient and Oriental Music*. Issued in England by HMV as nine 78-rpm discs (HMS 1-9) and as a boxed set of two LPs (HLP 1/2); in the USA as a boxed set of two LPs (RCA Victor LM-6057 [mono] or LSC-6057 [stereo]).

IV
Sound Recordings and Naturalized Epistemology

FRANCIS RUMSEY

Faithful to His Master's Voice?
Questions of Fidelity and Infidelity
in Music Recording

T HIS chapter is about the concept of fidelity in recorded music: the central question is whether fidelity is the aim of sound recording. Fidelity to what, one might ask? There are many different ways of conceptualising fidelity, and it is illuminating to examine the relationships between fidelity and preference, fidelity and quality, and spatial and timbral fidelity.

There is an unwritten assumption that the aim of recorded music is to provide an experience of listening that is as close as possible to that of natural listening – perhaps to the 'concert hall' experience. Absolute fidelity to the natural or original environment, however, is rarely – if ever – achieved and may not even be desirable. Listening experiences afforded by reproduced music are potentially different from those in 'natural' environments and could even be experienced as better or hyper-real. Furthermore, most commercially recorded music has no natural reference against which to compare it, since it has been created from scratch in a studio.[1] In some contexts live performance is expected to be faithful to recorded music, rather than the other way around. What, then, is the reference? How should one judge the quality of a recording?

Aspects of fidelity

The concept of fidelity has been of fundamental importance in defining the role of sound recording and reproduction. Fidelity can be defined variously as relating to faithfulness, as well as to accuracy in the description or reporting of facts and their details. In sound recording, it concerns the extent to which technical equipment is capable of accurately capturing, storing and reproducing sounds. Such definitions imply that sound reproduction is concerned with the accurate rendering of a sound source or sound field that occurred in the natural acoustical world. They stem from the primary role that sound recording and reproducing equipment had when it was first introduced – that of storing and reproducing a musical performance or someone's speech. Recording equipment was (and still is, to some extent) used to capture an event for posterity.

Floyd Toole describes his concept of fidelity in a paper on listening tests, and states that in addition to rating various aspects of sound quality 'listeners conclude with an overall "fidelity rating" intended to reflect the extent to which the reproduced sound resembles an ideal. With some music and voice the ideal is a recollection of live sound, with other source material the ideal must be what listeners imagine to be the intended sound' (Toole, 1982: 440). Fidelity is thus defined in relation to a memorized or imagined ideal reference. Toole's fidelity scale, shown in Figure 1, enables a hybrid of a value judgement (e.g. using terms like 'worse') and a faithfulness judgement (e.g. 'faithful to the ideal'), ruling out the possibility of 'less faithful' meaning 'better' (although this appears to be an unlikely combination, it highlights the assumption implicit in this type of scale.) It assumes that listeners know what is correct reproduction, and that what is correct is good. In some of his later papers on the subject, Toole goes on to show that listener preference and technical measures of fidelity can be closely related, at least in the case of loudspeaker evaluation, and that among listeners with similar hearing characteristics there are fewer differences of opinion than might be expected (e.g. Toole, 1986).

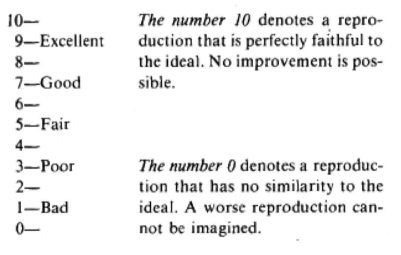

Figure 1: Toole's 1982 fidelity scale

Alf Gabrielsson and Bo Lindström define fidelity as 'the similarity of the reproduction to the original sound...the music sounds exactly as you heard it in the same room where it was originally performed' (Gabrielsson and Lindström, 1985: 52), but acknowledge the difficulty in judging this when listeners do not know what the music sounded like in reality: another example of the assumption that sound reproduction is designed primarily to reproduce something that actually happened and that listeners can remember it.

Tomasz Letowski (1989) distinguishes between sound quality and sound character, the former having an affective or hedonic component related to a value judgement or an emotional response and the latter being purely descriptive. The need for this crucial distinction between objective judgements and hedonic responses arises in a number of places in the sound quality literature, highlighted either by its presence or absence from the discussion. For example, the international standard for evaluation of small impairments in sound quality (ITU-R BS.1116[2]) uses a global quality rating called 'basic audio quality' that conflates the concept of annoyance with that of detection of an impairment. This scale is often termed 'mean opinion score' scale, showing more clearly that an opinion rather than an objective judgement is sought. At the top of the scale is the term 'imperceptible', which suggests that no impairment is detectable, while the next point on the scale is 'perceptible but not annoying', which is both an auditory threshold statement and an opinion about annoyance value. This makes it hard to separate information about auditory thresholds from those about hedonic response. The sister standard to this (ITU-R BS.1534), which is concerned with medium impairments, is more straightforward in this respect, having a quality scale running from 'excellent' to 'bad'. The fact that the mean opinion score scale is predominantly a preference scale is supported by results from Francis Rumsey et al. (2005a) where it was shown that naïve listener preference could be predicted moderately accurately using a regression model based on expert listener ratings of basic audio quality.

Other authors have tried to preserve the distinction between hedonic and descriptive responses in their analyses of sound quality. For example, Jan Berg and Rumsey (2006) used a form of verbal protocol analysis inspired by Elena Samoylenko et al. (1996) for the splitting of terms arising from a sound quality description experiment into appropriate bins for analysis. The protocol adopted is depicted in Figure 2, where terms are split into descriptive and attitudinal groups. Within the attitudinal category are the sub-categories of emotional/evaluative attributes and naturalness. The former include terms that the listeners used to describe their liking/ disliking for the sounds as well as their evaluation of them using terms such as good or bad, whereas naturalness-related terms were put in a bin of their own.

Naturalness turned out to be an important factor for many listeners in the experiments by Berg and Rumsey, and could not easily be classed as a purely descriptive, value-free feature (and therefore put in one of the left-hand bins). The concept of naturalness in sound reproduction was also addressed by Kalle Koivuniemi and Nick Zacharov, who stated that it 'describes how well the perceived events conform to what the subjects consider as realism' (Koivuniemi and Zacharov, 2001: 9). Naturalness, it is thus suggested, is related to a higher-level cognitive response whereby the 'plausibility' of lower-level factors is somehow weighed in relation to a remembered experience of natural listening conditions. Naturalness and liking were found by Berg and Rumsey to be highly correlated, suggesting that at least their listeners had an expectation that sound reproduction should seem 'natural'. This finding suggests that auditory cues in reproduced sound that contradict those encountered in the natural environment, or that are combined in an unnatural way, would be responded to negatively by listeners.[3] However, the context of the experiment was such that the sounds of live musical instruments, ensembles and speakers in rooms were reproduced, thereby leading listeners to expect something approaching real-world auditory cues. This says nothing about the reproduction of content that has been artificially contrived, and that has no natural anchor against which to compare the result.

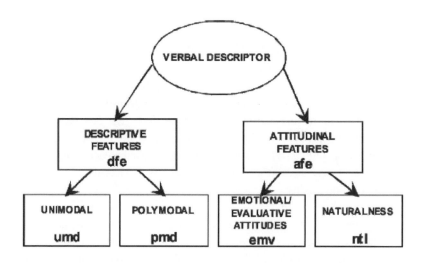

Figure 2: Berg and Rumsey's basic protocol for separating descriptive and attitudinal responses to sound quality

Letowski (1989) describes two primary aspects of sound character in his MURAL model shown in Figure 3, dividing sound character attributes into timbre and spaciousness groups. Timbral attributes are primarily related to sound colour while spatial attributes relate to features of the stereophonic image. Until recently, the spatial dimension of sound quality has not received as much attention as other facets (Rumsey, 2002). This may be partly because most sound reproduction, having only two channels, has not been very sophisticated spatially. With the advent of multichannel surround sound and various other types of 3D audio, this becomes potentially more important. While the timbral quality of sound reproduction can now approach an ideal, its spatial quality can leave a lot to be desired.

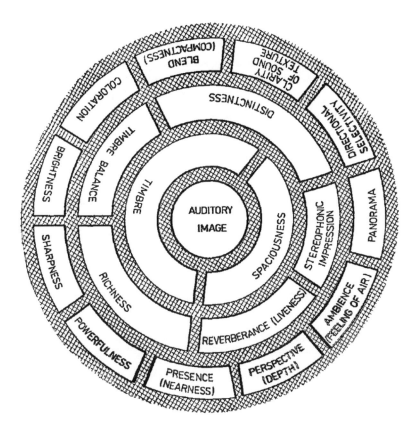

Figure 3: Letowski's MURAL

Rumsey et al. (2005b) attempted to quantify the relative importance of spatial and timbral fidelity in sound reproduction, using surround sound programme material that had been impaired in quality both spatially and timbrally. It was found that spatial fidelity to an unimpaired reference recording accounted for about 30 per cent of the global attribute 'basic audio quality' when rated by expert listeners, with timbral fidelity accounting for the remaining 70 per cent. Fidelity in these experiments was defined in terms of similarity of the impaired recordings to the reference. Spatial fidelity was divided into two parts: frontal and surround spatial fidelity, the former referring to spatial impairments within the frontal arc subtended by the left and right front loudspeakers, and the latter to those outside that arc. Frontal spatial fidelity turned out to be more important than surround spatial fidelity, although it was noted that the subjects were trained listeners who were likely to concentrate on the accuracy of stereophonic imaging in the frontal arc in preference to surround effects, partly owing to their familiarity with two-channel stereo recording.

When naïve listeners' responses were analysed it was noticed that frontal spatial fidelity ceased to feature in a regression model predicting their preference, whereas surround spatial fidelity made a substantial contribution. Clearly these listeners did not mind at all about changes to the frontal stereo image, as they had not been trained to listen to it, or to realise that it mattered. Instead, they liked a generally surrounding effect in the reproduction. This helps reinforce the point that it may matter whose opinion is sought when evaluating sound quality and that hedonic responses are liable to be more varied than descriptive judgements. In the food industry, for example, it is common to use naïve subjects representative of different populations to evaluate consumer preference because it is known that this depends greatly on demographic and socio-economic factors (Meilgaard et al., 1999). Nevertheless, it has been argued that audio presents a different case since it involves technical notions of correct reproduction and fidelity that have no parallel in food science (e.g. Olive, 2003).[4]

Fidelity in recording and reproduction equipment

Early advertisements for gramophones and phonographs displayed a touching naïveté when it came to the idea of sonic fidelity. People were quoted swearing that it was impossible to tell the difference between the crackly, distorted reproduction of a singer and the original performance. An advertisement for an early phonograph is shown in Figure 4, emphasising that the machine is capable of 'enunciating and pronouncing every word perfectly'.[5] While such early recording devices were remarkable for their day, one thing they did not offer was 'high fidelity' in the current understanding of the term. Limited bandwidth, high distortion, speed variations and an appalling signal-to-noise ratio would have given rise to a result that, to our modern ears, would be regarded as poor. It seems likely, however, that listeners to the early phonograph were responding to the identity of the voices they heard reproduced – if they could tell who was speaking then it was considered a faithful reproduction, despite the noise and distortion. 'Oh, that sounds just like Nancy,' they might have said, feeling that this was as much as could be expected. They were, after all, listening to a device generally known as a 'talking machine'. Nonetheless, the uncritical approbation accorded to these systems suggests that the perceptual reference for high quality has shifted over the years. The sound quality that would be regarded as high today is arguably higher than that experienced in the 1960s.

Philips, one of the two companies responsible for the Compact Disc, for example, is widely known in the audio industry for the rash advertising claim it made when the CD was first launched – 'Pure, Perfect Sound, Forever'[6] – suggesting the ultimate in sound storage technology. Although a great step forward from the long-playing vinyl record that preceded it, we can now say with reasonable assurance that the two-channel CD, with its 44.1 kHz sampling rate and 16-bit resolution, is neither perfect nor lasts for ever. The same company, 20-years later, promoted the Super Audio CD, with higher resolution and more audio channels, offering an enveloping 'surround sound' listening experience. Furthermore, there is talk these days of 'mere CD quality', placing this former bastion of sound quality somewhere down the pecking order. The dynamic and frequency ranges of Super Audio CD equal or exceed that of human hearing, yet many people find it difficult to tell the difference in sound quality between new formats like this and the CD (Nishiguchi and Hamasaki, 2005). This is because we are in an era of diminishing returns in the domain of sound quality.

It is now technically feasible to deliver sound quality to the consumer that meets or exceeds the requirements of human hearing in terms of frequency range, distortion levels and dynamic range (Stuart, 1997). This is one way in which a 'high fidelity' audio system might be defined – a psychoacoustically 'transparent' signal chain that carries signals from one end to the other in such a way that any distortion is inaudible. This relates to the electrical system that transports audio signals. There is still potentially some improvement that could be made to the electroacoustical means for capturing and reproducing sounds (the transducers – microphones and loudspeakers). Such devices are means of sampling sound fields and reproducing them at certain points in space, and it is still unclear what the ideal directional characteristics of microphones and loudspeakers should be, for example. The characteristics of transducers are often chosen on the basis of empirical and artistic judgements. This is because stereophony (the means by which the spatial aspects of a sound field are represented) is often limited to the creation of a spatial perceptual illusion, rather than the reconstruction of a physically accurate spatial sound field.[7] The final hurdle to be crossed in the development of a truly 'high fidelity' audio system almost certainly lies with the spatial aspects of sound quality, which has been limited by the two channel formats in place for much of the history of sound reproduction (Davis, 2003).

The irony is that now high technical fidelity is possible, few people seem to care very much about it. The new super-high resolution formats such as DVD-Audio and Super Audio CD, for example, have been relatively unsuccessful as consumer products.[8] This lack of consumer concern with the highest fidelity has probably always been a problem for the audio industry, although it is exacerbated by the fact that few people now take the time to sit down in an ideal listening position and listen to a recorded performance from beginning to end, relishing the 'concert hall experience' in their living rooms. The majority of product development and consumer interest in audio is in what might be termed the 'mid-fi' region of the market, where good but not ultimate quality is delivered in a variety of ways. The car is becoming a common listening room for many, and headphones a common means of delivery. Reproduction in these contexts is likely to be a compromise and there is increasing interest in optimising such environments for highest consumer preference, rather than highest fidelity (which do not always turn out to be the same thing, as discussed below).

Figure 4: An early advertisement for a recording machine

Contextual requirements and biases

What people like and what is most accurate in technical terms have sometimes been confused in the history of discussions about sound reproduction, particularly in the hi-fi press. As early as 1957, for example, Roger Kirk showed that learning and familiarity played an important role in determining the sound quality people preferred to listen to. Students who had spent a period of time listening to restricted frequency range audio systems demonstrated a preference for those compared with full-range systems (Kirk, 1957). Using proper experimental controls and blind testing under controlled conditions, however, Sean Olive (2003) found that there is a fairly consistent relationship between measured loudspeaker performance and listener preference, for both trained and untrained listeners. This suggests that there are at least some contexts in which there is a relationship between technical fidelity of audio products and listeners' hedonic judgements about sound quality.

Biases in judging sound quality can also arise as a result of other sensory inputs or expectations. In an interesting series of experiments by Toole and Olive (1994), in which they compared listener preferences for loudspeakers in both blind and sighted conditions, it was found that being aware of the model of loudspeaker under test affected the results as much as any other variables such as listening position or programme material. People's responses were so strongly biased by their expectations of certain brands or models that their judgements of sound quality were sometimes radically altered from their ratings under blind conditions. This also applied to the experienced listeners, suggesting that even people who 'know what sounds good' can have their opinions altered by their expectation or visual bias. 'Obviously', said the authors, 'listeners' opinions were more attached to the products that they could see, than they were to the differences in sound associated with program' (Toole and Olive, 1994: 13).

There is an argument to be made for a consideration of context or fitness for purpose when deciding how good sonic fidelity needs to be. While the trained sound engineer may care deeply about the last decibel of dynamic range and the minutiae of stereophonic imaging, the average consumer is often totally unaware that stereophonic imaging is important, for example (as demonstrated recently in Rumsey et al., 2005b). Many people listen to sound these days through little headphones connected to an MP3 player, and although this limits the potential for sonic fidelity it is a popular way of listening to music. In the absence of anything to compare it with, mediocre sound quality (in absolute terms) may be regarded by the general population as good. For the average listener, once above a certain threshold, perhaps sound quality only needs to be 'good enough'.

It could be argued that the sound system for 'shoot-em-up'-style computer games, for example, needs lots of bass so that the explosions sound exciting. It might also need to have the potential to generate sources in different locations around the player's head, as well as to deliver a sense of immersion, but the game player may have little need for a concept of fidelity to a natural environment provided the sound enhances his enjoyment of the game. The game is, at least partially, an unreal environment in the first place, and the aural environment has been created artificially. In this case, any concept of fidelity has more to do with ensuring that the game creator's intentions concerning the sound are reasonably faithfully conveyed to the player, although there is probably quite a wide range of tolerance in practice. The player, of course, has no idea what the game creator intended. Conversely, for the 'hi-fi' enthusiast (who, it is often joked, is more interested in the technical performance of the equipment than in the music listened to) the requirements are somewhat different. An expectation may exist about the accurate reconstruction of some remembered sonic context, most likely a concert hall performance of music. There is a mental anchor in the listener that rightly or wrongly fixes the reference point for high fidelity, drawing a distinction between listening contexts that will be returned to later.

Fidelity of commercial recordings and reproduction formats

While technical fidelity can be quantified in terms of distortions in the signal chain, and is capable of being very high, there are many reasons why the limitations of recording techniques and reproduction formats may make it necessary to consider alternative ideas about fidelity.

Commercial recording engineers rarely attempt to represent the true nature of an original sound field. Even the majority of classical recordings, for all their supposed purism, are made with a collection of distant and close microphones, mixed to make the result sound pleasing according to the judgement of a recording engineer. While this is usually done with an idea of representing the sound in the performance hall with some degree of accuracy, the result is in fact an artificial creation that is designed to accommodate the limitations of reproduction systems. People liked Decca classical recordings, for example, because they were made with spaced omnidirectional microphones that give lots of bass, and create a spacious, pleasing sound on two-channel stereo systems. No-one, though, could claim that they are accurate representations of the original sound field.

There are other contextual reasons why listening to recordings is different from real-life listening. Firstly, the visual cue is usually lacking, and this leads to the need for an enhancement or alteration of some auditory cues about the sources and the space in which they are sounding. Secondly, when all reverberation is coming from in front of the listener, as it is in two-channel stereo reproduction, an unnatural balance is often required to make the sources clear enough. Thirdly, the performance element and sense of occasion is missing. There are no people eating sweets in adjacent seats, and the experience of sitting in a large crowd is not there. It seems a bit like the difference between watching a football match on television and being in the crowd. On the television there is a much better view of the game, but you miss a chance to be beaten up and join in the cheering. These are all factors that to some degree or other contribute to the experience of naturalness or realism.

Compromise in relation to absolute fidelity of sound reproduction is sometimes necessary because of limitations in commercially available systems that do not have to do with frequency range, noise and distortion. Although, as mentioned above, it is true that the technical performance of high fidelity systems can approach or exceed the limits of human hearing, the spatial performance of such systems can still be quite limited. Since spatial performance appears to account for an appreciable part of overall sound quality this has to be taken seriously.

Recent developments now mean that enhanced spatial reproduction is possible; yet, even 5.1-channel surround sound is only an extension of two-channel stereophony, and still has many of its limitations. Using five loudspeakers in the locations specified in the ITU BS.775 standard describing 5.1 surround sound (or 3-2 stereo), it is possible to create a reasonable impression of a diffuse sound field, as shown by Koichiro Hiyama et al. (2002). This means that it should be possible to generate the psychoacoustic impression of being in an immersive reverberant sound field, such as encountered in a large hall, by means of only a few loudspeakers, even though five loudspeakers are not enough to reconstruct such a sound field with physical accuracy. It is, however, not possible to create accurate source images all around a listener, and 5.1 surround is only really designed to enable this in the frontal arc. Other locations are more of a lottery. Furthermore, the height dimension is entirely missing. This format does not aim at accurate physical reconstruction of a sound field. In fact, it builds on long-established psychoacoustic techniques of stereophonic illusion that are used to generate sufficient of the perceptual cues needed to convince the hearing mechanism. Most stereo and surround reproduction formats, therefore, are inherently inaccurate when it comes to reconstructing sound fields, so the reproduced sound experience is at least partially an illusion of sorts.

Headphone listening also suffers from spatial compromises. Although it is possible to use headphones to generate so-called binaural cues at the listener's ears, which might be very similar to those encountered in natural listening, there are many reasons why this is a problem in practice (Rumsey, 2001). Firstly, each listener's ears are different, giving rise to different spatial cues. Only recordings made with microphones in ears identical to the listener's will have accurate spatial fidelity. Further issues arise because head movements that are used for accurate spatial perception are hard to employ in sound reproduction and headphones couple imperfectly with the ears and differ in design. There are many more subtle factors. Most commercial recordings are not mixed binaurally, for example, even though a lot of music listening is now done on headphones; the stereo image one hears is, therefore, one that was designed for reproduction on loudspeakers. In headphone listening, each ear hears only one channel's signal, whereas with loudspeakers both ears hear both loudspeakers. This gives rise to a fundamental problem with much headphone stereo, whereby the image is inside the head and has an artificial separation between the ears.

One point rarely considered is the possibility that reproduced sound could be better than 'the original' – i.e. that listening to a recording of something might be better than experiencing it 'in the flesh'. The sound quality in the best seat in the best concert hall may not always be particularly wonderful, and a listener may find himself preferring the results he can get from his hi-fi system. This can also apply to pop and rock music, where the auditory experience of live concerts may be different from what is heard on a band's recordings. Most of the tricks that make such music sound good are done in the studio, and it is rare for bands to be able to do them all live, including the feat of singing in tune (which has been revolutionised by a studio plug-in known as Antares Auto-Tune). The live event is a visceral experience that has probably as much to do with being part of a gathering involving lots of other people as it is about sound quality. It is different in many ways from the experience of listening alone to a CD.

Anchors for fidelity

As previously mentioned, most discussions about the fidelity of reproduced sound implicitly or explicitly assume that a 'gold standard' exists against which the reproduced sound experience should be judged. For the classical music listener this is perhaps the concert hall experience, but it is less clear what should be the reference or anchor point for other kinds of content. Producers and recording engineers will usually say that the aim should be to convey their intentions as accurately as possible to the listener, so that what is heard in the reproduction space is very similar to what the producer heard in the control room when the recording was made (or at least that the recording contains sufficient information to enable this to happen). There is a good argument for this sort of fidelity because presumably the effort spent by a producer and engineer to make a certain sort of sound and to fine tune every nuance in the mix is not to be wasted. The fruits of their hard work should ideally be preserved. If this is considered from the consumer's point of view, however, it is clear that the consumer/listener has absolutely no idea what the producer intended. What would be their reference for high fidelity? It could be argued that it either does not exist and is simply 'the best' they have heard, or is, for example, the sound experienced at the dance club where they last heard that track played. If it sounded like that they might be very pleased. Since many people listen with headphones these days, perhaps their anchor for 'correct' sound reproduction is what they hear on headphones, and loudspeaker sound fields are an anomaly.

As an informal test to find out what a typical consumer expects when listening to music on headphones, I asked my daughter, who is nineteen and listens to an iPod a lot, what she thought about the idea of fidelity (I explained what I meant). A number of interesting things came out, among them being the idea that she thought it should sound as if the band was in front of her. When I asked her if that's what it really sounded like, she decided it was not, and that it actually sounded like most of the band was down the back of her neck, with a guitar in each ear. 'But that's OK', she said, 'that's normal. They all sound like that. I suppose that's what I expect it to sound like. If it didn't it would be weird.' This is just an example to show how a listener's reference point, or what she expects from reproduced sound, may be different from the supposed anchor of a live experience. Listeners have perhaps come to like certain types of reproduced sound for their own sake.

The idea that typical listeners have a floating anchor point for sound quality is borne out in the results of an experiment conducted by Kathryn Beresford et al. (2006a) in which a very large number of naïve listeners (around 200 college students) were asked to listen to a pop track that had been degraded in sound quality to different degrees. They listened to it either in a high-quality listening room or in a quality vehicle (a Mercedes saloon). The sound quality degradations consisted of middle frequency spectral alterations designed to introduce a series of peaks and dips into the spectrum, some of them quite severe and very unpleasant-sounding to most of the expert listeners who tried them out beforehand. As the naïve listeners just heard one example from the set of possibilities, they were not comparing it to anything, but simply rating on a simple sound-quality scale what they heard while sitting in a typical listening position. The primary aim of this experiment was to try to find out whether the listening context of the high-quality room or the car had a biasing effect on quality judgements, due to expectations or visual biasing. Perhaps the heavily impaired sounds would be rated better in the car than in the listening room because people expected less from car sound systems.

In fact, there was almost no significant difference between any of the stimulus gradings and no difference between the contexts. The results averaged out somewhere above the middle of the quality scale, roughly in the 'good' region (one step below the top 'excellent' grade). Even the really heavily impaired stimuli were rated in a similar region overall. This led the authors to suppose that in the absence of any reference point, a form of 'contraction bias' took place in the responses, leading people to grade conservatively, somewhere in the upper middle of the scale. The two high-quality environments provided a context that led them to expect the sound quality to be good, so much so that even stimuli that experienced listeners regarded as very unpleasant were given quite high grades. The naïve listeners either could not hear the quality degradations applied to the sound, or did not believe what they were hearing. Interestingly, when experienced listeners were asked to grade the same stimuli using a more conventional multiple-stimulus test comparing all the stimuli and an unimpaired reference, the grades for sound quality spanned the expected range of the scale, all the way from excellent to bad.

A final example helps to show where things stand today with regard to fidelity in reproduced sound. It rather turns the whole matter on its head. Robert Ellis-Geiger (2005) explains how it is common in film scoring for composers to use sampled and synthetic sound generators, with MIDI-control from a computer, to mock up the score for a director. He explains that a composer may get chosen for a job on the basis of how good the mock-up sounds and that composers such as Hans Zimmer freely integrate synthetic resources with real orchestral recordings in their film scores. The upshot of this is that in some cases the success of a final orchestral recording of a film score is likely to be judged on its fidelity to the synthetic mock up, rather than the other way around. Where then is the reference point when the 'natural' is judged in relation to the synthetic?

Responses to novel sound fields

As a rule, the traditional concert-hall paradigm for reproduced sound fields of classical music places the musicians in the front image, with some sort of hall reverberation around them. If this is done in surround sound then the same paradigm is usually adopted, with the rear loudspeakers being used for ambient sound. Why is this done? Presumably to emulate a familiar listening context and to persuade people that they are listening to a performance. (This assumes, of course, that consumers set up their surround systems with the loudspeakers in the right place, which is a rash assumption.) In an experiment conducted by Beresford et al. (2006b), listeners were asked to rate their preferences for different novel surround-sound balances of classical music, some of them with the musicians arranged all around the microphone array so as to place the listener in the centre of the ensemble or choir, while others were more conventionally arranged. Naïve listeners' responses were compared with those of trained listeners and it was found that the naïve listeners tended to prefer the unusual balances with sources all around them (very unlike the concert hall paradigm), whereas the trained listeners (who were final-year sound recording students) preferred conventionally reproduced scenes with the musicians in front of them.

This is an example of how training and conditioning lead to an expectation that reproduced sound will have a certain fidelity. The trained listeners in the above example had been given a lot of time to get used to the conventional two-channel stereo paradigm and all the recordings they normally made were done so as to put the musicians in front. The naïve listeners perhaps had no such preconceptions, due to the lack of training in technical listening, and had no difficulty accepting and even liking recordings that broke the conventional mould in terms of scene layout. For naïve listeners the predominant factor in a regression model predicting 'purchasability' (of the recordings) was the subjective variable 'envelopment', whereas for trained listeners the most important factors were 'locatedness' (of the musicians), 'naturalness' and timbral balance. The naïve listeners liked to be immersed in or enveloped by sound sources, whereas the trained listeners liked to be able to hear the locations of sources, have them sound natural (presumably this meant 'where they should be'), and be timbrally accurate. Since naïve listeners form the majority of the market for sound recordings this result has to be taken seriously. This is not to argue for an out-and-out consumerist view of sound recordings as a commodity, but it presents an alternative position to the traditional notion of fidelity, which suggests that sound recordings could be designed for optimum consumer preference, rather like wine or beer. People, after all, consume reproduced sound like any other commodity these days.

Interactive audio

As time progresses, the idea of a sound recording as a static artwork to be experienced 'as the producer intended' seems likely to be complemented, or even replaced by an increasing range of alternatives involving listener interaction. This may not happen overnight but it is sure to happen as technology shifts the burden of rendering the reproduced sound from the transmitting to the receiving end of the signal chain. For example, treble and bass controls were once the only way in which the listener could modify reproduced sound either to compensate for inadequacies in the reproducing equipment, or to suit his taste. Now there are sophisticated multi-band equalisation options on the iPod, designed to enhance different styles of music (e.g. 'rock', 'jazz', 'classical', etc.). This already suggests that a position is taken: either the producer did not get it right in the first place, or the equipment is incapable of transmitting what the producer intended, or more likely listeners/consumers just want something to fiddle around with and like to intervene in the selection of their 'brand' of sound quality. Home cinema systems have various sound-field controls that allow the listener to add room effects, in the form of artificial reverberation, making the sound appear to be in different space. While many of these may be somewhat unpleasant, and regarded as gimmicks by the informed listener, they point the way to what may become much more successful and sophisticated consumer signal processing in the future.

New digital representation formats such as MPEG-4 have a means of transmitting sound objects rather than complete sound recordings (Koenen, 2001). These objects are the elements of a sound scene, such as the instruments in a band or the speakers in a teleconference. The idea is that because an excessive amount of information is required to transmit very complex spatial scenes in their original form for advanced multichannel sound systems (such as wavefield synthesis), the job of rendering the scene for reproduction should be passed to the replay end of the chain. The rendering engine in the player does the best job it can of reconstructing the intended scene under the control of separate information, which tells it where objects are to be placed and what to do to them. Effects can be added or natural reverberation convolved with the sources to add environmental cues. The end result is a more-or-less satisfactory replica of the intended scene, depending on the quality of the information provided and the abilities of the rendering engine. Basic replay systems would render the scene less satisfactorily than more advanced ones, which allow for a range of different delivery channels all the way from the mobile phone to the sophisticated home entertainment room. This versatile rendering can be extended to include interactions by the consumer, who may be involved in the reconstruction or manipulation of the audio information, either musically or sonically, or under control of a game or other activity.

Faithful to his master's voice?

The foregoing discussion has highlighted some different notions of fidelity in sound recording and reproduction, showing how a fixed and inflexible conception of the purpose of sound recordings leads to a somewhat limited understanding of the way in which people really relate to them in practice. Although sound recording and reproduction started out as a means of *reproducing* the voices or sounds of things people knew, and could therefore recognise, it has moved well beyond to a realm of essentially artificial representation of content. The reference point for deciding what is good or appropriate quality depends greatly on the listening context, mode of listening and application area. There is an argument for treating sound recordings as consumer commodities, optimised for the market they are designed to serve – for maximum consumer satisfaction. Increasingly sound recordings are downloadable and disposable; here today and gone tomorrow. The majority of them are not primarily intended as records for posterity and there is no *de facto* requirement that they conform to traditional notions of what is correct. I like instant coffee as a drink in its own right, and do not worry about the fact that it does not taste exactly like ground coffee. It has its place, and the best instant coffee is really nice. Similarly, I like to listen to movie surround sound with the subwoofer turned up too high and the surround levels about 3 dB higher than they are supposed to be, because it sounds good at the listening levels I use. Reggae listeners turn up the bass so that it bends the windows of their cars; this is how they like it.

As interactive media take an ever-larger hold on the market, and as the number of different delivery channels increases, the range of qualities available will inevitably grow. 'Hi-fi' is already a very marginalised and elitist realm, but it is good to know that someone cares. Without a reference point for sound quality, listeners adapt to what is on offer and rapidly accept it as the norm, as long as its quality is tolerably good (and sometimes even if it is not, as shown above). Because listeners generally have no idea about what was intended in the first place, they are remarkably ready to accept recordings that lack fidelity in the absolute sense, provided they suit the purpose for which they are used. While this might be seen as a charter for mediocrity, it is intended more as a realistic evaluation of the notion and role of fidelity in a world that is remarkably different from the days of the phonograph. Perhaps it will be possible to work harder at optimizing sound quality for the task or application in hand, rather than assuming it is always necessary to aim for an outmoded concept of high fidelity.

Notes

1   The 2005 RIAA (Recording Industry Association of America) consumer profile survey, available at http://www.riaa.com, indicates that less than 5 per cent of the US market is accounted for by recordings that traditionally capture the sound scene of a natural acoustical performance, at least to some degree, such as classical and jazz music recordings. The remaining 95 per cent is accounted for by genres that are traditionally created in the studio using multitrack recording techniques, leading to constructed sound scenes that may have little or no relationship to natural acoustical spaces or performances.

2   The International Telecommunications Union publishes standards that can be used in the evaluation of perceived sound quality. These are principally designed for the evaluation of the impairments caused by low-bit-rate audio codecs such as the widely used 'MP3' and other similar processes employed in consumer audio equipment and broadcasting.

3   For further discussion of the methods used in the evaluation of sound quality and the relationship between auditory cues and listener responses, see Bech and Zacharov (2006).

4   Accurate audio reproduction, in terms of technical faithfulness to a reference sound source of some kind, can be quantified, at least in some respects, and it is often assumed that the most accurate is the most desirable. However, there is no reference 'Chicken Kiev', for example, in the food industry to which all other Chicken Kievs might be compared.

5   For a more detailed exposition of the development of recording machines, see Gelatt (1977).

6   This is the title of a Philips CD (F351 812 187-2) issued on a limited basis in the early 1980s, and designed to demonstrate the sound quality of the Compact Disc.

7   For further coverage of the challenges and limitations of spatial audio, see Rumsey (2001) and Rumsey (2006).

8   In 2005, Super Audio CD and DVD-Audio accounted for only 2 per cent of recorded music sales in the US (RIAA, see note 1 for source).

References

Bech, S. and Zacharov, N. (2006) *Perceptual Audio Evaluation*. Chichester: Wiley.

Beresford, K., Ford, N., Rumsey, F. and Zielinski, S. (2006a) 'Contextual Effects on Sound Quality Judgements: Listening Room and Automotive Environments', paper 6648 presented at the 120th Audio Engineering Society Convention, Paris.

Beresford, K., Rumsey, F. and Zielinski, S. (2006b) 'Listener Opinions of Novel Spatial Audio Scenes', paper 6687 presented at the 120th Audio Engineering Society Convention, Paris.

Berg, J. and Rumsey, F. (2006) 'Identification of Quality Attributes of Spatial Audio by Repertory Grid Technique', *Journal of the Audio Engineering Society* 54 (5): 365–79.

Davis, M. (2003) 'History of Spatial Audio Coding', *Journal of the Audio Engineering Society* 51 (6): 554–69.

Ellis-Geiger, R. (2005) 'Film Music Scoring Using a Digital Audio Workstation', paper 6388 presented at the 118th Audio Engineering Society Convention, Barcelona.

Gabrielsson, A. and Lindström, B. (1985) 'Perceived Sound Quality of High Fidelity Loudspeakers', *Journal of the Audio Engineering Society* 33 (1): 33–53.

Gelatt, R. (1977) *The Fabulous Phonograph*. London: Cassell.

Hiyama, K., Setsu, M. and Hamasaki, K. (2002) 'The Minimum Number of Loudspeakers and Its Arrangement for Reproducing the Spatial Impression of Diffuse Sound Field', paper 5674 presented at the 113th Audio Engineering Society Convention, Los Angeles.

Kirk, R. (1957) 'Learning a Major Factor Influencing Preferences for High Fidelity Audio Systems', *Journal of the Audio Engineering Society* 5 (4): 238–41.

Koenen, R. (2001) 'MPEG-4 and its Operational Environments', *Proceedings of the Audio Engineering Society 18th International Conference*, Burlingame, CA. Paper 1863.

Koivuniemi, K. and Zacharov, N. (2001) 'Unravelling the Perception of Spatial Sound Reproduction: Language Development, Verbal Protocol Analysis, and Listener Training', paper 5424 presented at the 111th Audio Engineering Society Convention, New York.

Letowski, T. (1989) 'Sound Quality Assessment: Cardinal Concepts', preprint 2825 presented at the 87th Audio Engineering Society Convention, New York.

Meilgaard, M., Vance Civille, G. and Carr, B.T. (1999) *Sensory Evaluation Techniques*. Boca Raton: CRC Press.

Nishiguchi, T. and Hamasaki, K. (2005) 'Differences of Hearing Impressions Among Several High Sampling Digital Audio Formats', paper 6469 presented at the 118th Audio Engineering Society Convention, Barcelona.

Olive, S. (2003) 'Differences in Performance and Preference of Trained versus Untrained Listeners in Loudspeaker Tests: A Case Study', *Journal of the Audio Engineering Society* 51 (9): 806–25.

Rumsey, F. (2001) *Spatial Audio*. Oxford: Focal Press.

– (2002) 'Spatial Quality Evaluation for Reproduced Sound: Terminology, Meaning and A Scene-Based Paradigm', *Journal of the Audio Engineering Society* 50 (9): 651–66.

– (ed.) (2006) *Spatial Sound Techniques. An Anthology of Articles on Spatial Sound Techniques, Part 2: Multichannel Technologies*. New York: Audio Engineering Society.

Rumsey, F., Zielinski, S., Kassier, R. and Bech, S. (2005a) 'Relationships Between Experienced Listener Ratings of Multichannel Audio Quality and Naïve Listener Preferences', *Journal of the Acoustical Society of America* 117 (6): 3832–40.

– (2005b) 'On the Relative Importance of Spatial and Timbral Fidelities in Judgments of Degraded Multichannel Audio Quality', *Journal of the Acoustical Society of America* 118 (2): 968–77.

Samoylenko, E., McAdams, S. and Nosulenko, V. (1996) 'Systematic Analysis of Verbalizations Produced in Comparing Musical Timbres', *International Journal of Psychology* 31: 255–78.

Stuart, J.R. (1997) 'Coding Methods for High Resolution Recording Systems', paper 4639 presented at the 103rd Audio Engineering Society Convention, New York.

Toole, F. (1982) 'Listening Tests: Turning Opinion into Fact', *Journal of the Audio Engineering Society* 30 (6): 431–45.

– (1986) 'Loudspeaker Measurements and Their Relationship to Listener Preference, Part 1', *Journal of the Audio Engineering Society* 34 (4): 227–35.

Toole, F. and Olive, S. (1994) 'Hearing is Believing vs. Believing is Hearing: Blind vs. Sighted Listening Tests, and Other Interesting Things', paper 3894 presented at the 97th Audio Engineering Society Convention, San Francisco.

DOROTTYA FABIAN

Classical Sound Recordings and Live Performances: Artistic and Analytical Perspectives

T HERE is a plethora of questions to ask when embarking on a study of sound recordings within the paradigm of historical musicology, some of which are also concerns of philosophy. What sort of documents are sound recordings? What do they represent? How much and in what sense do they differ from live performances? How is the sound stored on them to be analysed? How is that sound affected by production and replay equipment and circumstances? On the following pages I will investigate how recordings of Western classical music are perceived, especially in terms of their relationship to live performances. First I will look at ontological and epistemological matters. As these have already been discussed at length by philosophers such as Stan Godlovitch (1998) and Stephen Davies (2001) and in the volume edited by Michael Krausz (1993), I shall focus on questions that are important for my thesis. This posits that from the standpoint of a researcher of performance styles, sound recordings are valid documents because they are representative of particular artists' technique and interpretative approaches and thus can be regarded as 'performances'. This section will be followed by the presentation of two sets of empirical data: a report on a survey conducted among professional recording artists and a brief analysis of a few selected recordings to exemplify similarities between live and studio performances. The aim, therefore, is not so much to revisit theoretical questions that philosophers are better qualified to deal with but rather to bring in the pragmatic perspective of a 'musicological listener' (Cook, 1992: 152ff) and of some recording artists so as to stimulate further phenomenological discussions of issues that are of interest to performance researchers.[1]

Theoretical background

In Western historical musicology the study of sound recordings is a new field still in need of advocacy and justification. Leo Treitler, for instance, notes that traditional musicological ontology regards recordings as 'faithful *records* of performances, which are renderings of scores, which in turn are representations of works' (Treitler, 2002: 55). According to this ontology, music is not a performance art. The work, or the object of study, resides in the notated composition, i.e. the score, rendering the study of performance secondary, if at all important, to the study of composition. This essentially Platonist view regards musical works to be abstract sound-structures and as such remains indifferent to the variability of production as long as the appropriate relationships, such as pitch, rhythm, tempo, dynamics and so on are accurately instantiated (Gracyk, 1997: 140). Philosophers often seem to hold this view of music. Nelson Goodman (1976), for instance, argues for the object of contemplation to be defined as the class of performances that comply with the score identifying the work. Focusing on the composition as represented by its score, however, tends to neglect the affective component of European literate music. Acknowledging the importance of this element leads to the observation that the emotionally cathartic and stimulating aspects of music reside in the productive and perceptual acts. This recognition fosters interest in the performative and experiential facets of music-making and listening. Authors such as Lydia Goehr (1992), José Bowen (1999), Daniel Leech-Wilkinson (2001) and Nicholas Cook (2001), among many others, have started to question the validity of the work concept and to advocate the importance of studying music in performance; to regard each enactment or performance as an alternative manifestation of the composition. This position considers the score to be a *script* rather than a text and fosters a paradigm where the 'ontological hierarchy [that] attributes a "greater degree of reality" to the work than to its instances...collapse[s]' and 'works [are taken] as directive sets' (Godlovitch, 1998: 88). Moreover, the growing evidence of over 100 years of performance history on record has prompted a shift also in epistemology where recordings, as the artworks, are the 'primary objects of study' (Treitler, 2002: 55).

The score gained central position in musicological ontology because it was fixed, dissectible, and accessible to contemplation and analysis while performance was not. Performed music unfolds in time and is, by nature, ephemeral. The shift in epistemology referred to above implies that the advent of recording technology changed this dichotomy forever. Yet is it really the case? Recently, philosophers and theorists questioning the nature of a musical 'work' (abstract composition or its performed instances) have had to augment their field of investigation to address the additional problem of defining musical performance, particularly in relation to its technologically mediated instantiations.

Live performance versus sound recording

Theodore Gracyk defines musical performance as

> A public situation in which an audience attends to the actions of one or more performers during which specified sounds are intentionally generated for the express purpose of being attended to as music by the audience.

> (Gracyk, 1997: 139)

Accordingly 'the two most obvious deficiencies of recordings are the lack of visual data and the absence of the social event of the performance space' (Gracyk, 1997: 139). As Gracyk himself notes, this definition is problematic because it does not take into account the 'audience' present during a studio recording – engineer and producer, i.e. people very much 'attending to' the sounds generated as music. It also neglects to account for private recordings (which may very well be recordings of performances, i.e. uninterrupted renderings of pieces played with the intention to perform them, even if there is nobody *to* whom the performance is presented) and live broadcast performances because these seem not to meet another 'necessary condition': although the situation allows for the audience to participate *in real time*, it does not share the space of the performers (Godlovitch, 1998: 140). Furthermore, there could be situations when the audience of a sound recording may participate in a social event, namely as when people listen together to a recording. The performer is not present in the flesh, but, in my experience, the listeners feel and think they are listening to his or her interpretation and quite readily sublimate the technological product for the live event.

Are they listening to a performance? Although the participants of such an occasion are likely to answer 'yes', most theorists would argue in the negative and cite the recording conditions as proof that no 'real' performance took place. Godlovitch posits, for instance, that for a performance to take place, the proper order of the piece has to be observed and performed in a continuous manner, among other requirements (Godlovitch, 1998: 11–51). However, recording is a complex practice and what happens in the studio is often reported in a subjective way. It may be more useful to focus on the nature of the end product and not how it came about. The end result, the recording itself and its (social) function may satisfy almost all of Godlovitch's criteria of a performance and thus may be regarded valid as the research object when studying performance: accordingly, a recording is usually perceived to be a '(sonic event),...caused by human(-like) being [playing a] musical instrument [with] "creditworthy physical skill"'; to be 'an instance of some identifiable musical work, intended as an instance of such a work [and] successful as a constraint-model of such a work;...intended for some third-party listener...[and] listened to by some third-party listener exercising active concentrated attention' (Godlovitch, 1998: 49).

Although a recording is not presented before some third-party listener, it is presented *to* them, i.e. the intention and assumption is that people will listen to it. To acknowledge the existence of an 'audience' of recordings is paramount. The perspective of those who choose to listen to records rather than to live performances is unduly neglected in the literature. Sociological and psychological investigations (e.g. DeNora, 2000; North and Hargreaves, 1997; Sloboda and O'Neill, 2001) have provided much insight into the use and significance of music for listeners, but these studies tend to focus on the daily practice of the public at large rather than the professional musician or the 'focussed' listener.[2] What is clear, nevertheless, is that the majority of people consume larger quantities of 'canned' rather than 'live' music.

Thus, Gracyk's points that a 'live' audience is important primarily for the performer and that its absence 'makes the world of the performer, not the world of the listener, aesthetically poorer' (Gracyk, 1997: 148), are useful and need to be highlighted. Davies does not agree and emphasizes instead that

> the two contexts [live concert versus studio recording] call for different approaches to the music's interpretation. They offer contrasting opportunities and challenges to the performer, which, in turn, give rise to distinctive virtues (and vices) in the interpretations that are suitable.
>
> (Davies, 2001: 311)

True, but the perspective of the listener–consumer is again relegated to the background in favour of the performer's perspective. Moreover, Davies sets conditions under which the 'auditor' is *allowed* to enjoy a recording:

> Provided she is aware of the way the possibilities and demands of the studio differ from those of live performance, so that she *does not mistake studio recordings for documentary traces of live performances*, the auditor can find much that is enjoyable and different in studio recordings.
>
> (Davies, 2001: 313, italics added)

Why does a listener need permission to enjoy a recording but not a live performance? Why and in what sense would her experience diminish if she regarded the sound event emanating from the disc as a representation of artistic performance, as a kind of document that 'traces' characteristics of possible 'live performances'? Davies does not provide answers to these questions. In my later comments on selected recordings I will try to justify why I regard them as valid objections to his views.

The status of recordings is problematic because the medium contradicts elementary aspects of performance, namely its fleeting quality and unrepeatability. One can select any fragment of a recorded performance, and each gesture, pitch, rhythmic inflection, dynamic nuance, and tempo fluctuation can be listened to repeatedly and studied on its own or in conjunction with other features. But how can such minutiae explain the overall impression of a momentary experience of sound that unfolds in time? This question belies one similarity between live and recorded performance: they both can be listened to as events, as instantiations of compositions. If the record player happened to destroy the disk by the end of the sound event, the listener would have no opportunity to hear it again. Such a situation is, of course, hypothetical. Therefore, instead of the mentioned similarity it is more common to refer to the fundamental differences between live performance and studio recording: (1) a recording can be listened to over and over again, while a live performance cannot; and (2) in the studio the artist is free to repeat any segment until satisfaction is achieved while in a live concert this is not possible. How could a recording serve the study of performance when it is not a record of a continuous, uninterrupted rendering of a piece but has been edited from several takes often recorded over several days, at times months apart?

While these concerns are often voiced in relation to long-playing records and especially CDs, recordings from the pre-magnetic tape era are commonly taken as true representatives of performing traditions. Yet there is ample evidence that artists of that period felt uneasy in the studio because the conditions were unnatural and strenuous, potentially causing them to play rather differently from normal (Day, 2000; Philip, 2004). There are accounts of endless repetitions and awkward postures or positions as well as unusual interference during performance such as the rolling of the artists on a platform closer to or away from the horn as required by the limitations of the acoustic recording equipment. Discussing the early decades of the twentieth century, James Kraft, for instance, quotes several American artists who regarded recording as 'stressful work,...'"an awful battle" [that] stifled creativity' (Kraft, 1996: 61). He notes that '[i]nstrumentalists who did make records discovered at once that recording was quite different from other forms of performing' – a formulation that still considers recording a *form of performance*.

Most theorists are also concerned about the loss of the visual and physical aspects of performance when dealing with recorded music in audio format. Richard Leppert argues in *The Sight of Sound* (1993) that 'precisely because musical sound is abstract, intangible, and ethereal – lost as soon as it is gained – the visual experience of its production is crucial...for locating and communicating the place of music' (cited in Katz, 2004: 19). Davies goes as far as to claim that 'one cannot fully apprehend music without knowing how it is elicited from the instruments' but later admits that listening to a live broadcast may not 'produce significant difference in [the] listening experience...provided [the listener] can make the appropriate auditory discriminations and knows the kind of things he would see, moment by moment, were he present' (Davies, 2001: 297–8). Research also shows that general listeners find a performance more expressive when visual clues are available, and rate the expressiveness higher when gauged from visuals alone rather than through listening (Davidson, 1993). It is not difficult, then, to appreciate that studio recordings are different from concert performances. Can they nevertheless be regarded as performances?

The listener versus the performer

So audiences are affected by the demeanour of the performer, the excitement of being witness to the artist's concentration; but what about 'professional' listeners? I, for one, can fully associate with the writer from 1931: 'Alone with the phonograph, all the unpleasant externals are removed...You are alone with the composer and his music. Surely no more ideal circumstances could be imagined' (cited in Katz, 2004: 17). The only adjustment I would make is to substitute the composer for the performer as I am more often interested in the interpretation than the composition when I am listening to records. Nevertheless, am I listening to an interpretation, a performance? Or am I listening to a recording that is made up of segments performed by the named artist but supervised and edited by a producer and/or sound engineer? Can I still claim that my study (measurements and all) reports on that artist's musical concept and technical execution?

The results of a recent study provide an unusual perspective and pertinent data for pondering these questions. A series of experiments tested pianists' ability to recognize their own playing (Repp and Knoblich, 2004). The researchers 'recorded 12 pianists playing 12 mostly unfamiliar musical excerpts, half of them on a silent keyboard' (Repp and Knoblich, 2004: 604). On subsequent occasions 'several months later...the pianists [were] asked to use a 5-point scale to rate whether they thought they were the person playing each excerpt...Absence of sound during recording had no significant effect' on their ability to recognise their own playing (Repp and Knoblich, 2004: 604). In addition, the results demonstrated that 'pianists played about equally well with and without sound...showing little effect of auditory feedback deprivation on expressive performance' (Repp and Knoblich, 2004: 608). Furthermore, 'a tendency toward better self-recognition in pieces that were more familiar' was also shown (Repp and Knoblich, 2004: 607). Importantly, in the two follow-up tests the pianists were presented with edited interpretations; the experimenters eliminated from the stimuli all 'differences in tempo, overall dynamic (i.e. intensity) level, and dynamic nuances', parameters that arguably contribute most decisively to expressive performance (Repp and Knoblich, 2004: 604). On these occasions, therefore, the pianists had to recognize their own interpretation from individual differences in articulation and expressive timing. Their ability to do so was not affected. Bruno Repp and Günther Knoblich argued that the pianists may 'recognize their own performances' not because of remembering the recording session (i.e. not because of episodic memory) but rather because of their 'perception of action identity': their own performances 'create a stronger resonance in their action system than other performances'. In other words in such cases 'there is a closer match between anticipated and perceived action effects' (Repp and Knoblich, 2004: 607). The results thus suggest a close similarity between internal simulation or imagery and actual playing.

These conclusions bear upon several tenets which I am advocating in this chapter. In particular they support the validity of regarding a sound recording released with the artist's approval to be a document of that artist's performance (in general) as it is likely that he or she would recognise it as theirs.

Before looking at the perspective of the performers in a little more detail, it may be useful to clarify my standpoint regarding the listener. Admittedly it is not concerned with the 'average' listener. As mentioned above, they are discussed by many sources, while few take into account the 'musicological listener'. Since my main question in this 'reflection' is whether sound recordings are valid documents for the study of performance style, I focus on this somewhat rare and neglected species of listeners.

Many people prefer listening to CDs and find that it is often difficult to concentrate enough at concerts because of the external environment (coughing, lolly-wrapping, even silent nodding to the music, etc.). The location of their seat may also limit the listening experience. What is more important to note though is the subjectivity of the experience. A concert may be 'superb' for one listener while 'ordinary' for another and something in between for the performer (Tomes, 2004). However, it is not so much the individual difference that is of interest here but that the same listener may perceive the same performance differently on another occasion (e.g. a later broadcast). Research suggests that the loss of visual stimuli lessens the expressive effect of the performance (Davidson, 1993) although it is also known that many close their eyes to intensify their aesthetic experience. So it may be that it is the listener who is not in the same receptive mood on different occasions. Although the listener's perceptiveness may seem secondary to the standard of performance, the proposition can be defended by examining the phenomenon in the context of repeated listening to recordings. The conditions are the same, the listener is the same and, crucially, the interpretation is the same. Yet on one occasion the listener may hear the performance to be inspired and on another occasion it may seem indifferent; or striking aspects of it may become less or more noticeable. What do such experiences tell us about the nature of sound recordings and performances? Are they indeed dissimilar in terms of the 'end product', the musical experience? If the affect depends so much on the listener and not just the performer, is it still important to note that '[e]very live performance is different from every other. Yet every time a recording is replayed, the actions that originally produced the sounds remain unchanged' (Katz, 1999: 106)? What is 'real' about a performance and what are its aspects that are only in the eye/ear of the beholder or in the mind/psyche of the performer? Holding off the discussion of a few specific examples to account for some of the 'real' or measurable elements in recorded interpretations, it is important to turn first to the examination of the performer's perspective on live performance and recording.

As one of the recurring themes in discussions of sound recordings in relation to live performances is repeatability, it is worth capturing some of the frequently mentioned points in this regard. Apart from the emphasis on technical perfection that 'stifles spontaneity and excitement', repeatability is also often called upon when justifying literalistic renderings of scores. Alfred Brendel claims to have aimed at avoiding any 'exaggeration' in the recording studio because these might not 'bear frequent hearing' (Brendel, 1990: 200–2). Christopher Hogwood is also on record stating that although 'wild risks' and 'fantastic cadenzas' are likely to bring forth applause in a concert, these 'nearly always pall on repeated hearing' (cited in Day, 2000: 158). 'Idiosyncratic musical gestures…may not wear well over frequent and repeated hearings', agrees Mark Katz (1999: 106), who cites David Soyer, the cellist of the Guarneri Quartet: 'Recordings have a tendency to iron out the eccentric, idiosyncratic, personal things' because they may sound 'grotesque or mannered' on repeated hearing (Katz, 1999: 107). Some believe that Wilhelm Furtwängler's 'intense and revelatory' interpretations made his live performances memorable but caused his recordings to 'wear out' (Hitchcock, 1980: 69–70). Davies lists many similar claims and argues that one buys records to 'add a work to one's collection' and therefore a 'conservative' performance 'might become desirable' (Davies, 2001: 304). But is there empirical evidence for any of this? Or does it simply reflect the perception of certain people generalized into assertions that are made in the name of all listeners (or serving the priorities of recording companies and the market economy)? How often do people listen to the same recording? How much repeated listening does a recording have to 'endure'? Are not collectors famous for treasuring records that are idiosyncratic? Why is Glenn Gould such a phenomenon if listeners so easily tire of unusual interpretations? How come that Furtwängler's recordings are nevertheless legendary and ever newer generations of musicians still purchase them when available? If technical perfection is so important, how is it that Sviatoslav Richter's recordings, which are almost exclusively releases of live concert broadcasts and often include messy notes, have a market? All in all I would think that serious consumers of music willingly listen to recordings more than once *if* the interpretation is striking. This position may represent my bias, but I usually look forward to hearing again a strange timing, an additional accent, a beautifully shaped ornament, or an inner voice that I cannot hear in any other version, and so on. Without individual interpretative solutions – whether generated in a 'spontaneous' live concert or 'edited' in the studio – the performance is but a sounding demonstration of a piece which is often all too familiar.

Another commonly mentioned matter is the different atmosphere. Artists often seem to emphasize the disparity between how they feel during a concert versus a studio recording. Some admit that the studio 'permits a sharper focus on making music', a kind of 'monastic dedication which is oblivious of audience' (Yehudi Menuhin cited in Katz, 1999: 111). Those who favour concerts tend to mention the importance of an audience, the presence of which is also emphasized by philosophers as a basic criterion for a performance to take place (e.g. Godlovitch, 1998: 42). For others it is crucial to have a sense of the whole piece, the 'big picture'. Charles Rosen, for instance, asserts of doing takes of whole movements and then whole sections that can be used for edits (Rosen, 2002: 143–73). Susan Tomes provides a fascinating and candid description of her experiences in the studio. Although at times she sounds quite negative ('I don't think recording is compatible with being musically profound') and rightly critical of the minimal time allocated to making a record, eventually she admits, with some bewilderment, that the discs released *do represent* the 'interpretation that [I and my colleagues] wanted to record' (Tomes, 2004: 149). Many others insist that they only record pieces that they have performed in concert several times prior to the recording session (e.g. Malcolm Bilson, personal communication). To me all three scenarios imply that a recording reflects the artist's current conception–interpretation of the given piece. And as such I would regard them as performances. However, these are selective comments of only a few musicians whose views are available in print. Can they be considered typical?

The survey

When I was asked to contribute a chapter to this book I decided to try and collect some empirical evidence regarding the differences between concert performances and studio recordings from the perspective of professional musicians. I collected responses from 39 recording artists from the USA, UK, Europe and Australia to a pilot questionnaire circulated to them by mail and email.[3] Conscious of their time, I limited the questionnaire to a double-sided A4 page, consisting of demographical, categorical (yes/no) and 'rated-on-a-scale' questions with additional qualitative (open-ended) questions that were *optional* (see Appendix for a sample of the Questionnaire). Only soloists and/or chamber musicians (mostly keyboard and string but also voice) and conductors were recruited; one participant was involved in both classical and jazz recordings. They recorded for various labels, such as Nonesuch, Deutsche Gramophone, Hungaroton and ABC Classics. Age and gender data were not gathered but the participants included both older and younger artists. Their years of recording experience (mean = 9.75) and the number of CDs released (mean chamber/solo CDs = 9.25) are summarised in Table 1. Overall more than 70 per cent of the participants have released more than 10 CDs and thus can be regarded as seasoned recording artists.

Question	< 5	5 to 10	10 to 20	> 20	*N/A*
For how many years have you been making recordings?	5.13%	23.08%	38.46%	33.33%	
Approximately how many solo/chamber CDs have you released?	10.26%	20.51%	38.46%	25.64%	5.13%
Approximately how many concerto CDs have you released?	17.95%	17.95%	7.69%	5.13%	51.28%

Table 1: Percentage of responses to demographic questions

The results of the closed questions are summarised in Table 2. Although some of the participants found it difficult to answer with simple 'yes' or 'no' to questions that probed issues that are far from being black and white, the responses do indicate trends and consensus in most cases: 97.4 per cent agreed that recordings were different from live performances (Q1) but the majority (74.4 per cent) thought that recordings, or at least some of them, were nevertheless performances (Q2). There was also general agreement regarding differences in intention under different circumstances (Q3–4, 6): 58.97 per cent claimed to perform with different intentions in the studio (Q3), 69.2 per cent to do so in front of an audience (Q4), and 61.5 per cent when a concert was being recorded (Q6).

Questions 1–8 and 12	*Yes*	*No*	*Some*	*Maybe*	*N/A*
Q1: Do you think recordings are different from (live) performances?	97.44%		2.56%		
Q2: Do you think recordings are not really performances?	25.64%	64.12%	10.26%		
Q3: In terms of intentions, do you play differently in the recording studio than in a concert?	58.97%	38.46%	2.56%		
Q4: In terms of intentions, do you play differently in front of an audience than when performing alone in a studio?	69.23%	28.25%	2.56%		
Q5: Are you taking more risks in the studio than in live concerts?	12.82%	79.49%	5.13%	2.56%	
Q6: If a live performance is being recorded and/or broadcast, does this influence your playing (compared to studio recording and/or concerts without recording)?	61.54%	38.46%			
Q7: Have you ever released a recording that you were pressured to release (i.e. were not satisfied with its musical/artistic or audio qualities at the time of release)?	48.72%	53.85%			
Q8: Would you agree with the view that a recording is a representation of an ideal performance by a given artist at a particular point of his or her career or musical development?	56.41%	33.33%	5.13%		5.13%
Q12: Are there pieces on your repertoire that you couldn't release on record without editing?	51.28%	20.51%		23.08%	5.13%

Table 2: Percentage of responses to categorical questions

Interestingly, most (79.5 per cent) reported taking fewer risks in the studio, in spite of the potential for correction. There might be several reasons for this, including time constraints and tight budgets limiting the opportunity for experimentation. In any case the situation supports the notion that in the studio an established interpretation is recorded, which might not be as 'inspired' as the 'ideal' concert achievement but is, nevertheless, a rendering the performer feels 'at ease' to give. This interpretation of the results is supported by the responses to Q8 (whether a recording may be regarded as a representation of a given artist's ideal performance at the time): 56.4 per cent responded in the affirmative. However, 33.3 per cent of them held the opposite view. Perhaps the wording of the question (especially the expression 'ideal') was inappropriate. What I wanted to find out was the degree to which they felt recordings represented their interpretative conception of the piece at the time of recording. It seemed important to know to what extent artists identified with their interpretations on records if one was to draw conclusions from the analysis of these recordings regarding the artists' aesthetic approach. The near half-half response to Q7 (whether they have ever released CDs with which they were not satisfied) did not make the situation more comfortable from this point of view.

On the other hand, the answers to Q9–11 (Figure 1) seem to indicate some contradiction in the artists' self-report (as well as possible lack of clarity in the formulation of certain questions). More than three quarters of the participants claimed that the recordings represented well or very well their interpretation (81.6 per cent) and technical command (76.3 per cent) of the pieces at the time of recording (Q9, 11), and 63.2 per cent believed that the relationship between their concert performances and studio recordings were close (Q10). Apart from the wording, perhaps the opportunity to respond on a scale rather than with a simple yes/no contributed to the slightly different weighting in the answers to Questions 7–8 versus 9–11. In any case, the responses to Questions 9–11 reinforce the majority reply to Q8 and provide support for the view that recordings are valid documents for the investigation of performance styles and aesthetic approaches.

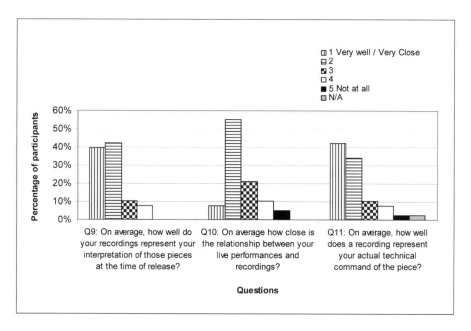

Figure 1: Summary of responses to scaled questions

The survey aimed to explore the perceived differences between concert performance and studio recording with three additional open-ended questions. These were nominated to be *optional* because of the potential time commitment involved in providing a reasoned answer. About 50 per cent of the participants offered responses to some or all of them. The questions asked participants to reflect on the *basic differences* (Optional Q1); potential differences in *intentions* and/or *approach* (Optional Q2); and the impact of *audience presence* (Optional Q3).

Some responded with one un-itemized reflection highlighting aspects of differences they considered undesirable and their approach to overcoming them. Others addressed the questions in more specific terms. The overarching responses captured aesthetic and experiential differences: 'In concert one tries to let go and express soul'; 'A concert contains more chances but enables the sounding of longer/larger scales/phrases'; 'I have always felt that a recording is like a film, a concert like a play'. Unmistakably, their main concern was to *eliminate* potential differences in the end product as far as the audience/listener may be concerned: 'I would prefer releasing live recordings'; 'I try never to record anything that I have not played several times in concert beforehand'; 'I find that my best live performances (which I try to give in early takes of complete movements, the only way I agree to record) have more spontaneity and expressive contrasts than edited versions'; '[In the studio] you have to imagine an audience. You have to create the same energy and magic as live'; 'I try for the same flair and excitement when making a CD'. The reflections also touched upon underlying social issues – 'ultimately music is a participatory experience while listening to a CD...[provides for] passive experiences'.

The more specific responses echoed these points and assisted in identifying six central issues of concern:

- *Risk taking*: 'I take more risks with a live audience – faster tempos etc.'; 'Concert performance [is] usually more careful'; 'You can take more risks [in the studio] knowing that if it does not work you get another chance'. (Compare these opposing views with the 79.49 per cent agreement shown at Q5, see Table 2.)

- *Nervousness*: 'Sometimes it is easier to be more relaxed [in the studio]'; 'Nerves often play a part in live performance and very very rarely in recording'.

- *Repeatability*: '[Recording is] less about immediate entertainment, more about long-term quality'; 'The permanence of the recording'; 'You can do it again in recording'; 'It can get stale with repeats in the studio'; 'Nice to be able to fix up details which can go wrong in live performance'.

- *Technical precision*: 'At most recordings the desire for technical perfection overrides the importance of "unrepeatable" musical moments'; 'In the studio one tries to reach technical fluidity and perfection'.

- *Spontaneity* and *excitement*: 'Concert performances are more liberated (free), the studio recording always wants to be too precise – and never succeeds enough. What sounds vital in the studio replay sounds dead from the CD in a few weeks'–months' time'; 'A concert brings a level of excitement, of a desire to give all and even take risks which does not always or readily happen in the studio'.

- *Audience impact*: 'The reactions of an audience, the silence, the attention are inseparable from the atmosphere of a concert which impacts on the musician and the music as well'; '[I get] a huge buzz and adrenalin [rush] from the presence of live audience'; 'It is hard to capture the electricity in many recording sessions – the energy that [develops] between performer and audience'; '[There is] a tendency to be more careful in a recording as you know that the CD listener...is a more critical and clinical audience'.

A few participants also mentioned unwanted noise such as coughing and the crackling of chairs during concerts or breathing into the microphone, foot tapping, and so on in the studio, and the fact that studio recordings do not provide the 'true sound of all instruments' nor record the 'piece in sequence'. The difference in concentration and energy requirements was also mentioned: 'Recording is an endurance/stamina activity while a live concert performance is more like a sprint'.

What emerges from these answers is a complex picture that refines the results of the categorical responses. Often it is not so much the differences but the similarities between concert and recording that are highlighted. This is particularly evident in the reflections of the more experienced artists and especially when they discuss their *intentions* or approaches to recorded and live performances:

I have come to expect and desire the same intentions/approach in both forms of music making. Although in a live performance I am less concerned about note-perfection than I am in studio recording. I will now take risks in recordings or I prepare myself (for the most part) so that I can take risks.

They mention the need to capture a stage presence even on record; to have the 'same intuition or empathy'; 'to give everything to the music and to the audience... because the audience is always there even if it is delayed by recording'. It is clear that these artists focus on the end product, the impression their performance or recording has (or will have) on the audience/listener: 'One should have the same impact with a studio recording (regardless of the desire for greater precision) as with a concert, if this is at all possible. I, at least would aim for that'.

Quite a few participants commented on the opportunity to self-analyse in the studio and how it may bear upon their interpretation: 'In a studio situation I arrive with an interpretative concept which I then develop during my recording in response to the technical constraints as well as possibilities'; 'In the studio there is more of a sense of going through a goal-oriented process. I want to study the way my interpretation develops'. The enthusiasm with which they described the impact of a live audience on their performance supports Gracyk's view that the absence of an audience impoverishes the world of the performer. Most responses emphasized the positive effects of audience presence. They believed the audience 'inspired' them, made the performance event 'more exciting' and 'communication easier'. One respondent echoed Godlovitch's statement about performers' intentions regarding their audiences, namely that they always 'wish to do something to and for that audience', even when they 'play alone' (Godlovitch, 1998: 42): 'I don't think anyone would play without the audience in mind – I approach everything I do as if someone will be listening'. This of course means thinking of the audience and 'performing to it' even in a recording session. Would this not make the record a representation of a performance?

Other respondents also appear to be in dialogue with Godlovitch. He continues the above point by arguing that to control the audience, 'its response, to work its feelings' is not possible in its absence. 'One cannot equivalently dazzle oneself virtuosically as one can a listener, nor lead on or surprise' (Godlovitch, 1998: 42). Perhaps it is this sensation and experience to which participants of the survey refer when they state: '[The audience] makes me be present and enjoy the experience of now rather than worrying about judgment in the future'; '[The audience] makes it interactive which might also lead to different solutions in the interpretation'.

Nevertheless, as one of the most experienced participants remarked, 'the one (and arguably only) essential of performance is to make people listen: achieve that and you have succeeded'. If people listen to a recording, in particular if they want to listen to it repeatedly, the performer has fulfilled the 'essential of [a] performance'.

How can this be achieved? The participant continues: 'When you sense the audience [to be] really intent on the music that can be exhilarating and inspiring. Clearly that is harder to achieve when playing to a microphone: so I try to think not of the microphone but of the others present [i.e. producer, engineer], who, after all, are ideal audience because so committed to a good result'. Clearly, performers, or at least some of them, aim to involve the (future) listeners of their recordings in an *experience of performance*.

Since the survey did not gather information on the perspectives of listeners, the data does not fully validate Gracyk's (1997) tenet that it is only the world of the performer that becomes poorer when people turn away from live events and listen to recorded music. However, diminishing concert audiences together with the overwhelming success of iPods and other forms of technologically mediated listening seem to indicate audience satisfaction with 'canned' music and lend support to Gracyk's analysis. Apart from reflecting fashionable social behaviour, this situation may also indicate limited difference in the *musical* experience of a concert audience and the CD listener. To examine this possibility in a little more detail, in the remaining section I discuss a few specific examples to account for some of the measurable musical elements in performances. It is hoped that the observations will contribute positively to my argument that recordings do represent performances and are therefore suitable documents for the historical study of changing interpretative styles.

Analysis of recordings made in live and studio contexts

Artistic solutions in music performance are notoriously difficult to describe in words and the language is prone to become discursive–descriptive rather than analytical. The lack of consistency in word usage from writer to writer – even from apparently similar cultural backgrounds – is a serious problem (Brock-Nannestad, 2006). Until now the desire to rectify this situation has led to statistical explorations of listeners' responses (mostly to compositions rather than performances, e.g. Gabrielsson, 2001; Juslin, 2001; Schubert, 2001; Sloboda and O'Neill, 2001) and measurements of performance features that contribute to perceived expressiveness, such as tempo fluctuation, dynamics, articulation, timing, and rhythmic flexibility.

A large body of literature exists that models expressiveness in music performance on the basis of measured parameters in specially created MIDI or Disklavier files (for a summary, see Clarke, 2004). Publications providing measurement data of performance features on commercially released CDs are fewer (e.g. Johnson, 2002; Repp, 1992). Yet such measurements are necessary because they provide empirical evidence for, and often against, claims about performance trends and individual characteristics. Extensive analysis of tempo fluctuations in orchestral repertoire enabled, for instance, the questioning of the status quo that regards

Arturo Toscanini the 'father' of 'strict' tempo. In contrast, the data indicated clearly that Herbert von Karajan, rather than anybody else, was the first whose tempos remained relatively steady throughout a movement (Bowen, 1996: 132). Systematic examinations of vibrato practice among violinists revealed that the frequency and intensity of its use depended on repertoire at least as much as on the period of recording or the generation of violinists (Fabian, 2005, 2006; Katz, 2003, 2004; Milsom, 2003). Calculating dotting ratios from measured note durations made it possible to investigate anew the performance of dotted rhythms in Baroque music and throw a different light on a vexed debate by pointing out the existence of a hitherto unacknowledged auditory illusion (Schubert and Fabian, 2001; Fabian and Schubert, 2008). The data could also be used to test listeners' perception of musical character in relation to changing performance features in various interpretations of the same piece (Fabian and Schubert, 2003).

But how do 'live' recordings of a piece compare to studio versions by the same artist? Are concert performances truly that much more 'spontaneous'? Unfortunately, it is not easy to locate comparable matches because ideally the date of the two recordings should be close, and although there are potentially thousands of concert recordings in big broadcasting archives these are difficult to access if at all possible. Therefore, one (famous) example will have to suffice. Gould released his first studio recording of Johann Sebastian Bach's *Goldberg Variations* in 1955 (Sony SMK 52 594). During the following years he performed the work on European concert tours, including the Salzburg Festival in 1959. This concert has been released on Sony Classical (SMK 52 685). The comparison reveals mostly similarities. Except for Variation 25, the tempos of each section are practically identical (Figure 2), the approach to interpretation akin: fast, crisp playing, dynamics remaining mostly homogeneous in faster movements and more varied in slow ones, little pedal, hardly any fermatas or ritardandos, linking many variations without a break, clear part-playing, strong but flexible pulse and a variety of touch serving rhythmic definition and rhythmic grouping. Rubato and accents highlight metric groups and strengthen the projection of each variation's rhythmic and affective character, which show strong similarities across the two versions.

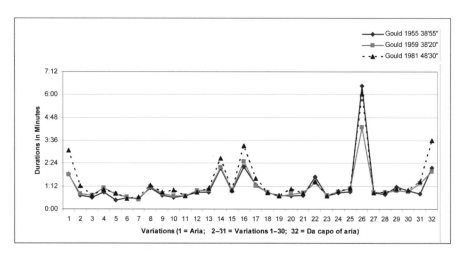

Figure 2: Comparison of durations in Gould's three interpretations of J.S. Bach's *Goldberg Variations*. The durations of repeats in the 1981 version have been eliminated to make the data comparable.

The minute differences between these two versions become insignificant in light of his second studio recording, which he prepared in 1981 (Sony SMK 52 619). By then he was nearly fifty and had developed alternative ideas about many sections of the piece. The recording is a testimony of his new interpretative concept (Bazzana, 1997). Tempos are often slower (see Figures 2 and 3), the overall approach more 'expressive', and the character of several movements more 'meditative' (e.g. Aria, Variation 15). Repeatedly, he brings out different voices and uses different articulation or dynamics in a given variation (e.g. Variation 13), or chooses a slower tempo to enable a similar strategy to be more obvious (e.g. Variation 19). At other times he performs the repeat of the first half of a variation – which he never does in the earlier versions – with a contrasting reading of the score (e.g. Variations 18, 21). Although the trademarks of his Bach-playing are still there, such as the clarity of texture and part-playing, varied articulation and touch, the lack of ritardandos and fermatas and the quasi attacca linking of all movements, the overall interpretation is so different that it is customary to group Gould-fans according to a preference for the early or the late version.

Perhaps surprisingly, a closer examination of one excerpt reveals a discrepancy between generalized statements (based on perception of affect as well as aural analysis) and measured performance features. In a study by Fabian and Schubert (2003), 98 tertiary music students rated all three versions of Gould's interpretation of Variation 7 from the *Goldberg Variations* as being like a siciliano or pastorale; 'serene', 'calm' and 'relaxed'. At the same time, acoustic measurements of tempo, loudness, dotting and articulation showed differences in performance.[4] Figure 3 illustrates the similarities and differences in execution: the biggest difference across all three versions is in tempo, which slows progressively. There is little difference in articulation, all being fairly legato – although the 1955 studio recording less so than the other two. Dynamic levels are similar in the later two versions but the dotting ratio is the same in the earlier two. Overall it seems that Gould had been envisaging a 'calm' siciliano-like interpretation of Variation 7 which he progressively heightened by playing slower, softer and more legato.[5] A breakthrough in achieving his goal might have been the realisation to under-dot the recurring 6/8 pattern and thus smooth out the rhythmic character. That this solution may be regarded a 'breakthrough' is proposed on grounds that, out of the 34 recordings made by various artists between 1933 and 2000 that Fabian and Schubert examined, Gould's 1981 version is the only one which is not over-dotted, while there are others which are even slower, softer or more legato. The most important lesson is, however, that listeners are able to perceive his artistic intention regardless of the measurable differences in execution. The trend towards a more serene reading of Variation 7 is also in line with the overall judgment, stated earlier, of his last recording of the *Goldberg Variations* to be more 'meditative' and introspective than those from the 1950s, whether from the studio or a live concert.

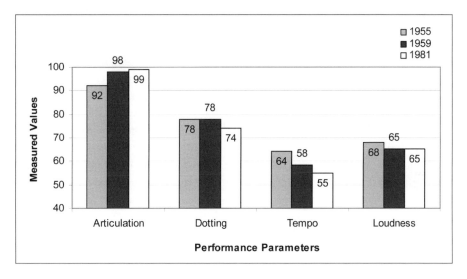

Figure 3: Mean articulation and dotting ratios, tempo and loudness in Gould's interpretations of Variation 7 from J.S. Bach's *Goldberg Variations* (1955 and 1981 studio recordings; 1959 live concert). The higher the articulation ratio the more legato is the performance (100 = maximum legato, i.e. no measurable gap between one note's off-set and the following note's onset. Literal (theoretical 3:1) dotting ratio = 75. Tempo values refer to beat per minute. Loudness is measured in Sones.

Dramatic changes in artistic approach are not uncommon, of course, and there are many instances where studio recordings document this process. Gustav Leonhardt's recordings of the *Goldberg Variations* or Nikolaus Harnoncourt's renderings of Bach's B Minor Mass are good cases in point. In both instances, the listener deals with studio recordings prepared at particular junctions in the artists' careers. Leonhardt recorded the *Goldberg Variations* three times at about twelve years' intervals: First in 1953 (Vanguard OVC 2004), then in 1965 (Teldec 4509 97994-2) and finally in 1978 (Deutche Harmonia Mundi GD77149). At the time the first version was made, Leonhardt was a fresh graduate of the Basel Schola Cantorum, a specialist institution for the study of early music. Yet, as I discuss it elsewhere at length (Fabian 1997; 2003), this recording offers little in terms of historically informed practice and represents, rather, the literalistic style of the 1950s (see, for instance the much more legato playing of Variation 7 in 1953. The dotting ratio and tempo do not change much in the later versions, but articulation becomes much more staccato contributing to a more 'characterized' or strongly shaped interpretation [cf. Figure 4]). During the ensuing years Leonhardt completely overhauled his playing style. On the 1965 recording his overall approach is relaxed and simple, the tempi only slightly faster than in 1953 and he hardly adds any extra ornaments (see Figure 5 for a comparison of durations). The essential difference lies in his articulation and greatly differentiated touch. Expressivity is achieved through flexible, well-defined, clearly delineated small groups of notes embedded in a strong sense of pulse and metric hierarchy. The articulation is locally nuanced; there are inflections, expressive timing, and rhythmic rubato while his earlier reading is strict in terms of tempo and rhythm.[6] At the time of release his new interpretation was radically different but so convincingly anchored in the historical style as it is currently understood that eventually the approach became the established standard. So much so that even Leonhardt did not change it significantly. The 1978 version is indeed very similar to that of 1965; perhaps at times a little more restrained, at other times a little faster, but essentially the same affects, groupings, inflections, clearly delineated parts and small musical units / phrases. To me the underlying similarities between the later two versions are evidence in support of the view that a recording is a testimony of the artist's interpretative concept. Some detail may be slightly different, more or less successful – just like from one concert to the next – while the essentials do not change, just as they remain stable in live performances, too. In this sense the released recording is also a unique 'version' or 'manifestation', even if one can hear it again and even if its creation may have involved many repetitions and edits.

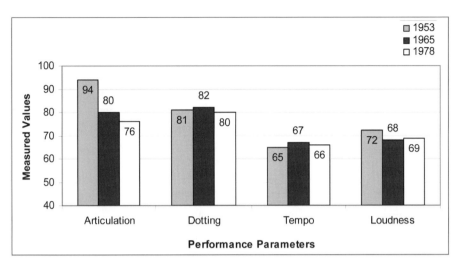

Figure 4: Mean articulation and dotting ratios, tempo and loudness in Leonhardt's three studio recordings of Variation 7 from J.S. Bach's *Goldberg Variations*. The higher the articulation ratio the more legato is the performance (100 = maximum legato, i.e. no measurable gap between one note's off-set and the following note's onset). Literal (theoretical 3:1) dotting ratio = 75. Tempo values refer to beat per minute. Loudness is measured in Sones.

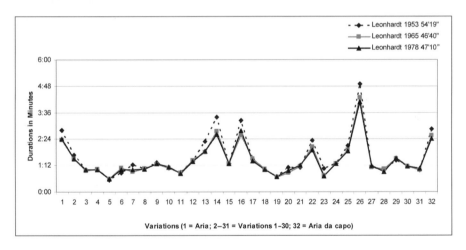

Figure 5: Comparison of durations in Leonhardt's three interpretations of J.S. Bach's *Goldberg Variations*. Durations of occasional repeats in the 1953 version have been eliminated.

Harnoncourt's first, 1969 recording of Bach's *B minor Mass* (Teldec 4509-95517) signified a similar watershed in the work's performance history. According to Butt, '[t]he contrast with [other] recordings...could hardly be more pronounced: not only is the texture immediately lighter...and the style of articulation more locally nuanced, but also many fundamental features of tempo and rhythm are "new"' (Butt, 1991:

40). Between the 1960s and 1980s Harnoncourt was a leading advocate of using historical instruments and knowledge in performance. However, in later years he seems to have been emphasizing a balanced approach, embracing artistic intuition and 'passion' as much as 'knowledge' (Malina, 2002). This is evidenced in most of his more recent recordings, including the 1986 second version of Bach's B minor Mass (Teldec 8.35716). This interpretation may seem like a 'reaction' to the first. The radical fast tempi and detailed, at times austere articulation of the earlier version give way to luscious dynamic fluctuations, longer phrases, and occasional smooth legato (compare, for instance the fugal part of Kyrie 1). Rather than adopting the vanguard historically informed position of soloistic (one per part) performance, he conducts a fairly large ensemble. The use of a mixed choir also contradicts 'historical knowledge'. In justifying his interpretation Harnoncourt argues:

> In its sensual religiosity, the *B Minor Mass* is not an example of Protestant church music. It was for this reason that we used not boys but women for the soloists...we consciously avoided performing the work with a boys' choir and used a mixed chorus since we believe that women's voices have such clear intonation that they can more clearly reproduce the rhythmic structure and coloratura passages, while at the same time bringing to bear on the work a grown-up's sensuality. For me, that is now an essential aspect of this work.
>
> (cited in Lewinski, 1986: 9)

The last sentence implies that the recording is a document of his then current artistic concept, at least in this respect.

Concluding remarks

At the beginning of Chapter 7 of his book Davies states that '[a]pparently we regard recorded performances as fair substitutes for live ones' but in footnote 1 on the same page he lists 'the few [philosophers] who are sensitive to the fact that recordings are very different from live performances' (Davies, 2001: 295). He continues:

> The significance of this technologically facilitated shift in the means by which we hear music will be missed if recordings are thought to be on a par with, or are heard as reproductions of, live performances.
>
> (Davies, 2001: 295–6)

In this chapter I have argued that the epistemological and ontological differences between live performances and recordings may be less important to performance practice researchers than theorists and philosophers posit. I have brought forth a variety of reasons for justifying the claim that the type of sound recordings discussed here may be regarded as documents of performance trends and interpretative styles or concepts. Johnson seems to agree when he writes: 'Recordings clearly reveal a wealth of information about changing performance practices' (Johnson, 2002: 208). The findings that performers can easily identify their own recordings as being their performances (Repp and Knoblich, 2004) together with the strong agreement among survey participants that their recordings represent well their interpretation of the pieces recorded (Q9) indicated significant support for such a view. The results of the analysis of multiple versions of the same piece recorded by the same performer over an extended period of time (Leonhardt, Harnoncourt) lent further credibility to this standpoint. The comparison of concert and studio recordings of the same piece by the same artist (Gould) signalled strong interpretative and technical commonality between 'performance' and 'recording' but more evidence is needed before confident conclusions may be drawn regarding such comparisons.

Johnson also seems to agree with my thesis, echoed by surveyed artists when reflecting on their intentions, that what matters is the end product and how it is heard or received. He writes of 'the *holistic listening experience* offered by the *recording itself*' and identifies the most difficult but most significant question researchers of performance face: 'how individual factors...combine to generate' such an experience (Johnson, 2002: 208, italics added).

Furthermore, the chapter highlighted differences in the perspectives of performers, listeners and theorists and the insufficient evidence for certain tenets: emphasizing the permanency of recordings, theorists and performers sometimes claim that listeners would tire of hearing 'idiosyncratic' interpretations. Yet it was proposed that the contrary may be just as possible. Moreover, Igor Stravinsky maintained that the 'life-expectancy of a recording' was not more than that of a 'motor car' (cited in Davies, 2001: 303), implying that people are always looking for something 'new', regardless of whether what they currently have is 'exotic' or 'conservative' (Davies, 2001: 304). Time and again, theorists make the assumption that 'one listens to a recording with the expectation of hearing it again – with an awareness of the reproducibility of its content – and this inevitably affects how one experiences and evaluates it' (Davies, 2001: 304). Apart from questioning the universal validity of such arguments I have endeavoured to show other reasons for listening, for instance a curiosity to know how a particular performer interprets a piece. The result may be that one never wants to hear it again.

Other philosophical concerns regarding the differences between live classical music performance and sound recording and either's relationship to the 'work' (or impact on the nature of the work), although perhaps crucial from an epistemological or ontological point of view, seemed quite beside the point for the historical musicologist, listener and even the performer. Tenets that the 'creative aspect' of a performance is 'permanently fixed and thereby ossified' when 'the real-time performance is recorded', or 'because the listener experiences the disc as constantly reproducible, she cannot hear the performer's decisions as spontaneous, so they lose their immediacy and vibrancy' (Davies, 2001: 304) are theoretical assertions and seem to have little bearing on 'real-life' listening experiences or the intentions of the performer. Overall, the chapter highlighted that the academic study of musical performance is in its infancy. There are many more pertinent questions being asked than satisfactory answers provided. Whether discussing live performances or studio recordings 'we know more about what can be *measured*...but very little about what listeners of all kinds *hear* in them' and what the intentions of the performers were (Clarke, 2002: 195). Without clarifying these, the philosophical and critical contemplation regarding the differences between the two 'products' will remain incomplete.

Appendix – the questionnaire

Thank you for taking the time to respond to this questionnaire. Please answer the formative questions honestly. Your identity will remain anonymous. The questionnaire is only a crude instrument to save time while exploring the reality of a few fundamental claims. There are also optional qualitative questions at the end. I would much appreciate it if you could answer those as well, however briefly. If you would like to add anything further please write freely on a separate sheet. Thank you!

Demographic questions:

1. For how many years have you been making recordings?
   (Please circle or mark with bold one option.)
   fewer than 5   5–10   10–20   more than 20

2. Approximately how many CDs have you released?
   Solo/chamber: < 5   5–10   10–20   more than 20
   Concerto: < 5   5–10   more than 10

Categorical and Scaled Questions:

1   Do you think recordings are different from (live)   Yes   No
    performances?

2   Do you think recordings are not really performances?   Yes   No

3   In terms of intentions, do you play differently in the   Yes   No
    recording studio than in a concert?

4   In terms of intentions, do you play differently in front of an   Yes   No
    audience than when performing alone in a studio?

5 Are you taking more risks in the studio than in live concerts?   Yes   No

6 If a live performance is being recorded and/or broadcast,   Yes   No
does this influence your playing (compared to studio
recording and/or concerts without recording)?

7 Have you ever released a recording that you were pressured   Yes   No
to release (i.e. were not satisfied with its musical/artistic or
audio qualities at the time of release)?

8 Would you agree with the view that a recording is a   Yes   No
representation of an ideal performance by a given artist at a
particular point of his or her career or musical development?

9. On average, how well do your recordings represent your interpretation of
those pieces at the time of release?
(Please circle a number, 1 = very well, and 5 = not at all well.)
1   2   3   4   5

10. On average how close is the relationship between your live performances and
recordings?
(Please circle a number, 1 = very close and 5 = very different.)
1   2   3   4   5

11. On average, how well does a recording represent your actual technical
command of the piece?
(Please circle a number, 1 = very closely and 5 = not at all closely.)
1   2   3   4   5

12. Are there pieces on your repertoire that you couldn't release on record
without editing?
Yes   No   Maybe

13. What is your relationship, on average, to others involved in the recording
process?
Chamber partners:
Equal   superior   subordinate
Conductor:
Equal   superior   subordinate
not applicable

Producer:
Equal   superior   subordinate
Engineer:
Equal   superior   subordinate

Optional qualitative questions

(Please answer freely; dot points would be just as useful as a written-out paragraph/
sentence.)

1. In your experience, what are the main differences between your performance
    at a concert and in the studio?
2. What sorts of differences could you identify regarding your intentions/approach
    to a live performance (with audience) versus a studio recording?
3. How do you think the presence of a live audience (whether present or listening
    through broadcast) impacts on your performance?

Notes

1   As this article was going to press I came across an MA dissertation (Curran, 2007) that
    provides further data on musicians' attitudes to recordings. The similarity of findings
    underlines the importance of engaging with the experiences of performers and serious
    listeners in philosophical discussions.
2   As a rare exception in dealing with classical rather than popular music consumption, a
    recently published study examined the audience of the 'Music in the Round' chamber
    music festival held in 2003 at Sheffield in the UK (Pitts, 2005). However, a detailed study
    of the listening patterns and experiences of 'focused listeners' to electronically mediated
    music is not yet available. Clarke's (2002) essay, 'Listening to Performance', is again more
    theoretically oriented and the empirical data he provides by way of reference to published
    case studies are concerned with perception rather than listening habits or attitudes.
3   I would like to thank Natalie Shea (ABC Classics), András Székely (Hungaroton/Magyar
    Zene), Aaron Williamon (Royal College of Music), Neal Peres da Costa (Conservatorium of
    Music, Sydney University), Eric Clarke (Sheffield University) and Jonathan Ong (University
    of New South Wales) for their assistance in recruiting participants and Emery Schubert
    for his advice while devising the questionnaire. I would also like to thank the participants,
    including my renowned musician friends and acquaintances – who should all remain
    anonymous – for taking time to respond. Furthermore, I would like to express my gratitude
    to the editor and two anonymous reviewers for their most constructive comments and
    suggestions on an earlier version of the paper.
4   Note on-sets and offsets were measured in audio editing software (Sound Edit 16) to
    calculate dotting and articulation ratios, loudness was measured in Sones, and tempo
    was calculated from duration. The full methodology is described in a study comparing
    measurements in 34 recorded interpretations of Variation 7 (Fabian and Schubert, 2008).

5 Variation 7 in the Bärenreiter NBA Urtext edition (1977) includes the inscription 'al tempo di giga' which Bach inserted in his own copy of the work (see Christoph Wolff's editorial comments).

6 Three short excerpts (bars 1–16) from Variation 6 illustrating the stylistic difference between his 1953 and 1965 and the similarities of his 1965 and 1978 recordings can be listened to on the website: http://empa.arts.unsw.edu.au/research/em/bachgbsound.html

References

Bazzana, K. (1997) *Glenn Gould: The Performer in the Work*. Oxford: Clarendon Press.

Bowen, J.A. (1996) 'Tempo, Duration and Flexibility: Techniques in the Analysis of Performance', *Journal of Musicological Research* 16 (2): 111–56.

_____ (1999) 'Finding the Music in Musicology: Performance History and Musical Works', in N. Cook and M. Everist (eds) *Rethinking Music*, pp.424–51. Oxford: Oxford University Press.

Brendel, A. (1990) *Music Sounded Out: Essays, Lectures, Interviews, Afterthoughts*. London: Robson Books.

Brock-Nannestad, G. (2006) 'W.R. Anderson as a Record Critic', Message to the *Musical Performance on Record Discussion List* (29 June 2006). URL: http://www.jiscmail.ac.uk/archives/mus-perf-rec.html

Butt, J. (1991) *Bach: Mass in B Minor*. Cambridge: Cambridge University Press.

Clarke, E. (2002) 'Listening to Performance', in J. Rink (ed.) *Musical Performance: A Guide to Understanding*, pp.186–96. Cambridge: Cambridge University Press.

_____ (2004) 'Empirical Methods in the Study of Performance', in E. Clarke and N. Cook (eds) *Empirical Musicology: Aims, Methods, Prospects*, pp.77–102. New York: Oxford University Press.

Cook, N. (1992) *Music, Imagination, and Culture*. Oxford: Clarendon Press.

_____ (2001) 'Between Process and Product: Music and/as Performance', *Music Theory Online* 7 (2), URL (consulted August 2007): http://www/societymusic theory.org/mto/

Curran, T.W. (2007) *Recording Music: Musicians' Attitudes and Approaches*. Unpublished MA dissertation, University of Sheffield.

Davidson, J.W. (1993) 'Visual Perception of Performance Manner in the Movements of Solo Musicians', *Psychology of Music* 21 (2): 103–13.

Davies, S. (2001) *Musical Works and Performances: A Philosophical Exploration*. Oxford: Clarendon Press.

Day, T. (2000) *A Century of Recorded Music: Listening to Musical History*. New Haven: Yale University Press.

DeNora, T. (2000) *Music in Everyday Life*. Cambridge: Cambridge University Press.

Fabian, D. (1997) 'Changing Style in Performing J.S. Bach's Music, 1945–1978: The Goldberg Variations', *The Consort* 53: 23–39.

_____ (2003) *Bach Performance Practice 1945–1975: A Review of Sound Recordings and Literature*. Aldershot: Ashgate.

_____ (2005) 'Towards a Performance History of Bach's Sonatas and Partitas for Solo Violin: Preliminary Investigations', in L. Vikárius and V. Lampert (eds) *Essays in Honor of László Somfai: Studies in the Sources and the Interpretation of Music*, pp.87–108. Lanham, Maryland: Scarecrow Press.

_____ (2006) 'The Recordings of Joachim, Ysaÿe and Sarasate in Light of their Reception by Nineteenth-Century British Critics', *International Review of the Aesthetics and Sociology of Music* 37 (2): 189–211.

Fabian, D. and Schubert, E. (2003) 'Expressive Devices and Perceived Musical Character in 34 Performances of Variation 7 from Bach's Goldberg Variations' *Musicae Scientiae* (Special Issue 2003–2004): 49–68.

_____ (2008) 'Musical Character and the Performance and Perception of Dotting, Articulation and Tempo in Recordings of Variation 7 of J.S. Bach's *Goldberg Variations* (BWV 988)', *Musicae Scientiae* 12 (2): 177–206.

Gabrielsson, A. (2001) 'Emotions in Strong Experiences with Music', in P. Juslin and J. Sloboda (eds) *Music and Emotion: Theory and Research*, pp.431–49. Oxford: Oxford University Press.

Godlovitch, S. (1998) *Musical Performance: A Philosophical Study*. London: Routledge.

Goehr, L. (1992) *The Imaginary Museum of Musical Works: An Essay in the Philosophy of Music*. Oxford: Clarendon Press.

Goodman, N. (1976) *Languages of Art*. Indianapolis: Hackett.

Gracyk, T. (1997) 'Listening to Music: Performances and Recordings', *Journal of Aesthetics and Art Criticism* 55 (2): 139–50.

Hitchcock, H.W. (ed.) (1980) *The Phonograph and our Musical Life: Proceedings of a Centennial Conference 7–10 December 1977*. New York: Institute for Studies in American Music, City University of New York (I.S.A.M. Monographs: No. 14).

Johnson, P. (2002) 'The Legacy of Recordings', in J. Rink (ed.) *Musical Performance: A Guide to Understanding*, pp.197–212. Cambridge: Cambridge University Press.

Juslin, P. (2001) 'Communicating Emotion in Music Performance: A Review and a Theoretical Framework', in P. Juslin and J. Sloboda (eds) *Music and Emotion: Theory and Research*, pp.309–37. Oxford: Oxford University Press.

Katz, M. (1999) *The Phonograph Effect: The Influence of Recording on Listener, Performer, Composer, 1900–1940*. Unpublished PhD dissertation, The University of Michigan.

_____ (2003) 'Beethoven in the Age of Mechanical Reproduction: The Violin Concerto on Record', *Beethoven Forum* 10: 38–54.

_____ (2004) *Capturing Sound: How Technology Has Changed Music*. Berkeley: University of California Press.

Kraft, J. (1996) *Stage to Studio*. Baltimore: Johns Hopkins University Press.

Krausz, M. (ed.) (1993) *The Interpretation of Music: Philosophical Essays*. Oxford: Oxford University Press.

Leech-Wilkinson, D. (2001) 'Using Recordings to Study Musical Performances', in A. Linehan (ed.) *Aural History: Essays on Recorded Sound*, pp.1–12. London: British Library.

Leppert, R. (1993) *The Sight of Sound: Music, Representation, and the History of the Body*. Berkeley: University of California Press.

Lewinski, W.-E. von (1986) 'Bach: B Minor Mass' – Liner Notes to Harnoncourt's B minor Mass Recording, Teldec 8.35716, pp.6–9.

Malina, J. (2002) 'Mi, belgák, így zenélünk: Villáminterjú Nikolaus Harnoncourt-ral' ['We Belgians Play Music Like That: Snapshot Interview with Nikolaus Harnoncourt'], *Muzsika* 45 (5): 20–1.

Milsom, D. (2003) *Theory and Practice in Late Nineteenth-Century Violin Performance: An Examination of Style in Performance 1850–1900*. Aldershot: Ashgate.

North, A. and Hargreaves, D. (1997) 'Experimental Aesthetics and Everyday Music Listening', in D. Hargreaves and A. North (eds) *The Social Psychology of Music*, pp.84–103. Oxford: Oxford University Press.

Philip, R. (2004) *Performing in the Age of Recording*. New Haven: Yale University Press.

Pitts, S.E. (2005) 'What Makes an Audience? Investigating the Roles and Experiences of Listeners at a Chamber Music Festival', *Music and Letters* 56 (2): 257–69.

Repp, B. (1992) 'Diversity and Commonality in Music Performance: An Analysis of Timing Microstructure in Schumann's "Träumerei"', *Journal of the Acoustical Society of America* 92 (5): 2546–68.

Repp, B. and Knoblich, G. (2004) 'Perceiving Action Identity: How Pianists Recognize their Own Performances', *Psychological Science* 15 (9): 604–9.

Rosen, C. (2002) *Piano Notes: The Hidden World of the Pianist*. London: Penguin Books.

Schubert, E. (2001) 'Continuous Measurement of Self-Report Emotional Response to Music', in P. Juslin and J. Sloboda (eds) *Music and Emotion: Theory and Research*, pp.393–414. Oxford: Oxford University Press.

Schubert, E. and Fabian, D. (2001) 'Preference and Perception in Dotted 6/8 Patterns by Experienced and Less Experienced Baroque Music Listeners', *Journal of Music Perception and Cognition* 7 (2): 113–32.

Sloboda, J. and O'Neill, S. (2001) 'Emotions in Everyday Listening to Music', in P. Juslin and J. Sloboda (eds) *Music and Emotion: Theory and Research*, pp.415–29. Oxford: Oxford University Press.

Tomes, S. (2004) *Beyond the Notes*. Woodbridge: The Boydell Press.

Treitler, L. (2002) 'Early Recorded Performances of Chopin Waltzes and Mazurkas: The Relation to the Text', *Journal of the American Liszt Society* 51: 55–75.

Discography

Gould, G. (1955) J.S. Bach: *Goldberg Variations* (Aria with 30 Variations, BWV 988), Sony SMK 52 594, 1992.

_____ (1959) J.S. Bach: *Goldberg Variations* (Aria with 30 Variations, BWV 988), SMK 52 685, 1993.

_____ (1981) J.S. Bach: *Goldberg Variations* (Aria with 30 Variations, BWV 988), Sony SMK 52 619, 1993.

Harnoncourt, N. (1969) J.S. Bach: *Messe in h-moll* (Mass in B minor, BWV 232), Teldec 4509-95517, 1994.

_____ (1986) J.S. Bach: *Messe in h-moll* (Mass in B minor, BWV 232), Teldec 8.35716, 1995.

Leonhardt, G. (1953) J.S. Bach: *Goldberg Variations* (Aria with 30 Variations, BWV 988), Vanguard OVC 2004, 1992.

_____ (1965) J.S. Bach: *Goldberg Variations* (Aria with 30 Variations, BWV 988), Teldec 4509 97994-2, 1995.

_____ (1978) J.S. Bach: *Goldberg Variations* (Aria with 30 Variations, BWV 988), Deutche Harmonia Mundi GD77149, 1990.

SIMON TREZISE

Distortions and Masks: Transmutations of the 'Performing Breath' in the Studio Take[1]

Recordings and musical performance

THE concession that historical recordings constitute a crucial source for musicological investigation of performance practice dates from around 1992 when Robert Philip's influential *Early Recordings and Musical Style* was published. For perhaps the first time in a scholarly monograph, early recordings provided source material for discussion of the history of musical performance.[2] In 2001 Daniel Leech-Wilkinson wrote optimistically of the study of recordings, at the same time challenging the claims of 'authentic' performance practice: 'the more original performances we hear, the less evident it is that historically informed performance carries any special ethical value' (Leech-Wilkinson, 2001: 6). In the same paragraph he stated that 'we know how Elgar's music sounded in his own time' (Leech-Wilkinson, 2001: 6). We 'know' because we have it on record. In a characteristically challenging essay, Nicholas Cook implies that we 'know' Igor Stravinsky's performances of his own music through recordings, a view implicitly endorsed by the composer, who attributed to his recordings an authority complementary to the notated score (Cook, 2003: 176–91).[3]

This chapter presents an epistemological study of recording. It questions the 'knowing', the assumption of familiarity with the performance of musicians, many long dead, that recordings have engendered. Leon Botstein's scepticism highlighted by his argument that recordings are a 'species of text' and 'ultimately fragmentary and inevitably distorted' (Botstein, 1999: 5) has influenced this study, even though the conclusions I arrive at may not provide final corroboration for his views. Botstein concludes his polemical 'Musings' with the statement that listening to and analysing a 'few recordings...are alluring but misleading shortcuts to an understanding of the history of performance...They are, finally, incomplete fragments of a musical culture' (Botstein, 1999: 5). The outlook adopted here is more favourable, but only once the nature of the 'text' is better understood. Space constraints dictate a highly selective approach, so attention is principally given to the 'take', which will be defined below. Given the speculative nature of the task, much of what follows probes and questions the recording process; answers are not so easily supplied, but the first step towards 'knowing' is surely doubting.

We should begin with an evocation of live musical performance, as it is a common assumption that a recording presents a reproduction of the act of musical (or other) performance, an assumption characteristically connoting live musical performance. Musical performance as defined by Stan Godlovitch in his philosophical study entails 'sounds, agents, works, and listeners' (Godlovitch, 1998: 11): 'Performance sound ceases with the cessation of its generative source, the activity of music-making, and hence is causally dependent upon that source' (Godlovitch, 1998: 13–14). In the spirit of his work, but not the letter, I shall characterise a live performance, conceived here normatively: one attends a concert. There is ritual and society. People read programme notes, which prepare them for Ludwig van Beethoven's Seventh Symphony. As the conductor enters, the audience applauds. The conductor turns to the orchestra and the audience is still. The 'performance' has already begun when, into the expectant hush, Beethoven's music begins. Since the listener can see the orchestra, she relates sound to source as the music starts to enfold her; sonorities are uniquely plotted in time, space, and vision. With the exposition of the first movement underway, there is a dramatic pause on a dominant-seventh chord before the counterstatement of the first subject in bar 88. Even before the *fortissimo* entry of the full orchestra that follows, the activity of the players prepares her for it: trumpets are raised and ready for their repeated As, and the players look expectantly at the conductor. A timeline unfolds that cannot be broken or extended beyond the demands of the score as interpreted by conductor and players. I call this the 'performing breath', the period from the attention call to relaxation at the work's end. Questions concerning the transformation and subversion of this 'performing breath' in recordings lie behind the following discussion of studio recordings.

The role of technology

Since recording technology has never been perfect – it cannot provide a transparent aural version of the concert hall for one's living room – technological limitations determine the first layer of distortion in the recording process. The acoustic process of recording, which pertained until the adoption of the microphone in 1925, had numerous limitations, including restricted frequency and dynamic ranges, monaural sound, and a playing time that rarely exceeded five minutes and was generally closer to four. In an orchestral work, musicians had to cluster around the sound-receiving horn, and the orchestration was often amended, for example to make bass frequencies more robust.

Improvements in recording technology are well documented. Electrical recording came in 1925; tape later enabled musicians to record in longer spans; the LP consolidated advances inherent in tape recording; stereo arrived commercially in 1958; and so on.[4] In spite of this constant 'ascent', sound quality has not been as significant a 'mask' as one might expect. At key points in the history of the gramophone, important commentators and consumers have testified to levels of satisfaction with technology as it was; listeners and performers became acclimatised to prevailing technology and even resented progress, at least temporarily. Edward Elgar professed himself content with the state of the art in the early 1920s (Moore, 1974: 39–40). For some listeners a technical equilibrium was upset by the new method of recording that arrived in 1925, as is evidenced by one G.C. Monkton of Bromley, Kent, who wrote:

> To my mind modern recording in bulk is worse, not better, than the old. Look at Coldstream Guards now and two or three years ago; mellowness and reality have given place to screaming.

> (Monkton, 1926: 380)

Monkton was not alone in his views, for many other correspondents and reviewers also felt that a retrograde step had been taken.[5] Compton Mackenzie, founder and editor of *The Gramophone*, was similarly reserved about the LP when it finally arrived in Britain (see his editorials in issues of 1950).

78s and the studio process

At this stage I set aside the issue of sound quality, for it simplifies, masks, and certainly distorts, but does not seem to twist the significance of recorded content to the same extent as other parameters. Chief among these parameters is how studio sessions dictate the way music is recorded. During the 78 era,[6] there were time constraints of two types: the period for which the musicians were booked and the quantity of music it was deemed economically viable to record; and the inevitable constraint of the four- to five-minute 12-inch side, which remained into the post-war period (until 1948 the only consumer recording product was the 78, mainly in 10" and 12" sizes). Commercial and technical issues were conflated in these concerns, with significant repercussions for the way music was recorded.

These issues can be broadly canvassed with session sheets from a 1939 recording of *Ein Heldenleben* conducted by Artur Rodzinski (American Columbia). Whereas most session sheets only give information about successful takes, these sheets are graphically unsanitised (Table 1).

ARTIST: The Cleveland Orchestra   Date: Dec 11 1939
Hour: 2:00 – 5:00

Disc No.	Cut No.	O.K. Cut	TITLE – MOVEMENT		Part of Set	Time	COMMENT
1	1		Playback				
1	2	*OK	Ein Heldenleben XCO 25790-1		1	4:10	
1	3	OK	"	XCO 25790-2-3?	1	4:14	better
2	1		"		2	4:02	p 46 @check more or le [sic]
2	2		"		2		breakdown
2	3	OK	"	XCO 25791-1-2	2	4:22	different ending 5 before 24
3	1	OK	"	XCO 25792-1	3	4:07	roughly OK some extraneous noises; solo fiddle fair
3	2		"		3	4:14	much better – end just before 31 a couple of plucks from solo fiddle
4	1		"		4		Breakdown
4	2		"	XCO 25793-1	4	3:25	
4	3	*	"		4	3:25	ends before 38
5	1		"	Festes Zeitmass – bad	5		
5	2	*	"	Festes Zeitmass p 95 XCO 25794-1	5		
			Date ended at 5:00				

ARTIST: The Cleveland Orchestra   Date: Dec 12 1939
Hour: 2:00 – 5:00

Disc No.	Cut No.	O.K. Cut	TITLE – MOVEMENT		Part of Set	Time	COMMENT
6	1	OK	Ein Heldenleben				Breakdown
6	2	OK	"	XCO 25795-1	6	4:17	to #77
6	3		"				Breakdown
6	4		"		7		7th side to #88 – kill everything else on disc 6
7	1	OK	"	XCO 25796-1	7	4:07	a little ragged ensemble to 88

7	2	OK	"	XCO 25796-2	7	4:11	better ensemble – first part not so brilliant
8	1		"		8		8th side to 97
8	2	OK	"	XCO 25797-1	8	4:15	after 97 fairly good
8	3		"		9		to end 105 – went over kill rest record
9	1	OK	"	XCO 25798-1	9	4:00	to 105
9	2		"		10	4:20	fairly good but tympani
10	1	OK	"	XCO 25799-1	10		from 105

Table 1: Session sheets for US Columbia recording of Strauss, *Ein Heldenleben*, 11–12 December 1939

Columbia at this time 'did not use wax masters at 78 rpm, but instead used a pair of $33^{1/3}$ rpm, 16-inch transcription-disc recorders to capture the sound from the session microphones. When the session was over, the discs were sent to studios in New York where the designated XCO tracks were dubbed onto 78 master discs and then made into 78 shellac records', with, as the sheets show, some modest scope for editing where a side ends. 'Disc No.' refers to the sequence of the discs recorded at the session; 'Cut No.' refers to track number recorded onto each disc.[7] The sheets show that the first session yielded five publishable sides and the second the remaining five for *Heldenleben* (with some usable alternative takes). Comments indicate changes of mind over side length, overruns, concerns over balance and ensemble, disruptive noises, and other problems. Although not shown in these sessions, Columbia could evidently boost certain instruments at the mixing desk, and technical requests from conductors are admitted, as when Fritz Reiner asks for the last side of the *Tannhäuser* 'Bacchanal' (Venusberg Music) to be recorded at the 'lowest possible level'.[8] Above all else, these sheets show the extent to which matters had to be organised on the fly, and how breakdowns, extraneous noises, and overruns placed pressure on musicians and producer.

Side-breaks of 78s transferred to LP and CD are often concealed by skillful engineers, who sometimes create almost seamless continuity across them in symphonic and other works. They mask the 78 rpm record's temporality, which was far removed from the performing breath of live performance. Until the advent of LP in 1948, 78s transmitted their musical performance in four-minute segments (10-inch 78s in three minutes or so), for even when auto-changers were employed there was a gap before the next record in the sequence started to play. The 78 audience never heard the counterstatement of the first-subject group in the exposition of Beethoven's Seventh Symphony follow directly from the pause in bar 88. Whilst some performers attempted to maintain momentum and simply interrupted the musical flow across the side-break whenever possible, many reflected these conditions in other ways, such as by slowing down, which resulted in a side having a measure of autonomy.

The idea that a side should have this autonomy was most pervasive in the acoustic period, when producers and musicians were reluctant to produce recordings that required or implied continuity over the side, and often cut movements to fit a single side. As longer and complete works were recorded, with the concomitant need for side turns, performers and arrangers regularly supplied endings for sides, which implied that 'the fragment' might be enjoyed independently (sometimes catalogue numbers for apparently successive sides are not contiguous, which again supports the counterintuitive view that continuation and continuity were not axiomatic).[9] In 1913 Alfred Hertz conducted the Berlin Philharmonic in a series of recordings of extracts from *Parsifal*. The 'Good Friday Music' was spread over two single-sided discs with no pretence at continuity, for the dominant harmony at bar 664 is arranged so as to lead to a cadential B major chord, a resolution absent in the original:

Example 1: Richard Wagner, bar 662 plus 4 additional bars, Good Friday Music, Act III, *Parsifal*, arranged for Grammophon 040798

The next side starts at bar 674 and continues to around bar 770, where the original is altered to supply another perfect cadence, this time in D major:

Example 2: Wagner, bar 766 plus 4 additional bars, Good Friday Music, Act III, *Parsifal*, arranged for Grammophon 040799

Both sides are thereby rendered partially self-sufficient. Mark Obert-Thorn in his transfer for Naxos craftily recomposes *Parsifal* and reinterprets the 78s by allowing the clarinet melody that opens the second side to emerge from the last chord of the first, thus creating seamless continuity between the two sides:[10]

Example 3: Wagner, 4th additional bar after bar 662, 674–7, Good Friday Music, Act III, *Parsifal*, rearranged for Naxos 8.110049–50 by Mark Obert-Thorn

The recording information for these records is given in Table 2:

| Grammophon 040798 | side 1 | bars 570–662+4 |
| Grammophon 040799 | side 2 | bars 674–766+4 |

Table 2: Wagner, 'Good Friday Music', Act III, *Parsifal*, Berlin Philharmonic Orchestra conducted by Hertz, 12–16 September 1913

The transfer process masks another facet of the side turn, namely the manner in which it was managed in terms of the location of the break in the score and the commensurate implications this had for the performance. This might involve repetition to help articulate the break; recomposition, such as was encountered in the *Parsifal* example; dovetailing, whereby part of the continuation is played at the end of one side and another part of the continuation coincident with it at the start of the second side; and simple breaking off (interruption). Tables 3 and 4 show where side breaks occur in Felix Weingartner's and Arturo Toscanini's studio recordings of Beethoven's Seventh Symphony, both made in 1936.[11]

Side	Side starts at	Side ends at	Type of break
side 1	movt 1, b. 1	movt 1, b. 88, 3rd quaver	interruption
side 2	movt 1, b. 88, 4th quaver	movt 1, b. 280, 1st quaver	repetition
side 3	movt 1, b. 277, 4th quaver	movt 1, end	
side 4	movt 2, b. 1	movt 2, b. 138, 1st crotchet	repetition
side 5	movt 2, b. 137, 1st crotchet	movt 2, end	
side 6	movt 3, b. 1	movt 3, b. 351, 1st crotchet	repetition
side 7	movt 3, b. 348, 3rd crotchet	movt 3, end	
side 8	movt 4, b. 1	movt 4, b. 198, 1st crotchet	repetition
side 9	movt 4, b. 198, 1st crotchet	movt 4, end	

Table 3: Beethoven, Symphony No. 7, Vienna Philharmonic Orchestra conducted by Felix Weingartner, side breaks, recorded 24–6 February 1936, Musikvereinsaal, Vienna, Columbia LX484–488

side	side starts at	side ends at	type of break
side 1	movt 1, b. 1	movt 1, b. 88, 3rd quaver	interruption
side 2	movt 1, b. 88, 4th quaver	movt 1, b. 300, 3rd quaver	interruption
side 3	movt 1, b. 300, 4th quaver	movt 1, end	
side 4	movt 2, b. 1	movt 2, b. 100, 2nd crotchet	interruption
side 5	movt 2, b. 101	movt 2, b. 223, 2nd crotchet	interruption
side 6	movt 2, b. 224	movt 2, end	
side 7	movt 3, b. 1	movt 3, b. 408, 3rd crotchet	interruption
side 8	movt 3, b. 409, 1st crotchet	movt 3, end	interruption
side 9	movt 4, b. 1	movt 4, b. 223, 2nd crotchet	interruption
side 10	movt 4, b. 224, 1st crotchet	movt 4, end	

Table 4: Beethoven, Symphony No. 7, New York Philharmonic conducted by Arturo Toscanini, side breaks, recorded 9–10 April 1936, Carnegie Hall, New York, Victor 14097–14101

Toscanini was granted one more side for the work than Weingartner, which is given to the second movement; it allows for 'clean' breaks for all the side turns in the sense that they occur during musical silence or between phrases. Most of the turns are treated differently by Weingartner and Toscanini. At the end of the second side of the first movement Weingartner breaks off at the start of the recapitulation, a point of great tension (Example 4).

Example 4: Beethoven, Symphony No. 7, first movement, bars 277–8, end of side 2 (Weingartner)

The third side begins with a repetition of the upbeat semiquavers in b. 277 (Example 5).

Example 5: Beethoven, Symphony No. 7, first movement, bars 277–9, start of side 3 (Weingartner)

This keeps side lengths close to four minutes, but had he extended the duration of the second side by just over 20 seconds, he might have availed himself of a less disruptive (to our ears at least) break. Weingartner's interpretation of the repeated passage is varied between the two sides: while at the end of side 2 the semiquavers are played in the prevailing tempo, at the beginning of side 3 the first semiquavers of the group are played more slowly and with greater weight; the first few measures of the recapitulation are ca. dotted crotchet = 90 rather than 100 as at the end of side 2 and elsewhere. The same music is, therefore, performed and heard differently. Weingartner's break in the slow movement repeats a cadential figure in the B section. The first time the figure is played, at the end of side 4, the two quavers are slightly held back to yield a greater sense of cadencing (they are ca. 25 per cent slower than side 5), but when they are repeated on side 5, they are in tempo, and more suitable for the context, which is flowing and continuous at this point (Examples 6 and 7).[12]

Example 6: Beethoven, Symphony No. 7, second movement, bars 135–8, end of side 4 (Weingartner)

Example 7: Beethoven, Symphony No. 7, second movement, bars135–8, start of side 5 (Weingartner)

Weingartner's break in the Scherzo (Example 8) also uses repetition, this time of the *forte* reprise of the main Scherzo motive (Example 9).

Example 8: Beethoven, Symphony No. 7, third movement, bars 347–51, end of side 6 (Weingartner)

Example 9: Beethoven, Symphony No. 7, third movement, bars 348–51, start of side 7 (Weingartner)

Extended study of side breaks based on many recordings fails to yield evidence of a consistent practice. Nevertheless, it is clear that aesthetic considerations did not automatically favour optimisation of musical continuity, as Dan Godfrey's recording of Wolfgang Amadeus Mozart's Symphony No.41 'Jupiter' for HMV dramatically demonstrates. The recording session took place on 4 February 1927 at the Scala Theatre in London, and the side breaks occur as follows:

Side	Side starts at	Side ends at	Type of break
side 1	b.1	b. 120, 4th crotchet	
side 2	b. 121, 1st crotchet	b. 243, 4th crotchet	interruption
side 3	b. 212, 1st crotchet	end	repetition

Table 5: Mozart, Symphony No. 41 K. 551, first movement, Godfrey and Symphony Orchestra,[13] 4 February 1927, Scala Theatre (demolished 1969), London, Columbia L1938–1939

Playing through the first three sides consecutively, purchasers of this Columbia set heard 32 bars twice. There is a loud clump in b. 214 on side 2, suggesting some accident in the recording venue, which the producer might have wanted to remedy in a later take, but there is no obvious reason why he did not re-record side 2 before moving on. The side breaks are strange in others ways, for it would have been reasonable to have taken only two sides for the first movement. As it is, the exposition is complete on one side, yielding a playing time of just 2:42. (Did Godfrey and his producer want the listener to have the option to perform a manual exposition repeat?) The overlap may have been made with the intention of creating a new side 2 without the last 32 bars, which would have optimised studio time, but perhaps time ran out. The matrix cards are H7242 to H7249 and feature the matrices in serial order; they confirm that the records were made on the same day, and consequently there was a large workload at the Scala Theatre, which may explain why side 2 was not redone and an aberrant side break was passed.[14] Alternatively, as other examples suggest, perhaps this was not deemed aberrant: a review by K.K. in the November 1927 issue of *The Gramophone* tacitly acknowledges the odd side break, for it gives score references for each turn, as was the journal's custom at the time, but the reviewer makes no reference to it in his review, preferring to note details of orchestration and the fact that '[i]t would have gone so much better with Beecham' (230).

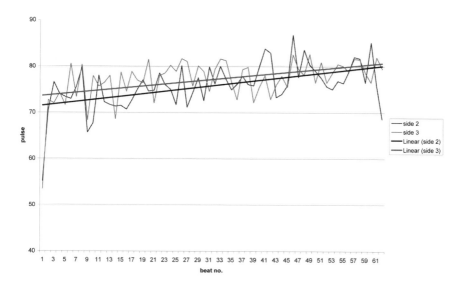

Figure 1: Mozart, Symphony No. 41 K. 551, first movement, bars 212–43, tempo graph

Figure 1 shows that the 32 repeated bars are played differently in the two performances. Trendlines show how the level of acceleration is greater on side 2 than on side 3, and measures 216–21 are consistently slower on side 2 than side 3. The greater animation of side 2 indicates momentum gained in performance towards the end of the side; the beginning of a new side requires momentum to be built afresh. Taken in conjunction with Weingartner and others, a pattern emerges.

The 'take'

A reductive analysis of the studio process leads us to an aspect we might call the 'highest common factor', namely the 'take'. The concept is arguably the principal signifier in the chain that leads from the inception of a recording to the finished, marketed product. In live performance the 'take' is, in a sense, the performing breath, from the pianist first poised over the keys to the moment of their release after the final notes have been played. Andre Millard describes the take as the 'basic unit of recording' (Millard, 2005: 262), the moment from when the red light goes on to the moment it goes off.

Franz Schalk's fascinating 1929 recording of Beethoven's Fifth Symphony (Hunt, 2000: 44) is pervaded by an uneasy sense of stress arguably rooted in the 78 format.[15] As the red light went on for the first side of the first movement of the symphony, he (or the orchestra) must have been caught unprepared, for only part of the orchestra comes in on time. Other aspects of this first side also suggest a conductor who needed to 'warm' to his task. Similarly, the second side, which starts at b. 253, is initially shaky. HMV planned to replace side 1 at a later date: in John Hunt's discography we read of an unpublished attempt to redo the side on 16 April 1931 (Hunt, 2000: 49). Lest it be thought that this recording (and others chosen for analysis here) were selected for their idiosyncrasies and departures from norms, it should be stressed that these features are a part of the fabric of recording in the 78 era: they are facets of the 'masks and distortions' evoked in the title of this chapter.

Discussion of takes leads us to a curious twist in the story of Toscanini's recording of Beethoven's Seventh Symphony discussed above. The performance was recorded with no obvious discontinuities in the presentation of the sound: balances are consistent. However, there are disconcerting changes in the version usually heard, which could hardly be missed by a listener on 78. The music is recorded at a higher dynamic level on the second disc and the music-making sounds more 'energetic'. Clarification calls for forensic evidence, as Peter Copeland calls it (Copeland, 2001: 107–15). The matrix numbers indicate that while side 1 was from the first take of the movement, sides 2 and 3 were from take 2. Although the recording setup was conventional – two 78 lathes – evidence indicates that Toscanini recorded each movement with only brief pauses between sides. Instead of using the second lathe to make a safety copy of a take, it was, therefore, used to allow the conductor a measure of continuity usually unobtainable in the recording studio of the time; all the conductor had to do was pause briefly to ensure that the second lathe was 'active' before the music-making continued. The most compelling evidence for this unusual practice in Toscanini's recording is that the reverberation from the end of side 1 is picked up at the start of side 2 before the new take officially begins.[16] Take numbers are therefore significant for a full movement rather than just individual sides.

In 1942 it was found that the matrix for side 1 take 1 was worn and the decision was to replace it with the matrix of take 2 rather than with a dubbing from take 1 (Obert-Thorn, 2001). It emerged that Toscanini had not superintended the original choice of take and actually preferred take 2: he said, 'I never like first side. Is too slow' (Haggin, 1959: 35). Comparison of the two takes reveals an astonishing 24-second difference, based almost entirely on the pacing of the slow introduction, although tempo fluctuations in the Vivace create the impression that this section is also faster in take 2.[17] In fact, Toscanini averages around dotted crotched = 96 for the Vivace before the side turn in both takes and quickly rises to well over 100 after it. Take 1 is less sharply chiselled in outline than take 2, for it takes Toscanini longer to find the regimentation of line and pulse that characterises his music making in general. This initially gives take 1 an exploratory quality more commonly associated with Wilhelm Furtwängler. Figure 2 shows the slower tempo and greater pulse fluctuations (measured in crotchets) in take 1 of bars 1–24. The trendline shows the slightly higher rate of acceleration in take 2, which reflects its greater rhythmic drive.

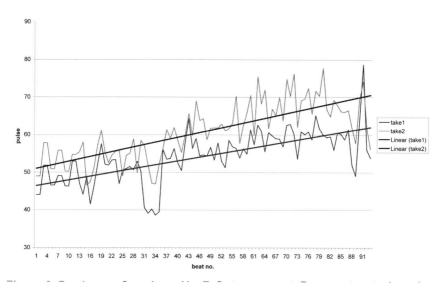

Figure 2: Beethoven, Symphony No. 7, first movement, Poco sostenuto, bars 1–24, tempo graph for takes 1 and 2 of Toscanini's 1936 recording

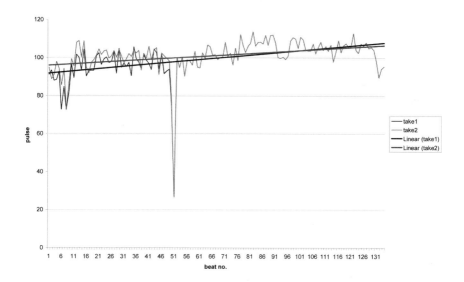

Figure 3: Vivace, bars 63–134: tempo graph for takes 1 and 2

Figure 3 illustrates differences in the Vivace, measured in dotted crotchets (after b. 51, where the side break occurs, take 2 is the only version available for measurement). The trendline shows the greater level of overall acceleration that results from playing take 2 of side 2 after take 1 of side 1. A variety of studio-driven priorities mediate and mask the succession of sounds on a 78. Among these, the constraints of technology and side length are the most audible but we can add others. For example, with detailed listening, it is possible to arrive at an interpretation of Schalk's recording of Beethoven's Fifth Symphony that contests a linearity of conception. Unlike Toscanini, who could browbeat his way through sessions and on some occasions refuse to record altogether, we may assume that Schalk complied with the commercial and artistic limitations imposed on him. Time was a dominant factor: there was time to rehearse and time to record, but there was always pressure and time often ran out. For all its lapses of ensemble, the first movement seems to have been conceived in a unified interpretative breath, but at the side break in the second movement there are subtle differences of pacing, articulation, and emphasis. There is also a dramatic shift in the spatial placement of the orchestra: while side 3 has the woodwind in close focus, side 4 has them in the distance with less immediacy in their sound. There is a similar shift in balance from side 4 to side 5. The reason for these differences, some of which might be masked by the post-war transfer engineer, can be seen in the production sheets (Table 6). Accordingly, the symphony was recorded over several months and Hunt's dating of the sessions as 26–28 October 1929 is therefore incomplete (Hunt, 2000: 44).

Side no.	Movement	Matrix	Session date
side 1	first pt 1	CW 2881-2	26 October 1929
side 2	first pt 2	CW 2882-1	26 October 1929
side 3	second pt 1	CW 2883-4	27 January 1930
side 4	second pt 2	CW 2884-5	26 October 1929
side 5	third pt 1	CW 2887-4	27 January 1930
side 6	third/fourth	CW 2888-2	28 October 1929
side 7	fourth pt 2	CW 2889-2	28 October 1929
side 8	fourth pt 3	CW 2890-2	28 October 1929

Table 6: Beethoven, Symphony No. 5, Vienna Philharmonic Orchestra conducted by Schalk, Konzerthaus, Vienna, HMV C2022–2025[18]

Different dates for completing a recording, indeed sometimes two recording sessions during the same day, and different musicians might result in changes of microphone balance and timbre, as could a change in cutting lathe. In Schalk's example, the recordings made in 1929 match up well together, but not with those done in the winter of 1930. Less obvious but just as tangible a product of the recording process is the ever-shifting relationship between rehearsal and recording, for they were generally combined in studio session, as the strange case of Robert Kajanus' Sibelius recording of 1932 illustrates.

Kajanus' sessions for his recording of Sibelius' Fifth Symphony with the London Symphony Orchestra took place on 22–4 June 1932. Recalling the pressure of time that often pertained in recording sessions[19] and the laxness of many English orchestras compared (especially) with their American and German counterparts,[20] one may infer the compromises involved in the recording. For example, side 3 (last part of the first movement) sounds rough as the string ensemble breaks down during the complex antiphony following cue K, and the orchestra falls apart at the end of the movement due to a late brass entry. Indeed, the final E-flat major chord from the brass fails to materialise. In this case, a single take represents the recording; if there was a take 2 it must have suffered from technical problems or been even more insecure to have been passed over. Preceding the take, there would probably have been a rehearsal for this very difficult music; on this occasion the rehearsal penetrated the take. Kajanus did not perform the symphony with the London Symphony Orchestra prior to the recording – there is no live-performance precedent. In fact, the orchestra had previously played the symphony only once with Sir Thomas Beecham on 23 November 1931 at the Queen's Hall.[21] Interpretation and performance were created, in haste it seems, in the studio – a pervasive feature of recordings before the advent of tape and one that also reflects performance practice at the time. Although the discussion of the take in connection with the 78 side has so far concerned its effect on musicians and music making, such as this Sibelius recording session with Kajanus, the 78 side was the primary unit of concentration and attention for the listener as well: even many years after 78s disappeared, users could recall the exact point a side change occurred in a work, even down to the physical position of the needle at a particular moment in the music.

A useful demonstration of the significance the physical medium had for the original listeners comes in this review by William Robert Anderson of Elgar's recording of his First Symphony:

> An astonishing Scherzo, with a bit of the real old Adamite Elgar for its second idea (side 5, half an inch in)...The middle section begins (side 5, half-way through) with the flutes' pastoral piping...A fourth theme is on clarinets, repeated by violins (side 5, two-thirds through). One of the delicious bits comes an inch from the end of this side.

> (Anderson, 1931: 531)

The take, the physical medium, and the performed work find geographical common ground in this system of reviewing, which was frequently employed in *The Gramophone* at this time (and was also used by record producers, who also had recourse to a ruler in discussion of their records).

Tapes and the studio process

In the 78 era the mapping of take to disc was relatively transparent. In the absence of mediation the musician's performance was transcribed onto a blank wax disc, which formed the basis for mass production. The exceptions are few, but one example is worthy of comment. Toscanini was unhappy with the weak timpani sound on two sides (including the last) of his recording of Tchaikovsky's *Romeo and Juliet* (1946) and forced Victor to dub them to new discs with additional timpani overdubbed, at some loss of audio quality (Haggin, 1959: 75). Dubbing of this sort was usually reserved for occasions when it was necessary to lower the dynamic level of a side or another straightforward adjustment. It was often at the expense of sound quality, and so was not encouraged. Such was Toscanini's influence and RCA Victor's desire to have Toscanini recordings to issue, an 'overdub' was permitted on this occasion and the result was remarkably well done.[22]

From the late 1940s the relation of a take to the physical medium of dissemination grows steadily hazier, and with it our interpretation of the mask. For 78s, mediation comes from the listeners and transfer engineer: equalisation, brightness, noise, and pitch are all adjustable and can transform the affective response to the material. For example, all 78s were made with the bass attenuated in order to reduce the width of the groove (the 'turnover curve' is the point where the frequency response goes from flat to reducing); although there were certain received curves in use by the record companies at various times, the most common in the late 1920s being the Westrex curve, it appears that engineers could tweak them at recording sessions; the transfer engineer has therefore to use his or her own judgement to arrive at a viable reciprocal of the turnover curve or curves. One of the main differences between transfers of 78s is the amount of bass they provide, which is a sign that the engineers have each interpreted the turnover curve differently.[23] Speed of playback is also critical: since not all 78s were recorded at 78 rpm, especially in the first 25 years or so, transfer engineers have to work out the correct playing speed; they often tune the A to 440 Hz, even though there were many variations in concert pitch in the first half of the century. There are many other ways transfer engineers can affect the sound of historical recordings as they refurbish them for CD and the Internet, not least in the amount of noise they remove and the means whereby this noise reduction is achieved.

When tape arrived, not only was there an intervening physical medium between the musicians and the commercial product, there was also the possibility of editing far beyond the capabilities of 78s. In the late 1940s, when tapes were new in the studios, some companies continued to record in short stretches often no longer than 78 sides, but soon the new medium was used to full advantage, to the extent that there was no longer a significant limit to the duration of a single take (this advantage continued into the digital era). Some producers favoured a system of recording whereby a movement, for example, was assembled like a patchwork from short takes; others recorded a long take first, often of a complete section or movement, and then used it as the basis for whatever patching was required. In both approaches the unity and linear directionality of a performance, as preserved on a single 78 side, can no longer be guaranteed.

The amount of mediation between the sound produced by performers in a recording venue and the product marketed on LP or CD is so extensive, especially with the vast range of possibilities inherent in digital sound processing, that only a tiny part can be mentioned here. To introduce the topic, I take a short article titled 'First Take: Anatomy of a Recording Session' (Nilsson, 1999), which documents The Concord Ensemble's debut recording for Dorian.[24] The recording was made in the Troy Music Hall (Troy, NY). In the article, M.A. Nilsson describes the positioning of the microphones, first contact in the transmission from human utterance to machine; apparently, the choice and placement of the microphones take a long time and determine the character of the sound perhaps more than any other decision in the long chain of technology that ensues. Then there are the takes. Nilsson evokes the Dorian recording of Victoria's Missa Dum complerentur (and we may view this as typical of many post-war recordings):

> producer Tina Chancey studies a score...She has just interrupted take 58. We can hear the stage creak as the singers relax. Chancey activates the microphone and says, 'Take it from 136 to the end. I want another crack at that nice low stuff. This will be take 59.'...[the old wooden hall emits a 'whiplike crack', which disrupts take 59, and take 60 is called, but the hall cracks again]...Take 61 provides a good, quiet finish. Take 62 covers the entire Gloria again.
>
> (Nilsson, 1999: 38–9)

Thus the process continues until after 'seven hours a night over five days' (Nilsson, 1999: 39) one hour of music is available for release.[25] We can examine this type of studio procedure in more detail in a major symphonic work, Sibelius' First Symphony, as it was recorded in 1978 by one of the most prolific recording conductors and orchestras of the twentieth century.

Eugene Ormandy recorded Sibelius' First Symphony four times: on 16 January 1935 with the Minneapolis Symphony Orchestra, and on 25 October 1941, 11 March 1962, and 17 April 1978 with the Philadelphia Orchestra. The last recording was made for RCA and produced by Jay Saks. The conductor's battered Breitkopf & Härtel score reveals its earlier orientation towards recording for 78, for inside the front cover there are timings for 78 sides, and side-break indicators occur throughout the score for each of the ten sides of the 1935 recording (the timings are close to the recording);[26] these points are also marked with double vertical lines in the score. By 1978 RCA confined its recording activities to works that Ormandy was performing in concert to avoid wasting studio time. After the recording sessions in the now-demolished Scottish Rite Cathedral in central Philadelphia, Saks listened to the tapes and decided which ones to use in the published recording. He marked his decisions in red in the score, which were then acted upon by the tape engineer. The master tape thus assembled was sent to a disc cutter, who produced the matrix from which stampers were subsequently produced; he usually adjusted equalisation and dynamic range for optimal LP playback. An acetate was generated from this master and sent to Ormandy,[27] along with the producer's score containing the markings,[28] for comment. Ormandy's practice, as he related it to John and Susan Edwards Harvith in 1976, was to listen carefully to the acetate on a quadraphonic setup supplied by RCA, make 'little notes' in the producer's score, give his impressions in a memo, and finally send them back with the test record (Harvith and Harvith, 1987: 148). Since the score and test record remained with the composer it is hard to say whether Ormandy expressed a view on this recording (I could detect no obvious differences between the acetate and finished LP). Perhaps the long delay in bringing out the LP – it did not appear until 1984, just under a year before his death – may have something to do with this.

On other occasions after hearing a test record, Ormandy sometimes called for extensive changes, especially in the balance; in relation to a recording with Emmanuel Ax of Chopin's Piano Concerto No. 2 in E minor (13 February 1978) he wrote:

> I had difficulty hearing the accompaniment at all in less forte passages. I am afraid
> I must ask you to raise the orchestra almost all the way through. [E]specially the
> first violins which continue to remain below the rest of the strings level.[29]

Although his correspondence contains many references to balance problems, he does not question RCA's prerogative to set the balance, so long as he can tinker with it. Indeed, in the interview with the Harviths he defends the system of recording used by RCA: 'our ears have developed so much towards the present-day techniques of recording that we could not, we would not accept [a return to a single microphone as provocatively put to him by the Harviths]' (Harvith and Harvith, 1987: 148). As in Toscanini's dealings with the company, there is a reciprocity that maintains contemporary studio practice.

The edits for Ormandy's recording of the Scherzo of Sibelius' Symphony No.1 (5:34 in this performance) are given in Table 7. A large 'T' in the score indicates the point where the splice is to be made; on either side of it is the previous and following take name (e.g. 4-1) as chosen by Saks (Example 10).

Cue / Measure no.	After beat no. (3/4)	Take no. starts
-- / 1		3
B / 40	3	2 (with comment 'this piece of tk 3 swapped into tk 2')
B+2 / 42	3	3
E-2 / 106	3	1-3
E+13 / 120	3	1-12
G+12 / 154	3	2-1
I-8 / 171	3	3-2
K-1 / 202	3	4-1
M+9 / 243	1	5-1
M+10 / 244	3	6-1
M+27 / 261	2	6-2
M+28 / 262	3	6-1
M+29 / 263	3	6-2
N+9 / 298	3	6-1
O-7 / 293	3	6-2
Q+8 / 351	2	7-3

Table 7: Editing points in producer's score of Sibelius' Symphony No. 1 in E minor Op. 39, recording of 17 April 1978, Scottish Rite Cathedral, Philadelphia

Example 10: Sibelius, Symphony No. 1, Scherzo, bars 241–5, editing instructions in producer's score

In the absence of other documentation, we cannot say where one take started and ended, though the sequence suggests that the higher numbers sometimes started later in the movement. The suffixes indicate further attempts at a take, so there must have been at least twelve attempts at take 1. In view of the fact that each movement starts with a single digit, e.g. '3', rather than 3-1, it is possible that the suffix series implicitly runs from 0 rather than 1, though there may be another explanation. In the first movement the sequence runs as follows: 4, 4pu, 5-1, 4pu, 1-1, 2-1, 6-4, 6-2, 6-4, 2-1, 7-2, 7-1, 2-1, 8-2. This suggests that takes 1 and 2, if the numeric sequence has any meaning, were of a large part or all of the movement; from comments of other producers, it is likely that 'pu' denotes a version of take 4 that was previously considered 'possibly usable'.

The recording was made on eight-track tape recorders with the tracks grouped around the following instruments (there were also at least four effect microphones that covered the triangle, for instance, which could be switched on and off depending upon the instrumentation of a passage):

1. trumpets, horns
2. trombone, tuba, horns
3. woodwind (high)
4. woodwind (low), triangle
5. violins I, timpani
6. violins I, violins II, bass drum, cymbals
7. viola, cellos
8. double basses, cellos, harp

Each track had its own fader and equalisation controls on the mixer. Decisions for their use (beyond establishing a mean balance for the entire session) are, to some extent, indicated in the score. For example, at bars 304–7 (cue O+2), there are brackets around the violas in blue ink (shown in Example 11 with dashed lines), presumably because they are the principal voice, and instructions to lower timpani and harp on faders 5 and 8 respectively. Green markings and Ormandy's initials indicate the conductor's wish for the violas to be brought out. Saks' response appears to have been to lower the levels on the timpani and harp.

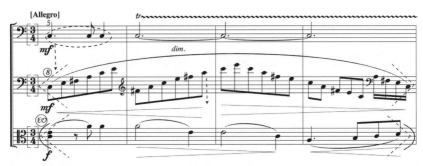

Example 11: Sibelius, Symphony No. 1, Scherzo, bars 304–7, balance adjustments in producer's score

Ormandy's presence at the playback or in discussion with the producer at another time is indicated by markings in green or pencil, sometimes in his own hand and often attached to his initials, such as at C +9 in the first movement, where he added a cymbal crash and wanted it adequately reflected in the mix reaching the tape. Other annotations in Ormandy's hand may be in response to the acetate sent along with the score for his final comments and approval, but there are few comments that appear to fall into this category.

With sixteen segments of tape, numerous changes of levels, and other manipulations, the sonic object arising from this kind of process is far removed from the performing breath of live performance. Unity of time and space has long since departed. We possess a text that has been multiply dismantled and reassembled and the order of music-making is no longer governed by a single timeline. Besides, there is no single seat in the stalls surrounded by the acoustic cues of the hall, with at least twelve microphones ensuring that the orchestra is dissected and scrutinised for us (Ormandy mentions eighteen microphones in his interview with the Harviths (1987: 147)). But it must also be considered that before starting a new take, say at m. 106 of the Scherzo, Ormandy would have been able to listen to the preceding measures, so it was possible to pick up from a previous take. Repeated listenings to the lacquer, the LP, and CD reissues have not revealed any obvious discontinuity in the recording: the splices listed in Table 7 are not *obviously* audible to me, and Ormandy's beat is so flexible that even where there seems to be a difference in pulse across an editing point, such as from take 2-1 to 3-2 at b. 171, it is not inconsistent with other changes of pulse in passages not divided by an edit. Nevertheless, an interesting test is to compare a recording of a live performance, broadcast just a couple of days before his Columbia recording, with the last two studio recordings. In Figure 4, the tempo graphs compare a long passage in the Scherzo's central section in the three recordings:

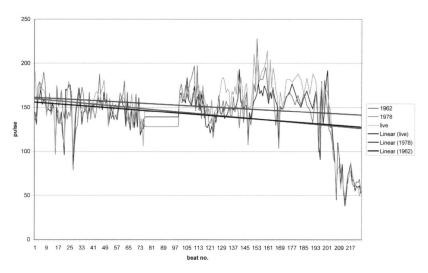

Figure 4: Sibelius, Symphony No. 1, Scherzo, bars 170–244, tempo graph of 1962 broadcast performance, 1962 Columbia recording, and 1978 RCA recording. Pulse is given in crotchets, beat no. refers to crotchets from the first beat of b. 161. (The long horizontal plot from beat 76 refers to the long trill for clarinet and bass drum in bars 195–202, during which there is no discernible pulse.)

The two studio performances are very similar in many details. The trendlines, for example, display an average pulse in the section, which is crotchet = 142 in 1962 and 143 in 1978. In contrast, the live performance is more animated in the latter part. Here the average pulse is crotchet = 151 and the trendline is correspondingly different. There is limited evidence that Ormandy's live performance follows a different pattern to the studio versions, aside from the tendency to opt for a faster pulse as the music progresses. Without access to more information, it is hard to say how the studio process, e.g. the stop-start nature of the takes, impinged on the interpretation, but the difference is suggestive.

Ormandy's recording of Sibelius' First Symphony, discussed at length here because it seems to be representative of many thousands of recordings made in similar ways, is a technological product that recalls so many aspects of the sonic imprint of a live performance that the listener accepts its surrogacy. Nevertheless, the following extracts from a paper given by the Welsh-based record company Nimbus at an audio conference in Japan characterise the criticism such recordings sometimes provoke:

> A musical performance is something that not only happens in a specific time but also a specific place...A performance is an emotional and intellectual experience, complete from start to finish. Any disruption of that by editing parts from elsewhere, can only lessen its emotional impact.

(Griffiths, 1995: 34–5)

Whether so much editing, combined with the spatial disorientation caused by the microphones, 'lessen[s] its emotional impact' is a subject that requires detailed research. For Eric Clarke, the answer lies in the separation of recording and 'real performance':

> The highly edited multi-take recording is not a 'stitch-up': it is a deliberately and carefully constructed sounding of the music...Studio processes are completely intertwined with what are conventionally regarded as performance factors, and the result is simply a different kind of object/event as compared with a real performance.

(Clarke, 2002: 187)

This separation is convenient, but it offers little succour for historians of musical performance working on recordings, who would be obliged to reorientate their scholarship to the history of musical performance on record.

Conclusion

Godlovitch rejects the notion that recordings of performances are performances; they are, he writes, 'just traces or records of performances, and no more performances in their own right than photos are the objects photographed' (Godlovitch, 1998: 14). Ranged against Godlovitch and Botstein's pessimistic view of recordings as fragmented texts, the work of Philip, Cook, and José Bowen makes a direct connection between recordings and how musicians performed, presumably in live performance. Between the two extremes there is surely a compromise.

There is no reason why we should mistrust every sign of performance we believe we hear on records; but the record's codes cannot be devolved back through a transformational language to live performance without detailed consideration of the medium. Recordings are technical surrogates, artistic identikits of live performance.[30] With Stravinsky's recordings, we know from surviving documents and reports on the sessions that they were recorded under pressure of time, extensively edited, and not all the rehearsals, indeed not even all the takes, were conducted by Stravinsky (Stuart, 1991; Taruskin, 1995). The studio-recording system intervenes, as it does for Elgar, whose 'alternative' takes – usually rejected takes that have survived (Moore, 1963: 34) – indicate how interpretative details varied within a few minutes of studio time, making the frozen nature of the recording chosen for release an obstacle to 'knowing' how Elgar, with his flexible conception of the music, played it.

So we might have arrived back at the characterisation of recording as a snapshot. In this chapter I presented some of the forensic work that can be done on recorded performances, and in the process posed questions about the epistemology of recording. I argued that we may come to know a great deal about performance from recordings, but not without consideration of the medium. Assimilating the examples discussed above of the studio-recording process, and decoding the information they contain, lead us to the central mystery of the recorded work: it is disembodied and yet it mimics crucial aspects of the experience of live music. The possibility of a First World War soldier listening to Elgar in his Belgian trench depended on a multilayered metamorphosis encompassing both dismemberment and experiential reconstruction, the former spanning many months and the latter an instant. The translation of the music to disc was a long process, involving its dismemberment to suit an acoustic recording and playback system, not to mention the long production and distribution route and the geographical dislocation from London to Belgium that followed. For the soldier the act of recreation involved in his listening would happen instantaneously: he would accept the horn's testimony, which might move, comfort, and distract him. The human agency involved in the recording might affect him just as if the performers had been magically transported to his trench. The soldier's experience of the music-making could be described as an act of faith in which the outward appearance of reality is set aside (for that appearance might be of a wind-up acoustic gramophone on a rickety table amidst mud and bayonets) in favour of an emotional identification with an invisible group of performers. Experiencing the recording intensely, he feels he knows all there is to know about the music.

Move ahead seventy years and relocate the listeners in a comfortable living room with two speakers on either side of a fireplace and how much more do they know? The performing narration presents them with events A–B–C (which can be taken to be any parts of the music stitched together by the tape engineer or 78 sides pieced together by a transfer engineer) in the Scherzo of Sibelius' First Symphony or in Beethoven's Fifth – the recordings by Ormandy and Schalk discussed above; the listener's cognition of them will construct event B as a linear consequence of event A, conceived in real time as if an uninterrupted human agency operated across the two events. In the Beethoven example, A and B are different in sonority and in other ways, but the musical brain clings to their connectedness and attempts to find points of coherence. If the disruption of the sequence is too great, such an attempt might break down, of course, but we are speaking of an underlying predisposition to believe what we hear. The 'real' nature of the sequence may be indicated by excavating the data surrounding the recording, which reveals that the sessions at which the two events were recorded were separated by a year. The performance, which we wish to believe reflects the activities of a single musical exhalation, is in reality the outcome of two widely separated musical actions: during the intervening period the musicians playing in the orchestra might have changed, the conductor was a year older and wiser, and the microphones were differently positioned in the hall. The organic unfolding of live performance, in which one event is motivated by a previous one in a single realisation of a score is an illusion.

In listening to the recording of Sibelius' First Symphony our senses, our neurological act of recreation, make us imagine the performing breath as if the A–B–C sequence took place in real time, in consistent space. Documentation of the recording tells us that this is not so: B was recorded out of sequence with A and C. This is the fabrication, the montage-like method by which tape recordings were made. No matter how carefully the editing is done, the final cut is not the result of a single performing breath. The disembodiment of the performer calls forth a fictional narrative from the listener or, to put it another way, the addressee constructs a signification system that relies on interpretative codes learnt from a different stimulus, namely a live musical performance.[31] With an awareness of the recording process and contingent identification of the masks and distortions, it is possible that new codes might be learnt and therefore the signification altered, creating a distinction between a sort of 'expert' knowledge and a more instinctive response. What this chapter has endeavoured to explore and challenge is the naturalistic epistemology of recording, held to account here through a testimony-led use of alternate evidence. It encourages the researcher to view a recording as a text the signs of which are subject to codes not only of musical performance but of the recording process. The text changes as it mutates through different channels (changing times bring different playback mechanisms and modified expectations), such that the application by a mischievous audio engineer of shellac surface noise to a modern recording can fool the addressee into attributing greater authority to the interpretation than the original because an interpretative code has instilled this quality in historical recordings; one might almost term them 'olfactory' signs.[32]

It would take many words to weigh the shifting channels of recording as the messages progress from studio to listener. For the performer, the artistic compromises are often just as complex and masked. The never-ending reciprocity of records places the performer in the position of auditor as well as music-maker; he or she can rarely be detached from the 'two ends' of the horn and microphone. So the performer's performing response to recording is just as distorted and masked as the addressee's response to the record: the performer on record is not the transmitter, in the way he might be in an auditorium; rather he is embroiled in a medium in which human agency and machine collaborate according to complex and usually hidden codes. The music discussed in this chapter is often considered organic in the way it unfolds in time: each event is motivated by a preceding one. If merely the correct notes are played, performance naturally reproduces this kind of organic unfolding in a primitive form, but performers, as Nimbus implies, add an additional linearity of cause and effect, such that an unnotated *accelerando* in bar 25 may, according to the impulse of the moment, precipitate a compensatory *ritardando* in b. 27. If b. 27 is recorded at a different take, the performer has to remember a performing act that is already history (even if the memory is stimulated by a playback from the control room). Thus, the performer acts out a consequent of something remembered, minutes, hours, perhaps even a year after the antecedent. For Ormandy, on the evidence of his recording of Sibelius' First Symphony, we may tentatively suggest that he diminished the gap between antecedent and consequent in favour of a repeatable product: the *accelerando* he practised live is attenuated and hence constitutes an easier (or safer) 'load' for the recording producer. The performer, therefore, errs on the side of the conservative and the safe, for the urgency of the instant – the sudden impulse of a live performance – might undermine the process. On this issue we have to be content with broad generalisation: there are numerous inspired and wonderful recordings. There are too many different routes through this subject to arrive at a conclusion that satisfies every situation, but if a pattern has emerged from the foregoing, it is that the performer must often be constrained by recording in terms of space, in terms of repeatability (you cannot change your mind from take to take), and in other ways.

That this understanding is of more value to researchers and the insatiably curious is undeniable; that recordings continue to prove irresistible as artistic documents is proof of the mercurial attraction of human performance in all its manifestations.

Notes

1   I am most grateful to the following for unstinting advice and access to materials: Nancy Shawcross and John Pollack of the Annenberg Rare Book and Manuscript Library of the University of Pennsylvania; Roger Beardsley, George Brock-Nannestad, Adrian Farmer, Michael Gray, Áine Heneghan, Ted Kendall, Daniel Leech-Wilkinson, Ward Marston, Mark Obert-Thorn, David Patmore, Libby Rice, and John Rink.

2   This was preceded by Philip's short article in *Early Music* (1984), a journal that had been slow in recognising recordings as important source material for the study of performance. Prior to that, Philip's PhD dissertation (Cambridge University, 1974) was the first to study recordings.

3   See also Cook (1995); Day (2000) especially the chapter 'Listening to recordings': 199–256; Johnson (2002); Philip (2004).

4   For a brief summary of technical developments up to around 1962 see Bachman et al. (1978: 9–15). The same volume deals with distortion and other characteristics of recording up to the late 1970s (Roys, 1978). Other historical studies of recording include Copeland (2001), Day (2000), Gelatt (1977) and Millard (2005).

5   It later emerged that this was due in part to the acoustic playback systems not being suitable for, or adapted to, electrical recordings.

6   One might also refer to this as the 'shellac era', though towards the end of the period, before the introduction of the LP and EP, shellac came to be replaced by vinylite.

7   I am indebted to Michael Gray (Voice of America Library and Audio Services) for sending me copies of these sheets and his description of the recording techniques and record keeping used by Columbia, which is quoted here (private email).

8   Pittsburgh Orchestra, 9 January 1941.

9   Bengt Hambræus discusses the importance of the arrangement in the early twentieth century. It helps, he argues, to explain the ready acceptance of abbreviated works for reduced forces for the early gramophone. His discussion concentrates on Elgar's heavily abridged acoustic concerto recordings (Hambræus, 1997: 85–94).

10 Naxos 8.110049–50.

11 In his chapter 'Listening to Toscanini', Harvey Sachs makes detailed comparisons between Toscanini's 1936 recording and others by Furtwängler, Otto Klemperer, Strauss, Bruno Walter, and Weingartner (Sachs, 1993: 167–80).

12 I used two systems to measure tempo fluctuations: Windows software TempoTapper by Tiasoft provides a readout of the pulse as one taps on a computer keyboard, but it does not retain the information in any form. For more accurate measurement I use Rod Johnson's Windows programme Sforzando: this records one's taps as a sequence of time co-ordinates, which can be imported into Excel and displayed as a graph after conversion. More recently I have used Sonic Visualiser, developed at the Centre for Digital Music, Queen Mary, University of London. It operates in a manner similar to Sforzando but offers many more possibilities for displaying and analysing the results. José Antonio Bowen (1996) calls such

graphs 'tempo maps' and explores the methodology and implication of such analysis.

13 The matrix cards have 'Royal Philharmonic Orchestra' crossed out and replaced by 'Symphony Orchestra'.

14 I am most grateful to Roger Beardsley for this information.

15 The dates given in Hunt's discography are incomplete. This subject is discussed further below.

16 Beecham's famous pre-war RCA *Don Quixote* (1932) exhibits the same technique.

17 The two versions have been published on CD: Naxos 8.110840.

18 The two missing matrix numbers were allocated to another session on 28 October 1929 with Clemens Kraus conducting Richard Strauss (Hunt, 2000: 45).

19 Millard writes that the 'workday of the studio, in the UK at least, was divided into 3-hour sessions which extended from early in the morning to late at night. Each session was expected to produce four takes good enough for mastering' (Millard, 2005: 269).

20 See Philip (2004: 63–71) for a discussion of British orchestras in the early twentieth century.

21 I am indebted to Libby Rice of the London Symphony Orchestra for this information (regional information about the orchestra's activities was not available from this source at the time of writing).

22 Of great interest is a recording of the dubbing session in which an engineer explains to Toscanini why it would be necessary to wear a headphone during the dubbing. On the same recording we hear Toscanini rehearsing the NBC Symphony Orchestra's timpanist. This fascinating piece of recording history can only be heard in the Rodgers and Hammerstein Archives of Recorded Sound, New York Public Library.

23 Transfer engineers do a considerable amount of equalisation after setting a turnover curve. For most classical recordings on HMV, right up to the end of the 78 era, the attenuation starts somewhere around middle C from where the bass is reduced by 6 dB per octave. Later recordings also boosted the treble to improve the signal-to-noise ratio in playback, but the majority of HMV recordings of classical music kept the treble flat and should be played in this way (though filtering should be applied to frequency ranges above the recorded musical signal).

24 The Concord Ensemble is an all-male vocal ensemble.

25 For other accounts of recording in the post-war era and rich insights into the role of the producer, see Grubb (1986). Suvi Raj Grubb was first Walter Legge's assistant and then his successor at EMI.

26 For his next 78 recording RCA reduced the number of sides to 8, though overall timings do not vary greatly, except in the first movement, which is faster in 1941.

27 Ms. Coll. 440, Eugene Ormandy Collection of Test Pressings and Private Recordings, Item 69, Rare Books and Manuscript Library, University of Pennsylvania.

28 Ms. Coll. 60 Box 287, Eugene Ormandy Collection of Scores, Rare Book and Manuscript Library, University of Pennsylvania.

29 Unpublished letter to Jay Saks, RCA producer, 15 June 1978, Ms. Coll. 91 F.1219, Rare Book and Manuscript Library, University of Pennsylvania.

30 A fascinating and provocative study of the consumerisation of music through recording may be found in Eisenberg (2005). See especially Chapter 8 'Phonography', 89–131.

31 My normalisations might be deemed flawed if the addressee has never attended a live performance of music but still enjoys recordings; but the principle of the argument holds even if we have to sieve through the codes afresh.

32 Extraneous noise not associated with an audience or ambience is readily interpreted as part of a recording, but experience shows that we now view historical recordings as holding greater authority than modern ones: surface noise of a certain sort therefore transmits meaning way beyond dating the source.

References

Anderson, W.R. (1931) Review article, _The Gramophone_, 531–2.

Bachman, W.S., Bauer, M.M. and Goldmark, P.C. (1978) 'Disc Recording and Production', in H.E. Roys (ed.) _Disc Recording and Reproduction_, pp. 9–15. Stroudsburg: Dowden.

Botstein, L. (1999) 'Musings on the History of Performance in the Twentieth Century', _Music Quarterly_ 83 (1): 1–5.

Bowen, J.A. (1996) 'Tempo, Duration, and Flexibility: Techniques in the Analysis of Performance', _Journal of Musicological Research_ 16 (2): 111–56.

Clarke, E.F. (2002) 'Listening to Performance', in J. Rink (ed.) _Musical Performance: A Guide to Understanding_, pp.185–96. Cambridge: Cambridge University Press.

Cook, N. (1995) 'The Conductor and the Theorist: Furtwängler, Schenker and the First Movement of Beethoven's Ninth Symphony', in J. Rink (ed.) _The Practice of Performance: Studies in Musical Interpretation_, pp.105–25. Cambridge: Cambridge University Press.

_____ (2003) 'Stravinsky Conducts Stravinsky', in J. Cross (ed.) _The Cambridge Companion to Stravinsky_, pp.176–91. Cambridge: Cambridge University Press.

Copeland, P. (2001) 'Forensic Evidence in Historical Sound-Recordings', in A. Linehan (ed.) _Aural History: Essays on Recorded Sound_, pp.107–15. London: British Library.

Day, T. (2000) _A Century of Recorded Music: Listening to Musical History_. New Haven: Harvard University Press.

Eisenberg, E. (2005) _The Recording Angel: Music, Records and Culture from Aristotle to Zappa_. New Haven: Yale University Press.

Gelatt, R. (1977) _The Fabulous Phonograph, 1877–1977_. New York: Macmillan.

Godlovitch, S. (1998) _Musical Performance: A Philosophical Study_. London: Routledge.

Griffiths, A. (1995) _Nimbus: Technology Serving the Arts_. London: Deutsch.

Grubb, S.R. (1986) _Music Makers on Record_. London: H. Hamilton.

Haggin, M.H. (1959) _Conversations with Toscanini_. Garden City, NY: Doubleday.

Hambræus, B. (1997) _Aspects of Twentieth Century Performance Practice: Memories and Reflections_. Sweden: Royal Swedish Academy of Music.

Harvith, J.H. and Harvith, S.E. (1987) *Edison, Musicians, and the Phonograph: A Century in Retrospect.* New York: Greenwood Press.

Hunt, J. (2000) *Vienna Philharmonic and Vienna State Opera Orchestras.* London: John Hunt.

Johnson, P. (2002) 'The Legacy of Recordings', in J. Rink (ed.) *Musical Performance: A Guide to Understanding*, pp.197–212. Cambridge: Cambridge University Press.

Leech-Wilkinson, D. (2001) 'Using Recordings to Study Musical Performance', in A. Linehan (ed.) *Aural History: Essays on Recorded Sound*, pp.1–12. London: British Library.

Millard, A.J. (2005) *America on Record: A History of Recorded Sound.* Cambridge: Cambridge University Press.

Monkton, G.C. (1926) Letter to *The Gramophone* 3: 380.

Moore, J.N. (1963) *An Elgar Discography.* London: British Institute of Recorded Sound.

_____ (1974) *Elgar on Record: The Composer and the Gramophone.* Oxford: Oxford University Press.

Nilsson, M. (1999) 'First Take: Anatomy of a Recording Session', *Early Music America* 5 (2): 37–40.

Obert-Thorn, M. (2001) Producer's note in *Beethoven: Symphony No. 5, Symphony No. 7.* Naxos 8.110840.

Philip, R. (1974) 'Some Changes in Style of Orchestral Playing 1920–1950 as Shown by Gramophone Recordings'. Unpublished PhD dissertation, Cambridge University.

_____ (1984) 'The Recordings of Edward Elgar (1857–1934): Authenticity and Performance Practice', *Early Music* 12 (4): 481–9.

_____ (1992) *Early Recordings and Musical Style: Changing Tastes in Instrumental Performance, 1900–1950.* Cambridge: Cambridge University Press.

_____ (2004) *Performing Music in the Age of Recording.* New Haven: Yale University Press.

Roys, H.E. (ed.) (1978) *Disc Recording and Reproduction*, Stroudsburg: Dowden.

Sachs, H. (1993) *Reflections on Toscanini.* Rocklin: Prima Publishing.

Stuart, P. (1991) *Igor Stravinsky: The Composer in the Recording Studio.* New York: Greenwood Press.

Taruskin, R. (1995) *Text and Act: Essays on Music and Performance.* London: Oxford University Press.

Discography

Beecham, T. (1932) Strauss *Don Quixote*, with the Royal Philharmonika, Victor 7589-7593.

Elgar, E. (1930) Elgar Symphony No. 1 with London Symphony Orchestra, HMV D 1944–1949.

Godfrey, D. (1927) Mozart Symphony No. 41 with Symphony Orchestra, Columbia L1938–1941.

Hertz, A. (1913) Wagner Good Friday Music, *Parsifal* with Berlin Philharmonic Orchestra, Grammophon 040798–9.

Kajanus, R. (1932) Sibelius Symphony No. 5 with London Symphony Orchestra, HMV DB 1739–1741.

Ormandy, E. (1978a) Chopin Piano Concerto No. 1 with E. Ax (piano) and Philadelphia Orchestra, RCA RL 12868.

_____ (1978b) Sibelius Symphony No. 1 with Philadelphia Orchestra, RCA RL 14901.

Reiner, F. (1940) Wagner Venusberg Music, *Tannhäuser* with Pittsburgh Orchestra, unissued.

Rodzinski, A. (1939) Strauss *Ein Heldenleben* with The Cleveland Orchestra, Columbia 11482-D–11486-D.

Schalk, F. (1929) Beethoven Symphony No. 5 with Vienna Philharmonic Orchestra, HMV C2022–2025.

The Concord Ensemble (1999) Victoria Missa Dum complerentur, Dorian 90274.

Toscanini, A. (1936) Beethoven Symphony No. 7 with New York Philharmonic, Victor 14097–14101.

_____ (1946) Tchaikovsky *Romeo and Juliet* with NBC Symphony Orchestra, Victor 11-9976-9978.

Weingartner, F. (1936) Beethoven Symphony No. 7 with Vienna Philharmonic Orchestra, Columbia LX484–488.

V
Practising Music, Recording Music

MİNE DOĞANTAN-DACK
Recording the Performer's Voice

Certain subtleties of expression cannot really be described; they must be heard.

Daniel Gottlob Türk (1789/1982: 337)

WHEN Jonathan Dunsby published his book titled *Performing Music: Shared Concerns* over a decade ago, he had reservations about the use of the term 'discipline' in reference to 'performance studies'. He cautioned his readers by writing:

> I trot out the term 'discipline' of musical performance studies as if it clearly existed, but it is as well to state that this term at present stands merely for 'subject' or 'topic'. 'Discipline' carries the implication of a received body of knowledge and an orderliness in whatever is conducted in its name, however subversively. I shall repeatedly comment on the fact that this does not really seem to have been the case in musical performance studies.

> (Dunsby, 1995: 17)

The intervening decade, however, witnessed a complete reversal of this situation, with performance studies rapidly emerging as a thriving research area marked by systematic investigation, methodological rigour and discursive cohesion. Consequently, students of musical performance at the beginning of the twenty-first century have an unprecedented wealth of 'received body of knowledge' on which to base their research. This includes extensive theoretical knowledge about the practice strategies of performers, the motor skills involved in playing musical instruments, the psychological and social factors that influence the way performers work, the acoustical properties and gestural elements of so-called expressive performance, and changing performance styles (e.g. Davidson, 2004, 2005; Day, 2000; Jørgensen and Lehmann, 1997; Parncutt and McPherson, 2002; Philip, 1992, 2004; Rink, 1995, 2002; Williamon, 2004). Indeed, such wide-ranging interest in matters of performance led various scholars to posit a change in the 'musical object' of research, implying a fundamental shift in the ontological status of music (Cook, 2001, 2003, 2007; Cook and Clarke, 2004). Musicology, according to this view, is steadily moving away from a score-based conception of music to one that regards it as in essence a performance art.

Without doubt, the most important factor that enabled knowledge production in contemporary performance studies, and thereby facilitated its establishment as 'a musicological discipline in its own right' (Rink, 2004: 36), has been recording technology and the recorded artefacts it makes available. Although more recent digital technologies in the form of sophisticated software programs, which allow researchers to 'navigate and browse recordings' (Cook, 2007: 186) and provide visual representations of data, play an important role in extending the boundaries of what can be observed in and through recorded performances, the very existence of artefacts that can be used as objects of research in performance studies has been contingent upon the representational possibilities offered by audio recording technologies. Studying musical performance from the live event involves formidable difficulties, most obvious among them being the problem of obtaining and stabilising data from the fleeting performance for research purposes. In the absence of a seizable phenomenon which represents the vanished event, and to which one can keep returning for detailed scrutiny, live musical performances resist sufficient objectification to become the focus of research.[1] Arguably the most potent significance of sound recording since its beginnings has been the objectification and reification it affords performances by providing detailed acoustic representation of music as performed. These acoustic representations form the 'primary source documents for the study of performance' (Narmour, 1988: 318), the basic 'repository of evidence' (Leech-Wilkinson, 2001: 1) for researchers. In the words of Eric Clarke '[t]he perennial problem with the study of performance is its temporality and hence ephemerality, and if nothing else, concrete performance data [obtained from recorded performances] at least gives analysts and other parties the assurance that they are dealing with the same thing' (Clarke, 1995: 52). Without recording technology and recorded artefacts, we simply would not know what we now know about musical performances.

Since performance studies as a discipline relies to such a great extent on recordings as documents of performances, one would expect performers and their musicianship to be at the heart of the discipline's epistemological profile and the discourse that embodies it. As one of the most obvious answers one can give to the question 'What (who) do we hear in and through recordings' is 'The performer's music making', it seems only natural to expect performers to play a significant role in effectively shaping the nature of research, the mechanisms of knowledge production, and the sensibilities of the dominant disciplinary discourse. Such, however, has not been the case. Close study of musical performances over the last decade did not bring along a similar focus on performers in that their musical activities and musicianship continue to be represented, in theoretical writings, in terms of received notions, tools and concepts that historically were developed to understand the composer's musical activities. Performance making is still largely conceived in terms of fidelity to the composer's intentions as revealed in the score, rather than as a creative practice shaped by complex factors that include not only expert knowledge about performance traditions, but also a continual striving towards singularity driven by an embodied aesthetic–epistemological quest to create musical meaning. John Rink has written in this connection that 'certain authors have all but robbed performers of their musical personae and artistic prerogatives, transforming them into museum curators, laboratory subjects, theorists and analysts, at the expense of their identities as musicians...And if such constraint is the end result, can we claim that performance studies has much to do with actual performance?' (Rink, 2004: 41)

The history of the relationship between recordings and the dominant disciplinary discourse in contemporary performance studies is yet to be written, but I would argue that the critical emphasis placed on two characteristics made possible for the first time by recordings, namely the repeatability and the spatial–temporal–social decontextualisation of the sounds of a performance, are more than likely to have played a significant role in reinforcing a work-based conception of music during the twentieth century: by insinuating the severance of the singular ties between the performer and the recorded performance, the technology presumably encourages one to hear the latter first and foremost as abstract musical structure. Clarke has written that with recordings '[t]he emphasis on abstraction and ineffability, which are powerfully associated with the ideology of music's autonomy and absolutism, is given extra impetus when the music is itself abstracted from the physical and visual circumstances of its production, and when all possibilities for communication between performers and audience have been eliminated' (Clarke, 2007: 50).

The relationship between the dominant ideology/discourse in performance studies and recording technology is set into relief when one explores the ways performers were represented in the music theoretical discourses of the pre-recording era, when live performance provided the only kind of context where one could encounter not only music, but also music making with all its artistry and magic. During the pre-recording part of music history, as the visible material cause of the sounding music, the performer was firmly connected to her performance in the musical experience of the listener. As the idea of a historical concert repertoire established the canon of classical music during the course of the nineteenth century, and different performances of canonic works highlighted the extent to which performers indeed determine the musical experiences of audiences, the performer came to be established as an autonomous category independent of the composer. The roots of contemporary performance studies go back to this period when the activities of the performer began to receive attention not only in pedagogical but also in music theoretical and philosophical writings. Most remarkably, as the first systematic investigations of musical performance were carried out in the absence of recording technology, theorists were already able to formulate some of the fundamental hypotheses of recent research (Doğantan-Dack, 2006), demonstrating that although fraught with difficulties, basing the study of musical performance on the live event is by no means impossible. For instance, the method employed by the Swiss theorist Mathis Lussy in this connection consisted of recording some of the details of timing, dynamics and phrasing he observed during live performances by diligently annotating musical scores for forty years. As I shall discuss in a future publication, Lussy's writings include invaluable materials, which up to now have not been brought to the attention of musicologists: the scores he annotated during performances shed light on the interpretative decisions made by some of the most important performers of the nineteenth century, among them Hans von Bülow and Anton Rubinstein, the two giants of Romantic pianism. In some cases, the annotations concern the same passages of music as interpreted by different pianists, forming the first historical examples of comparative performance analysis. While precious as musicological documents, Lussy's annotations are nevertheless powerless to re-create an experience of the astounding musicianship of the said pianists, which written accounts describe. And without any acoustic documentation of their artistry, Bülow and Rubinstein are no longer within the chain of knowledge production *as performers*, though their ideas on music (Bülow, 1895–1908; Rubinstein, 1891) retain their potential to influence musical thought.[2]

A study of the music theoretical discourses of the nineteenth century reveals that performers enjoyed a short-lived authority in matters of musical epistemology, and were elevated to the status of being the true source of musical knowledge. Music analysis and theory, particularly in connection with musical rhythm, were evidently informed by the performance practice of the day, and the musical score was regarded as subject to the authority of the performer who made it intelligible to the listener. The abundant performance editions from this period, in which the composer's presumed incorrect barring and time-signature would be corrected by the editor – for example, Riemann's editions (*Phrasierungsausgaben*) of Mozart (1883), Beethoven (1885) and Haydn (1895) Piano Sonatas – are the best-known examples of the kind of practice where the performer is granted the freedom to alter certain aspects of the notated score for purposes of musical intelligibility, overriding the authority of the composer in determining the essential features of the musical 'work'. A typical statement from this period demonstrating the epistemological status of the performer's practice reveals how radically our conception of this status has changed since then:

> It is truly astonishing that Brahms, so rich in his rhythmic conceptions, has written [the beginning of *Hungarian Dance* No.6] in 2/4. Quibblers say: 'if Brahms wished so!' Can Brahms or any other genius wish for the impossible, the absurd, that which is against nature? Brahms, like Beethoven, etc. could have had moments of distraction. It's up to us to resist their incorrect incitements. It is highly probable that Brahms played this piece differently than he wrote it. In any case, Bülow, who studied with Brahms, played it as we have shown.
>
> (Lussy, 1903: 17)[3]

Determining to what extent recording technology played a part in transforming the way musicological discourse came to represent the performer's role during the twentieth century requires extensive research into historical documents. It is, nevertheless, indisputable that the age of recording generated a discourse where the relationship between the performer and musical knowledge embedded in performance became obscured at best, and non-existent at worst. Recorded performances, regarded as 'acoustic texts' (Cook, 2007: 184), have become epistemologically disconnected from their 'authors' in that the prevailing disciplinary agenda reiterates the conspicuous absence of performers in performance studies. Cook, for example, has written: 'much as I applaud the efforts that have been made in the last decade or two to develop a musicology of performance, we are vulnerable to the claim that the voices of performers have not really been heard' (Cook, 2005: 23). Stipulating the absence of performers while building the discipline's main research agenda on recorded performances is indeed an indication that performance studies is still overwhelmingly based on the ideology of 'the work' and its attendant bias towards the composer's epistemological primacy: accordingly, a recorded performance is regarded primarily as an acoustic representation of the musical score, and thereby a mediated manifestation of the composer's authority. Substituting the term 'acoustic texts' for 'recorded performances' – and implying that they are 'authored' by performers – is far from redressing the balance in favour of a footing of equality for the performer, since the kind of epistemological connection that is assumed to exist between a notated musical text, i.e. the score, and its author, i.e. the composer, is not easily and comfortably transferable to the realm of so-called acoustic texts: while any musicological work on a score starts from the assumption that it inheres an intelligible, rational musical design based on the composer's creative activity, no musicological study assumes that the recorded performance inheres an intelligible, rational and creative performer as its generating cause. The latter rather has to be argued for and demonstrated with ample evidence. As music theory and compositional practice developed hand in hand during the last four hundred years – from the Middle Ages onwards, theoretical attempts to understand the technical features and structural organisation of existing compositions were made with the pedagogical aim of providing models for aspiring composers – and since music analysis as a discipline took shape only as the composer's score came to be regarded as a 'final, fixed, immortal text' (Bowen, 1999: 429), the basic paradigms of intelligibility that composers have been working with and are able to notate with more or less precision, namely abstract relationships of discrete pitches and durations, turn out to be the very ones that are recovered/recoverable by analysts from a score.[4] Sharing these symbol-oriented paradigms conceptually with the composer, theorists and analysts generally do not find it problematic to understand the composer's musical activities in their own terms. In this sense, the history of Western musical thought has been the site for the privileged relationship between the composer and the musicologist.

On the other hand, the basic components that preoccupy performers in their efforts to create musical meaning and intelligible musical gestures and shapes, namely tone colour, touch, articulation, and dynamic sense of phrasing and form are not recoverable easily – if at all – from the acoustic text, i.e. the recorded performance. More significantly, performers and musicologists have never interacted sufficiently to develop the tradition of a shared conceptual plane.[5] Being insufficiently equipped to 'read' the 'acoustic text' in terms of the variables used by the performer to create meaning, musicologists, it seems, fail to recognise the markers in the recorded performance that point to the agent responsible for them, i.e. the performer. It is, therefore, not surprising that as far as the dominant disciplinary discourse in contemporary performance studies is concerned, recorded performances, even if conceived as acoustic texts, exist without their authors and are 'mute' in that they do not make the performer's voice heard; a recorded performance does not make the intelligible design, and musical knowledge behind it apparent to musicologists, who by and large rely on tools appropriate for exploring another kind of musical activity to understand what the performer does. Even if musicology has indeed left behind its almost obsessive focus on the score and moved on to a conception of music as a *performance art* (Cook and Clarke, 2004: 10), it nevertheless remains the case that researchers in performance studies are reluctant to represent performers as authorities in the generation of musical meaning and knowledge, and as creators on a par with composers, all the while using their recorded performances as basic research materials. Consequently, the prevailing disciplinary ideology assigns minimal epistemological worth to the *musical voice* of a performer, and requires her to have a textual voice shaped by the dominant discourse before confirming her presence within the discipline.[6]

Even though sound-recording technology is often regarded as having broken the singular, causal ties between the performer and her performance in the listener's experience by abstracting the acoustical features of a performance from its original place, time and social context of occurrence, as the direct and immediate consequence of the performer's actions, a performance – whether live or recorded – is always indissolubly linked to its maker. Research in sound perception and cognition provides substantial evidence that images of sound and sound production are closely linked such that actions of the performer that produce the musical sounds are represented as part of the musical sounds themselves in the listener's experience (Godøy, 2001). Listening to recorded performances is, among other things, aurally witnessing the performer's actions, and observing her enactment of the music. As Rolf Inge Godøy has argued 'there are motor schemata which run parallel to "pure" sound, constituting a "silent choreography" of sound-production integral to notions of musical sound' (Godøy, 2001: 243). In a similar vein, Shove and Repp wrote that

> [n]o one needs to see how high the feet are being raised to hear someone walking or to sense the continuity of the leg movements between the discrete footsteps. The series of footsteps is a natural, lawful consequence of the continuous movements of the legs (indeed, of the whole body). In this respect, their timing and amplitude 'specify' the continuity of movement. The same, we submit, is true of performance movement: the timing and amplitude of the sound-producing attacks lawfully specify the movement spanning a group of attacks, which one can hear as a unit of motion – as a gesture. Some may object to this claim on the

(false) assumption that all one hears are the attacks, for they alone produce the sound. However, attacks are nested events, constrained by, affected by and thus lawfully specific to the performer's actions. To hear the attacks is to hear the performer move.

(Shove and Repp, 1995: 60)

Hence, while one can choose to focus on abstract pitch and durational relationships in listening to a recorded performance, this does not mean that one can perceptually or cognitively erase the kinetic, bodily trace of the performer in the sound. It is important to note that the sounds and sound-producing actions heard in and through a recording do not simply *refer* to the performer: they rather *constitute* the performer and her musicianship. The performer *qua* performer comes into being simultaneously with the sounds she makes; the kinaesthetic markers that are embedded in the sonorous qualities of musical sounds are essential for the identity of the performing musician. As Naomi Cumming has observed the performer's 'identity as a musician cannot be known apart from the sounds she makes' (Cumming, 2000: 26). Ontologically, performers, whether they are seen or not, are firmly connected to their performances. Recordings, therefore, need to be recognised not merely as documents of performances that took place in some specific time and place, in one or several takes, but also as documents of the performer's musical voice and expert knowledge. As Peter Johnson observed, the musical voice of a performer

is unmistakable once we have heard it, regardless of whether it is on CD or in a live performance. It is this performing voice that recordings capture so effectively and which becomes present every time we play a record or a CD. A recording is, literally, *of* the performer or ensemble engaged in interpreting the work.

(Johnson, 2002: 197)

In the words of Tim Day, the particular value of sound recordings lies in their potential to demonstrate 'stylistic traits in contexts, as part of an artist's voice or personality' (Day, 2000:149).

While it may be difficult – if not impossible – for non-performing researchers to immediately recognise the embodied expert knowledge that went into shaping the sonorous qualities of a recorded performance and the performer's conception of the music on record, the aesthetic–critical judgements made by a pianist listening to the recorded voice of another pianist, for example, would be motivated by a shared epistemological plane that is characterised by procedural action representations, originating in the expert production of musical sound sequences on the piano (Jäncke, 2006; Palmer, 2006; Schlaug, 2006). These action representations, which are continuously activated during listening, form the conditions of possibility for the acquisition of new knowledge about the art of piano playing while listening to recorded performances. In the words of Cumming, for a performer listening 'a knowledge of what *might have been* in the performance of [a] sound is able tacitly to inform the moment of hearing it' (Cumming, 2000: 55). Unless one has first-person experience of music making on the piano, the mere observation of the actions and sounds of a pianist would not lead to this kind of comparative cognition of her musicianship, which unfolds as one listens to a live or recorded performance. While one can still describe the musical movements, gestures and sounds observed accurately in terms of timing and dynamics in the absence of such first-person knowledge, one would have difficulty in attributing *pianistic* meaning to them. To use a term from ecological theory (Clarke, 2005; Gibson, 1986), a recorded performance *affords* expert learning and comparative enacting of the music for a performer, and – unlike in the case of a listener – does not 'hold perception and action apart' (Clarke, 2007: 49).[7]

The insistence on representing the performer's identity as a musician through a textual voice has been most acute in the literature on performance and analysis, a research area the aims of which have never been well defined in my view. The great majority of research in this area is built on the assumption that musical performance does not involve and reveal knowledge in the same way as music analysis, and that a performance is epistemologically creditworthy only when its sonic characteristics are justified by a rational, analytical, discursive knowledge basis, inevitably provided by the analyst. Janet Schmalfeldt's frequently cited article of 1985 titled 'On the relation of analysis to performance: Beethoven's Bagatelles Op.126, Nos. 2 and 5' is a paradigm case for the kind of musicological discourse that renders the credibility and worth of the performer's musical activity contingent upon her displaying – in discursive language – an understanding of the score that is reached by means of institutionally established music analytical methods. As is well known, in the article Schmalfeldt alternately assumes 'the roles of two musicians – a Performer whose forthcoming concert includes Beethoven's Six Bagatelles op.126, and an Analyst who is preparing a study of the same' (Schmalfeldt, 1985: 2). Throughout the text, the 'fictive Analyst' (Schmalfeldt, 2005: ¶ 3) enlightens the fictive Performer, who repeatedly expresses her gratitude for the insights and knowledge the Analyst provides. When the Performer asks herself what she has done to ensure that she can recreate the complete work as if it were her own, and on what basis she performs the work as she does, she replies by stating: 'If I succeed in finding confidence for the performance of the Second Bagatelle, it will be because I have tried more than ever to find an analytic basis for performance decisions' (Schmalfeldt, 1985: 19). I shall not dwell on the fact that such statements represent wishful thinking by analysts rather than the conditions of success on stage, nor on the fact that for a performer, the experience of owning a piece of music is born of a highly affective, embodied investment that leaves her aesthetic–kinaesthetic signature in the musical sounds, of an affective commitment to make the piece 'work', and not from an analytic contemplation of the score. To be sure, various musicologists have noted that the relationship between the fictive analyst and the fictive performer in Schmalfeldt's 1985 article is not one of equal partnership (Cook, 1999; Lester, 1995; Rink, 2002; Rosenwald, 1993) since throughout the text it is the analyst who speaks with authority about musical structure and interpretation and enlightens the performer. Rosenwald, for instance, wrote that the fictive performer is 'throughout the experiment the analyst's student, in one case cheerful and in the other mildly troubled. In neither case is she asking questions other than those the analyst would pose in any case' (Rosenwald, 1993: 61).

There is, however, a more fundamental representational problem in Schmalfeldt's text that, to my knowledge, has not been noted by any researcher in the field: this concerns the ontological state of the two fictive characters, and their epistemological credibility. How fictional indeed are the two characters created by Schmalfeldt, and how fictional are their analyses and performances? I would argue that since they do not occupy the same ontological and epistemological plane, the Analyst and the Performer in fact are not equally fictional. In the article, the distinction between the fictional Analyst – a persona created by Schmalfeldt – and the (implied) author collapses as the Analyst displays highly specialised expert analytical knowledge about the musical work under investigation. Representation of such expert knowledge by the persona becomes at the same time a representation of the intelligence, knowledge and opinion of the authorial perspective that holds together all the elements of the analytical discourse we, as readers, are aware of. There is, in this sense, no difference between the perspectives of the fictive Analyst and of Schmalfeldt on Beethoven's Bagatelles. Epistemologically, once such a creditworthy analysis is provided, whether the analyst is fictive or not becomes irrelevant in terms of the expert knowledge offered through the analysis.

But is the same true for the fictive Performer? Following the Performer's response to the Analyst, Schmalfeldt writes that 'The Performer gives a complete rendition of Bagatelle no.2, op.126' (Schmalfeldt, 1985: 19), inviting the reader to imagine a performance not only informed and inspired by the Analyst's expert knowledge and insights, but one that is aesthetically satisfying. In other words, we are asked to believe that a fictive performance by a fictive performer is epistemologically feasible. However, as the expert knowledge of the performer *qua performer* cannot be revealed other than through the sounding music, i.e. as writing alone cannot represent her performance expertise, the fictional Performer in Schmalfeldt's article remains distinct from the (implied) author – and thus truly fictional. The problem is not resolved by the information that Schmalfeldt herself sometimes performs: without actually hearing the interpretation of the fictive Performer and its relationship to what she has to say about the second Bagatelle in the article, we cannot draw from her textual voice a musical voice, and refer to her as a 'performer'. The epistemological paradox of the article is that a fictional performer whose performance is not actually heard is not musically credible, while a performer who performs cannot be fictional because of the indissoluble link between her embodied presence and the musical sounds she produces. To be fair, in 1985, when Schmalfeldt published this pioneering

article on performance and analysis, technologies for accompanying texts with
sound examples were not as advanced and readily available as they are now. However,
for any present-day researcher who wishes to prescribe performance decisions by
relying on the authority of analytical findings based on the score, there is no excuse
for not demonstrating through a recorded performance of her own how exactly such
analytical knowledge is translated into a sounding performance of the piece.

II

I have so far claimed that the performer's musicianship cannot be known independently
of the musical sounds she makes, and argued that as far as musicologists are concerned
sound recordings – the primary source documents for research in performance
studies – do not reveal performers' expert knowledge about music and music-making.
By way of countering the prevailing ideology that requires the performer to justify
her performance through a discursive textual voice, I have implied that a recorded
performance is its own demonstration, its own argument, if you like, in its specifically
musical 'language'. Nevertheless, the fact remains that the philosophical foundations
of knowledge production and research in Western thought, which prize reason
and propositional knowledge over and above affect and know-how, do not easily
accommodate modes of knowledge presentation that lie outside the verbal realm. In
this sense, the musical voice of the performer that is revealed through recordings does
not suffice to make her heard as an equal partner to the musicologist in knowledge
production. To challenge the disciplinary *status quo*, which is deeply rooted in this
tradition giving priority to discursive knowledge, and to reclaim for performance
studies the long-neglected epistemological primacy of the act of music making require
using the tools of that very tradition, namely arguing and convincing. It will indeed
take much discoursing to establish the fact that the possibility of any musicological
knowledge about music is contingent upon the existence of a musical way of knowing
that originates in music making. Rather than regarding this as a discouraging state
of affairs that reflects the knowledge–political agenda of positivistic musicology and
retreating to the realm of mere 'doers' (Kerman, 1985: 195–6), performers can take it
as an opportunity to set aside their notorious image as inarticulate musicians, and fill
in the epistemological gap in performance studies by articulating their perspective on
matters of performance through a *performer's discourse*. The establishment of such a
discourse is essential if performers are to assume greater priority within the discipline
– which in turn is essential, according to Rink, for the discipline itself to continue to
thrive (Rink, 2004: 41).

The dominant discourse in performance studies is the expression of a primarily
textual culture, and as such it seeks to 'read' recorded performances and construe
their different levels of signification from a textual understanding of them. In
contrast to this, the performer's discourse would originate in an aural culture,
celebrating a system of values that do not require meaning to be primarily read but

heard, a culture where new knowledge is aurally recorded; here, it is the performance that makes possible and drives the linguistic discourse. As such, a performer's discourse destined to play a role within the discipline needs to have both linguistic and non-linguistic components, and present the performer's voice both musically and verbally: it would have to provide an aural–discursive construction of the performer's perspective and identity as a musician.

To be sure, performers have been writing about their art and in that sense they are not as a rule inarticulate doers. However, most of this literature does not involve disciplinary concerns – an imperative to contribute to performance studies by presenting the performer's perspective to theorists and practitioners of music alike – and consequently does not find acceptance in musicological circles as presenting a legitimate knowledge producing perspective. In defining the nature of a performer's discourse that would find a space within the discipline of performance studies, it would not be desirable to attempt to delimit in advance the epistemological profile it would acquire, since it is difficult, if not impossible, to filter out the knowledge background of each performer–researcher who will take part in the formation of such a discourse: inevitably, some will have been trained as historical musicologists relying on the established terminologies and conceptual framework of musicology, some as music psychologists, and some as practitioners articulating their experiences as creative artists. Motivated by a particular knowledge background, a particular performer's perspective on music and performance will involve many different kinds of assumptions, information, images, and associations, which will contribute in unique ways to the formation of her performance interpretations, and performance signature; the representation of this perspective in language will accordingly involve a particular blend of knowledge, a particular *epistemological relief.* Moreover, the different kinds and modes of knowledge, which such a relief would project, do not necessarily form a hierarchy of importance. Clarke has noted, for instance, that

> a person's knowledge of Hegelian dialectics might influence the performance of a Beethoven sonata, since sonata form structures can themselves be seen as an example of the operation of a dialectical process. The same might be equally said of a performer whose knowledge of biology led him/her to interpret a through-composed piece according to a metaphor of organic growth.

(Clarke, 1993: 208)

As such, it would limit the epistemological inquiry to dictate that only certain components of a performer's knowledge background are suitable for inclusion in a disciplinary discourse. On the other hand, starting without limits means that one cannot predict at the outset to what extent performers will be able to overcome the constraints of the dominant disciplinary ideology. In my view, the most fruitful approach in representing the performer's voice textually is to aim to record what otherwise would not be articulated in the discipline, i.e. the phenomenology of performing and the performer's perspective on the cognitive–affective dimensions of music making.

In this undertaking, recordings play an indispensable role in integrating the musical voice of the performer with her textual voice. This new role would inevitably generate new meanings that go beyond the ones recordings have traditionally been assigned as either 'sound photographs' of musical performances (Fred Gaisberg in Day, 2000: 33), or created aesthetic objects à la Gould, or interpretations of a musical performance (John Culshaw in Day, 2000: 43). For instance, a recording that is intended and produced as part of a performer's discourse – as part of her knowledge production process – would be conceived as representing an intermediary arrival point, a narrative cross section from the unfolding 'life' of a piece of music in the hands of a particular performer,[8] rather than 'the carefully controlled final state of a performer's interpretive activity' (Clarke et al., 2005: 31). As an integral part of the performer's research, recording would also provide the performer with the opportunity to theorise about performance practices by challenging, questioning, and even negating known ways of interpreting music, and presenting performance practices that are clearly driven by research imperatives – a practice that is not always viable in commercially oriented classical recordings. Recordings would thereby become a means of knowledge presentation and dissemination in performance studies.

III

The second movement of Ludwig van Beethoven's Piano Sonata Op.13 in C minor, the *Pathétique*, involves one of his best-known themes (Figure 1), and its rhythmic ambiguities have generated performance-oriented analyses in the writings of theorists such as Lussy (1912) and Hugo Riemann (1919). Other – score-based – analyses of the movement have been given by Donald Tovey (1931), Jeffrey Kresky (1977) and Bengt Edlund (1997). There is no space – nor is there any necessity – to exercise yet another score-based analysis of the movement here. As my own performance interpretation originates in an embodied, pianistic understanding of the music, I am rather interested in discoursing about the meanings that emerge from the act of performing it. In this unexplored territory, such well-known pieces reveal significations that have been concealed by a veil of familiarity.

Figure 1

The tempo–expression mark Beethoven gave to the second movement of the *Pathétique*, i.e. *Adagio cantabile* (moderately slow in a singing style), appears sparingly in his piano music,[9] although he used it more frequently in his music involving strings and wind instruments.[10] While the marking is sometimes interpreted as a performance direction to bring out the melody against the accompaniment, it more significantly represents an incitation to imitate the singing voice. My conception of the second movement of the *Pathétique* grows out of the implications of its *Adagio cantabile* marking, and can be expressed as a concise image of progression from restraint to relative freedom as I explain below. Such nut-shell conceptions of form that guide performance have been criticised as having a 'summary nature' and therefore no theoretical rigour (Cook, 1999: 13–15). It is important to note, however, that understanding of musical form in terms of a concise image, verbal or musical narrative, is not to be equated with a 'performer's analysis' – it is rather a mental representation that functions like a road map during performance, guiding the performer in her quest to create musical meaning. It is a way of representing the whole of the music to be performed to oneself before one plays the first note, as during a performance, there is no time to activate and play from a representation either of a Roman numeral analysis or of the levels of a Schenkerian one.

Another misconception that has to be amended is the idea that the performer's interpretative activity concerns local details rather than larger-scale structural relationships of a piece of music. Cook, for instance, has written that

> [w]hile the developing analytical literature on performance tends to focus on issues of structural interpretation, often on a relatively large-scale, there is a strong argument that large-scale structure is to a high degree hard-wired into music as composed, and that the performer's ability to generate musical meaning depends much more on the handling of details. (Another way of saying this is that the analytical literature on performance reflects the agenda of score-based analysis rather than that of performance).
>
> (Cook, 2007: 189)

Whether there are systematic relationships and possible interdependency between the local and global expressive variations observed in a performance has not been investigated extensively in research. Nevertheless, the idea that the large-scale structure, or form, is hard-wired into music is difficult to hold: if this were the case, the large-scale form of a piece of music would always be identified in the same way by different analysts, and different performers would always work from one and the same formal understanding of it. While certain pieces of music may indeed display clear large-scale structural relationships, which can be identified, say, as sonata-form, some other pieces might inhere multiple analyses in this respect: the important point is that, in either case, the way a performer handles local details is very much related to her conception of large-scale relationships – or her lack thereof.

One of the major interpretative decisions the performer of the second movement of Beethoven's Piano Sonata Op.13 makes, for example, concerns how each occurrence of the main theme is to be treated in performance, which means developing a conception of the relationship between its five appearances, spanning 66 out of the 73 bars that make up the movement; this certainly constitutes an understanding of the large-scale structure.

The formal identity of *Pathétique*'s *Adagio cantabile* movement has been a matter of controversy among analysts: some, including Tovey (1931) and Cole (2001), have identified it as a 'Rondo' – a sectional form where the first section or refrain recurs (rather than returns) between contrasting sections – while others regard it as a large ABA form subsuming all five occurrences of the theme, the fourth of which represents a return after departure. The implications of this situation for performance resonates particularly well with Tim Howell's observation that, for a performer, relying on 'someone else's analysis, even if specifically targeted as "performer friendly", is almost the equivalent of asking someone else to practice on your behalf' (Howell, 1992: 702). Should the performer treat all of the occurrences of the theme as repetitions (as in Rondo form)? Or does the fourth occurrence involve a sense of return as in ABA? Here, the performer, it seems, has to turn to herself as the authoritative source in developing a performance interpretation. One can provide score-based arguments for one or the other of these interpretations – stronger ones for one of them in my view – but the point is that neither of these score-based interpretations could form a *necessary* basis for a performance interpretation, which can arise only from an intimate familiarity with the piece acquired through performance.

Some answers regarding the form of the second movement of the *Pathétique* begin to suggest themselves when the pianistic implications of the tempo–expression mark *Adagio cantabile* are considered. The direction to play the movement in a singing style is naturally associated with a musical texture that can be identified, in terms of the listening experience, as melody and accompaniment, the two components being experienced in their distinct textural functions within a unified whole. However, the pianistic phenomenology is far from this kind of standard, text-book description, as throughout the performance of the movement the melody never acquires a distinct textural role, never gains independence to 'sing' on its own. The melody can be brought out without difficulty, but this is not equivalent to singing on the piano: what is required is rather a sustained level of kinaesthetic tension that will translate into a sustained level of force, effecting dynamically uniform and steady connections between the successive tones. It is worth noting that a *cantabile* performance does not necessarily depend on the composed structure having a particularly 'vocal' quality: the composer can ask for a *cantabile* performance of a scale, of an atonal melody, etc. In the second of movement of the *Pathétique* Sonata, phenomenologically, the fingers of the right hand, which also have to take part in playing the accompaniment, cannot 'grow into' the keys as they would normally do when singing on the piano; the wrist is also not free to 'breathe' as in normative pianistic *cantabile* practice. Compare this, for example, with the beginning of the second movement of Beethoven's Piano Trio Op.1 No.1 (Figure 2), which is also marked *Adagio cantabile*, where the fingers and wrist of the right hand are totally free to accomplish singing on the piano.

Figure 2

However, in the fourth and fifth occurrences of the theme in the second movement of the *Pathétique*, a phenomenological change in the performance of the melody takes place: the accompaniment, now in triplets, allows the 'singing' fingers playing the melody more elasticity to sustain a certain level of kinaesthetic tension, and the wrist more 'space' to breathe. Hence, pianistically one notes a progression from restraint to more freedom to sing: the accompaniment, which at first creates a restricting environment for the melody, becomes relatively liberating towards the end and gives the melody the chance to thrive 'vocally'. It should be noted that as the melody never acquires total freedom for a *cantabile* performance, Beethoven's *Adagio cantabile* marking remains, in one sense, an imagined guiding force, rather than an actually, and fully, enacted one.

How does one now proceed from these observations, which still do not necessarily imply a specific performance for the piece? Pierre Boulez has written that 'one's [analytical] studies are of merely technical interest if they are not followed through to the highest point – the *interpretation* of the structure; only at this stage can one be sure that the work has been assimilated and understood' (Boulez, 1975: 18). There are innumerable ways for a performer to construct an interpretation of her observations, analytical or otherwise, that would guide the temporal unfolding of the music during a performance. As I have argued earlier, this interpretation would ideally be represented in a compact form, so that it could be called upon with ease while performing. How the performer interprets her observations about a piece of music very much depends on her aesthetic preferences: for instance, should the relative pianistic freedom gained by the melody in bar 51 of the second movement of the *Pathétique* be interpreted as a goal, and expressed through the creation of a sense of direction towards bar 51, or should it be understood more as an event that just comes to pass, as it were? What were Artur Schnabel's aesthetic assumptions when he introduced long drawn-out lines, and waves of dynamic changes in his 1934 recording of the second movement of the *Pathétique* (in Schnabel, 2002)? What aesthetic preferences drove Claudio Arrau in his 1963 recording of the *Pathétique* (in Arrau, 1989) to choose for the second movement so slow a tempo as to create a quasi stasis, a feeling of labouring throughout?

My aesthetic preference in this regard is in favour of an interpretation that sees bar 51 as a return after departure, as a goal expressed through a sense of direction in performance, which is consistent with a narrative understanding of the melody as thriving in the rhythmic space opened up by the triplet accompaniment in bar 51. I have found that in performance this conception invariably leads me to override Beethoven's *piano* dynamic marking in bar 51 and keep the dynamic level *forte* till the coda. To those who might object to this performance choice on the basis of a *Werktreue* ideology, one only needs to point out that the notion of 'faithfulness to the composer's intentions as revealed in the score' is relative: Schnabel, who was considered – and considered himself – as one of the early practitioners of *Werktreue*, rarely followed the dynamic details of this movement as notated. Furthermore, there are performance traditions for many works that have not grown out of what is written in the score, such as the tradition of playing the opening of Sergei Rachmaninoff's Second Piano Concerto Op.18 in C minor much slower that the rest of the movement. As far as the *Pathétique* Sonata is concerned, 'it is far from obvious which elements Beethoven and his contemporaries considered essential for the integrity of a musical work' (Bowen, 1993: 141). Besides, one can give a musically meaningless performance of a piece of music, while playing all the pitches, rhythms and dynamics as notated. An aesthetically satisfying performance does not necessarily rise upon the pillars of *Werktreue* ideology. A performer rather aims to *make* a piece work aesthetically, to create a sounding phenomenon that is effective, moving – even enchanting and transforming – the conditions for which do not necessarily lie in a knowledge of how the score was interpreted by the composer's contemporaries, or how the piece works compositionally. All musical knowing originates in the embodied act of performance making, when the hand makes contact with the musical material, and begins to mould it. A recorded performance is a dynamic trace of this moulding and of the musical knowledge – of the 'intimate familiarity' (Brendel, 1990: 224) – that guides the process. It is the *raison d'etre* for the textual aspects of the performer's discourse. Hence, my recorded performance of the second movement of Beethoven's Piano Sonata Op.13,[11] which can be heard on the accompanying CD (track 1), is that from which all textual aspects of this performer's discourse follow. The greatest challenge for performance studies is to recognise and theorise the musical way of knowing which recorded performances entail, so as to place it at the epistemological foundations of the discipline. Performance studies will thrive to the extent that it successfully represents the musical activities and experiences of not only those who listen to and theorise about live and recorded performances, but also of those who ultimately make musical experiences possible, namely performers.

Notes

1   I use the term 'objectification' to refer to the process of forming a conceptual object of understanding.

2   Though it is reported that Bülow (Day, 2000: 1) recorded on a cylinder, this has never been found.

3   Translation from the French original by the author.

4   The discussion concerns conventionally notated scores, and excludes electroacoustic, electronic and open works.

5   In reality, and broadly speaking, composers and performers work with all parameters of music; there is, nevertheless, an important difference of degree in the kinds of parameters with which each is preoccupied.

6   In contrast to this, no musicologist has ever complained that the voices of composers have not been heard in the discipline (even though the number of composers who have actually written about music and/or about their practice is very few), since the musical voice of a composer is seen as sufficient to establish his identity as an epistemologically creditworthy musician. Note that the issue I raise here is independent of the often-stated idea that performers as 'doers' are reluctant to talk about music.

7   In this connection, also note the recent neuroscientific evidence, which indicates that in expert performers, brain activation patterns for auditory and motor tasks are so similar that it becomes hard to tell which is which: 'For the expert performers, perception and action seem to be just two aspects of one integrative skill' (Bangert, 2006: 179).

8   Such a conception might, of course, also reflect the reality of various commercially available recordings.

9   Among his piano sonatas, it marks only the second movement of Op.13, and the slow four-bar introduction of Op.78 in F sharp.

10   See, for example, the second movement of his Piano Trio Op.1. No.1 in E flat; the second movement of his String Quartet Op.18 No. 2 in G; the second movement of his Wind Septet Op.20 in E flat; his Romance for violin and orchestra Op.50 in F; the third movement of his Cello Sonata Op.69 in A; and the second movement of his Trio for two oboes and English horn Op.87 in C.

11   Recorded as a single take at Middlesex University in April 2008. I am grateful to recording engineer Peter Williams for his assistance during the recording of this movement.

References

Bangert, M. (2006) 'Brain Activation during Piano Playing', in E. Altenmüller, M. Wiesendanger and J. Kesselring (eds) *Music, Motor Control and the Brain*, pp.173–88. New York: Oxford University Press.

Bowen, J.A. (1993) 'The History of Remembered Innovation: Tradition and Its Role in the Relationship between Musical Works and Their Performances', *The Journal of Musicology* 11: 139–73.

_____ (1999) 'Finding the Music in Musicology: Studying Music as Performance', in N. Cook and M. Everist (eds) *Rethinking Music*, pp.424–51. Oxford: Oxford University Press.

Boulez, P. (1975) *Boulez on Music Today.* Trans. S. Bradshaw and R.R. Bennett. London: Faber. Original (1963) as *Penser la Musique Aujourd'hui.* Paris: Gonthier.

Brendel, A. (1990) *Music Sounded Out.* London: Robson Books.

Bülow, M. von (ed.) (1895–1908) *Hans von Bülow: Briefe und Schriften,* 8 vols. Leipzig: Brietkopf und Härtel.

Clarke, E. (1993) 'Generativity, Mimesis and the Human Body in Music Performance', *Contemporary Music Review* 9: 207–21.

_____ (1995) 'Expression in Performance: Generativity, Perception and Semiosis', in J. Rink (ed.) *The Practice of Performance*, pp.21–54. Cambridge: Cambridge University Press.

_____ (2005) *Ways of Listening: An Ecological Approach to the Perception of Musical Meaning.* New York: Oxford University Press.

_____ (2007) 'The Impact of Recording on Listening', *Twentieth Century Music* 4 (1): 47–70.

Clarke, E., Cook, N., Harrison, B. and Thomas, P. (2005) 'Interpretation and Performance in Bryn Harrison's *être-temps*', *Musicae Scientiae* 9 (1): 31–74.

Cole, M.S. (2001) 'Rondo', in S. Sadie and J. Tyrrell (eds) *The New Grove Dictionary of Music and Musicians*, 2nd ed. URL (consulted January 2007): http://www.grovemusic.com

Cook, N. (1999) 'Words About Music, or Analysis Versus Performance', in N. Cook, P. Johnson and H. Zender (eds) *Theory into Practice: Composition, Performance, and the Listening Experience*, pp.9–52. Leuven University Press.

_____ (2001) 'Between Process and Product: Music and/as Performance', *Music Theory Online* 7 (2). URL (consulted January 2007): http://www.societymusictheory.org/mto

_____ (2003) 'Music as Performance', in M. Clayton, T. Herbert and R. Middleton (eds) *The Cultural Study of Music: A Critical Introduction*, pp.204–14. New York: Routledge.

_____ (2005) 'Prompting Performance: Text, Script, and Analysis in Bryn Harrison's être-temps', *Music Theory Online* 11 (1). URL (consulted January 2007): http://www.societymusictheory.org/mto

_____ (2007) 'Performance Analysis and Chopin's Mazurkas', *Musicae Scientiae* XI (2): 183–207.

Cook, N. and Clarke, E. (2004) 'Introduction: What is Empirical Musicology?' in E. Clarke and N. Cook (eds) *Empirical Musicology: Aims, Methods, Prospects*, pp.3–14. Oxford: Oxford University Press.

Cumming, N. (2000) *The Sonic Self: Musical Subjectivity and Signification.* Bloomington: Indiana University Press.

Davidson, J.W. (ed.) (2004) *The Music Practitioner. Research for the Music Performer, Teacher and Listener.* Aldershot: Ashgate.

_____ (2005) 'Bodily Communication in Musical Performance', in D. Miell, R. MacDonald and D.J. Hargreaves (eds) *Musical Communication*, pp.215–28. Oxford: Oxford University Press.

Day, T. (2000) *A Century of Recorded Music: Listening to Musical History.* New Haven: Yale University Press.

Doğantan-Dack, M. (2006) 'The Body Behind Music: Precedents and Prospects', *Psychology of Music* 34 (4): 449–64.

Dunsby, J. (1995) *Performing Music. Shared Concerns.* Oxford: Oxford University Press.

Edlund, B. (1997) *'Sonate, que te fais-je?* Toward a Theory of Interpretation', *Journal of Aesthetic Education* 31 (1): 23–40.

Gibson, J.J. (1986) *The Ecological Approach to Visual Perception.* Hillsdale, NJ: Erlbaum.

Godøy, R.I. (2001) 'Imagined Action, Excitation, and Resonance', in R.I. Godøy and H. Jørgensen (eds) *Musical Imagery*, pp.237–50. Lisse, Netherlands: Swets & Zeitinger.

Howell, T. (1992) 'Analysis and Performance: The Search for a Middleground', in J. Paynter, T. Howell, R. Orton and P. Seymour (eds) *Companion to Contemporary Musical Thought* vol.2, pp.692–714. London: Routledge.

Jäncke, L. (2006) 'The Motor Representation in Pianists and String Players', in E. Altenmüller, M. Wiesendanger and J. Kesselring (eds) *Music, Motor Control and the Brain*, pp.153–72. New York: Oxford University Press.

Johnson, P. (2002) 'The Legacy of Recordings', in J. Rink (ed.) *Musical Performance: A Guide to Understanding*, pp.197–212. Cambridge: Cambridge University Press.

Jørgensen, H. and Lehmann, A.C. (eds) (1997) *Does Practice Make Perfect? Current Theory and Research on Instrumental Music Performance.* Oslo: Norwegian State Academy of Music.

Kerman, J. (1985) *Contemplating Music: Challenges to Musicology.* Cambridge, Mass.: Harvard University Press.

Kresky, J. (1977) *Tonal Music: Twelve Analytic Studies.* Bloomington: Indiana University Press.

Leech-Wilkinson, D. (2001) 'Using Recordings to Study Musical Performances', in A. Linehan (ed.) *Aural History: Essays on Recorded Sound*, pp.1–12. London: The British Library.

Lester, J. (1995) 'Performance and Analysis: Interaction and Interpretation', in J. Rink (ed.) *The Practice of Performance: Studies in Musical Interpretation*, pp.197–216. Cambridge: Cambridge University Press.

Lussy, M. (1903) *L'anacrouse dans la musique moderne.* Paris: Heugel.

_____ (1912) *La Sonate Pathétique de L. van Beethoven Op.1. Edition Rythmée et Annotée par Mathis Lussy.* Posthumous. Paris: Costallat.

Narmour, E. (1988) 'On the Relationship of Analytical Theory to Performance and Interpretation', in E. Narmour and R. Solie (eds) *Explorations in Music, the Arts, and Ideas: Essays in Honor of Leonard B. Meyer*, pp.317–40. New York: Pendragon Press.

Palmer, C. (2006) 'The Nature of Memory for Music Performance Skills', in E. Altenmüller, M. Wiesendanger and J. Kesselring (eds) *Music, Motor Control and the Brain*, pp.39–53. New York: Oxford University Press.

Parncutt, R. and McPherson, G.E. (2002) *The Science and Psychology of Music Performance. Creative Strategies for Teaching and Learning.* Oxford: Oxford University Press.

Philip, R. (1992) *Early Recordings and Musical Style: Changing Tastes in Instrumental Performance 1900–1950.* Cambridge: Cambridge University Press.

———— (2004) *Performing Music in the Age of Recording.* New Haven: Yale University Press.

Riemann, H. (1919) *L. van Beethovens sämtliche Klavier-Solosonaten.* Berlin: Max Hesses Verlag.

Rink, J. (ed.) (1995) *The Practice of Performance: Studies in Musical Interpretation.* Cambridge: Cambridge University Press.

———— (ed.) (2002) *Musical Performance: A Guide to Understanding.* Cambridge: Cambridge University Press.

———— (2004) 'The State of Play in Performance Studies', in J.W. Davidson (ed.) *The Music Practitioner: Research for the Music Performer, Teacher and Listener*, pp.37–51. Aldershot: Ashgate.

Rosenwald, L. (1993) 'Theory, Text-Setting and Performance', *The Journal of Musicology* 11 (1): 52–65.

Rubinstein, A. (1891) *Die Musik und ihre Meister. Eine Unterredung.* Leipzig: Senff.

Schlaug, G. (2006) 'Brain Structures of Musicians: Executive Functions and Morphological Implications', in E. Altenmüller, M. Wiesendanger and J. Kesselring (eds) *Music, Motor Control and the Brain*, pp.141–52. New York: Oxford University Press.

Schmalfeldt, J. (1985) 'On the Relation of Analysis to Performance: Beethoven's Bagatelles Op.126, Nos. 2 and 5', *Journal of Music Theory* 29: 1–31.

———— (2005) 'Response to the 2004 SMT Special Session "Performance and Analysis: Views from Theory, Musicology, and Performance"', *Music Theory Online* 11 (1). URL (consulted January 2007): http://www.societymusictheory.org/mto

Shove, P. and Repp, B.H. (1995) 'Musical Motion and Performance: Theoretical and Empirical Perspectives', in J. Rink (ed.) *The Practice of Performance*, pp.55–83. Cambridge: Cambridge University Press.

Tovey, D. (1931) *A Companion to Beethoven's Pianoforte Sonatas.* London: Associated Board of RAM and RCM.

Türk, D.G. (1982) *School of Clavier Playing or Instructions in Playing the Clavier for Teachers and Students.* Trans. R.H. Haggh. Lincoln: University of Nebraska Press. Original (1789) as *Klavierschule, oder Anweisung zum Klavierspielen für Lehrer und Lernende, mit kritischen Anmerkungen.* Leipzig: Schwickert.

Williamon, A. (ed.) (2004) *Musical Excellence: Strategies and Techniques to Enhance Performance.* Oxford: Oxford University Press.

Discography

Arrau, C. (1989) *Beethoven Piano Sonatas: Appassionata, Pathétique, Moonlight.* Philips CD 422 970-2.

Schnabel, A. (2002) *Beethoven Piano Works, vol.3. Historical Recordings 1932–1935.* Naxos Historical CD 8.110695.

JOHN YOUNG

Inventing Memory: Documentary and Imagination in Acousmatic Music

Recorded sound and musical practice

SOUND recording has radically changed the production and reception of music, and in electroacoustic genres composers have witnessed an unparalleled growth in the range of viable sounds and processes. The application of the term 'music' to this new sound landscape has often created more confusion than clarification regarding the intentions and methods of its practitioners. One of the most persistent debates in electroacoustic music revolves around the aesthetic implications of this point in that the propensity for recording to isolate sounds from any physical, generative context presents new perspectives on absolutist and referentialist aesthetic stances.[1]

These perspectives can be summarised through a simple distinction:

(1) Recording provides 'raw' materials that deliver the complex structures of natural sounds to the composer in a fixed form, allowing them to be treated as abstract objects, placed or reshaped into a self-contextualising structure.

(2) By capturing sounds of actions and objects, recording engages our habitual mechanisms of sound-source recognition, which may embrace associative meanings we ascribe to sounds in daily life, with the potential to evoke 'images' that may be available as form-bearing elements through reference and narrative.[2]

One common element in these two perspectives is the fact that recording fixes sound events in time. Sound is captured intact directly from a physically 'real' source, which may contain never-to-be-repeated subtleties and inflections, now available for infinite re-audition and placement in new contexts. Moreover, the fixing of sound through recording is different in essence to the fixed nature of a musical score, since precise details of articulation and timbre become fully determined attributes of the sound, which may subsequently influence the quality and sonic attributes of electroacoustic transformations. The central idea of this chapter is that in terms of its fundamental aesthetic implications as musical material, sound recording functions as a mirror held up to real-world events and offers a means of exploring the nature of lived experience. This is expressed here in terms of two general aspects of consciousness, namely experience and memory. These respectively characterise the capacity for sound recording to facilitate repeated listening to a potentially very accurate recreation of the original acoustical stimulus and, by virtue of the microphone's clinical reception of the signals that reach it, the potential for sound recording to function as a sonic notepad for things we remember and forget.

Pierre Schaeffer's pioneering work in developing a theory and compositional practice in electroacoustic music had a powerful influence on the development of sound recording as an original musical medium. It led to the formulation of a number of significant theoretical constructs in conjunction with practical experimental work (Schaeffer, 1966) and to the establishment of the *Groupe de recherches musicales* (GRM) as a centre for music production within Radio France. Schaeffer's aim was to develop electroacoustic music in ways that did not incorporate source recognition as a factor in the structural design or meaning of a work. In developing a musical theory out of work with recorded sounds, he considered the potential of recording to separate sound from its physical origins as a path to rendering sound a self-contained phenomenological entity. The term 'acousmatic' was adopted by Schaeffer to characterise the natural consequence of the occlusion of a sound's physical origins by audio recording. This, he proposed, was a crucial step towards working with any sound exclusively in terms of its sonic rather than its referential qualities (Schaeffer, 1966: 98). He proposed the term 'reduced listening' [*écoute réduite*] (Schaeffer, 1966: 270) as a musically focused way of engaging with acousmatic sounds, which he termed 'sound objects' [*objets sonores*].

Despite the thorough way in which Schaeffer articulated his vision, his application of reduced listening has not found complete accord with the practice of electroacoustic music in subsequent years, and there has been a wealth of compositional output that pragmatically affirms the expressive and poetic value of embracing our tendency to associate sounds with their sources (Truax, 1996; Wishart, 1996). As early as the 1960s, acting against the prevailing aesthetic of abstraction within the GRM, Luc Ferrari recognised the potential for poetic use of representation in acousmatic music:

> From 1963 on I listened to all the sounds which I had recorded, I found that they were like images. Not only for me who could remember them, but also for innocent listeners. Provide images, I told myself, contradictory images which catapult in the head with even more freedom than if one really saw them...There I had the complete scale from the abstract to the concrete, which allowed me to make an absurd discourse based on images which were absurd or put in absurd situations...For example, the wave from a heavy sea...I had never heard before, it was possible to cut...a wave starting from complete silence and going back to it. Because the sea produces a continuity of sound. But there it was a question of a poetic apparition. There was a confrontation between extreme realism and a complete utopia.

> (Ferrari, 1996: 100–1)

Trevor Wishart has argued that sound source recognition is integral to human audition and therefore quite naturally has a potential role in the creation of meaningful forms (Wishart, 1996: 129ff).[3] In developing this idea he has proposed the notion of 'sonic landscape' as the source from which we *imagine* a sound to come – a pragmatic way of acknowledging the potential ambiguity of acousmatic sound, but also a lever to exploit its imaginative potentials. Over the last two decades the field of soundscape studies, pioneered in the work of R. Murray Schafer (Schafer, 1994), has also had a strong influence on electroacoustic music, and to date it is in the creative and literary work of Barry Truax (Truax, 2001) that the potential for synergy between electroacoustic composition and the analytical methodologies of soundscape studies is most powerfully exemplified. By paying attention to the significance of the associative and contextual dimensions of sound in natural and man-made environments, soundscape studies has shown that both the formal and functional aspects of natural sounds are significant as vehicles for meaning, offering an holistic approach to the way we might view the interaction of morphological and referential dimensions of sound when composing with recorded environmental sounds. Hildegard Westerkamp has characterised the genre of soundscape composition by saying that 'its essence is the artistic, sonic transmission of meanings about place, time, environment and listening perception' (Westerkamp, 2002: 52). Notions allied to soundscape philosophy have also brought electroacoustic music closer to phonography, in which sound recording is used as a means of capturing and relaying to an audience sounds from interesting environmental and cultural situations.

By removing actual physical contexts, but not necessarily that which is contextual within sound itself, the acousmatic phenomenon behaves as a catalyst for an intensified and focused experience of any aspect of the sound world around us. Imaginative scenarios can easily spiral out of listening to a recording, as the sound's generative actions or contexts may be surmised, encouraging broad reflection on our real-world experience.[4] In this way, any imagery that we conjure up during listening tells us something not just about the sounds, but also about something fundamental to our own response mechanisms. Allowing the recording process to open up new vistas for associative meaning and imaginative engagement, the acousmatic phenomenon, which has the capacity to bring about changes in context that are both physical (detached from their physical source) and temporal (detached from their original time) is imbued with the potential to trigger emotive responses.

Recording as artefact of experience

Walter Benjamin's insights into the nature of reproduction technologies such as photography and cinema offer critical tools by which significant aspects of sound recording as a creative implement can be established. Benjamin argued that reproductions of artworks detached them from the authentic *aura* of the original: 'In even the most perfect reproduction, *one* thing is lacking: the here and now of the work of art – its unique existence in a particular place' (Benjamin, 1936/2002: 103).

Hence, the singular authenticity of a painting or sculpture may be seen to result directly from the artist's touch and physical engagement with materials, standing as a unique embodiment of imagination and creative travail. But in photography and cinema, he argued, the capacity for precise reproduction from, say, a negative means that such artefacts do not possess the aura of authenticity bestowed by the singularity of, for example, a painting.[5] But the notion of authenticity was a double-edged sword for Benjamin. In the emergence of works 'designed for reproducibility' (Benjamin, 2002: 106), such as photography and cinema, he recognised on the one hand a loss of historical connection with the 'sphere of tradition' surrounding the artwork, and on the other hand a liberation of art from its role in archaic, and – as implied – arcane ritual.[6] The other side of Benjamin's argument is that art that makes reproduction technology intrinsic to the creative process directs us away from the ritual associations of the singular original, and toward new kinds of intensified images that can throw new light on our lived experience; such images are achievable only through the prosthetic of a technology capable of directly capturing and reflecting the experience of visual and auditory stimuli around us.[7]

> Whereas it is a commonplace that, for example, we have some idea what is involved in the act of walking (if only in general terms), we have no idea at all what happens during the split second when a person actually takes a step. We are familiar with the movement of picking up a cigarette lighter or a spoon, but know almost nothing of what really goes on between hand and metal, and still less how this varies with different moods. This is where the camera comes into play, with all its resources for swooping and rising, disrupting and isolating, stretching or compressing a sequence, enlarging or reducing an object. It is through the camera that we first discover the optical unconscious, just as we discover the instinctual unconscious through psychoanalysis.[8]
>
> (Benjamin, 2002: 117)

This view of the potential of cinema points to a way of extending Benjamin's concept of authenticity to include what might be termed an *aura of experience* made possible through recording media. The elements that comprise a sequence such as Benjamin describes above – physical actions, the nature of their capture and media-based reconstruction – are original acts in themselves, drawing directly on our engagement with and experience of worldly things. The capacity of recording technology to transmit back to us 'sampled' sounds or images as traces of sensory experience invites us to think about the way we understand the nature of reality, as events and impressions we form about them are made available for re-evaluation. Listening back to a sound recording of an event just witnessed is something engaging just because it affords the otherwise-impossible opportunity to re-hear something extracted and made seemingly permanent out of the flow of time (or perhaps to hear something on which attention was not originally focused). Similarly, a recording of an event that was not seen or heard first hand can be vicariously appreciated as a 'window' on this technological mediation of experience or as affirmation of evidence of an event. The composer, then, may work with sound not just as aural 'matter', but as an experiential trace in which time, place, personalities and other aspects of generative and contextual substance may have a meaningful role. Yet even the most straightforward sound or image capture is never a completely transparent, unmediated view of 'reality'. There is always the choice of perspective from which the recording is made, an inevitable framing in time of the way a sequence is edited/montaged, and the spatial/contextual reduction imposed by constraints such as lens focal length or the stereo window of sound reproduction. The medium itself frames the representation. In fact, Benjamin argued that in cinematic terms it is only through the process of montage, where new and heightened relationships between images and actions are constructed, that a work of 'art' is produced (Benjamin, 2002: 110). As such, technique and artistic insight are required to 'make something' from these kinds of technologically mediated and manipulated materials that is more than the sum of its parts.

Music's connection to the traditional notion of authenticity is complex since the experience of music does not spring from the score itself but from its realisation in live performance.[9] The traditional processes of musical invention, notation and instrumental realisation open up various layers in which notions of authenticity may operate. Thus, it is the experience of live performance that is normally considered to carry an 'aura', leading often to a sidelining of acousmatic music, where the active, visible performing agents are absent (McNabb, 1986: 144). What I want to argue here is that the role of recording in acousmatic music is not just a convenience of support, but that the genre creates a platform in which the recording, as a window on documented experience, represents by necessity a fixed 'snapshot' of a sound event, captured and framed by its detachment from the passing of time. One of the most original and essential attributes of the acousmatic genre is, therefore, its capacity to deal with themes of an experiential and phenomenological nature, through evocation of images and by allowing us to recognise reflections of lived experience in audio documents. Just as Benjamin, quoted above, spoke of the 'optical unconscious', this view of sound recording provides a mechanism for the composer to explore the relationship between the narrative, the associations of recognisable sound events and the substance and structure of these sounds in phenomenological terms.

A seminal work in that respect is Ferrari's *Presque rien No. 1: Le lever du jour au bord de la mer* (1970)[10] which is made from deftly edited recordings made in the early hours of the morning during a period of stay in a Dalmatian fishing village.[11] Though the sounds in this work are detached from their source place and time, they remain sufficiently recognisable for the listener to vicariously form an understanding of the evolving scenario that is presented. While the piece reflects the composer's very intense response to the emergence of daily sounds out of nocturnal silence as experienced in the original environment (Warburton, 1998), it also projects some imaginative intervention; in fact, the more one listens to this work, the more one hears (or imagines) a guiding, 'orchestrating' hand at work, and a clear sense of being invited to listen into the layers of sound presented. For example, in the second and third sections, voices (first speaking and then singing) are heard in a naturalistically contrapuntal texture with cicada sounds. Whether presented literally from recorded document or mixed by the composer, the effect is of a realistic event, framed and heightened by its recontextualisation in recorded form. This effects a transformation from the functional to the aesthetic: sounds coexist and we may choose to find satisfying 'rightness' – a musicality perhaps – in the concerted effect. Moments of rupture are felt most keenly in the second section, announced by an audible overlap of materials at the moment of transition between sections one and two. At 23", a diesel engine starts abruptly and alarmingly close by, and without visual knowledge of the presence of a large vehicle next to us, this effects an immediate change in the perception of our position within the soundscape, which, until that point, had consisted of objects and events at moderate distance from the point of audition. Suddenly, events are brought into true physical proximity to the listener, who is not solely located within a comfortable vista. But most tellingly, the trace of intervention is felt in the cloud of cicada sounds that engulfs the final minutes of the work, offering an exaggerated immersion in one component of the sound field. This represents a significant shift from the evolving counterpoint of voices and other signs of life passing by the composer's window, as the impression is created of a listening perspective now more decisively directed by the artist. Whereas we previously were witness to an array of sounds that articulated a wide-ranging environmental scene (from a boy's echoing shouts to the clucking of boat engines), we are now submerged in an atmosphere that obliterates a sense of perspective between objects, and places us in a myriad of intense, close-up sound particles. In that sense, the most decisive gesture in the work is the abrupt cut of the ending, tearing us sharply from the privilege of engaging with the artist's experience.

The potential of sound recording and associated electroacoustic processing to allow the composer to explore the listening process by forming and unlocking new aural relationships might be elucidated by Robert Hughes' assessment of Cézanne:

> The Renaissance admired an artist's certainty about what he saw. But with Cézanne...the statement: 'This is what I see,' becomes replaced by a question: 'Is this what I see?' You share his hesitations about the position of a tree or a branch; or the final shape of Mont Ste-Victoire, and the trees in front of it. Relativity is all.

> (Hughes, 1991: 18)

Due to its capacity to cross between referentialist and absolutist aesthetic mechanisms, electroacoustic music also has an innate potential to bring us to a new understanding of the relativity of perception. As Wishart has noted, the acousmatic 'effect' is often to create ambiguities of source recognition (Wishart, 1996: 148), capable of blurring any definitive line between the referential and the abstract, so that when we hear a sound to which we cannot conclusively ascribe a source, we may still find in it characteristics of energy input, flow and release, motion through pitch space or a sense of the physical scale of the 'object' producing the sound.[12]

In addition, the way referential sounds themselves are presented can impart imagery in different ways. For instance, Jonty Harrison's *Unsound Objects* (1995) and *Hot Air* (1995) present discourses based on juxtaposition and melding of fragments of realistic recordings and layers of electroacoustic transformations. Frequently the images these sounds present are what we might regard as iconic – vivid in their realism, but polished and extracted from any wider context (for example, in *Hot Air* the struck match at 7'17"). A 'fantasy' environment facilitated by sound transformation and mixing is harnessed by the composer to project an air of playful ambiguity in the way sound sources appear to 'interact', such as the folding together of roughly handled party balloons and fireworks in *Hot Air* (at 12'). Yet, there are places in these works where the images come a step closer to a sense of the contextual reality from which they are drawn. For instance, in *Hot Air*, the act of recording is evidenced by the presentation of a brief interaction at 2'35" between a child and (we might reasonably assume) the composer: 'What are you doing?'...'Recording the thunder'. And in the closing minutes of *Unsound Objects* (from 10'30"), a collection of iconic fragments – footsteps in gravel, waves and seaside fun – merge to corroborate in the projection of a believably coherent scenario, tilting the emphasis to a sense of documentary, presenting for us images of reality and the more authentic 'trace' of the direct reflection. Furthermore, concentrated listening changes perceptions and can be the conduit for the forging or discovery of relationships between sounds, and the identification and utilisation of sound transformation processes suitable to a specific compositional scenario. In this way (to paraphrase the quotation from Hughes, above), 'this is what I hear' shifts to 'is this what I hear?' expressed, as in the works of Harrison, by the establishment of an interplay between layers of realistic sound, their connotations and denotations, and transformations.

Strong listening experiences in daily life are often a crucial catalyst for the use of sound recording in artistic contexts. The shift from 'listening' to 'recording' denotes a creative action, rendering sound an intact reflection of experience as well as an object that can be taken apart and reassembled. Westerkamp describes the subtlety of articulation with which she frequently works as an interaction between composerly intent and 'the power of the sound materials themselves to shift that intent by virtue of their inherent meanings, as well as through discovery and surprise in the compositional process' (Westerkamp, 2002: 53). Katharine Norman puts this in perspective in relation to Westerkamp's work *Talking Rain* (Westerkamp, 1997):

> It appears to take the lightest touch – just a few steps down the path between a recording and a composition – to turn a documented landscape into a new journey. It's a matter of surreptitiously offering a new approach, one that a listener might come across while passing through familiar territory...At the opening of *Talking Rain* there is the sound of tapping rain on a roof in the foreground. It

traces one, recognizably musical, path through many other water sounds. Its rhythm invites other sounds to join it as music. And yet this rhythmic musical tapping is also merely the sound of rain on a roof.

(Norman, 2004: 79–80)

Westerkamp acknowledges an imperative to demonstrate the way listening influences each point in the process of composing with environmental sounds (Norman, 2004: 80–1). There is a delicate balance between allowing the natural morphology of sounds to remain intact – to 'speak' – whilst articulating a new context for the materials that will maximise their impact, laying bare the composer's listening as an essential agent in the creative process. The act of recording is, then, a pointer to distinctive sounds, which in the larger scheme of things may be barely noticeable without the time and space to explore and locate them, or without the microphone to pinpoint and capture them. To further paraphrase Hughes: this is not just a case of 'this is *what* I hear', but 'this is *how* I hear.'

Another work which clearly articulates this kind of approach is Westerkamp's *Kits Beach Soundwalk* (1989). Here, the composer announces her presence in the scene – 'It's a calm morning. I am on Kits Beach in Vancouver' – and throughout the listener's attention is drawn to many of the sonic subtleties of the location: the relative loudness of distant Vancouver traffic, the quiet popping of water over barnacle shells. Formally, the work hinges on the notion of escape through an awareness of and ability to appreciate sonic detail, which turns on reference to the technology itself: 'We can just go into the studio and get rid of the city – pretend it's not there, pretend we are somewhere far away' (3'00"). Parallels are drawn with listening through musical repertoire (specifically Xenakis and Mozart) and the evocations of dreams, further symbolising notions of escape in the fantasy, and the pleasure and meaning that we may find in deep contemplation of sound. In general, these processes represent forms of hyper-contextualisation enabling the listener to engage with the recording, and provide a focused conduit to the way functional, mundane experience can be transformed into aesthetic awareness. When the city 'noise' is reintroduced at the end as an object of play, the circle of imaginative mastery of the soundscape is complete. This is no simple document of an environmental soundwalk; it is a virtual, electroacoustically dramatised critical reflection on place, time and feeling, as sensed and articulated through sound.

Recording as artefact of memory

In Jorge Luis Borges' short story 'Funes el memorioso' ['Funes the memorious'] (1944/1964) the subject is a young man whose comprehension of the world is entirely through memory; each encounter with each object and each part of every object is remembered exactly, and these are perceived as though for the first time. In short, he is a 'recorder' of sensory input that finds no correlation between discrete actions or physical things. Borges' conception of such extreme phenomenological awareness emphasises that this is precisely the antithesis of the way 'normal' memory informs our immediate experience, enabling generalisation, grouping, and cataloguing that allow specific details of events and objects to pass into impressions and feelings, and to function as a sounding board for the imagination, while at the same time bestowing a sense of permanence onto objects, to make sense of the apparent, phenomenal continuity of our surroundings. Sound recording gives us the magic of being connected to a ruthlessly objective memory, affording us a view of reality which is simultaneously heightened in that we can review and shift the focus of our attention as we replay events, and also less 'real' because of the inevitable loss of the immediacy of the unstoppable and irretrievable present.

By identifying in recording the potential to re-examine experience, we find a powerful trigger for the associative and emotional properties of memory. As the fixing of sound through recording allows us to deepen our experience, it also forms an extension of memory and, as Truax suggests, a channel between past and present:

> The very experience of time becomes a paradox. We have access to sounds of the past, but all of them seem to be part of the present in some great collage of juxtapositions. And yet, we are emotionally susceptible to the bringing back to life of a sound, perhaps a familiar voice, that has long since been silenced. We understand a picture to be merely that, a representation that we have never experienced until we see it...But a recorded sound, even if imperfect in its reproduction, is close enough to our own experience to be capable of bringing back all of the original context and the feelings associated with it. Therefore, to many people, a sound recording seems a more powerful link to the past.

(Truax, 2001: 130)

Awareness of experience ebbs away in the continuity of life, and memory can become a startling mix of the wholly precise, the indistinct and what we fabricate by way of compensation. But recordings are also prone to their own forms of signal degradation and loss through instabilities and frailties of storage media; inadequacies in the chain of signal transduction, such as tape hiss, record surface noise, wow and flutter; and errors that arise from digital data that cannot be read correctly. As things stand, the phases in the evolution of recording media produce a range of seemingly naturalistic archaeological strata, as very early recordings are scarce, limited in the range of reproduced frequencies and dynamic range of any particular era, and frequently heavily 'decayed'. Gradually time and technology might be seen to clear the 'mists' to the extent that technological transparency might conceivably have been reached. The traces left by the imperfections of recording media, however, are still potent artefacts, capable of reminding us that we are listening back through time. The catalogue of all recorded sounds forms a repository of experience that is fragmentary, frayed around the edges, and evaporating with age.

The trace of technology in conjunction with the fragility of experience is felt keenly in Rachel McInturff's *By Heart* (1996). In this work, a young girl obviously traumatised by domestic violence, is recording her feelings while shut way in the midst of a brutally abusive confrontation.[13] We hear a male voice shouting in another part of the house, her quiet voice, and the (lo-fi) technological imprint of the cassette recorder (through tape hiss, hum and the initial 'wow' characteristic of commencing recording with cheap tape transports). Her experience appears to be to document her own predicament, the anger around her, and her own resolve to create a reflection of her predicament and perhaps to strengthen herself through the process of making this experiential evidence. The listener, on the other hand, is eavesdropping on these two spaces simultaneously as we are aware of both the private space the girl has made for herself and the space outside filled with anger. The tangible presence of recording technology is critical in shaping a perception of the event as something 'coming to life' and we put ourselves into the scene through an empathy with the girl. The content of this work is so powerful that it can touch us through the technological haze. Paradoxically, the technological imprint itself emphasises the immediacy and apparent honesty of the material. We hear enough to be able to assemble the context, which stimulates an urge to listen more intently; to hear 'through' the lo-fi 'gauze' imposed by the tape recorder helps summon an imaginative response, acutely underlining the desperate nature of the situation. Thus, an image of a real experience is not dependent on 'high fidelity' reproduction but on our interpretation of the way the recording allows us access to the girl's experience.

Private moments revealed through sound recording are also found in *Parade* (1982) by John Cousins. The work is constructed from letter tapes made to send back to his home in New Zealand while the composer was on an extended trip to North America in 1972/3 – a time when the compact cassette had already become a ubiquitous and conveniently portable recording tool, and letter tapes of this kind were becoming a commonplace, seemingly a more personable way to correspond. This material revolves around Cousins' descriptions of events and experiences on that trip, particularly his encounters with aspects of American culture.

The work involves the literal presentation of recordings which, at the time, were not made with a view to their inclusion in any form of artwork: a light-hearted encounter with springs protruding from a hotel mattress, attempts to eat a spicy hot dog, descriptions of American football and ice hockey, an outdoor recording of a vociferous Christian preacher, snatches of TV sports commentaries and recordings of a football trophy parade. There is virtually no content that presents interaction between Cousins and any other person, emphasising the nature of the work as a reflection on solitary experiences, with the composer consistently narrating events in first person. Structurally, *Parade* is set out as a series of six vignettes, separated by short silences but unified by the presence of the central personality and by the reappearance of much of the material in altered contexts. There is also direct reference to the recording medium through the use of tape recorder switch-on/off sounds placed at the beginnings and endings of some of the vignettes, and the tape recorder is actually mentioned in one of the recordings (8'30"), emphasising the documentary origins of the materials.

Naturalistic recordings and electroacoustic transformations/distortions interact in a collage structure, with the transformation process providing a platform for the growth of dense textures in which voices are embedded. For example, the section starting at 2'38" opens with the hotel bed-springs 'encounter' and is progressively layered with further descriptions of the hotel, recordings of carillon and street music, and streams of abrasively distorted vocal sounds forming a richly contoured noise texture. The section approaches a point of spectral saturation by 4'30" and although the texture is extremely dense the voice of the preacher (previously heard at 1'54") can be heard embedded within it. The abstract texture falls away at 5'17", exposing the voice of the preacher yelling not-previously-heard words in a slightly more reverberant acoustic setting than in the earlier presentation of him. The final section (10'53 – 14'10") takes this process into the parade itself, with a crescendo of rapid changes in the apparent recording perspective, multiple layers of superimposition and recapitulations of materials previously heard, underpinned by the beat of a pounding bass drum, which closes the work with an image of a gradually receding procession. This kind of process is representative of the way materials are handled in *Parade*. Recordings are presented unembellished, but reappear or are pre-empted in transformed and collaged versions and are woven through abstract textures.

The contents of the field recordings themselves, although spontaneous, immediate and genuine, do not convey an overt sense of narrative or psychological development. Instead, we are witness to sequences of sonic snapshots, which, through processes of enrichment and obfuscation, collage and transformation, layering, cross-referencing and submergence in a cloak of rich and complex noise, consort to present us with images of the real and the surreal – or perhaps more tellingly, with metaphors for memory and emotive response. The fact that the same snatches of recordings are reiterated in new contexts epitomises the creative, fluid and contextual nature of memory; the specific experiences are the same, but the context in which they are recalled, and therefore the perspectives offered on them, have altered.

Ricordiamo Forlì: experience, memory and narrative

Ricordiamo Forlì (2005) is a hybrid documentary, radiophonic, electroacoustic work I have composed, attempting to reconstruct the wartime story of my own family through historical and contemporary recordings and an oral history narrative.[14] In the process of creating this work, I drew on the ideas set out above: namely, the capacity for recording to carry sound across time and location and to create new, heightened meaning in the service of the representation of experience and evocation of memory. That concept grew out of my first visit to the Italian city of Forlì in 2002. This was where my parents met in 1944, my mother an Italian civilian and my father a soldier in the Allied forces. The catalyst for this work was my experience of standing in Piazza Saffi, the central square of Forlì, and hearing bells from churches around the city, clearly audible across great distances. This gave me a strong sense of experiencing the sounds as something resonant of the place and its history, and the intimate connection to my own family background as though these sounds were 'voices' from the past – something permanent and alive – evoking a sense of being touched by something that others had experienced with the same immediacy over many years and through the violence of the war.

This poetic idea – that sound can remain as a 'living' entity and a quasi-tactile connection to the past – led me to search the archives of war correspondence reports held in New Zealand and in Britain[15] for materials relating to the 1943–5 Italian Campaign, in particular for materials which might in some way reflect interactions between soldiers and civilians, or contain actuality recordings from the relevant regions of the country. I wanted to try and connect aspects of my direct experience of Forlì with the impressions made on me through my parents' stories, their memories and interpretations of the events they endured, as well as to project, contextualise and 're-experience' historical events through the use of original wartime sound recordings. I also wanted to amplify and dramatise the emotional web of the events that are described and suggested, through electroacoustic music derived from both the historical materials and my own recordings made in Forlì. A unifying 'acousmêtre'[16] commentary fleshes out events and maintains narrative continuity, allowing the environmental, historical and imaginary settings of the work to be contextualised.

The work is structured around a central story that is reserved for the last third of the piece. My parents (Alex and Tarcisia) met in a farmhouse at Malmissole in 1944 (today a small collection of houses in the outskirts of Forlì). She was evacuated there following Allied bombing of Forlì and he was an 8th Army soldier using the farmhouse as shelter. When my mother and her family moved back into Forlì after the city's liberation, she and my father were able to continue seeing each other, since appalling weather brought about a military stalemate in the winter of 1944–5. On one of those occasions my mother was to have visited her sister who had relocated with her children to a large apartment complex. Instead, however, she pleaded with her mother to be allowed to see 'the New Zealand soldier' and that day, at about that time, the apartment block was bombed, killing two out of the three members of my family living there. My parents' meeting may have saved my mother's life and the work as a whole aims to sketch a context around the providence of that single event.

Most of the contemporary referential materials in this work were recorded on three trips to Forlì, and are used to support key themes around the ambience and sense of location as experienced through sound. In particular, the bells of Forlì's Duomo play a central role as a specific icon drawn from the town[17] for their more general symbolisms (a call to worship; sounds that define and express space and distance; sounds that express lament or jubilation) and as a malleable sound identity (its rhythmic pattern and its spectral makeup). A further unifying musical device is the use of the 'kiss' theme from Verdi's *Otello*, recorded on an out-of-tune upright piano. The theme is presented complete at various points in the work, but the notes are also reordered into a new thematic identity that seeps through much of the work. While the bell might be thought of as something 'spiritual' (a sound, although humanly initiated, relatively detached from human presence in actuality), the piano presents itself as something more grounded on a human scale, tactile, detuned and fallible. A useful connection between these two sounds was the significance of the note C-sharp in the 'kiss' theme, which is one of the approximate spectral centres of the bell of the Duomo that is used extensively as a sound icon and as a component in mixing and signal processing. The attack-resonance morphological identity of the bell also allowed for various kinds of spectral fusions between it and piano notes, such as the slow unfolding of bell partials out of the high C-sharp of Verdi's theme in the passage commencing at 36'53" (Track 2 on the accompanying CD). Linking these two sonic identities materially has the potential to evoke for the listener not just a sense that the sounds are inhabiting the same 'mixed' space, but that they are fused metaphorically and are indicative of an imaginative world, or a world of memory in which identities may cross over each other.

A number of other supporting sound references were employed: for example, weather (rain, thunder), bicycles, the resonant interiors of churches, footsteps and record-surface noise from the war correspondence recordings. These, along with the core sounds of bells, the piano and voices, form a network of identities that are transformed and interrelated using a wide range of processing methods. These generally lean on the associative aspects of the sounds but they also steer sounds toward more abstractly shaped patterns of extension, expectation and textural development. The main goal of these kinds of distinctions and relationships is to dramatise individual stories and provide aural images that link aspects of the larger narrative. For example, a short bridge section early in the work, at 2'17", is derived from various transformations of the spectral components of the bell. It aims to convey an image of a vaguely remembered or illusory reconstruction of bells, taking on an exaggerated, sinister quality following reference to Nazi atrocities in Forlì (Track 3).

The historical recordings themselves presented a number of distinct styles of reporting and reflecting on events, which offered me different perspectives on how to develop the narrative. As Klaus Schöning has observed, although *original tone* reporting 'can be an informative document on reality...what is reported is not identical with the entire authentic occurrence reported on' and recordings such as these are influenced by the reporting style and individual experiences of the speaker (Schöning, 1986: 37).[18] In this case, some were stiffly realised impersonal reports, while others were more emotive and poetic, relating personal narratives, such as Douglas Willis' story of a children's funeral procession in the rain, followed by a convoy of 8th Army vehicles, or Wynford Vaughan-Thomas' description of a farmhouse where an Italian family was sheltered in the cellar at 23'37" (Track 4). There were also 'actuality' recordings made during battles or in the presence of a public, such as the one involving the rather awkward but touching description by A.L. Curry of New Zealand soldiers entering Florence after its liberation, found in the work at 26'37" (Track 5).

I was seeking an expression of collective memory and for the preserved traces of events, which, outside of the recollections that had been passed to me by my parents, might confirm the context if not the actuality of their experience. In all of these original recordings, the natural self-reference of the surface noises inherent in the decay processes of the particular recording medium (direct-to-disc gramophone recordings made in the field) brought an aura of experiential authenticity to them – acoustical traces fixed in time as unique documents of specific experience, functioning now for me as surrogate memory. The intention was for these elements not to be simply illustrative, but to have a universalising function by being bound into the story as elements of the wider narrative.

There were also many descriptive references to sound in these reports and these were a significant part of my parents' war memories. For instance, my mother felt intense fear at what she described as the 'metallic' sounds of shells and bombs landing close by; and my father experienced (assumed) psychological warfare near Forlì, with the sounds of trains being heard clearly in the distance, when all soldiers knew that railway lines in the area had been virtually obliterated over the preceding months. One further idea of this kind used in *Ricordiamo Forlì* was the story of an 'acousmatic' aeroplane of unknown origin, colloquially called 'Pippo' – probably an illusion as a single entity, and the result of rumour (Perry, 2003). Pippo was heard at night in the skies of Northern Italy, reported to occasionally drop bombs, or flares, which Alan Perry describes thus:

> Pippo functioned as an audible Panopticon – a Panacousticon – droning omnipresent above the blackout. Very few people claim ever to have seen Pippo, but they swear they heard his drone each evening. Like a prison guard, Pippo surveyed the Italian inmates gripped by fear as they lived under the conditions of German occupation, civil war, and Allied bombardment. He made his presence known audibly as he passed over and visibly in any damage ascribed to him. But he remained unverifiable, for people thought that he was always present. As one man [Carlo Mingardi] remembers...'One night I was in the country and went outside. I did not see or hear a thing. And yet, I swear that if I had really really wanted, I could have heard something'.

(Perry, 2003: 132)

The story of Pippo was developed as one section of the work, both as a contextual 'aside' to the narrative, and a place in the work where the tension felt through the sound of an unseen enemy added a new element of drama. This extract, from 20'20", includes the narration of Franco Bianchini (Track 6).

A central idea in *Ricordiamo Forlì* is the projection of experience through recordings that function as containers of memory, through oral history in the form of reminiscence and original wartime recordings as 'surviving' artefacts. These support a central theme of the work, namely the striving for normal human relationships in the midst of extreme fear and anxiety. An interview recorded with my father in 2005, shortly after one of our visits to Forlì, provided a natural structure for the last half of the work, leading with clarity through a series of events enhanced by poignant specific memories, representing moments relived as reminiscence. Edward S. Casey characterises reminiscing as something distinct from the more functional, or even involuntary act of remembering. To relive the past in reminiscence, he claims, is

> a matter of *actively re-entering* the 'no longer living worlds' of that which is irrevocably past. In reliving the past, we try to re-enter such worlds not just as they were – which is, strictly speaking, impossible – but as they are now rememberable in and through reminiscence...[R]eminiscing can be said to be a way, an essentially privileged and especially powerful way, of *getting back inside our own past more intimately, of reliving it from within.*

> (Casey, 2000: 107, 109)

It was from exactly that kind of analysis that the whole ensemble of materials in *Ricordiamo Forlì* was conceived. The work represents an attempt to gain insight into the way a specific soundscape experience functioned as a trigger for imagination by bringing together two core dimensions of the experience of past events: human memory articulated through reminiscence and its evidential mirror in sound recording. We are made aware of both past and present when we are confronted with reminiscence as in my father's commentary. This extract from 39'51" is an example: the subject matter is 'the past' but it is relived at a time detached from that past (Track 7). At the same time, 'reliving' is supported by memory-images and emotions that shape the substance and nature of the recollection. Conversely, the war correspondence reports as artefacts originate from the actual time and place of the war, with media and signal degradation that further contextualises them. In this work, they provide a sense of some of the missing experiential foundation that gives meaning to the articulation of memory through reminiscence. These two types of oral history material are separated by sixty years of intervening time, forming opposite ends of the 'documentary' telescope. Since the work is set in a nominal 'present', in reference to which the war took place six decades earlier, sound recording itself provides both a vehicle for the immortalisation of reminiscence, and a window on the traces of historical events as they occurred. In addition, the more abstract materials and transformed sounds are a means of reinventing the aura of experience and memory, as a foil to narrative and offering more connotative and metaphorical sonic environments. These musically shaped transformative extensions of the materials provide a reflective space for the listener in the presence of the unfolding story, with past and present projected as existing in a continuous interaction between a place, its soundscape and memory, such as in this example from 15'08" evoking the harsh winters of the 1943–5 Italian campaign (Track 8).

Like the other works discussed in this chapter, *Ricordiamo Forlì* draws on the propensity for sound recording to reproduce traces of lived experience, making that experience available for repeated scrutiny and questioning, allowing us to explore all the referential, sensual and connotative dimensions of sound – in one sense a metaphor for the capacity of human memory and imagination to cross-fertilise in the search for meaning in our condition. In an age of 'sound bites' and a plethora of synthetic audiovisual experience via broadcast and other electronic media, the scope for sound recording to function as an active extension of our sensibilities, and – through creative consideration of its potentials – as a means to gain a deeper understanding of our place in the world, confirms its crucial role in the development of electroacoustic arts.

Notes

1   See Meyer (1994) for further discussion of these aesthetic views.

2   The notion of the 'sound image' in this sense is developed in Young (2007).

3   Schaeffer acknowledged this kind of listening but deliberately steered his theory away from an integration with it as a musical tool: 'In fact, Pythagoras' curtain is not enough to discourage our curiosity about causes, to which we are instinctively, almost irresistibly drawn. But the repetition of the physical signal, which recording makes possible, assists us here in two ways: by exhausting this curiosity, it gradually brings the sonorous object [*l'objet sonore*] to the fore as a perception worthy of being observed for itself; on the other hand, as a result of ever more attentive and more refined listenings, it progressively reveals to us the richness of this perception' (Schaeffer, 1966/2004: 78).

4   See Norman (1996) for a discussion of this idea.

5   Even though in the sphere of analogue sound recording we might find some element of Benjamin's aura attached to, say, an original master tape or to physically edited sub-mixes, these artefacts are not in themselves a tangible part of the way the musical work itself is mediated to an audience. Schaeffer also made a point of distinguishing magnetic tape as *support sonore* from the *objet sonore* – the latter being the real carrier of musical substance (Schaeffer, 1966: 95–6).

6   It is out of a defensive reaction to this latter paradigm, Benjamin argues, that hermetic, socially disengaged notions of artistic purity emerged (Benjamin, 2002: 106).

7   Benjamin's argument here was politicised in the sense that the artistic implications were progressive in conjunction with a direct accessibility to a wide audience afforded by the medium.

8   See Kittler (1986/1999: 87ff) for a description of Freudian methods that use sound recording as a therapeutic aid.

9 There are notable exceptions, such as the provocative stance on the legitimacy of recording (Gould, 1990), and the special status of the studio-produced recording in popular music.

10 A date given immediately after a work's title refers to its date of composition. The discography cites its date of release on the recording that is consulted.

11 Described by Ferrari in Warburton (1998).

12 Schaeffer's four 'listening modes' attempt to summarise these divisions of emphasis in listening (Schaeffer, 1966: 112–28).

13 A full analysis of this work can be found in Lochhead (2005).

14 Ricordiamo Forlì © 2005, John Young, Giosuè Carducci (APRA) / 2007 YMX MéDIA (SOCAN). First released in 2007 on the disc 'Lieu-temps', empreintes DIGITALes, IMED 0787. http://www.empreintesdigitales.com

15 Sourced in the Imperial War Musuem's Sound Archive and the Sound Archive of New Zealand.

16 This term is used by Michel Chion to describe the setting of a detached 'super-voice' in cinema (Chion, 1990/1994: 129–31).

17 The original bell tower of the Duomo was in fact blown up in late 1944 by the retreating Nazi army.

18 The radio commentary made at the scene of the Hindenburg airship disaster of 1937 is a particularly dramatic example.

References

Benjamin, W. (2002) 'The Work of Art in the Age of Its Technological Reproducibility', in H. Eiland and M.W. Jennings (eds) *Selected Writings, Volume 3, 1935–1938*, pp.101–33. Cambridge, MA: Belknap Press of Harvard University Press. Original (1936/1989 posthumous) as 'Das Kunstwerk im Zeitalter seiner technischen Reproduzierbarkeit', in R. Tiedemann and H. Schweppenhäuser (eds) *Walter Benjamin, Gesammelte Schriften, volume 7*, pp.350–84. Frankfurt am Main: Suhrkamp.

Borges, J.L. (1964) 'Funes the Memorious', in D.A. Yates and J.E. Irby (eds) *Labyrinths*, pp.87–95. London: Penguin. Original (1944) as 'Funes el memorioso' in *Ficciones*. Buenos Aires: Editorial Sur.

Casey, E.S. (2000) *Remembering: A Phenomenological Study*. Bloomington: Indiana University Press.

Chion, M. (1994) *Audio-vision: Sound on Screen*. Trans. C. Gorbman. New York: Columbia University Press. Original (1990) as *L'Audio-Vision*. Paris: Nathan.

Ferrari, L. (1996) 'I was Running in So Many Directions', *Contemporary Music Review* 15 (1–2): 95–102.

Gould, G. (1990) 'The Prospects of Recording', in T. Page (ed.) *The Glenn Gould Reader*, pp.331–53. New York: Vintage.

Hughes, R. (1991) *The Shock of the New: Art and the Century of Change*. London: Thames and Hudson.

Kittler, F.A. (1999) *Gramophone, Film, Typewriter*. Trans. G. Winthrop-Young und M. Wutz. Stanford: Stanford University Press. Original (1986) as *Grammophon Film Typewriter*. Berlin: Brinkmann & Bose.

Lochhead, J. (2005) 'Found Sound and the Aestheticization of the "Real": McInturff's *By Heart*.' Paper presented at the Critical Studies/Experimental Practices (CS/EP) Intermedia Festival. University of California, San Diego.

McNabb, M. (1986) 'Computer Music: Some Aesthetic Considerations', in S. Emmerson (ed.) *The Language of Electroacoustic Music*, pp.141–53. London: Macmillan.

Meyer, L.B. (1994) *Music, The Arts and Ideas*. Chicago: University of Chicago Press.

Norman, K. (1996) 'Real-World Music as Composed Listening', *Contemporary Music Review* 15 (1–2): 1–27.

_____ (2004) *Sounding Art: Eight Literary Excursions Through Electronic Music*. Aldershot: Ashgate.

Perry, A.R. (2003) 'Pippo: An Italian Folklore Mystery of World War II', *Journal of Folklore Research* 40 (2): 115–48.

Schaeffer, P. (1966) *Traité des objets musicaux*. Paris: Seuil.

_____ (2004) 'Acousmatics', in C. Cox and D. Warner (eds) *Audio Culture: Readings in Modern Music*, pp.76–81. New York: Continuum. Original (1966) as 'Acousmatics', in *Traité des objets musicaux*, pp.91–8. Paris: Seuil.

Schafer, R.M. (1994) *The Soundscape: Our Sonic Environment and the Tuning of the World*. Rochester, VT: Destiny.

Schöning, K. (1986) 'On the Development of Acoustic Literature in Radio: The German Hörspiel', *Michigan Quarterly Review* 25 (1): 28–39.

Truax, B. (1996) 'Soundscape, Acoustic Communication and Environmental Sound Composition', *Contemporary Music Review* 15 (1–2): 49–65.

_____ (2001) *Acoustic Communication*. Westport, CT: Ablex.

Warburton, D. (1998) 'Luc Ferrari' [Interview, 22 July 1998], *Paris Transatlantic*, URL (consulted October 2005): http://www.paristransatlantic.com/magazine/interviews/ferrari.html

Westerkamp, H. (2002) 'Linking Soundscape Composition and Acoustic Ecology', *Organised Sound* 7 (1): 51–6.

Wishart, T. (1996) *On Sonic Art*. Amsterdam: Harwood.

Young, J. (2007) 'Reflections on Sound Image Design in Electroacoustic Music', *Organised Sound* 12 (1): 25–33.

Discography

Cousins, J. (1993) 'Parade' on *Sleep Exposure*. Ode Records CD MANU 1436.

Ferrari, L. (1995) 'Presque rien No. 1' on *Presque rien*. INA-GRM, CD INA-C 2008 275 482.

Harrison, J. (1996) 'Hot Air' and 'Unsound Objects' on *Articles Indéfinis*. Empreintes Digitales CD IMED 9627.

McInturff, R. [1997] 'By Heart' on *Music from SEAMUS 6*. Society for Electroacoustic Music in the United States CD EAM 9701.

Westerkamp, H. (1997) 'Talking Rain' on *Harangue 1*. Earsay CD es-98001.

_____ (1996) 'Kits Beach Soundwalk' on *Transformations*. Empreintes Digitales CD IMED 9631.

Young, J. (2007) 'Ricordiamo Forlì' on *Lieu-temps*. Empreintes Digitales DVD-A IMED 0787.

SABINE SCHÄFER AND JOACHIM KREBS

Deleuze and the Sampler as an Audio-Microscope:
On the Music-Historical and Aesthetic Foundations of Digital Micro-Acoustic Recording and EndoSonoScopy as the Process of Analysis and Production[1]

The properly musical content of music is plied by becomings-woman, becomings-child, becomings-animal; however, it tends, under all sorts of influences, having to do also with instruments, to become *progressively* more molecular in a kind of cosmic lapping through which the inaudible makes itself heard and the imperceptible appears as such: no longer the songbird, but the sound molecule.

Gilles Deleuze and Félix Guattari (1980/1987: 248)[2]

I

As early as the 1820s, one of the main representatives of German Romantic philosophy, Georg Wilhelm Friedrich Hegel, in his lectures on aesthetics, stated the following remarkable and far-reaching facts:

In certain stages of art-consciousness and presentation, the abandonment and distortion of natural formations is not *unintentional* lack of technical skill or practice, but intentional alteration which proceeds from and is demanded by what is in the artist's mind.

(Hegel, 1832–45/1975: 74)

About a century later, Walter Benjamin elaborated these ideas further in his epoch-making, visionary study 'The Work of Art in the Age of Mechanical Reproduction' and remarked that '[t]o an ever greater degree the work of art reproduced becomes the work of art designed for reproducibility' (Benjamin, 1939/1982: 226). He also stated that around 1920 the standard of technical reproduction had already succeeded in making the entirety of existing artworks its object, and that such reproduction would also have to find its own place among creative techniques, resulting in radical changes in the effect that artworks have (Benjamin, 1982: 221–2).

From the beginning, it was thus obvious to the visionary thinkers and artists of the time that those technological inventions and developments that are based on the principles of electricity should not be used merely to reproduce existing artworks in larger quantities for their commercial exploitation. Instead, they believed that the new technical opportunities should mainly serve the qualitatively intensified production of works of sound art specifically created for the electrical medium (the 'instrument') of the loudspeaker. Accordingly, the loudspeaker, for example, would become a mediator of music specifically produced for it instead of remaining 'just' an authentic intermediary for vocal and instrumental music.

The rapid developments that took place during the course of the twentieth century in the electrical creation of sounds, as well as the recording, broadcasting and communication of music – in diverse genres such as dance and popular music, film and video, electronic/electroacoustic music, and computer multimedia art – confirm this in many different ways. Electronically created sounds are today omnipresent as part of film, television, stage and radio plays, and also in their function as electronic signals, such as we find in mobile-phone ring tones and in acoustic design. (In this they are similar to the world-wide Anglo-American pop music, which is mainly created by electronic instruments and practically depends on technical media for its entire existence, communication and mass distribution.)

Hence, artificially shaped movements of air (sound waves – and what else would the art form of music be in a fundamental, physical sense?) that are, for example, directly and immediately produced by a singer or instrumentalist, and are *not* just generated through a resonating membrane, streaming towards us from loudspeakers, have today become a rare and 'exclusive' event. The manifold and new correlations and interdependencies between music and technological development, and the modified receptive behaviour of new types of listeners, caused for instance by the independence of space and time, have frequently been the object of research and description. These include interpretations that are adapted to this kind of listener, arrived at by interpreters who are 'playing it safe' in that they are more interested in a 'faithful rendition' of a work by means of recognisable similarities to their previously published interpretations, with which the audience is already familiar, than in taking up the position of a spontaneous and creatively emphatic '(inter)mediator' for the work. This essay will primarily consider the effects of technical progress on the *actual* process of creating the artwork.

Accordingly, if one searches the history of music for the beginnings and first examples of 'acoustical artworks' (in Benjamin's sense as briefly described above), which, for example, do not use electrical recording devices merely as an intermediary for the acoustical documentation *of* music(al performances), and do not demote loudspeakers to instruments used for 'musical coverage', but which above all employ 'the power of nature' phenomenon of electricity to produce the actual artificial tones, sounds and noises, one inevitably encounters two kinds of 'acoustic art' in the original realm of 'Central European Art Music' that emerged roughly at the same time as applied art forms, including the radio play and film music. These are *elektronische Musik* as it first developed in Germany, and *musique concrète* with its French origins. Both represent the first genuine (and pure) categories and forms of music for the loudspeaker as an 'instrument'. Since in these genres composers/producers themselves are no longer in need of interpretative mediation for their acoustic artworks, which are fixed in their form and development through recording devices and storage media, the composer is always also the performer and interpreter, as it were, of his/her own work. Not only is s/he able to secure potential 'version(s)' of his/her work, which s/he records in an optimal way, and the greatest degree of authenticity in their performance, but s/he also has more flexibility and independence in making available and distributing his/her works of audio art.[3]

It appears to be a fact, too, that the so-called amateur is immediately able to grasp the 'coherence' of electronically produced sounds coming from a loudspeaker even upon first hearing, and the force of habit does the rest to create the impression that these are 'better' suited to the electrical instrument of the loudspeaker, when compared to instrumental sounds. And is it not curious indeed that piano music, for example, reproduced via a loudspeaker makes the latter sound like a piano, but not look like it? Instead, it still looks like a loudspeaker!

Admittedly, in all these cases the electromagnetic reproduction device will only 're-create' what was produced at an earlier time, but it does not 're-produce' anything that could exist without the former. Instead, it 'produces' the 'original' itself in conjunction with the loudspeakers. Musique concrète is a special case in this context. Based on the technologically grounded noise art of Futurism promoted by Filippo Tommaso Marinetti and Luigi Russolo around 1912–13, Pierre Schaeffer created the 'music of noises' in France from 1948 onwards (he himself referred to it as 'musique concrète' after 1949). By contrast with the electronically created sound material of *elektronische Musik*, Schaeffer took his sound and noise material from all that is audible, recorded with electric microphones. In his collages of sound and noise, produced from all sorts of everyday noise, sounds of nature like the wind, rain, the rushing of water, and sounds of animals and humans, he sought 'direct' contact with sound material without any electrons as intermediaries (Schaeffer, 1952). Thus, in addition to the 'instruments' of the microphone and the loudspeaker, the techniques of manipulation and splicing by means of the tape recorder became relevant for creative production and performance. In this kind of music, even though the sound material was not produced electronically, we encounter more than just artificially arranged 'reproductions' of natural sounds and noises, as one might at first be inclined to assume. Instead, we find original and autonomous works of sound art that could only be produced with the help of the newly developed instruments, which in turn could not have been designed and built without appropriate technological developments in this field.

Composers and sound artists have always taken advantage of the various possible interactions and reciprocal relationships between the 'personal–abstract', i.e. the imaginary in art production, and the 'collective–concrete', i.e. the materialised and continually progressive technical developments (such as instrument making), and their artistic inspirations have found expression in the creative implementation of these interactions. These radical developmental leaps have repeatedly presented sound art with new instrumental possibilities for the sonic realization of the purely imaginary, the 'utopian', and the (pre)thought. Thus, Robert Moog's invention and development of the synthesizer during the late 1960s was regarded as an intellectual and almost instrumental accelerator for the developments in electronic music.

This is neither the place nor the occasion to continue examining aspects of purely electronically created music, because in our joint TopoSonicComposition projects since 1995 we have consistently and consciously given up *purely* electronically produced sound material. The synthesizer as an instrument was regarded as *the* revolution in the field of electronic music, as an 'instrumental authority' that provoked radical changes. In contrast to this, the impact of the (acoustic) production process of digital sampling technology is still completely underestimated by many. This technology developed around 1985 in conjunction with computer-aided advances, and led to radical changes and the emergence of artistically innovative production possibilities. It proved to be truly 'epoch-making' for the production and distribution of music world wide. In this process, the central production unit is represented by the computer, in the form of an applied 'musical instrument' and a MIDI-controlled, digital sound processor: in short, a 'sampler'.

The sampler represents, as it were, a circular, closed and thus independent production unit for digital recording, storage, modification and reproduction of (analogue) sound events of any kind. It would, therefore, have been the ideal instrument for Schaeffer's above-mentioned *musique concrète*. However, after he started to include electronically produced sounds and noises in his works from 1956 onwards, Schaeffer in 1958 had already re-named his 'Groupe de recherches de musique concrète', founded in 1951, as 'Groupe de recherches musicales' (Eimert and Humpert, 1973: 215ff.; Riemann, 1967: 618–19). Some people, therefore, believed that the 'historic task' of *musique concrète* was more or less complete and that its short history spanning one decade should officially be declared as over. We completely disagree with that! For is it not true that once again the newly constructed, computer-aided instruments for the recording, production and re-production of sounds and noises – instruments based on the rapid digital-technological developments of the 1980s – were the ones that were able to provide the necessary innovative impact from mid-1980s onwards? The purpose was to create a new acoustic art form – a *purely* auditory art of sound – that solely consists of artificially arranged ('composed') natural sounds and noises. And is it not equally true that through the digitised process of production and ordering of events, these sounds and noises become, in their 'innermost' selves, synchronised, artistic elements to be placed in a network, since all media and instruments used for their production are based on the same logical, digital principles? (What a greatly enlarged opportunity!)

Unfortunately, the first developmental years of the sampler as a creatively usable instrument were the last years of the 1980s, and the first of the 1990s, a time when – similar to the previous developmental history of the synthesizer in the early 1970s – it was under the dictates of a commercially optimised exploitation of music through the minimisation of costs associated with production processes. Due to digitised and 'pixel-exact' access to all parameters of every abstractly imaginable and concretely available (or made available) audio material in all their acoustic dimensions and materializations, it became possible to generate, for example, so-called 'acoustic clones' of real instruments. These then serve as tonal surrogates for the now-superfluous musicians and their instruments. The imaginary presence of such 'clones' created 'only' through sound allows those cheap imitations to yield a very remarkable 'real' simulation of 'authentic' instrumental sound. (No more, but no less either!) Such presence is caused by physical (visual) absence, since it is only conveyed 'indirectly' through sound and loudspeaker (invisible, but audible (!) existence). The 'misuse' of the sampler as a superficial and simplistically ostentatious, pseudo-modern 'sound producer', exhibiting its continually available, cost-effective use in the computer generated creation of short-lived, mass-produced items for video, film and television that are manufactured solely with commercial aspects in mind, has also become the conventional practice of our time. In the still relatively short history of the evolution of digital sampling and sound-processing technologies, spanning barely two decades so far, there is no telling (even for a sound artist who thinks and works as a visionary) which artistic–dynamic–innovative potential for the future of music in general and sound art in particular is still dormant in the mechanical–artificial aspects of the sampler–loudspeaker 'instrumental duo'.[4]

Elementary, direct, pixel-exact ('particle-exact') access to endogenous–acoustic (micro)dimensions of 'sound' in itself – whether pre-recorded 'natural' sounds or electronically produced 'artificial' sounds – was already suggested in other contexts and made possible by digital-technological developments. This gives the potential for networks of spatio-temporally synchronized, hierarchy-free complexes, and is due principally to the generally *unspecific* sound character of the sampler. For example, in contrast to the synthesizer and conventional musical instruments, the sampler itself does not create its own specific and individually identifiable sounds, timbres and colours. Instead, within all the aforementioned limitations with respect to the 'faithful rendering' of naturally created sounds via electroacoustic loudspeakers, it reproduces, preferably one-to-one, the analogue sound event, which was previously digitally recorded in the traditional way with the help of microphones (a record-and-playback machine, as it were).

By contrast to analogue recording technology, during the process of digital recording an analogue signal is transformed into a digital signal, and individual sounds are depicted as numbers and recorded as numerical codes. This results in not only a 'linear' and less-distorted sound quality, and thus a 'higher' fidelity of sound reproduction, but also in the availability for a highly differentiated creative processing of the digitally stored sound materials, which at first appear unlimited regarding human thought categories. Unlike traditional tape technologies, artistic possibilities of access and production are hugely extended, and even amateurs immediately realize and understand these (quality-enhancing) dimensions when, for example, they compare the lack of potential for the modifications of their older, analogue photographs with what is offered in this connection by modern digital image editing programmes that can easily be realised nowadays with any PC and appropriate software.

Since the 1990s, technologies for the digital modification and computer generation of images became the standard in international, mostly commercially oriented, professional video, film and TV productions. However, there are comparatively few artistic examples in the field of 'pure' art music that utilise, in an artistically valid manner, the innovative–technological and, above all, the utopian–artistic possibilities for creating synergies between the production unit, the sampler, and the instrument of mediation, the loudspeaker. Still in its simplest form and with little memory, the sampler was used – if at all – rather sporadically from the mid-1980s onwards, mainly in live-electronic experimental jazz and improvisational music as well as in multimedia performance and action-art scenes.[5]

Mainly due to an improved technological development in the manufacturing of storage chips, and the resulting huge extension of memory capacities and production possibilities, the musician, composer and soundscape artist Joachim Krebs managed from the mid-1990s onwards (first mainly in his electroacoustic sound art project 'Artificial Soundscapes') to develop and formulate an extremely extended and therefore radically modified artistic and music–aesthetic approach to electroacoustic sound art – both in theory and practice – based on the now full-fledged and highly evolved technology of sampling.

To immediately counter any misunderstanding that might arise: naturally, we are not interested in an uncritical, exclusively affirmative relationship with technological development as such. We have no intention of supporting a solely mechanistically motivated, continually 'improving' concept of development marked by belief-in-progress, which surely appears infantile today in the twenty-first century, given the definitely negative global effects that are (also) happening. Much less should we want to advocate the thesis that 'new' music would almost automatically be generated through new technologies or new instruments. Quite the reverse: on the one hand, it took years of practice and experience with the artistic use of the sampler (since 1985) in many live concerts and studio productions, and on the other hand an intellectual–theoretical background formed by the writings and 'colossal' philosophical system of the great visionary French thinker Gilles Deleuze, to develop a 'pure' sound art directly in the musical tradition of, for example, the Italian Futurists from about 1910, of Dadaistic phonetic sound poetry of the 1920s, of tape-based sound/noise collages of French *musique concrète*, and of the electroacoustic compositions of Luc Ferrari and Iannis Xenakis, to name but a few. A purely 'acoustic art' that gives precedence to the sensory impression involved in the sheer process of listening. And all this with the smallest contribution from the visual–performative and the multimedia character of installation, and finally combined and composed from natural sound and noise materials recorded and modified with the sampler.

II

So far, we have focused on the relationship between 'autonomous' production of art and technical progress, especially with respect to the radically innovative possibilities for recording, production and reproduction offered by digital sampling technology. Whereas the previous remarks were related rather more to historical–philosophical, music technological and music sociological thought, the following pages are mainly devoted to the above mentioned philosophical and theoretical foundations that, among other reasons, were behind the original development of the process of 'EndoSonoScopy' (interior sound representation), which we use in our work and describe below.

In 1920 Paul Klee (undoubtedly one of the most important twentieth-century artists) formulated that momentous – and soon-to-be-famous – principle about his quest for another ('true') reality that must be hidden behind the accustomed appearance of things, a quest that at first sight seems infantile: 'Art does not reproduce the visible but makes visible' (Klee, 1920/1961a: 76). With this statement, Klee pointed out the shortcoming that we described earlier, namely that the production of art – whether with or without the use of technology – would fall far too short of its aim if it stopped at *only* the purely illustrative reproduction of surfaces and superficial manifestations of nature or matter. It would attempt to doubly and unnecessarily imitate only those phenomena that could also exist without art (or technology), the result being never quite the same as the original. However, apart from the aspect of 'making visible' the previously 'invisible' (and that should not be imagined as a cheap magician's trick), Klee first of all intended to point out the process-like and immanent movements inherent in the actual, artistically structured 'event of making visible' itself.

The main concern here is, therefore, the representation of dynamic 'ways of becoming', and not the static condition of 'being'. For example, one should not reproduce the flower, but the 'blossoming',[6] not the river, but the 'flowing', not the dog, but the 'barking',[7] etc. At the same time, the following statement by Klee involves an important 'utopian spark', to use a term by Ernst Bloch: 'Besides, I have no desire to show this man as he is, but only as he might be' (Klee, 1956/1961b: 95).

Deleuze and Guattari, in whose writings Klee appears in various contexts, wrote in *A Thousand Plateaus*: 'then, adopting an "earthbound position," the artist turns his or her attention to the microscopic, to crystals, molecules, atoms, and particles, not for scientific conformity, but for movement, for nothing but immanent movement' (Deleuze and Guattari, 1987: 337). This passage makes it very clear that this is not only about things that are 'concealed' or another reality behind objects, but instead about (concretely, as it were!) the concealed, originating directly from the micro-dimensions of the 'interior', and about the dynamic process of setting free some intrinsic, hitherto 'unthinkable powers' and the 'realization/externalization of inner intensities'.[8]

From their own (internal) centre, with a momentum and self-intensifying development, ever more extensive and consistent materials come into being, which in turn release ever more intensive powers and energy, or are able to create them in the first place. Consequently, the continuously varied generation of matter turns into an active, 'synergetic–symbiotic' and direct relationship of material and force instead of being solidified in a formal, static–mechanistic separation, a pseudo-dialectical 'contrast of dichotomy' – here: matter, there: form. 'It is now a question', as Deleuze and Guattari continue, 'of elaborating a material charged with harnessing forces of a different order' (Deleuze and Guattari, 1987: 342).

What might all of this mean for the physical medium of 'artificially moved air' and thus, in the broadest sense, for the art of music, which represents itelf as a temporal–dynamic 'acoustic time art/art of time', characterised especially by and in the linearly directed flow of time? Deleuze, who repeatedly described in his writings the manifold kinds of relationships between his philosophical thoughts and the medium of sound, wrote the following in his chapter with Guattari titled '1837 – Of the Refrain' from *A Thousand Plateaus*:

> Music molecularizes sound matter and in so doing becomes capable of harnessing nonsonorous forces such as Duration and Intensity. *Render Duration sonorous.*
>
> (Deleuze and Guattari, 1987: 343)

> The molecular material has even become so deterritorialized that we can no longer even speak of matters of expression, as we did in romantic territoriality. *Matters of expression are superseded by a material of capture.* The forces to be captured are no longer those of the earth, which still constitute a great expressive Form, but the forces of an immaterial, nonformal, and energetic Cosmos...This is the postromantic turning point: the essential thing is no longer forms and matters, or themes, but forces, densities, intensities.
>
> (Deleuze and Guattari, 1987: 342–3)

And in the context of compositional processes employed by the French–American composer Edgar Varèse, he wrote about

> a musical machine of consistency, a *sound machine* (not a machine for reproducing sounds), which molecularizes and atomizes, ionizes sound matter, and harnesses a cosmic energy. If this machine must have an assemblage, it is the synthesizer. By assembling modules, source elements, and elements for treating sound (oscillators, generators, and transformers), by arranging microintervals, the synthesizer makes

audible the sound process itself, the production of that process, and puts us in contact with still other elements beyond sound matter.

(Deleuze and Guattari, 1987: 343)

Deleuze and Guattari wrote these statements in the 1970s. And as we described above, this was the first decade of the synthesizer's development. The (digital) era of the sampler, which began in the mid-1980s, had naturally not arrived yet. While developing the process of 'EndoSonoScopy' during the late 1990s, we quickly discovered how accurate Deleuze and Guattari's statements – concerning the synthesizer, for instance – were with respect to the instrument of the sampler, which was, obviously, completely unknown to them at the time. This specially designed micro-acoustic procedure for the recording and analysis of the largely unexplored and unknown (internal) micro-dimensions of 'naturally' created sounds and noises employs the sampler in an original, specific way, almost exclusively as a so-called 'audio microscope'.

The concept of a musical sound and consistency machine mentioned by Deleuze and Guattari, surely also in a metaphorical, even 'metamorphic' sense, and meant in a concrete and practical way related purely to electronically created 'sound matter', is realized here firstly in a 'real and practical' manner, and widened crucially by the extension of the term 'matter' to mean 'everything that sounds in this world', without limitations to 'man-made' sound matter that is generated usually electronically or instrumentally. Since the sampler generates the sound material, which is to be reproduced later, *exclusively* from acoustically 'foreign' materials that are previously digitally recorded – and does not create them itself like conventional instruments (this, of course, includes the synthesizer) – it is able, as an appropriate and central 'machine of sound molecularisation', to enter the omnipresent 'organic texture of sound' through a complex of computer-aided interfaces that can 'molecularise' – at least in acoustic terms – the fragment specimens (samples) taken from it. The sampler functions as a 'high-performance audio microscope' in this context, not only by digital 'internal sound' representation (EndoSonoScopy) and sound molecularisation, and making the 'inaudible' audible, but first and foremost, by rendering the process of sound production *itself* audible, and thereby preparing, even enabling, natural consistency formations, which the sound artist needs to produce artificially. Artificially creating the interdependent, natural–artificial consistency formations as a process of continuous variation, which permanently and dynamically fluctuates between the concrete and the abstract, is the prerequisite for evoking those unknown internal acoustic intensities and temporal permanencies. In their turn, these consistencies provide evidence of the existence of an imaginary–auditory landscape and vegetation that lives and thrives underneath the acoustical surfaces, as it were: the acoustically imagined habitat as an 'audio-sphere' for diverse 'audio-mutations' and acoustically oscillating, novel kinds of becoming and vanishing – a symbiosis between concrete naturalness and abstract artificiality.

It stands to reason that the basic audio materials for the creation of our TopoSonicCompositions should be taken from the spheres of nature, and especially from the animal world. And indeed, we received clear confirmation of the wide-spread scepticism many people display towards, for example, electronically produced sounds as 'synthetically dead material' even in our first trials with sound microscopy. For example, if you compare the internal richness of a grasshopper's 'song', which emerged over millions of years in a highly differentiated way, and is made audible for the first time by the process of sound microscopy, with the comparatively undifferentiated, monotonous and 'lifeless' sound signal of an electronic sound generator, or something similar, then, especially in the sound-microscoped, acoustical micro-levels of electronically produced sounds and noises, the lack of sound materials evoking 'inaudible–hidden' and 'unthinkable powers' becomes very obvious (clearly audible!). For the great opportunity of invoking those powers (at least acoustically) that are unthinkable for human beings is not to be found in the use of sound material imagined and produced by them in order to create audio artworks, but instead in immediately returning to the almost de-subjectivised material of expression existing in the diverse (sound microscoped) sounds of animals and noises of nature that lie beyond the imagination and productive powers of any human. The part of the production that is designated 'subjective and human' should then mainly be limited to the artistic–creative selection (what?) and artificial combination (when, where, who with whom / what with what?) of the previously molecularised, meticulously analysed and catalogued sound materials. In relation to this, one can listen to different sound examples on the attached CD. Tracks 9 to 11 feature, respectively, examples of the creative selection, and artificial combination of a single insect sound, which is layered with itself in a polyphonic mix in different degrees of augmentation. By contrast, track 12 is a SpacesoundMilieu with an artificial mixture of different kinds of animal and nature sounds.[9]

Another important advantage of utilising only the recordings of naturally produced sounds and noises from the three basic categories of natural resources (i.e. animal, nature and human) – particularly for the communication and reception our TopoSonic art – is the universal character of those sounds and noises with a natural origin, with which everyone is familiar and often intimate on an everyday basis. Despite the experimental and avant-garde aesthetic approach in all our TopoSonic artworks, this universal character allows many people spontaneous access to the actual TopoSonicComposition, without the need for certain previous, (nationally) marked, socio-cultural experience, let alone special expert knowledge that is often indispensable for an adequate reception of euro-centrically shaped new (classical) music.[10]

But what does one do now with all these sound materials one has selected, audio-microscoped, analysed, and catalogued according to artistic criteria (and which first appear to be rather diffuse and chaotic for human ears and minds) in order to create artificial elements out of them, and supply these with a potential for consistency, permanently fluctuating between the 'natural–concrete', which is already available, and the 'artificial–abstract', which must be artificially produced? Deleuze and Guattari wrote on this subject:

> Sometimes one overdoes it, puts too much in, works with a jumble of lines and sounds; then instead of producing a cosmic machine capable of 'rendering sonorous,' one lapses back to a machine of reproduction that ends up reproducing nothing but a scribble effacing all lines, a scramble effacing all sounds. The claim is that one is opening music to all events, all irruptions, but one ends up reproducing a scrambling that prevents any event from happening. All one has left is a resonance chamber well on the way to forming a black hole.
>
> (Deleuze and Guattari, 1987: 343–4)

> The material must be sufficiently deterritorialized to be molecularized and open onto something cosmic, instead of lapsing into a statistical heap. This condition is met only if there is a certain simplicity in the nonuniform material: a maximum of calculated sobriety in relation to the disparate elements and the parameters.
>
> (Deleuze and Guattari, 1987: 344)

> According to Varèse, in order for the projection to yield a highly complex form, in other words, a cosmic distribution, what is necessary is a simple figure in motion and a plane that is itself mobile; otherwise you get sound effects. Sobriety, sobriety: that is the common prerequisite for the deterritorialization of matters, the molecularization of material, and the cosmicization of forces.
>
> (Deleuze and Guattari, 1987: 344)

> Material thus has three principal characteristics: it is a molecularized matter; it has a relation to forces to be harnessed; and it is defined by the operations of consistency applied to it.
>
> (Deleuze and Guattari, 1987: 345)

Following the molecularisation of sound material, and the accompanying process of 'making audible/making thinkable' the inaudible and unthinkable powers that are to be captured, which in turn served for the acoustic evocation of (inaudible) concealed inner intensities, the compositional processes of 'auditory elementarisation' and artificial consistency formation gain increasing importance in the artificial creation of harmonious, and almost organically proliferating, growing TopoSonic artworks from those amorphous–heterogenous sound and noise materials. The process of TopoSonic elementarisation takes place during an artificially initiated production phase of TopoSonic intensification. During this phase, the acoustic presence of each individual sound element is increased through an intensifying transparency formation by selective partial amplification, attenuation or even elimination of individual acoustic parameters. Furthermore, the previously recorded particular 'acoustic aura (audio atmosphere)' surrounding each individual sound component gains noticeable plastic acoustic conciseness in the process of 'space microscoping' (or rather 'acoustic location microscoping'). One only retains and/or takes away the most elementary acoustic presences of the TopoSonic lines, locations, movements, durations, colours and velocities of the usable inner acoustic intensities in order to create naturally, and equally artificially, consistent TopoSonic habitats. This is achieved with the help of artificial blending of consistency formations that continue synchronous/asynchronous layering and the temporally successive series with a momentum of their own.

Even a TopoSonic environment first represents a condition of temporarily present and specific selection that appears static on the macro-structural level; it represents a blending and artificially composed combination of TopoSonic elements that are either similar or have been made similar to themselves, the latter via artificially created self-intensification (loops/warps) that have their own momentum, and via chains of repetition. The micro-structural internal levels of this TopoSonic environment of artificial and acoustically imagined habitats and artificially produced audio biospheres are, on the other hand, marked by a high level of 'internal' consistency that is also artificially produced. Such consistency is itself mainly characterised by the dynamic process of continuous variation of all vertical and diagonal 'harmonies', and simultaneously takes place in different time zones and dimensions with their own specific systems of time, relation and definition of speed(s).[11]

With respect to the question of artificial production of 'consistency formations' that points far beyond natural consistencies, may we add the following remarks as conclusion: two of the most important requirements for those artifically composable *consistencies* which at first appear in a continuously fluctuating acoustic 'twilight zone' – between pure concreteness and pure abstraction – are the acoustic processes of deconstruction and transformation. On the one hand, there is the process of the (partial) dissolution of the (non)sonic, *solely* concrete material of content and meaning, and on the other hand, their conversion into a purely sonic but *not just* abstract de-subjectivised material of expression, as it were. Both take place in the production process of TopoSonic molecularisation through audio microscoping, and the ensuing TopoSonic fragmentarisation with the possibly self-intensifying formation of loops, as described in detail above. For example, if you start, as in a picture puzzle, exclusively from a small detail (a 'sample', a so-called 'fragment specimen'), and are to guess visually the (whole) object that is reproduced only through fragments, and when the identification of the object is further complicated by enlargements and selective visual depiction of details (that serve to render visible the unknown dimensions of the exterior, visual form and shape of the object), then during the process of TopoSonic microscoping, the concrete acoustic material of content and meaning of the naturally created sounds and noises linked clearly to a living thing, to a natural (physical) phenomenon or a concrete object, is transformed into a *seemingly* different, concrete material of content, or often entirely dissolves – as the audio fragment becomes smaller and the magnification of sound microscoping higher – into more or less abstract material of expression:

> In the mind of each listener, even beyond (extra)musical meanings and contents, in a 'twilight zone', individual, audio-inspired imagination can unfold, in permanent fluctuation between (!) pure naturalness and pure abstraction. This is achieved all the more successfully as, for example, animal sounds, natural noises or the human voice when singing also become 'something else': pure line, pure space, pure colour, pure sound, pure rhythm, pure movement, pure becoming...pure state of being...The aim is no longer to develop a form or to impose a shape on matter, but to create 'ways of becoming' of foreign internal intensities and de-subjectivised affects. Form(s) should dissolve, for example, to render audible the tiniest variations of speed *between* combined (composed) locations, and push fast or slow movements to the state of immobility (stillness). The TopoSonic soundscape artificially created by the TopoSonicArtist thus appears to be an ensemble of de-subjectivised material of expression in a space, time and sound matrix (layered in all directions) of 'temporally' horizontal and rhythmic, melodic TopoSonicFigure and the 'spatially' vertical and resonant harmonic TopoSonicStructure.
>
> (Schäfer and Krebs, 2004)

Information about the sound examples on the accompanying CD:

Four Spacesound Milieus

Just as in all other works by the artist duo, these four SpacesoundMilieus focus on the predominantly unexplored and unknown micro-dimensions of animal and nature sounds. Applying their original process of sound microscopy (EndoSonoScopy), the SpacesoundArtists examine natural sounds and noises in order to trigger their intrinsic melodic, rhythmic and spatial 'inaudible intensities' and to realize the Spacesound composition on the basis of an artificially produced combination of consistencies that are found naturally and produced artificially. Every single SpacesoundMilieu is a small, closed – although open towards 'the other' at its margins – acoustic cosmos, 'unheard-of' sound worlds, which offers an extraordinary sound experience. For further information on the work: www.sabineschaeferjoachimkrebs.de

Notes

1 Translated from the German original by *ar.pege*, and edited by Ralf Nuhn, John Dack, and Mine Doğantan-Dack.

2 The authors wish to include here the German translation of this quotation from Deleuze and Guattari, which formed the basis of their chapter: ‚Der eigentlich musikalische Inhalt der Musik wird von Arten des Frau-Werdens, Kind-Werdens und Tier-Werdens durchlaufen, aber durch alle möglichen Einflüsse, die auch mit den Instrumenten zu tun haben, tendiert er immer stärker dazu, molekular zu werden, und zwar in einer Art von kosmischem Geplätscher, bei dem das Unhörbare hörbarwird und das Unwahrnehmbare als solches erscheint:nicht mehr der Singvogel, sondern das Klang-Molekül' (Deleuze and Guattari, 1992: 339).

3 The radically modified situation this brings about with respect to the possibilities of the production of music is often imperfectly understood, investigated and described in its aesthetic importance and relevance, by musicological philosophical research, for instance. In this new situation, the composer will henceforth be able to fix his completed artwork 'authentically' for posterity 'ad infinitum' – comparable to the man of letters or an artist. S/he no longer is dependent on the often 'problematic help' from interpreters to have his work come into existence in a sonic, materialised way.

4 Naturally, there are always the 'interfaces' of the human: a) as a sound artist (sender) and b) as an addressee (recipient). The human (sound artist) as the 'sender' forms a 'symbiotic production structure', as it were, together with the machine (production unit: sampler). And the loudspeaker as an instrument of mediation then forms a so-called 'mediation and communication structure' with the 'recipient' in the form of a 'listening human being'.

5 Author Joachim Krebs realised multimedia projects on a larger scale between 1985 and 1994 – for the new art of music and media – at internationally important performance venues where the sampler was used in live performances (e.g. courses for New Music in Darmstadt in 1988, and the 'Multimediale' festival of the Centre for Art and Media Technology, ZKM Karlsruhe in 1991.)

6 A kind of 'becoming a flower' represented by the process of blossoming.

7 One way of 'becoming a dog' is, for example, represented by the acoustic act of barking. The process of barking is an expression, i.e. the 'alienation' of an *inner* movement that results in an *external* movement, a movement of the air among others. The air in turn reaches and enters the ear of the listening human or animal. And thus, artificially formed/deformed air, caused by affects, is transformed into sound in an almost imaginary way.

8 Paul Klee: 'For we know that, strictly speaking, everything has potential energy directed towards the centre of the earth. If we reduce our perspective to microscopic dimensions, we come once more to the realms of the dynamic, to the egg and to the cell' (Klee, 1961b: 5).

9 Three SpacesoundMilieus (Tracks 9–11) with audio-microscoped sounds of insects:

Track 9: 'Uromenus rugosicollis' (1'56")

Track 10: 'Metrioptera roeseli' (1'56")

Track 11: 'Myrmeleotettix maculatus' (2'10")

One SpacesoundMilieu (Track 12) with audio-microscoped nature atmosphere (3'07")

10 'The same goes for literature, for music. There is no primacy of the individual; there is instead an indissolubility of a singular Abstract and a collective Concrete' (Deleuze and Guattari, 1987: 100).

11 If the epistemological statement according to which only the relationship of objects to each other, and not they themselves, can be recognised as 'those being *as such*', and that they are also determined by the position and the perspective of the perceiver, and if Albert Einstein is correct in stating that space, time and mass depend on the *condition of movement* of the observer and therefore are relative categories, one can say with regard to music that the interior conditions of movement, the inherent affects caused by the music and the inner emotionalities of the listener/recipient make it possible to observe the 'temporal relationships' of the most diverse relations between speeds – in an almost mentally qualified way.

References

Benjamin, W. (1982) 'The Work of Art in the Age of Mechanical Reproduction', in H. Arendt (ed.) *Illuminations*, pp.219–53. Trans. H. Zohn. Suffolk: Fontana. Original (1939/1974 posthumous) as 'Das Kunstwerk im Zeitalter seiner technischen Reproduzierbarkeit', in R. Tiedemann and H. Schweppenhäuser (eds) *Walter Benjamin, Gesammelte Schriften, vol. 1*, pp.471–508. Frankfurt am Main: Suhrkamp.

Deleuze, G. and Guattari, F. (1987) *A Thousand Plateaus. Capitalism and Schizophrenia*. Trans. B. Massumi. Minneapolis: University of Minnesota Press. Original (1980) as *Capitalisme et schizophrenie, tome 2: Mille plateaux*. Paris: Éditions de Minuit.

_____ (1992) *Tausend Plateaus*. Trans. G. Ricke and R. Voullié. Berlin: Merve Verlag.

Eimert, H. and Humpert, H.U. (1973) *Lexikon der elektronischen Musik*. Regensburg: Bosse.

Hegel, G.W.F. (1975) *Aesthetics: Lectures on Fine Art*. Trans. T.M. Knox. Oxford: Clarendon Press. Original (1832–45) published in *Georg Wilhelm Friedrich Hegel's Werke*. Berlin: Duncker & Humbolt.

Klee, P. (1961a) 'Creative Credo', in *Notebooks, vol. 1: The Thinking Eye*, pp.76–80. Trans. R. Manheim. London: Lund Humphries. Original (1920) as 'Schöpferische Konfession' in K. Edschmid (ed.) *Tribüne der Kunst und Zeit*, n.p.n. Berlin: Erich Reiss.

_____ (1961b) 'Towards a Theory of Form Production', in *Notebooks, vol. 1: The Thinking Eye*. Trans. R.Manheim. London: Lund Humphries. Original (1956) as *Form- und Gestaltungslehre vol.1: Das bildnerische Denken*. Basel: Schwabe Verlag.

Riemann, H. (1967) *Musiklexikon*. Mainz: Schott.

Schäfer, S. and Krebs, J. (2004) TopoSonic Spheres. Booklet for the CD/DVD of the same title.

Schaeffer, P. (1952) *A la recherche d'une musique concrète*. Paris: Editions du Seuil.

About the Authors

Marc Battier lives and works in France. He is professor of musicology and electroacoustic music at the University of Paris Sorbonne and head of the MINT research group. He started using computers in his compositional practice in 1970. His electroacoustic music has been played in most countries of Europe, and in Japan, China, Korea, Taiwan, the United States and Canada. In the late seventies, after having organized with Barry Truax a computer music conference in Denmark within an UNESCO world project, he worked first at Groupe de recherches musicales (France) as computer music assistant to François Bayle, then at IRCAM (France) with major composers such as Pierre Boulez, Pierre Henry, Karlheinz Stockhausen, and Jôji Yuasa. He was invited professor at the University of California at San Diego, at UC Irvine, and at University of Montreal. He is the co-founder of Electroacoustic Music Studies Network, and in 2005 founded the Electroacoustic Music Studies Asia Network (EMSAN). In 1992–3, he designed the twentieth-century collection of electronic musical instruments for the Museum of Music in Paris. He is now on the Acquisition Board of the museum where he aims to enrich the collection of twentieth-century musical instruments.

Websites: http://www.omf.paris4.sorbonne.fr/MINT
http://www.ems-network.org/
Email: marc.battier@paris-sorbonne.fr

Bruce Ellis Benson is Department Chair and Professor of Philosophy at Wheaton College, USA. He is the author of *The Improvisation of Musical Dialogue: A Phenomenology of Music* (Cambridge University Press, 2003); *Pious Nietzsche: Decadence and Dionysian Faith* (Indiana University Press, 2007); and co-editor of *Hermeneutics at the Crossroads* (Indiana University Press, 2006). His work on hermeneutics and aesthetics – particularly in relation to jazz – has appeared in such journals as the *Revue internationale de philosophie* and *Horizons philosophiques*.

Email: bruce.ellis.benson@wheaton.edu

John Dack was born in Kings Cross, London. He worked as photographer's assistant and guitar teacher before studying music as a mature student at Middlesex Polytechnic (BA Hons, 1980). His subsequent studies include: PhD with Denis Smalley, 1989; Post-graduate Diploma in Music Information Technology (distinction), City University, 1992; MSc (distinction), City University, 1994; MMus in Theory and Analysis, Goldsmiths College, 1998; MA in Aesthetics and Art Theory (merit), Middlesex University, 2004. Since 1998, he has been employed as Research Fellow at the Lansdown Centre for Electronic Arts, Middlesex University. In 2006 he was promoted to Senior Research Fellow. Visiting lecturer in the Music Departments of Goldsmiths College; City University, London, and the Guildhall School of Music and Drama, John Dack gave conference presentations in Britain, France, Germany, Spain, China and Turkey. His current research areas: history, theory and analysis of electroacoustic music; the music and works of the Groupe de Recherches Musicales; serial thought. In 2004 he was the director of the AHRC-funded 'Scambi Project' which is a continuing investigation into the 'open' work 'Scambi' by Henri Pousseur and the concept of the 'open' work in general.

Websites: www.cea.mdx.ac.uk
www.scambi.mdx.ac.uk
Email: j.dack@mdx.ac.uk

Mine Doğantan-Dack is a pianist (BM, MM The Juilliard School) and a music theorist (MA, Princeton University; MA, MPhil, PhD, Columbia University). She also holds a BA in philosophy from Boğaziçi University, Istanbul. She is the winner of the William Petschek award for piano performance, and regularly performs as a soloist and chamber musician. She recorded the music of J.S. Bach and Scriabin for WNCN, and various programs for the Turkish radio and television. She has published articles on the history of music theory, expressivity in music performance, and affective responses to music. Her book titled *Mathis Lussy: A Pioneer in Studies of Expressive Performance* was published in 2002 by Peter Lang AG. She is the editor of the online journal *Septet: An Interdisciplinary Journal of the Arts, Humanities and Social Sciences* published by Yeditepe University. She taught at Columbia University, New York and Yeditepe University, Istanbul and has been employed as a Research Fellow at Middlesex University since 2004. She is the founder of the Marmara Piano Trio (with Pal Banda, cello, and Philippa Mo, violin) and is currently working on a practice-based research project funded by the AHRC (Arts and Humanities Research Council) investigating the epistemology of live performance in the context of her piano trio. Mine was awarded Dozency in 2002, and Professorship in 2008 by the Turkish Ministry of Education.

Website: http://www.mdx.ac.uk/alchemy
Email: dogantanm@yahoo.com   m.dack@mdx.ac.uk

William Echard is Associate Professor of Music at Carleton University, Ottawa, Canada. His research centers on questions of signification in rock music and closely related traditions, with special interests in musical icons of space and movement, theories of persona and virtuality, and topic theory. His book titled *Neil Young and the Poetics of Energy* was published by Indiana University Press (2005). He is currently working on a SSHRC (Social Sciences and Humanities Research Council)-funded program of research concerning the theory of musical topics and its application to rock criticism of the 1960s and 1970s.

Email: wechard@ccs.carleton.ca

Dorottya Fabian is Associate Professor and lecturer in musicology at The University of New South Wales, Sydney, Australia. Her main research interest is performance styles on sound recordings. She aims to combine historical–analytical investigations with experimental examinations of listeners' perception. Her book titled *Bach Performance Practice, 1945–1975: A Comprehensive Review of Sound Recordings and Literature* was published by Ashgate (2003). Currently she is working on two large projects funded by the Australian Research Council. The first, in collaboration with Emery Schubert, aims to model expressiveness in performance of baroque and romantic repertoire through extensive analysis of performance features evidenced on commercially released sound recordings. The second project investigates prominent violinists of the past century interpreting Bach, Beethoven and Brahms sonatas with a view to establish individual artistic signatures and thus refine current notions about performance trends and their cultural contexts.

Email: d.fabian@unsw.edu.au

Michael Frith is an organist, composer and academic. He has performed throughout Britain and Europe, both as soloist and accompanist. His compositions include a considerable number of short choral pieces, mostly liturgical, which have been extensively performed world-wide, two large-scale works for chorus and orchestra, a Clarinet Sonata, a Viola Concerto and an Organ Symphony. His current research is in the field of nineteenth- and early twentieth-century French organ music, especially that of Franck and Messiaen. He is a Visiting Lecturer in Music at Middlesex University, and the editor of *Zemlinsky Studies* published by Middlesex University Press in 2007.

Email: michael.frith@waitrose.com

Tony Gibbs is an author, photographer, sound engineer and lecturer on sound art. He was a founder member (with Andrew Deakin and John Dack) of Middlesex University's pioneering BA Sonic Arts programme and has been its leader since 2002. In addition to a number of papers on sound and art, he has recently written one of the first introductory books on the subject: *Foundations of Sonic Arts and Sound Design* (AVA Books, 2007). Current projects include research on creative applications of sound in the pre-electronic era with particular reference to landscape, architecture and culture.

Email: t.gibbs@mdx.ac.uk

Theodore Gracyk is the Department Chair and Professor of Philosophy at the Minnesota State University Moorhead, USA. He has a PhD in Philosophy, University of California, Davis (1984). His doctoral dissertation focused on Kant's aesthetic theory. This work led to a number of publications on eighteenth-century aesthetics in such journals as *The British Journal of Aesthetics*, *The Journal of Aesthetics and Art Criticism*, and *The Monist*. Strong interest in the philosophy of music led to his first publication in that area, 'Adorno, Jazz, and the Aesthetics of Popular Music', which appeared in *The Musical Quarterly* in 1992. The majority of his subsequent published work explores issues concerning the aesthetics of popular music. Some of this work appeared in three books, *Rhythm and Noise: An Aesthetics of Rock* (Duke University Press, 1996), *I Wanna Be Me: Rock Music and the Politics of Identity* (Temple University Press, 2001), and *Listening to Popular Music* (The University of Michigan Press, 2007). *I Wanna Be Me* was named co-winner (with Gary Giddins) of the 2002 Woody Guthrie Award.

Email: gracyk@mnstate.edu

Anthony Gritten studied at Cambridge University, first as an undergraduate organ scholar and then with Alexander Goehr, writing a doctoral thesis on *Stravinsky's Voices*. He worked as a lecturer at the University of East Anglia in Norwich, latterly becoming Head of the School of Music, before taking up the post of Head of Postgraduate Studies and Research at the RNCM in Manchester until September 2008, when he moved to Middlesex University as Head of the Department of Performing Arts (Music, Theatre, Dance). His publications include two co-edited volumes of essays on *Music and Gesture* (Ashgate, 2006 and forthcoming), based on materials presented at the two international conferences on the subject that he organized in 2003 and 2006. He has published essays in the journals *Musicae Scientiae* and the *British Journal of Aesthetics*, and chapters in the edited volumes *Phrase and Subject: Studies in Literature and Music* (Legenda, 2006) and *In(ter)discipline: New Languages for Criticism* (Legenda, 2007). A Fellow of the Royal College of Organists, he gives ten recitals a year of music from Louis Couperin to Wolfgang Rihm and Mauricio Kagel, and has worked with Gaston Litaize, Jean Guillou, and Daniel Roth on their music. In October 2007 he played the complete works of Buxtehude in one six-and-a-half hour recital to celebrate the tercentenary of the composer's death.

Email: a.gritten@mdx.ac.uk

Andrew Kania has an MA from the University of Auckland and a PhD from the University of Maryland, and is Assistant Professor of Philosophy at Trinity University in San Antonio, USA. His principle research is in the philosophy of music, film, and literature. He has published in the *Journal of Aesthetics and Art Criticism* and the *British Journal of Aesthetics*, and is currently editing one collection of essays on musical ontology, and another on philosophical aspects of the film *Memento*.

Email: Andrew.Kania@Trinity.edu

Joachim Krebs (composer; sound-scape artist) was born in Germany. Between 1968 and 1978 he was a member of the German polit-rock band „Checkpoint Charlie". He studied piano and composition at the University of Karlsruhe. Study visits and fellowships took him to India and the USA. Since 1994 he has staged Space-sound compositions as enterable Space-soundBodies, concert installations and Space-soundObjects. Between 1995 and 1998 he developed the project titled 'Artificial Soundscapes' for spatial sound microscoping of natural sounds and noises ('EndoSonoScopy'), and since 1998 he has been collaborating with artist Sabine Schäfer. He performed at international festivals, including Berlin Festival Weeks, Audio Art Festival Warsaw, Nuova Consonanza Rome, Donaueschinger Musiktage (1983/1999), International Vacation Courses for Contemporary Music Darmstadt (1984/86/88), Munich Biennale, CCMIX Festival Paris, and ISCM World New Music Festival, Stuttgart (2006). He has permanent exhibitions at ZKM Karlsruhe and at Science Centre 'phaeno' Wolfsburg. He received various awards including the Beethoven-Prize, Bonn. His complete instrumental works between 1978 and 1989 are published by Peermusic Hamburg/New York.

Website: http://www.joachimkrebs.de
Email: artists@sabineschaeferjoachimkrebs.de

Robert Reigle completed his doctoral studies at the University of California Los Angeles, USA, and joined the faculty of the centre for Advanced Musical Research (MIAM) at Istanbul Technical University in 2002. He conducted his primary ethnomusicological research in Serieng village, Papua New Guinea, where he lived for three years and studied the sacred music repertoire wherein men modify the timbre of their voices to transform them from mere human voices into those of ancestor spirits. In 2005 he began to study *dengbêj* music in Turkey. His article on octave perception appeared in *Sonus*. He collaborates regularly with leaders of the phenomenological school of spectral composition, Iancu Dumitrescu and Ana-Maria Avram, and premiered works by them in Tokyo and Bucharest. His recordings as a saxophonist and composer have been reviewed in *The Wire*, *Downbeat*, and *Cadence*, among others. He founded improvisation ensembles in Istanbul, Los Angeles, Seattle, New York, and Lincoln.

Email: rreigle@gmail.com

Francis Rumsey is Professor and Director of Research at the Institute of Sound Recording, University of Surrey, UK. He was a Visiting Professor at the School of Music in Piteå, Sweden between 1998 and 2004. He specialises in the engineering and psychological aspects of sound quality evaluation and was appointed as a research advisor in psychoacoustics to NHK Science and Technical Research Laboratories, Tokyo, in 2006. Professor Rumsey was the winner of the 1985 BKSTS Dennis Wratten Journal Award, the 1986 Royal Television Society Lecture Award, and the 1993 University Teaching and Learning Prize. He is the author of over 200 books, book chapters, papers and articles on audio, and in 1995 he was made a Fellow of the Audio Engineering Society for his significant contributions to audio education. His book titled *Spatial Audio* was published in 2001 by Focal Press. He is also an organist and accompanist in the Guildford area. In 2005 he obtained a postgraduate diploma in counselling and psychotherapy, specialising in phenomenological aspects of psychotherapy.

Email: f.rumsey@surrey.ac.uk

Sabine Schäfer (composer and media artist) was born in Germany. She studied music at the University of Karlsruhe, with Wolfgang Rihm and Mathais Spahlinger. Between 1982 and 1991 she was active as composer–performer in the field of interdisciplinary performance art. Between 1989 and 1992 she developed a 24-channel spatial sound control system in relation to 'TopoPhonia', an art project about the spatialisation of sound, at the Centre for Art and Media - ZKM with Sukandar Kartadinata. Since 1991, she has created multi-channel Space-sound compositions staged as enterable Space-soundBodies, concert installations and Space-soundObjects, and since 1998 she has been collaborating with artist Joachim

Krebs. She performed at international festivals including Berlin Festival Weeks 1995, Warsaw Autumn 1996, MusikTriennale Cologne 1997, Nuova Consonanza Rome 1998, Donaueschinger Musiktage 1995/1999, Munich Biennale 2002, MIDEM Cannes 2004, CCMIX Festival Paris 2005, ISCM World New Music Festival, Stuttgart 2006. She has permanent exhibitions at ZKM, Karlsruhe and at Science Centre 'phaeno' Wolfsburg. Since 1994 she has produced radio plays in the field of sonic art. She is the recipient of various grants and awards including Siemens Media Art Prize, Prize of the Ars Acustica International WDR Cologne.

Website: http://www.sabineschaefer.de
Email: artists@sabineschaeferjoachimkrebs.de

Colin Symes teaches at Macquarie University, Australia. He is the author of *Setting the Record Straight: A Material History of Classical Recording* (Wesleyan University Press), which was the recipient of a 2005 Deems Taylor Award from the American Society of Composers, Authors and Publishers. His latest book (with Kalervo Gulson) *Spatial Theories of Education: Policy and Geography Matters* was published by Routledge in 2007. He recently published in journals such as the *Journal of Aesthetic Education, Popular Music, British Journal of Music Education, Discourse, Time and Society* and *Mosaic.*

Email: Colin.Symes@aces.mq.edu.au

Simon Trezise was born in Brighton, England. He studied at Keble College, Oxford, where he wrote his dissertation on Schoenberg's *Gurrelieder* under the supervision of Derrick Puffett. Since 1984 he has lectured at Trinity College, Dublin. He has published books on Debussy, the Cambridge Music Handbook on Debussy's *La mer* (1995) and edited the *Cambridge Companion to Debussy* (2003). Interests include Elgar, Wagner, romantic opera, music and text, film music and, more recently, the study of performance through recordings, which is reflected in a number of articles, papers, a book project on the conductor Eugene Ormandy, and the creation of an audio archive at Trinity College Dublin.

Email: simon.trezise@gmail.com

Tony Whyton joined the School of Media, Music and Performance at the University of Salford, UK in September 2007 after 10 years at Leeds College of Music. In his work at Leeds, Tony was responsible for the creation, management and strategic development of the Centre for Jazz Studies, and was the founding editor of the interdisciplinary journal *The Source: Challenging Jazz Criticism.* Tony has published articles and presented conference papers on a variety of topics, including jazz history, the politics of music education, the cultural influence of recordings and interdisciplinary approaches to music. His research has been disseminated internationally within university settings including Yale University, McGill University Montreal, Charles University Prague and the University of Jyvaskyla Finland. In May 2007, he was invited to the University of Melbourne as a visiting Research Fellow at the Victorian College of Arts. He now co-edits the internationally peer-reviewed *Jazz Research Journal* (Equinox) and is completing a book entitled *Jazz Icons*, to be published by Cambridge University Press in 2009.

Email: t.whyton@salford.ac.uk

John Young was born in Christchurch, New Zealand and studied at the University of Canterbury, completing a doctorate on the manipulation of environmental sound sources in electroacoustic music. He lectured at Victoria University of Wellington from 1990 to 2000 where he also directed the Electroacoustic Music Studios, prior to joining the Music, Technology and Innovation Research Centre at De Montfort University, Leicester, UK, where he is currently a Reader. He is a composer working primarily in acousmatic music, particularly on forms based around the interplay between recognizable natural sound sources and computer-based studio transformations. He has been a guest researcher at institutions and festivals throughout Europe and North and South America. He is the recipient of numerous international awards, notably the 1996 Stockholm Electronic Arts Award and the programme music award of the 2007 Bourges Electroacoustic Music Competition.

Email: jyoung@dmu.ac.uk

About the CD

Track 1:

Ludwig van Beethoven's Piano Sonata Op.13 in C minor, the *Pathétique*
Second movement: *Adagio cantabile*
Mine Doğantan-Dack, piano
Recorded on 20 April 2008 at Middlesex University

Tracks 2–8:

Excerpts from *Ricordiamo Forlì* (2005) by John Young
Giosuè Carducci (APRA) / 2007 YMX MéDIA (SOCAN)
First released in 2007 on the disc 'Lieu temps', empreintes DIGITALes, IMED 0787
http://www.empreintesdigitales.com

Tracks 9–12:

SpacesoundMilieus by Sabine Schäfer and Joachim Krebs (2007)

Three SpacesoundMilieus with audio-microscoped sounds of insects:
9. 'Uromenus rugosicollis'
    Duration: 1'56"
10. 'Metrioptera roeseli'
    Duration: 1'56"
11. 'Myrmeleotettix maculatus'
    Duration: 2'10"
And
12. One SpacesoundMilieu with audio-microscoped nature atmosphere
    Duration: 3'07"

Index of Terms

A

Acousmatic xvi, 35, 39, 84, 92, 314–16, 318–19, 327, 331, 356

Acoustic

——— art 334–6, 338

——— design 178, 334

——— environment xiv, 172–3, 175–6, 179

——— orchestration 51–3

——— portraits 180, 182

——— representation 294, 297

Action representation 299

Actuality 51

Actualization, musical xi, 22, 25–31, 33, 36–7

Aesthetic

———, absolutist 314, 319

——— appreciation xiv, 191, 200, 203–4

——— empiricism 16

——— evaluation 64

——— experience 38, 238

——— judgment 73, 82, 88, 91, 95, 299

——— preference 307–8

——— reception 189, 196

——— referentialist 314

——— response 64, 190, 243

——— status xi, xii–xiv, 42, 155, 159

Aesthetics x–xi, xiii, 38, 73, 190, 195, 197, 200, 333

———, cross-cultural 203

———, late-twentieth-century 44

———, musical 62, 189, 203

———, nominalist 44

Albert Hall 61, 174

Allographic artworks 23, 44, 48, 52, 54, 107

Analogue 69, 329, 336–8

Analysis

———, music 16, 91, 168, 195, 199, 296–7, 300

———, performance 232, 242, 246, 253, 272, 287, 296

———, performance and 300, 302

———, performer's 305

———, score 233, 301, 304–5

———, verbal protocol 215

Architecture 44

Articulation 91, 112, 237, 246, 248–52, 256, 274, 297, 314

Artistry 46, 83, 295–6

Arts

———, notational 45

———, performing 68

Artwork xi, 4, 11, 26–7, 65, 113, 156–7, 159, 162, 165, 180, 227, 233, 316–17, 323, 333–5, 342–3, 346

Audience (see also Auditor and Listener) 8–9, 11, 13–15, 43, 49, 55–6, 63–7, 69–70, 128, 144, 155, 160, 167, 205, 236, 245–6, 295

——— impact 244

Audio-microscope xvi, 333, 341, 346–7, 357

Audiophile 33

Auditor (see also Audience and Listener) 91, 235, 285

Auditory

——— cue 216, 222, 229

——— culture 22, 24

——— illusion 247

——— threshold 86, 215

Aura xii, 23, 65–7, 70–3, 77, 86–7, 316–18, 327–9, 344

Aural

——— analysis 248

——— culture xii, 302

——— deception 66

——— documentation 62

——— environment 221

——— experience 6

——— expression 196

——— perception xiii, 100, 181

——— technologies 41

Authenticity xi, xiii, 44–5, 52–3, 83, 93, 106–7, 160, 167, 317–18, 327, 335

Author 113, 150, 162, 297–8, 301

Authority 85, 93, 261, 285, 288, 296–8, 301–2, 306, 336

Authorship 147, 156

Autographic artworks xi, 23, 45, 48, 51, 54–5, 107

B

Baroque

———, church ceilings 34

———, era 46, 122, 198

———, music 247

Becoming, ontological xi, xvi, 25, 28, 34, 333, 339, 341, 345–6

Index of Names